CONTENTS OF VOL. VIII.

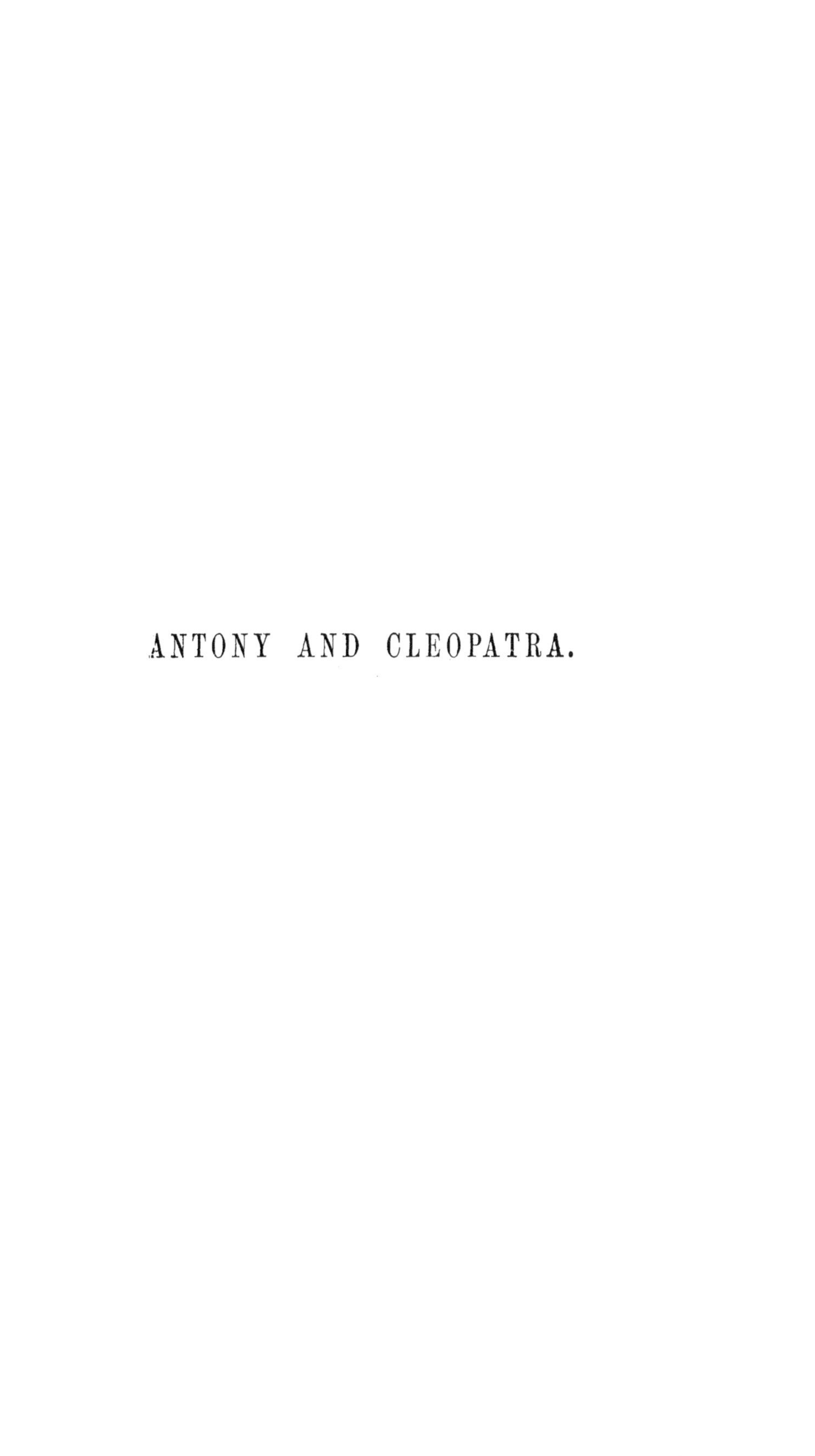

ANTONY AND CLEOPATRA.

"The Tragedie of Anthonie and Cleopatra" occupies twenty-nine pages in the folio of 1623; viz. from p. 340 to p. 368 inclusive, in the division of "Tragedies." Although at the beginning it has *Actus Primus. Scœna Prima*, it is not divided into acts and scenes, nor is the defect cured in any of the subsequent folio impressions of 1632, 1664, and 1685. They are all without any list of characters.

INTRODUCTION.

WE are without any record that "Antony and Cleopatra" was ever performed; and when in Act v. sc. 2, the heroine anticipates that "some squeaking Cleopatra" will "boy her greatness" on the stage, Shakespeare seems to hint that no young male performer would be able to sustain the part without exciting ridicule. However, the same remark will, more or less, apply to many of his other female characters; and the wonder, of course, is, how so much delicacy, tenderness, and beauty could be infused into parts which the poet knew must be represented by beardless and crack-voiced boys.

The period of the year at which "Antony and Cleopatra" was entered on the Stationers' Registers might lead to the inference, that, having been written late in 1607, it was brought out at the Globe in the spring of 1608, and that Edward Blunt (one of the publishers of the folio of 1623) thus put in his claim to the publication of the tragedy, if he could procure a manuscript of it. The memorandum bears date on the 20th May, 1608, and the piece is stated to be "a book" called "Anthony and Cleopatra." Perhaps Blunt was unable to obtain a copy of it, and, as far as we now know, it was printed for the first time in the folio of 1623.

It does not appear that there was any preceding drama on the story, with the exception of the "Cleopatra" of Samuel Daniel, originally published in 1594, to which Shakespeare was clearly under no obligation. Any slight resemblance between the two is to be accounted for by the fact, that both poets resorted to the same authority for their materials—Plutarch—whose "Lives" had been translated by Sir T. North in 1579. The minuteness with which Shakespeare adhered to history is more remarkable in this drama than in any other; and sometimes the most trifling circumstances are artfully, but still most naturally, interwoven. Shakespeare's use of history in "Antony and Cleopatra" may be contrasted with Ben Jonson's subjection to it in "Sejanus."

"Of all Shakespeare's historical plays (says Coleridge) 'Antony and Cleopatra' is by far the most wonderful. There is not one in which he has followed history so minutely, and yet there are few in which he impresses the notion of angelic strength so much—perhaps none in which he impresses it more strongly. This is greatly owing to the manner in which the fiery force is sustained throughout, and to the numerous momentary flashes of nature, counteracting the historic abstraction." (Lit. Rem. vol. ii. p. 143.)

DRAMATIS PERSONÆ.

M. Antony, Octavius Cæsar, M. Æmil. Lepidus,	Triumvirs.
Sextus Pompeius,	
Domitius Enobarbus, Ventidius, Eros, Scarus, Dercetas, Demetrius, Philo,	Friends of Antony.
Mecænas, Agrippa, Dolabella, Proculeius, Thyreus, Gallus,	Friends to Cæsar.
Menas, Menecrates, Varrius,	Friends to Pompey.

Taurus, Lieutenant-General to Cæsar.
Canidius, Lieutenant-General to Antony.
Silius, an Officer under Ventidius.
Euphronius, Ambassador from Antony to Cæsar.
Alexas, Mardian, Seleucus, and Diomedes, Attendants on Cleopatra. A Soothsayer. A Clown.

Cleopatra, Queen of Egypt.
Octavia, Sister to Cæsar, and Wife to Antony.

Charmian, Iras,	Attendants on Cleopatra.

Officers, Soldiers, Messengers, and other Attendants.

SCENE, in several Parts of the Roman Empire.

ANTONY AND CLEOPATRA.

ACT I.

SCENE I.—Alexandria. A Room in CLEOPATRA'S Palace.

Enter DEMETRIUS *and* PHILO.

Phi. Nay, but this dotage of our general's
O'erflows the measure: those his goodly eyes,
That o'er the files and musters of the war
Have glow'd like plated Mars, now bend, now turn
The office and devotion of their view
Upon a tawny front: his captain's heart,
Which in the scuffles of great fights hath burst
The buckles on his breast, reneges[1] all temper,
And is become the bellows, and the fan,
To cool a gipsy's lust. Look, where they come.

Flourish. Enter ANTONY *and* CLEOPATRA, *with their Trains; Eunuchs fanning her.*

Take but good note, and you shall see in him
The triple pillar of the world transform'd
Into a strumpet's fool: behold and see.

Cleo. If it be love indeed, tell me how much.

Ant. There 's beggary in the love that can be reckon'd.

Cleo. I 'll set a bourn how far to be belov'd.

Ant. Then must thou needs find out new heaven, new earth.

Enter an Attendant.

Att. News, my good lord, from Rome.

Ant. Grates me:—the sum

Cle. Nay, hear them, Antony:
Fulvia, perchance, is angry; or, who knows
If the scarce-bearded Cæsar have not sent

[1] *Denies.*

His powerful mandate to you, "Do this, or this;
Take in that kingdom, and enfranchise that;
Perform 't, or else we doom[1] thee."
Ant. How, my love!
Cleo. Perchance,—nay, and most like,—
You must not stay here longer; your dismission
Is come from Cæsar; therefore hear it, Antony.—
Where 's Fulvia's process? Cæsar's, I would say?—
Both?—
Call in the messengers.—As I am Egypt's queen,
Thou blushest, Antony, and that blood of thine
Is Cæsar's homager; else so thy cheek pays shame,
When shrill-tongu'd Fulvia scolds.—The messengers!
Ant. Let Rome in Tyber melt, and the wide arch
Of the rang'd empire fall! Here is my space.
Kingdoms are clay: our dungy earth alike
Feeds beast as man: the nobleness of life
Is to do thus; when such a mutual pair, [*Embracing*
And such a twain can do 't, in which I bind,
On pain of punishment, the world to weet,[2]
We stand up peerless.
Cleo. Excellent falsehood!
Why did he marry Fulvia, and not love her?—
I 'll seem the fool I am not; Antony
Will be himself.
Ant. But stirr'd by Cleopatra.—
Now, for the love of Love, and her soft hours,
Let 's not confound the time with conference harsh
There 's not a minute of our lives should stretch
Without some pleasure now. What sport to-night?
Cleo. Hear the ambassadors.
Ant. Fie, wrangling queen!
Whom every thing becomes, to chide, to laugh,
To weep; whose every fashion fitly[3] strives
To make itself, in thee, fair and admir'd.
No messenger; but thine, and all alone,
To-night we 'll wander through the streets, and note
The qualities of people. Come, my queen;
Last night you did desire it.—Speak not to us.
[*Exeunt* ANT. *and* CLEOP. *with their Train*
Dem. Is Cæsar with Antonius priz'd so slight?
Phi. Sir, sometimes, when he is not Antony,
He comes too short of that great property

[1] damn: in f. e. [2] *Know.* [3] fully: in f. e

Which still should go with Antony.

Dem. I am full sorry,
That he approves the common liar, who
Thus speaks of him at Rome; but I will hope
Of better deeds to-morrow. Rest you happy. [*Exeunt.*

SCENE II.—The Same. Another Room.

Enter CHARMIAN, IRAS, ALEXAS, *and a Soothsayer.*

Char. Lord Alexas, most sweet Alexas, most any thing Alexas, almost most absolute Alexas, where 's the soothsayer that you praised so to the queen? O! that I knew this husband, which, you say, must charge[1] his horns with garlands!

Alex. Soothsayer!

Sooth. Your will?

Char. Is this the man?—Is 't you, sir, that know things?

Sooth. In nature's infinite book of secrecy
A little I can read.

Alex. Show him your hand.

Enter ENOBARBUS.

Eno. Bring in the banquet quickly; wine enough, Cleopatra's health to drink.

Char. Good sir, give me good fortune.

Sooth. I make not, but foresee.

Char. Pray, then, foresee me one.

Sooth. You shall be yet far fairer than you are.

Char. He means, in flesh.

Iras. No, you shall paint when you are old.

Char. Wrinkles forbid!

Alex. Vex not his prescience; be attentive.

Char. Hush!

Sooth. You shall be more beloving, than belov'd.

Char. I had rather heat my liver with drinking.

Alex. Nay, hear him.

Char. Good now, some excellent fortune. Let me be married to three kings in a forenoon, and widow them all: let me have a child at fifty, to whom Herod of Jewry may do homage: find me to marry me with Octavius Cæsar, and companion me with my mistress.

Sooth. You shall outlive the lady whom you serve.

Char. O excellent! I love long life better than figs.

[1] change: in folios.

Sooth. You have seen, and proved a fairer former fortune,
Than that which is to approach.

Char. Then, belike, my children shall have no names. Pr'ythee, how many boys and wenches must I have?

Sooth. If every of your wishes had a womb,
And fruitful[1] every wish, a million.

Char. Out, fool! I forgive thee for a witch.

Alex. You think, none but your sheets are privy to your wishes.

Char. Nay, come; tell Iras hers.

Alex. We'll know all our fortunes.

Eno. Mine, and most of our fortunes, to-night, shall be, drunk to bed.

Iras. There's a palm presages chastity, if nothing else.

Char. Even as the o'erflowing Nilus presageth famine.

Iras. Go, you wild bedfellow, you cannot soothsay.

Char. Nay, if an oily palm be not a fruitful prognostication, I cannot scratch mine ear.—Pr'ythee, tell her but a work-day fortune.

Sooth. Your fortunes are alike.

Iras. But how? but how? give me particulars.

Sooth. I have said.

Iras. Am I not an inch of fortune better than she?

Char. Well, if you were but an inch of fortune better than I, where would you choose it?

Iras. Not in my husband's nose.

Char. Our worser thoughts heavens mend! Alexas,—come, his fortune, his fortune.—O! let him marry a woman that cannot go, sweet Isis, I beseech thee: and let her die too, and give him a worse; and let worse follow worse, till the worst of all follow him laughing to his grave, fifty-fold a cuckold. Good Isis, hear me this prayer, though thou deny me a matter of more weight, good Isis, I beseech thee!

Iras. Amen. Dear goddess, hear that prayer of the people; for, as it is a heart-breaking to see a handsome man loose-wived, so it is a deadly sorrow to behold a foul knave uncuckolded: therefore, dear Isis, keep decorum, and fortune him accordingly!

[1] fertile: in f. e.; foretell: in folio.

Char. Amen.

Alex. Lo, now! if it lay in their hands to make me a cuckold, they would make themselves whores, but they'd do 't.

Eno. Hush! here comes Antony.

Char. Not he, the queen.

Enter CLEOPATRA.

Cleo. Saw you my lord?

Eno. No, lady.

Cleo. Was he not here?

Char. No, madam.

Cleo. He was dispos'd to mirth; but on the sudden,
A Roman thought hath struck him.—Enobarbus!—

Eno. Madam.

Cleo. Seek him, and bring him hither. Where's Alexas?

Alex. Here, at your service.—My lord approaches.

Enter ANTONY, *with a Messenger and Attendants.*

Cleo. We will not look upon him: go with us.

[*Exeunt* CLEOPATRA, ENOBARBUS, ALEXAS, IRAS, CHARMIAN, *Soothsayer, and Attendants.*

Mess. Fulvia, thy wife, first came into the field.

Ant. Against my brother Lucius?

Mess. Ay:
But soon that war had end, and the time's state
Made friends of them, jointing their force 'gainst Cæsar;
Whose better issue in the war, from Italy
Upon the first encounter drave them.

Ant. Well, what worst?

Mess. The nature of bad news infests the teller.

Ant. When it concerns the fool, or coward.—On:
Things, that are past, are done, with me.—'T is thus;
Who tells me true, though in his tale lie death,
I hear him as he flatter'd.

Mess. Labienus
(This is stiff news) hath with his Parthian force
Extended[1] Asia from Euphrates;
His conquering banner shook from Syria
To Lydia, and to Ionia; whilst——

Ant. Antony, thou wouldst say,—

Mess. O, my lord!

Ant. Speak to me home, mince not the general tongue;

[1] *Seized.*

Name Cleopatra as she is call'd in Rome;
Rail thou in Fulvia's phrase, and taunt my faults
With such full license, as both truth and malice
Have power to utter. O! then we bring forth weeds,
When our quick winds lie still; and our ills told us,
Is as our earing.[1] Fare thee well awhile.

Mess. At your noble pleasure. [*Exit*

Ant. From Sicyon now the news? Speak there.

1 *Att.* The man from Sicyon!—Is there such an one?

2 *Att.* He stays upon your will.

Ant. Let him appear.—
These strong Egyptian fetters I must break,

Enter another Messenger.

Or lose myself in dotage.—What are you?

2 *Mess.* Fulvia thy wife is dead.

Ant. Where died she?

2 *Mess.* In Sicyon:
Her length of sickness, with what else more serious
Importeth thee to know, this bears. [*Giving a Letter*

Ant. Forbear me.—
[*Exit Messenger*
There 's a great spirit gone. Thus did I desire it:
What our contempts do often hurl from us,
We wish it ours again; the present pleasure,
By repetition souring,[2] does become
The opposite of itself: she 's good, being gone;
The hand would pluck her back, that shov'd her on.
I must from this enchanting queen break off;
Ten thousand harms, more than the ills I know,
My idleness doth hatch.—How now![3] Enobarbus!

Enter ENOBARBUS.

Eno. What 's your pleasure, sir?

Ant. I must with haste from hence.

Eno. Why, then, we kill all our women. We see how mortal an unkindness is to them: if they suffer our departure, death 's the word.

Ant. I must be gone.

Eno. Under a compelling occasion, let women die: it were pity to cast them away for nothing; though, between them and a great cause, they should be esteemed nothing. Cleopatra, catching but the least noise of this, dies instantly: I have seen her die twenty

[1] Ploughing our "quick winds" which dry the soil for the plough. [2] By revolution lowering: in f. e. [3] Dyce reads: Ho!

times upon far poorer moment. I do think, there is mettle in death, which commits some loving act upon her, she hath such a celerity in dying.

Ant. She is cunning past man's thought.

Eno. Alack, sir! no; her passions are made of nothing but the finest part of pure love. We cannot call her winds and waters, sighs and tears; they are greater storms and tempests than almanacs can report: this cannot be cunning in her; if it be, she makes a shower of rain as well as Jove.

Ant. Would I had never seen her!

Eno. O, sir! you had then left unseen a wonderful piece of work, which not to have been blessed withal would have discredited your travel.

Ant. Fulvia is dead.

Eno. Sir?

Ant. Fulvia is dead.

Eno. Fulvia!

Ant. Dead.

Eno. Why, sir, give the gods a thankful sacrifice. When it pleaseth their deities to take the wife of a man from him, it shows to man the tailors of the earth: comforting therein, that when old robes are worn out, there are members to make new. If there were no more women but Fulvia, then had you indeed a cut, and the case to be lamented: this grief is crowned with consolation: your old smock brings forth a new petticoat; and, indeed, the tears live in an onion, that should water this sorrow.

Ant. The business she hath broached in the state
Cannot endure my absence.

Eno. And the business you have broached here cannot be without you; especially that of Cleopatra's, which wholly depends on your abode.

Ant. No more light answers. Let our officers
Have notice what we purpose. I shall break
The cause of our expedience[1] to the queen,
And get her leave[2] to part: for not alone
The death of Fulvia, with more urgent touches,
Do strongly speak to us, but the letters, too,
Of many our contriving friends in Rome
Petition us at home. Sextus Pompeius
Hath given the dare to Cæsar, and commands

[1] *Expedition.* [2] love: in folio.

The empire of the sea: our slippery people
(Whose love is never link'd to the deserver,
Till his deserts are past) begin to throw
Pompey the great, and all his dignities,
Upon his son: who, high in name and power,
Higher than both in blood and life, stands up
For the main soldier; whose quality, going on,
The sides o' the world may danger. Much is breeding,
Which, like the courser's hair, hath yet but life,
And not a serpent's poison.[1] Say, our pleasure,
To such whose place is under us, requires
Our quick remove from hence.
Eno. I shall do it. [*Exeunt.*

SCENE III.

Enter CLEOPATRA, CHARMIAN, IRAS, *and* ALEXAS.

Cleo. Where is he?
Char. I did not see him since.
Cleo. See where he is, who 's with him, what he does:
I did not send you.—If you find him sad,
Say, I am dancing; if in mirth, report
That I am sudden sick: quick, and return. [*Exit* ALEX.
Char. Madam, methinks, if you did love him dearly,
You do not hold the method to enforce
The like from him.
Cleo. What should I do, I do not?
Char. In each thing give him way, cross him in nothing.
Cleo. Thou teachest, like a fool, the way to lose him.
Char. Tempt him not so too far; I wish, forbear:
In time we hate that which we often fear.
Enter ANTONY.
But here comes Antony.
Cleo. I am sick, and sullen.
Ant. I am sorry to give breathing to my purpose.—
Cleo. Help me away, dear Charmian, I shall fall:
It cannot be thus long; the sides of nature
Will not sustain it.
Ant. Now, my dearest queen,—
Cleo. Pray you, stand farther from me.
Ant. What 's the matter?

[1] An allusion to the ancient belief, that a horse hair laid into water, turned into a snake.

Cleo. I know, by that same eye, there 's some good news.
What says the married woman?—You may go:
Would, she had never given you leave to come!
Let her not say, 't is I that keep you here,
I have no power upon you; hers you are.
Ant. The gods best know,—
Cleo. O! never was there queen
So mightily betray'd; yet at the first
I saw the treasons planted.
Ant. Cleopatra,—
Cleo. Why should I think, you can be mine, and true,
Though you in swearing shake the throned gods,
Who have been false to Fulvia? Riotous madness,
To be entangled with those mouth-made vows,
Which break themselves in swearing!
Ant. Most sweet queen,—
Cleo. Nay, pray you, seek no colour for your going,
But bid farewell, and go: when you sued staying,
Then was the time for words; no going then:
Eternity was in our lips, and eyes;
Bliss in our brows bent; none our parts so poor,
But was a race of heaven: they are so still,
Or thou, the greatest soldier of the world,
Art turn'd the greatest liar.
Ant. How now, lady!
Cleo. I would, I had thy inches; thou shouldst know
There were a heart in Egypt.
Ant. Hear me, queen.
The strong necessity of time commands
Our services a while, but my full heart
Remains in use with you. Our Italy
Shines o'er with civil swords: Sextus Pompeius
Makes his approaches to the port of Rome:
Equality of two domestic powers
Breeds scrupulous faction. The hated, grown to strength,
Are newly grown to love: the condemn'd Pompey,
Rich in his father's honour, creeps apace
Into the hearts of such as have not thriv'd
Upon the present state, whose numbers threaten;
And quietness, grown sick of rest, would purge
By any desperate change. My more particular,
And that which most with you should safe my going,
Is Fulvia's death.

Cleo. Though age from folly could not give me freedom,
It does from childishness.—Can Fulvia die?
Ant. She 's dead, my queen.
Look here, and, at thy sovereign leisure, read
The garboils[1] she awak'd; at the last, best,
See, when, and where she died.
Cleo. O, most false love!
Where be the sacred vials thou shouldst fill
With sorrowful water? Now I see, I see,
In Fulvia's death, how mine receiv'd shall be.
Ant. Quarrel no more, but be prepar'd to know
The purposes I bear; which are, or cease,
As you shall give the advice: by the fire
That quickens Nilus' slime, I go from hence,
Thy soldier, servant; making peace, or war,
As thou affect'st.
Cleo. Cut my lace, Charmian, come.—
But let it be.—I am quickly ill, and well,
So Antony loves.
Ant. My precious queen, forbear;
And give true credence[2] to his love, which stands
An honourable trial.
Cleo. So Fulvia told me.
I pr'ythee, turn aside, and weep for her;
Then bid adieu to me, and say, the tears
Belong to Egypt: good now, play one scene
Of excellent dissembling; and let it look
Like perfect honour.
Ant. You'll heat my blood: no more.
Cleo. You can do better yet, but this is meetly.
Ant. Now, by my sword,—
Cleo. And target.—Still he mends,
But this is not the best. Look, pr'ythee, Charmian,
How this Herculean Roman does become
The carriage of his chafe.
Ant. I 'll leave you, lady.
Cleo. Courteous lord, one word
Sir, you and I must part,—but that 's not it:
Sir, you and I have lov'd,—but there 's not it;
That you know well: something it is I would,—
O! my oblivion is a very Antony,
And I am all forgotten.

[1] *Commotions.* [2] evidence: in f. e.

Ant. But that your royalty
Holds idleness your subject, I should take you
For idleness itself.
Cleo. 'T is sweating labour
To bear such idleness so near the heart,
As Cleopatra this. But, sir, forgive me;
Since my becomings kill me, when they do not
Eye well to you: your honour calls you hence;
Therefore, be deaf to my unpitied folly,
And all the gods go with you! upon your sword
Sit laurel'd victory, and smooth success
Be strew'd before your feet!
Ant. Let us go. Come;
Our separation so abides, and flies,
That thou, residing here, go'st yet with me,
And I, hence fleeting, here remain with thee.
Away! [*Exeunt.*

SCENE IV.—Rome. An Apartment in CÆSAR'S House.

Enter OCTAVIUS CÆSAR, LEPIDUS, *and Attendants.*

Cæs. You may see, Lepidus, and henceforth know,
It is not Cæsar's natural vice to hate
Our[1] great competitor. From Alexandria
This is the news: he fishes, drinks, and wastes
The lamps of night in revel; is not more manlike
Than Cleopatra, nor the queen of Ptolemy,
More womanly than he: hardly gave audience, or
Vouchsaf'd to think he had partners: you shall find there
A man, who is the abstract of all faults
That all men follow.
Lep. I must not think, there are
Evils enow to darken all his goodness:
His faults, in him, seem as the spots of heaven,
More fiery by night's blackness; hereditary,
Rather than purchas'd: what he cannot change,
Than what he chooses.
Cæs. You are too indulgent. Let us grant, it is not
Amiss to tumble on the bed of Ptolemy,
To give a kingdom for a mirth; to sit
And keep the turn of tippling with a slave;
To reel the streets at noon, and stand the buffet

[1] One: in f. e.

With knaves that smell of sweat: say, this becomes him,
(As his composure must be rare indeed,
Whom these things cannot blemish) yet must Antony
No way excuse his foils.[1] when we do bear
So great weight in his lightness. If he fill'd
His vacancy with his voluptuousness,
Full surfeits, and the dryness of his bones,
Fall[2] on him for 't; but, to confound such time,
That drums him from his sport, and speaks as loud
As his own state, and ours,—'t is to be chid
As we rate boys; who, being mature in knowledge,
Pawn their experience to their present pleasure,
And so rebel to judgment.

Enter a Messenger.

Lep. Here' s more news

Mess. Thy biddings have been done; and every hour,
Most noble Cæsar, shalt thou have report
How 't is abroad. Pompey is strong at sea;
And it appears, he is belov'd of those,
That only have fear'd Cæsar: to the fleets[3]
The discontents repair, and men's reports
Give him much wrong'd.

Cæs. I should have known no less.
It hath been taught us from the primal state,
That he, which is, was wish'd, until he were:
And the ebb'd man ne'er lov'd, till ne'er worth love,
Comes lov'd[4] by being lack'd. This common body,
Like to a vagabond flag upon the stream,
Goes to, and back, and lackeying[5] the varying tide,
To rot itself with motion.

Mess. Cæsar, I bring thee word,
Menecrates and Menas, famous pirates,
Make the sea serve them; which they ear[6] and wound
With keels of every kind: many hot inroads
They make in Italy; the borders maritime
Lack blood to think on 't, and flush youth revolt.
No vessel can peep forth, but 't is as soon
Taken as seen; for Pompey's name strikes more,
Than could his war resisted.

Cæs. Antony,
Leave thy lascivious wassels.[7] When thou once

[1] Malone reads: soils. [2] Call: in f. e. [3] ports: in f e. [4] dear'd in f. e.; fear'd: in folio. [5] lacking: in folio. Theobald made the change. [6] *Plough.* [7] vassailes: in folio; some eds. read: vassels.

Wast beaten from Modena, where thou slew'st
Hirtius and Pansa, consuls, at thy heel
Did famine follow; whom thou fought'st against,
Though daintily brought up, with patience more
Than savages could suffer: thou didst drink
The stale of horses, and the gilded puddle,
Which beasts would cough at: thy palate then did deign
The roughest berry on the rudest hedge;
Yea, like the stag, when snow the pasture sheets,
The barks of trees thou browsed'st: on the Alps
It is reported, thou didst eat strange flesh,
Which some did die to look on; and all this
(It wounds thine honour, that I speak it now)
Was borne so like a soldier, that thy cheek
So much as lank'd not.

Lep. 'T is pity of him.

Cæs. Let his shames quickly
Drive him to Rome. 'T is time we twain
Did show ourselves i' the field: and, to that end,
Assemble we[1] immediate council: Pompey
Thrives in our idleness.

Lep. To-morrow, Cæsar,
I shall be furnish'd to inform you rightly
Both what by sea and land I can be able,
To front this present time.

Cæs. Till which encounter,
It is my business too. Farewell.

Lep. Farewell, my lord. What you shall know mean time
Of stirs abroad, I shall beseech you, sir,
To let me be partaker.

Cæs. Doubt not, sir; I knew it for my bond.
[*Exeunt.*

SCENE V.—Alexandria. A Room in the Palace.

Enter CLEOPATRA, CHARMIAN, IRAS, *and* MARDIAN.

Cleo. Charmian!

Char. Madam.

Cleo. Ha, ha!—
Give me to drink mandragora.

Char. Why, madam?

Cleo. That I might sleep out this great gap of time,
My Antony is away.

[1] me: in folio, 1623.

Char. You think of him too much.
Cleo. O, 't is treason!
Char. Madam, I trust, not so.
Cleo. Thou, eunuch, Mardian—
Mar. What 's your highness' pleasure?
Cleo. Not now to hear thee sing: I take no pleasure
In aught an eunuch has. 'T is well for thee,
That, being unseminar'd, thy freer thoughts
May not fly forth of Egypt. Hast thou affections?
Mar. Yes, gracious madam.
Cleo. Indeed?
Mar. Not in deed, madam; for I can do nothing,
But what in deed is honest to be done;
Yet have I fierce affections, and think
What Venus did with Mars.
Cleo. O, Charmian!
Where think'st thou he is now? Stands he, or sits he?
Or does he walk? or is he on his horse?
O, happy horse to bear the weight of Antony!
Do bravely, horse, for wot'st thou whom thou mov'st?
The demi-Atlas of this earth, the arm
And burgonet[1] of men.—He 's speaking now,
Or murmuring, "Where 's my serpent of old Nile?"
For so he calls me. Now I feed myself
With most delicious poison:—think on me,
That am with Phœbus' amorous pinches black,
And wrinkled deep in time? Broad-fronted Cæsar,
When thou wast here above the ground, I was
A morsel for a monarch; and great Pompey
Would stand, and make his eyes grow in my brow:
There would he anchor his aspect, and die
With looking on his life.

Enter ALEXAS.

Alex. Sovereign of Egypt, hail!
Cleo. How much unlike art thou Mark Antony;
Yet, coming from him, that great medicine hath
With his tinct gilded thee.—
How goes it with my brave Mark Antony?
Alex. Last thing he did, dear queen,
He kiss'd,—the last of many doubled kisses,—
This orient pearl:—his speech sticks in my heart.
Cleo. Mine ear must pluck it thence.
Alex. Good friend, quoth he,

[1] *Helmet.*

Say, "the firm Roman to great Egypt sends
This treasure of an oyster; at whose foot,
To mend the petty present, I will piece
Her opulent throne with kingdoms: all the east,"
Say thou, "shall call her mistress." So he nodded,
And soberly did mount an arm-girt[1] steed,
Who neigh'd so high, that what I would have spoke
Was boastfully[2] dumb'd by him.
Cleo. What! was he sad, or merry?
Alex. Like to the time o' the year between the extremes
Of hot and cold: he was nor sad, nor merry.
Cleo. O well-divided disposition!—Note him,
Note him, good Charmian, 't is the man; but note him:
He was not sad, for he would shine on those
That make their looks by his: he was not merry
Which seem'd to tell them, his remembrance lay
In Egypt with his joy; but between both:
O heavenly mingle!—Be'st thou sad, or merry,
The violence of either thee becomes,
So does it no man else.—Met'st thou my posts?
Alex. Ay, madam, twenty several messengers.
Why do you send so thick?
Cleo. Who's born that day
When I forget to send to Antony,
Shall die a beggar.—Ink and paper, Charmian.—
Welcome, my good Alexas.—Did I, Charmian,
Ever love Cæsar so?
Char. O, that brave Cæsar!
Cleo. Be chok'd with such another emphasis!
Say, the brave Antony.
Char. The valiant Cæsar!
Cleo. By Isis, I will give thee bloody teeth,
If thou with Cæsar paragon again
My man of men.
Char. By your most gracious pardon,
I sing but after you.
Cleo. My sallad days,
When I was green in judgment:—cold in blood,
To say as I said then!—But come, away:
Get me ink and paper;
He shall have every day a several greeting,
Or I'll unpeople Egypt. [*Exeunt.*

[1] arm-gaunt: in f. e. [2] beastly: in f. e.

ACT II.

SCENE I.—Messina. A Room in POMPEY'S House.

Enter POMPEY, MENECRATES, *and* MENAS.

Pom. If the great gods be just, they shall assist
The deeds of justest men.
Mene. Know, worthy Pompey,
That what they do delay, they not deny.
Pom. Whiles we are suitors to their throne, decays
The thing we sue for.
Mene. We, ignorant of ourselves,
Beg often our own harms, which the wise powers
Deny us for our good; so find we profit
By losing of our prayers.
Pom. I shall do well:
The people love me, and the sea is mine;
My powers are crescent, and my auguring hope
Says, it will come to the full. Mark Antony
In Egypt sits at dinner, and will make
No wars without doors: Cæsar gets money, where
He loses hearts: Lepidus flatters both,
Of both is flatter'd; but he neither loves,
Nor either cares for him.
Men. Cæsar and Lepidus
Are in the field: a mighty strength they carry.
Pom. Where have you this? 't is false.
Men. From Silvius, sir
Pom. He dreams: I know, they are in Rome together
Looking for Antony. But all the charms of love,
Salt Cleopatra, soften thy warm[1] lip!
Let witchcraft join with beauty, lust with both:
Lay[2] up the libertine in a flood[3] of feasts,
Keep his brain fuming; Epicurean cooks,
Sharpen with cloyless sauce his appetite,
That sleep and feeding may prorogue his honour,
Even till a Lethe'd dulness.—How now, Varrius!

Enter VARRIUS.

Var. This is most certain, that I shall deliver.
Mark Antony is every hour in Rome
Expected; since he went from Egpyt, 't is
A space for farther travel.

[1] wand: in f. e. [2] Tie: in f. e. [3] field: in f. e.

Pom. I could have given less matter
A better ear.—Menas, I did not think,
This amorous surfeiter would have don'd his helm
For such a petty war: his soldiership
Is twice the other twain. But let us rear
The higher our opinion, that our stirring
Can from the lap of Egypt's widow pluck
The ne'er lust-wearied Antony.

Men. I cannot hope,
Cæsar and Antony shall well greet together:
His wife that 's dead did trespasses to Cæsar;
His brother warr'd upon him, although, I think,
Not mov'd by Antony.

Pom. I know not, Menas,
How lesser enmities may give way to greater.
Were 't not that we stand up against them all,
'T were pregnant they should square[1] between themselves;
For they have entertained cause enough
To draw their swords: but how the fear of us
May cement their divisions, and bind up
The petty difference, we yet not know.
Be it as our gods will have 't! It only stands
Our lives upon to use our strongest hands.
Come, Menas. [*Exeunt.*

SCENE II.—Rome. A Room in the House of LEPIDUS.

Enter ENOBARBUS *and* LEPIDUS.

Lep. Good Enobarbus, 't is a worthy deed,
And shall become you well, to entreat your captain
To soft and gentle speech.

Eno. I shall entreat him
To answer like himself: if Cæsar move him,
Let Antony look over Cæsar's head,
And speak as loud as Mars. By Jupiter,
Were I the wearer of Antonius' beard,
I would not shave 't to-day.

Lep. 'Tis not a time
For private stomaching.

Eno. Every time
Serves for the matter that is then born in 't.

Lep. But small to greater matters must give way.

Eno. Not if the small come first.

1 *Quarrel.*

Lep. Your speech is passion:
But, pray you, stir no embers up. Here comes
The noble Antony.

Enter ANTONY *and* VENTIDIUS

Eno. And yonder, Cæsar.

Enter CÆSAR, MECÆNAS, *and* AGRIPPA.

Ant. If we compose well here, to Parthia:
Hark you, Ventidius.

Cæs. I do not know,
Mecænas; ask Agrippa.

Lep. Noble friends,
That which combin'd us was most great, and let not
A leaner action rend us. What 's amiss,
May it be gently heard: when we debate
Our trivial difference loud, we do commit
Murder in healing wounds. Then, noble partners,
(The rather, for I earnestly beseech)
Touch you the sourest points with sweetest terms,
Nor curstness grow to the matter.

Ant. 'T is spoken well.
Were we before our armies, and to fight,
I should do thus. [*Shake hands.*[1]

Cæs. Welcome to Rome.

Ant. Thank you

Cæs. Sit.

Ant. Sit, sir.

Cæs. Nay, then—

Ant. I learn, you take things ill, which are not so,
Or, being, concern you not.

Cæs. I must be laugh'd at,
If, or for nothing, or a little, I
Should say myself offended; and with you
Chiefly i' the world: more laugh'd at, that I should
Once name you derogately, when to sound your name
It not concern'd me.

Ant. My being in Egypt, Cæsar,
What was 't to you?

Cæs. No more than my residing here at Rome
Might be to you in Egypt: yet, if you there
Did practise on my state, your being in Egypt
Might be my question.

Ant. How intend you, practis'd?

Cæs. You may be pleas'd to catch at mine intent,

[1] Not in f. e.

By what did here befal me. Your wife, and brother
Made wars upon me, and their contestation
Was theme for you; you were the word of war.
Ant. You do mistake your business: my brother never
Did urge me in his act: I did enquire it;
And have my learning from some true reports,
That drew their swords with you. Did he not rather
Discredit my authority with yours;
And make the wars alike against my stomach,
Having alike your cause? Of this my letters
Before did satisfy you. If you'll patch a quarrel,
No matter whole you have to make it with,
It must not be with this.
Cæs. You praise yourself
By laying defects of judgment to me; but
You patch'd up your excuses.
Ant. Not so; not so;
I know you could not lack, I am certain on't,
Very necessity of this thought, that I,
Your partner in the cause 'gainst which he fought,
Could not with graceful eyes attend those wars
Which fronted mine own peace. As for my wife,
I would you had her spirit in such another:
The third o' the world is yours, which with a snaffle,
You may pace easy, but not such a wife.
Eno. Would we had all such wives, that the men might go to wars with the women!
Ant. So much uncurbable, her garboils, Cæsar,
Made out of her impatience, (which not wanted
Shrewdness of policy too) I grieving grant,
Did you too much disquiet: for that, you must
But say, I could not help it.
Cæs. I wrote to you,
When rioting in Alexandria; you
Did pocket up my letters, and with taunts
Did gibe my missive out of audience.
Ant. Sir,
He fell upon me, ere admitted: then
Three kings I had newly feasted, and did want
Of what I was i' the morning; but, next day,
I told him of myself, which was as much
As to have ask'd him pardon. Let this fellow
Be nothing of our strife; if we contend,
Out of our question wipe him.

Cæs. You have broken
The article of your oath, which you shall never
Have tongue to charge me with.
Lep. Soft, Cæsar.
Ant. No, Lepidus, let him speak:
The honour's sacred which he talks on now,
Supposing that I lack'd it. But on, Cæsar;
The article of my oath.
Cæs. To lend me arms and aid when I requir'd them,
The which you both denied.
Ant. Neglected, rather;
And then, when poison'd hours had bound me up
From mine own knowledge. As nearly as I may,
I'll play the penitent to you; but mine honesty
Shall not make poor my greatness, nor my power
Work without it. Truth is, that Fulvia,
To have me out of Egypt, made wars here;
For which myself, the ignorant motive, do
So far ask pardon, as befits mine honour
To stoop in such a case.
Lep. 'T is nobly spoken.
Mec. If it might please you, to enforce no farther
The griefs between ye: to forget them quite,
Were to remember that the present need
Speaks to atone[1] you.
Lep. Worthily spoken, Mecænas.
Eno. Or, if you borrow one another's love for the instant, you may, when you hear no more words of Pompey, return it again: you shall have time to wrangle in, when you have nothing else to do.
Ant. Thou art a soldier only: speak no more.
Eno. That truth should be silent I had almost forgot.
Ant. You wrong this presence; therefore, speak no more.
Eno. Go to then; you[2] considerate stone.
Cæs. I do not much dislike the matter, but
The manner of his speech; for it cannot be,
We shall remain in friendship, our conditions
So differing in their acts. Yet, if I knew
What hoop should hold us staunch, from edge to edge
O' the world I would pursue it.
Agr. Give me leave, Cæsar,—

[1] *Reconcile.* [2] your: in folio.

Cæs. Speak, Agrippa.
Agr. Thou hast a sister by the mother's side,
Admir'd Octavia: great Mark Antony
Is now a widower.
Cæs. Say not so, Agrippa.
If Cleopatra heard you, your reproof
Were well deserv'd for[1] rashness.
Ant. I am not married, Cæsar: let me hear
Agrippa farther speak.
Agr. To hold you in perpetual amity,
To make you brothers, and to knit your hearts
With an unslipping knot, take Antony
Octavia to his wife; whose beauty claims
No worse a husband than the best of men,
Whose virtue and whose general graces speak
That which none else can utter. By this marriage,
All little jealousies, which now seem great,
And all great fears, which now import their dangers,
Would then be nothing: truths would be tales,
Where now half tales be truths: her love to both,
Would, each to other, and all loves to both,
Draw after her. Pardon what I have spoke,
For 't is a studied, not a present thought,
My duty ruminated.
Ant. Will Cæsar speak?
Cæs. Not till he hears how Antony is touch'd
With what is spoke already.
Ant. What power is in Agrippa,
If I would say, "Agrippa, be it so,"
To make this good?
Cæs. The power of Cæsar, and
His power unto Octavia.
Ant. May I never
To this good purpose, that so fairly shows,
Dream of impediment!—Let me have thy hand:
Further this act of grace, and from this hour,
The hearts of brothers govern in our loves,
And sway our great designs.
Cæs. There is my hand.
A sister I bequeath you, whom no brother [ANT. *takes it.*[2]
Did ever love so dearly: let her live
To join our kingdoms, and our hearts; and never
Fly off our loves again!

[1] of: in f. e. [2] Not in f. e.

Lep. Happily, amen.
Ant. I did not think to draw my sword 'gainst *Pompey;*
For he hath laid strange courtesies, and great,
Of late upon me: I must thank him, only
Lest my remembrance suffer ill report;
At heel of that, defy him.
Lep. Time calls upon us:
Of us must Pompey presently be sought,
Or else he seeks out us.
Ant. Where lies he?
Cæs. About the Mount Misenum.
Ant. What 's his strength
By land?
Cæs. Great, and increasing; but by sea
He is an absolute master.
Ant. So is the fame.
Would we had spoke together! Haste we for it;
Yet, ere we put ourselves in arms, despatch we
The business we have talk'd of.
Cæs. With most gladness;
And do invite you to my sister's view,
Whither straight I 'll lead you.
Ant. Let us, Lepidus,
Not lack your company.
Lep. Noble Antony,
Not sickness should detain me.
[*Flourish. Exeunt* CÆSAR, ANTONY, *and* LEPIDUS.
Mec. Welcome from Egypt, sir.
Eno. Half the heart of Cæsar, worthy Mecænas!—my honourable friend, Agrippa!—
Agr. Good Enobarbus!
Mec. We have cause to be glad, that matters are so well digested. You stay'd well by it in Egypt.
Eno. Ay, sir; we did sleep day out of countenance, and made the night light with drinking.
Mec. Eight wild boars roasted whole at a breakfast, and but twelve persons there; is this true?
Eno. This was but as a fly by an eagle: we had much more monstrous matter of feast, which worthily deserved noting.
Mec. She 's a most triumphant lady, if report be square to her.

Eno. When she first met Mark Antony, she pursed up his heart, upon the river of Cydnus.

Agr. There she appeared indeed, or my reporter devised well for her.

Eno. I will tell you.
The barge she sat in, like a burnish'd throne,
Burn'd on the water: the poop was beaten gold;
Purple the sails, and so perfumed, that
The winds were love-sick with them: the oars were
silver;
Which to the tune of flutes kept stroke, and made
The water, which they beat, to follow faster,
As amorous of their strokes. For her own person,
It beggar'd all description: she did lie
In her pavilion, (cloth of gold and[1] tissue)
O'er-picturing that Venus, where we see,
The fancy out-work nature: on each side her,
Stood pretty dimpled boys, like smiling Cupids,
With diverse-colour'd fans, whose wind did seem
To glow[2] the delicate cheeks which they did cool,
And what they undid, did.

Agr. O, rare for Antony!

Eno. Her gentlewomen, like the Nereides,
So many mermaids, tended her i' the eyes,
And made their bends adornings: at the helm
A seeming mermaid steers; the silken tackle
Smell[3] with the touches of those flower-soft hands,
That yarely[4] frame the office. From the barge
A strange invisible perfume hits the sense
Of the adjacent wharfs. The city cast
Her people out upon her; and Antony,
Enthron'd i' the market-place, did sit alone,
Whistling to the air; which, but for vacancy,
Had gone to gaze on Cleopatra too,
And made a gap in nature.

Agr. Rare Egyptian!

Eno. Upon her landing Antony sent to her,
Invited her to supper: she replied,
It should be better he became her guest,
Which she entreated. Our courteous Antony,
Whom ne'er the word of "No" woman heard speak,
Being barber'd ten times o'er, goes to the feast;
And for his ordinary pays his heart

[1] of: in f. e. [2] glove: in folio. [3] Swell: in f. e. [4] *Nimbly.*

For what his eyes eat only.
Agr. Royal wench!
She made great Cæsar lay his sword to bed;
He plough'd her, and she cropp'd.
Eno. I saw her once
Hop forty paces through the public street;
And having lost her breath, she spoke, and panted,
That she did make defect perfection,
And, breathless, power breathe forth.
Mec. Now Antony must leave her utterly.
Eno. Never; he will not.
Age cannot wither her, nor custom stale
Her infinite variety: other women cloy
The appetites they feed, but she makes hungry,
Where most she satisfies; for vilest things
Become themselves in her, that the holy priests
Bless her when she is riggish.
Mec. If beauty, wisdom, modesty, can settle
The heart of Antony, Octavia is
A blessed lottery to him.
Agr. Let us go.—
Good Enobarbus, make yourself my guest,
Whilst you abide here.
Eno. Humbly, sir, I thank you. [*Exeunt.*

SCENE III.—The Same. A Room in CÆSAR'S House

Enter CÆSAR, ANTONY, OCTAVIA *between them; Attendants.*

Ant. The world, and my great office, will sometimes
Divide me from your bosom.
Octa. All which time,
Before the gods my knee shall bow with prayers
To them for you.
Ant. Good night, sir.—My Octavia,
Read not my blemishes in the world's report:
I have not kept my square, but that to come
Shall all be done by the rule. Good night, dear lady.—
Good night, sir.
Cæs. Good night. [*Exeunt* CÆSAR *and* OCTAVIA

Enter a Soothsayer.

Ant. Now, sirrah: you do wish yourself in Egypt.
Sooth. Would I had never come from thence, nor you thither!
Ant. If you can, your reason?

Sooth. I see it in my motion, have it not in my tongue: but yet hie you to Egypt again.

Ant. Say to me, whose fortune shall rise higher, Cæsar's, or mine?

Sooth. Cæsar's.
Therefore, O Antony! stay not by his side:
Thy dæmon, that 's thy spirit which keeps thee, is
Noble, courageous, high, unmatchable,
Where Cæsar's is not; but near him thy angel
Becomes afeard,[1] as being o'erpower'd: therefore,
Make space enough between you.

Ant. Speak this no more.

Sooth. To none but thee; no more, but when to thee
If thou dost play with him at any game,
Thou art sure to lose; and, of that natural luck,
He beats thee 'gainst the odds: thy lustre thickens,
When he shines by. I say again, thy spirit
Is all afraid to govern thee near him,
But, he away, 't is noble.

Ant. Get thee gone:
Say to Ventidius, I would speak with him.—
[*Exit Soothsayer.*
He shall to Parthia.—Be it art, or hap,
He hath spoken true: the very dice obey him;
And in our sports my better cunning faints
Under his chance: if we draw lots, he speeds:
His cocks do win the battle still of mine,
When it is all to nought; and his quails ever
Beat mine, inhoop'd, at odds. I will to Egypt:
And though I make this marriage for my peace,

Enter VENTIDIUS.

I' the east my pleasure lies.—O! come, Ventidius,
You must to Parthia: your commission 's ready;
Follow me, and receive it. [*Exeunt.*

SCENE IV.—The Same. A Street.

Enter LEPIDUS, MECÆNAS, *and* AGRIPPA.

Lep. Trouble yourselves no farther: pray you, hasten
Your generals after.

Agr. Sir, Mark Antony
Will e'en but kiss Octavia, and we 'll follow.

Lep. Till I shall see you in your soldier's dress,
Which will become you both, farewell.

[1] a fear: in f e

Mec. We shall,
As I conceive the journey, be at Mount[1]
Before you, Lepidus.
Lep. Your way is shorter;
My purposes do draw me much about:
You 'll win two days upon me.
Mec. Agr. Sir, good success!
Lep. Farewell. [*Exeunt.*

SCENE V.—Alexandria. A Room in the Palace.

Enter CLEOPATRA, CHARMIAN, IRAS, *and* ALEXAS.

Cleo. Give me some music; music, moody food
Of us that trade in love.
Attend. The music, ho!

Enter MARDIAN.

Cleo. Let it alone; let's to billiards: come, Charmian.
Char. My arm is sore, best play with Mardian.
Cleo. As well a woman with an eunuch play'd,
As with a woman.—Come, you 'll play with me, sir?
Mar. As well as I can, madam.
Cleo. And when good will is show'd, though 't come [too short,
The actor may plead pardon. I 'll none now.—
Give me mine angle,—we 'll to the river: there,
My music playing far off, I will betray
Tawny-finn'd[2] fishes; my bended hook shall pierce
Their slimy jaws, and as I draw them up,
I 'll think them every one an Antony,
And say, Ah, ha! you 're caught.
Char. 'T was merry, when
You wager'd on your angling; when your diver
Did hang a salt-fish on his hook, which he
With fervency drew up.
Cleo. That time.—O times!—
I laugh'd him out of patience; and that night
I laugh'd him into patience: and next morn,
Ere the ninth hour, I drunk him to his bed;
Then, put my tires and mantles on him, whilst
I wore his sword Philippian.—

Enter ELIS, *a Messenger.*[3]

O! from Italy?—
Ram thou thy fruitful tidings in mine ears,
That long time have been barren.

[1] Mt. Misenum. [2] Tawney-fine: in folio. Theobald made the change. [3] *Enter a Messenger:* in f. e.

Mess. Madam, madam,—
Cleo. Antony 's dead ?—
If thou say so, villain, thou kill'st thy mistress :
But well and free,
If thou so yield him, there is gold, and here
My bluest veins to kiss ; a hand, that kings
Have lipp'd, and trembled kissing.
Mess. First, madam, he is well.
Cleo. Why, there 's more gold.
But, sirrah, mark, we use
To say, the dead are well : bring it to that,
The gold I give thee will I melt, and pour
Down thy ill-uttering throat.
Mess. Good madam, hear me.
Cleo. Well, go to, I will ;
But there 's no goodness in thy face. If Antony
Be free, and healthful, why so tart a favour
To trumpet such good tidings ? if not well,
Thou shouldst come like a fury crown'd with snakes,
Not like a formal man.
Mess. Will 't please you hear me ?
Cleo. I have a mind to strike thee, ere thou speak'st
Yet, if thou say, Antony lives, 't is well ;
Or friends with Cæsar, or not captive to him,
I 'll set thee in a shower of gold, and hail
Rich pearls upon thee.
Mess. Madam, he 's well.
Cleo. Well said.
Mess. And friends with Cæsar.
Cleo. Thou 'rt an honest man.
Mess. Cæsar and he are greater friends than ever.
Cleo. Make thee a fortune from me.
Mess. But yet, madam,—
Cleo. I do not like "but yet," it does allay
The good precedence ; fie upon "but yet !"
"But yet" is as a gaoler to bring forth
Some monstrous malefactor. Pr'ythee, friend,
Pour out the pack of matter to mine ear,
The good and bad together. He 's friends with Cæsar,
In state of health, thou say'st : and, thou say'st, free.
Mess. Free, madam ? no ; I made no such report :
He 's bound unto Octavia.
Cleo. For what good turn ?
Mess. For the best turn i' the bed

Cleo. I am pale, Charmian.
Mess. Madam, he 's married to Octavia.
Cleo. The most infectious pestilence upon thee!
[*Strikes him down.*
Mess. Good madam, patience.
Cleo. What say you?—Hence,
[*Strikes him again*
Horrible villain! or I 'll spurn thine eyes
Like balls before me: I 'll unhair thy head.
[*She hales him up and down.*
Thou shalt be whipp'd with wire, and stew'd in brine,
Smarting in lingering pickle.
Mess. Gracious madam,
I, that do bring the news, made not the match.
Cleo. Say, 't is not so, a province I will give thee,
And make thy fortunes proud: the blow thou hadst
Shall make thy peace for moving me to rage;
And I will boot thee with what gift beside
Thy modesty can beg.
Mess. He 's married, madam.
Cleo. Rogue! thou hast liv'd too long. [*Draws a Knife.*
Mess. Nay, then I 'll run.—
What mean you, madam? I have made no fault. [*Exit.*
Char. Good madam, keep yourself within yourself:
The man is innocent.
Cleo. Some innocents 'scape not the thunder-bolt.—
Melt Egypt into Nile! and kindly creatures
Turn all to serpents—Call the slave again:
Though I am mad, I will not bite him.—Call.
Char. He is afeard to come.
Cleo. I will not hurt him.—
These hands do lack nobility, that they strike
A meaner than myself; since I myself
Have given myself the cause.—Come hither, sir.

Re-enter Elis, *the Messenger.*[1]

Though it be honest, it is never good
To bring bad news: give to a gracious message
An host of tongues; but let ill tidings tell
Themselves, when they be felt.
Mess. I have done my duty.
Cleo. Is he married?
I cannot hate thee worser than I do,
If thou again say, Yes.

[1] *Re-enter Messenger:* in f. e.

Mess. He 's married, madam.
Cleo. The gods confound thee! dost thou hold there still?
Mess. Should I lie, madam?
Cleo. O! I would, thou didst,
So half my Egypt were submerg'd, and made
A cistern for scal'd snakes. Go, get thee hence:
Hadst thou Narcissus in thy face, to me
Thou wouldst appear most ugly. He is married?
Mess. I crave your highness' pardon.
Cleo. He is married?
Mess. Take no offence, that I would not offend you:
To punish me for what you make me do,
Seems much unequal. He is married to Octavia.
Cleo. O! that his fault should make a knave of thee,
That art not! What! thou 'rt sure of?[1]—Get thee hence:
The merchandise which thou hast brought from Rome,
Are all too dear for me: lie they upon thy hand,
And be undone by 'em! [*Exit Messenger.*
Char. Good your highness, patience.
Cleo. In praising Antony, I have disprais'd Cæsar.
Char. Many times, madam.
Cleo. I am paid for 't now.
Lead me from hence;
I faint.—O Iras! Charmian!—'T is no matter.—
Go to the fellow, good Alexas; bid him
Report the feature of Octavia, her years,
Her inclination, let him not leave out
The colour of her hair: bring me word quickly.—
[*Exit* ALEXAS.
Let him for ever go?—let him not—Charmian,
Though he be painted one way like a Gorgon,
The other way he 's a Mars.—Bid you Alexas
[*To* MARDIAN.
Bring me word, how tall she is.—Pity me, Charmian,
But do not speak to me.—Lead me to my chamber.
[*Exeunt*

[1] That art not what thou 'rt sure of: in folio.

SCENE VI.—Near Misenum.

Flourish. Enter POMPEY *and* MENAS, *at one side, with Drum and Trumpet: at another,* CÆSAR, LEPIDUS, ANTONY, ENOBARBUS, MECÆNAS, *with Soldiers marching.*

Pom Your hostages I have, so have you mine;
And we shall talk before we fight.
Cæs. Most meet,
That first we come to words; and therefore have we
Our written purposes before us sent,
Which, if thou hast consider'd, let us know
If 't will tie up thy discontented sword,
And carry back to Sicily much tall youth,
That else must perish here.
Pom. To you all three,
The senators alone of this great world,
Chief factors for the gods.—I do not know,
Wherefore my father should revengers want,
Having a son, and friends; since Julius Cæsar,
Who at Philippi the good Brutus ghosted,
There saw you labouring for him. What was it,
That mov'd pale Cassius to conspire? And what
Made the all-honour'd, honest, Roman Brutus,
With the arm'd rest, courtiers of beauteous freedom,
To drench the Capitol, but that they would
Have one man but a man? And that is it
Hath made me rig my navy, at whose burden
The anger'd ocean foams; with which I meant
To scourge th' ingratitude that despiteful Rome
Cast on my noble father.
Cæs. Take your time.
Ant. Thou canst not fear[1] us, Pompey, with thy sails;
We 'll speak with thee at sea: at land, thou know'st
How much we do o'er-count thee.
Pom. At land, indeed,
Thou dost o'er-count me of my father's house:
But, since the cuckoo builds not for himself,
Remain in 't as thou may'st.
Lep. Be pleas'd to tell us,
(For this is from the present) how you take

[1] *Alarm.*

The offers we have sent you.
Cæs. There 's the point.
Ant. Which do not be entreated to, but weigh
What it is worth embrac'd.
Cæs. And what may follow,
To try a larger fortune.
Pom. You have made me offer
Of Sicily, Sardinia; and I must
Rid all the sea of pirates; then, to send
Measures of wheat to Rome: this 'greed upon,
To part with unhack'd edges, and bear back
Targes undinted.
Cæs. Ant. Lep. That 's our offer.
Pom. Know then,
I came before you here, a man prepar'd
To take this offer; but Mark Antony
Put me to some impatience.—Though I lose
The praise of it by telling, you must know,
When Cæsar and your brother were at blows,
Your mother came to Sicily, and did find
Her welcome friendly.
Ant. I have heard it, Pompey;
And am well studied for a liberal thanks,
Which I do owe you.
Pom. Let me have your hand.
I did not think, sir, to have met you here.
[*They take Hands.*[1]
Ant. The beds i' the east are soft; and thanks to you,
That call'd me timelier than my purpose hither,
For I have gain'd by it.
Cæs. Since I saw you last,
There is a change upon you.
Pom. Well, I know not
What counts harsh fortune casts upon my face,
But in my bosom shall she never come,
To make my heart her vassal.
Lep. Well met here.
Pom. I hope so, Lepidus.—Thus we are agreed.
I crave, our composition may be written,
And seal'd between us.
Cæs. That 's the next to do.
Pom. We 'll feast each other, ere we part; and let us

[1] Not in f. e.

Draw lots who shall begin.

Ant. That will I, Pompey.

Pom. No, Antony, take the lot; but, first
Or last, your fine Egyptian cookery
Shall have the fame. I have heard, that Julius Cæsar
Grew fat with feasting there.

Ant. You have heard much

Pom. I have fair meanings, sir.

Ant. And fair words to them

Pom. Then, so much have I heard:
And I have heard, Apollodorus carried—

Eno. No more of that:—he did so.

Pom. What, I pray you?

Eno. A certain queen to Cæsar in a mattress.

Pom. I know thee now: how far'st thou, soldier?

Eno. Well,
And well am like to do; I perceive,
Four feasts are toward.

Pom. Let me shake thy hand:
I never hated thee. I have seen thee fight,
When I have envied thy behaviour.

Eno. Sir,
I never lov'd you much; but I have prais'd you,
When you have well deserv'd ten times as much
As I have said you did.

Pom. Enjoy thy plainness,
It nothing ill becomes thee.—
Aboard my galley I invite you all:
Will you lead, lords?

Cæs. Ant. Lep. Show us the way, sir.

Pom. Come.

[*Exeunt* POMPEY, CÆSAR, ANTONY, LEPIDUS, *Soldiers and Attendants.*

Men. Thy father, Pompey, would ne'er have made this treaty.—[*Aside.*]—You and I have known, sir.

Eno. At sea, I think.

Men. We have, sir.

Eno. You have done well by water.

Men. And you by land.

Eno. I will praise any man that will praise me; though it cannot be denied what I have done by land.

Men. Nor what I have done by water.

Eno. Yes; something you can deny for your own safety: you have been a great thief by sea.

Men And you by land.

Eno. There I deny my land service. But give me your hand, Menas: if our eyes had authority, here they might take two thieves kissing.

Men. All men's faces are true, whatsoe'er their hands are.

Eno. But there is never a fair woman has a true face.

Men. No slander; they steal hearts.

Eno. We came hither to fight with you.

Men. For my part, I am sorry it is turned to a drinking. Pompey doth this day laugh away his fortune.

Eno. If he do, sure, he cannot weep it back again.

Men. You have said, sir. We looked not for Mark Antony here: pray you, is he married to Cleopatra?

Eno. Cæsar's sister is call'd Octavia.

Men. True, sir; she was the wife of Caius Marcellus.

Eno. But she is now the wife of Marcus Antonius.

Men. Pray you, sir?

Eno. 'T is true.

Men. Then is Cæsar, and he, for ever knit together.

Eno. If I were bound to divine of this unity, I would not prophesy so.

Men. I think, the policy of that purpose made more in the marriage, than the love of the parties.

Eno. I think so too: but you shall find, the band that seems to tie their friendship together will be the very strangler of their amity. Octavia is of a holy, cold, and still conversation.

Men. Who would not have his wife so?

Eno. Not he, that himself is not so; which is Mark Antony. He will to his Egyptian dish again: then, shall the sighs of Octavia blow the fire up in Cæsar; and, as I said before, that which is the strength of their amity, shall prove the immediate author of their variance. Antony will use his affection where it is: he married but his occasion here.

Men. And thus it may be. Come, sir, will you aboard? I have a health for you.

Eno. I shall take it, sir: we have used our throats in Egypt.

Men. Come; let 's away. [*Exeunt.*

SCENE VII.—On Board POMPEY's Galley, lying near Misenum.

Music. Enter Two or Three Servants, with a Banquet.

1 *Serv.* Here they 'll be, man. Some o' their plants are ill-rooted already; the least wind i' the world will blow them down.

2 *Serv.* Lepidus is high-coloured.

1 *Serv.* They have made him drink alms-drink.

2 *Serv.* As they pinch one another by the disposition, he cries out, "no more:" reconciles them to his entreaty, and himself to the drink.

1 *Serv.* But it raises the greater war between him and his discretion.

2 *Serv.* Why, this it is to have a name in great men's fellowship: I had as lief have a reed that will do me no service, as a partizan I could not heave.

1 *Serv.* To be called into a huge sphere, and not to be seen to move in 't, are the holes where eyes should be, which pitifully disaster the cheeks.

A Sennet[1] *sounded. Enter* CÆSAR, ANTONY, POMPEY, LEPIDUS, AGRIPPA, MECÆNAS, ENOBARBUS, MENAS, *with other Captains.*

Ant. Thus do they, sir. [*To* CÆSAR.] They take the flow o' the Nile
By certain scales i' the pyramid: they know,
By the height, the lowness, or the mean, if dearth,
Or foison[2] follow. The higher Nilus swells,
The more it promises: as it ebbs, the seedsman
Upon the slime and ooze scatters his grain,
And shortly comes to harvest.

Lep. You have strange serpents there.

Ant. Ay, Lepidus.

Lep. Your serpent of Egypt is bred, now, of your mud by the operation of your sun: so is your crocodile.

Ant. They are so.

Pom. Sit,—and some wine!—A health to Lepidus.

Lep. I am not so well as I should be, but I 'll ne'er out.

Eno. Not till you have slept: I fear me, you 'll be in, till then.

Lep. Nay, certainly, I have heard, the Ptolemies' pyramids are very goodly things; without contradiction, I have heard that.

[1] *Trumpet blast.* [2] *Plenty*

Men. [*Aside.*] Pompey, a word.

Pom. [*Aside.*] Say in mine ear: what is 't?

Men. [*Aside.*] Forsake thy seat, I do beseech thee,
And hear me speak a word. [captain,

Pom. [*Aside.*] Forbear me till anon.—
This wine for Lepidus.

Lep. What manner o' thing is your crocodile?

Ant. It is shaped, sir, like itself, and it is as broad as it hath breadth; it is just so high as it is, and moves with its own organs: it lives by that which nourisheth it, and the elements once out of it, it transmigrates.

Lep. What colour is it of?

Ant. Of its own colour too.

Lep. 'T is a strange serpent.

Ant. 'T is so; and the tears of it are wet.

Cæs. Will this description satisfy him?

Ant. With the health that Pompey gives him, else he is a very epicure.

Pom. [*To* MENAS, *aside.*] Go, hang, sir, hang! Tell me of that? away!
Do as I bid you.—Where 's this cup I call'd for?

Men. [*Aside.*] If for the sake of merit thou wilt hear
Rise from thy stool. [me,

Pom. [*Aside.*] I think, thou 'rt mad. The matter?
[*Walks aside.*

Men. I have ever held my cap off to thy fortunes.

Pom. Thou hast serv'd me with much faith. What 's else to say?—
Be jolly, lords.

Ant. These quick-sands, Lepidus,
Keep off them, for you sink.

Men. Wilt thou be lord of all the world?

Pom. What say'st thou?

Men. Wilt thou be lord of the whole world? That 's twice.

Pom. How should that be?

Men. But entertain it,
And though thou think me poor, I am the man
Will give thee all the world.

Pom. Hast thou drunk well?

Men. No, Pompey, I have kept me from the cup.
Thou art, if thou dar'st be, the earthly Jove:
Whate'er the ocean pales,[1] or sky inclips,[2]

[1] *Encloses.* [2] *Embraces*

Is thine, if thou wilt have 't.
Pom. Show me which way.
Men. These three world-sharers, these competitors,
Are in thy vessel: let me cut the cable;
And, when we are put off, fall to their throats:
All then is thine.
Pom. Ah! this thou shouldst have done,
And not have spoke on 't. In me, 't is villainy;
In thee, 't had been good service. Thou must know,
'T is not my profit that does lead mine honour,
Mine honour, it. Repent, that e'er thy tongue
Hath so betray'd thine act: being done unknown,
I should have found it afterwards well done,
But must condemn it now. Desist, and drink.
Men. [*Aside.*] For this,
I 'll never follow thy pall'd fortunes more.
Who seeks, and will not take, when once 't is offer'd,
Shall never find it more.
Pom. This health to Lepidus.
Ant. Bear him ashore.—I'll pledge it for him, Pompey.
Eno. Here 's to thee, Menas.
Men. Enobarbus, welcome.
Pom. Fill, till the cup be hid.
Eno. There 's a strong fellow, Menas.
[*Pointing to the Attendant who carries off* LEPIDUS.
Men. Why?
Eno. He bears
The third part of the world, man: see'st not?
Men. The third part, then, is drunk: would it were all,
That it might go on wheels![1]
Eno. Drink thou; increase the reels.
Men. Come.
Pom. This is not yet an Alexandrian feast.
Ant. It ripens towards it.—Strike[2] the vessels, ho!
Here is to Cæsar.
Cæs. I could well forbear it.
It 's monstrous labour, when I wash my brain,
And it grows fouler.
Ant. Be a child o' the time.
Cæs. Profess[3] it, I 'll make answer; but I had rather fast
From all four days, than drink so much in one.
Eno. Ha, my brave emperor! [*To* ANTONY.

[1] A proverbial expression. [2] *Tap.* [3] Possess: in f. e.

Shall we dance now the Egyptian Bacchanals,
And celebrate our drink?

Pom. Let 's ha 't, good soldier.

Ant. Come, let us all shake hands,
Till that the conquering wine hath steep'd our sense
In soft and delicate Lethe.

Eno. All take hands.—
Make battery to our ears with the loud music;
The while I 'll place you: then, the boy shall sing;
The holding[1] every man shall bear, as loud
As his strong sides can volley.

[*Music plays.* ENOBARBUS *places them hand in hand.*

SONG, *by the Boy.*[2]

Come, thou monarch of the vine,
Plumpy Bacchus, with pink eyne:
In thy vats our cares be drown'd;
With thy grapes our hairs be crown'd;
Cup us, till the world go round; } The burden.
Cup us, till the world go round! }

Cæs. What would you more?—Pompey, good night.
—Good brother,
Let me request you off: our graver business
Frowns at this levity.—Gentle lords, let 's part;
You see, we have burnt our cheeks. Strong Enobarbe
Is weaker than the wine, and mine own tongue
Splits what it speaks: the wild disguise hath almost
Antick'd us all. What needs more words? Good night.—
Good Antony, your hand.

Pom. I 'll try you on the shore.

Ant. And shall, sir. Give 's your hand.

Pom. O, Antony!
You have my father's house.—But what? we are friends.
Come down into the boat.

Eno. Take heed you fall not.—

[*Exeunt* POMPEY, CÆSAR, ANTONY, *and Attendants.*

Menas, I 'll not on shore.

Men. No, to my cabin.—
These drums!—these trumpets, flutes! what!
Let Neptune hear, we bid a loud farewell
To these great fellows: sound, and be hang'd! sound out! [*A Flourish.*

Eno. Ho, says 'a!—There 's my cap.

Men. Ho!—noble captain! come. [*Exeunt*

[1] *Burden.* [2] *by the Boy:* not in f. e.

ACT III.

SCENE I.—A Plain in Syria.

Enter VENTIDIUS, *as it were in triumph, with* SILIUS, *and other Romans, Officers, and Soldiers; the dead Body of* PACORUS *borne before him.*

Ven. Now, darting Parthia, art thou struck; and now
Pleas'd fortune does of Marcus Crassus' death
Make me revenger.—Bear the king's son's body
Before our army.—Thy Pacorus, Orodes,
Pays this for Marcus Crassus.
Sil. Noble Ventidius.
Whilst yet with Parthian blood thy sword is warm,
The fugitive Parthians follow: spur through Media,
Mesopotamia, and the shelters whither
The routed fly: so thy grand captain, Antony,
Shall set thee on triumphant chariots, and
Put garlands on thy head.
Ven. O Silius, Silius!
I have done enough: a lower place, note well,
May make too great an act; for learn this, Silius,
Better to leave undone, than by our deeds acquire
Too high a fame, when him we serve 's away.
Cæsar and Antony have ever won
More in their officer, than person: Sossius,
One of my place in Syria, his lieutenant,
For quick accumulation of renown,
Which he achiev'd by the minute, lost his favour.
Who does i' the wars more than his captain can,
Becomes his captain's captain; and ambition,
The soldier's virtue, rather makes choice of loss,
Than gain which darkens him.
I could do more to do Antonius good,
But 't would offend him; and in his offence
Should my performance perish.
Sil. Thou hast, Ventidius, that
Without the which a soldier, and his sword,
Gains scarce distinction. Thou wilt write to Antony?
Ven. I 'll humbly signify what in his name,
That magical word of war, we have effected;
How, with his banners and his well-paid ranks
The ne'er-yet-beaten horse of Parthia

We have jaded out o' the field.
Sil. Where is he now?
Ven. He purposeth to Athens; whither, with what haste
The weight we must convey with us will permit,
We shall appear before him.—On, there! pass along.
[*Exeunt.*

SCENE II.—Rome. An Ante-Chamber in CÆSAR'S House.

Enter AGRIPPA, *and* ENOBARBUS, *meeting.*

Agr. What! are the brothers parted?
Eno. They have despatch'd with Pompey: he is gone;
The other three are sealing. Octavia weeps
To part from Rome; Cæsar is sad; and Lepidus,
Since Pompey's feast, as Menas says, is troubled
With the green sickness.
Agr. 'T is a noble Lepidus.
Eno. A very fine one. O, how he loves Cæsar!
Agr. Nay, but how dearly he adores Mark Antony!
Eno. Cæsar? Why, he 's the Jupiter of men.
Agr. What 's Antony? The god of Jupiter.
Eno. Spake you of Cæsar? How! the nonpareil!
Agr. O Antony! O thou Arabian bird!
Eno. Would you praise Cæsar, say,—Cæsar;—go no farther.
Agr. Indeed, he ply'd them both with excellent praises.
Eno. But he loves Cæsar best;—yet he loves Antony.
Ho! hearts, tongues, figures, scribes, bards, poets cannot
Think, speak, cast, write, sing, number, ho!
His love to Antony. But as for Cæsar,
Kneel down, kneel down, and wonder.
Agr. Both he loves.
Eno. They are his shards,[1] and he their beetle. So,— [*Trumpets.*
This is to horse.—Adieu, noble Agrippa.
Agr. Good fortune, worthy soldier; and farewell.

Enter CÆSAR, ANTONY, LEPIDUS, *and* OCTAVIA.

Ant. No farther, sir.
Cæs. You take from me a great part of myself;
Use me well in 't.—Sister, prove such a wife

[1] *Scaly wings*

As my thoughts make thee, and as my farthest band
Shall pass on thy approof.—Most noble Antony,
Let not the piece of virtue, which is set
Betwixt us as the cement of our love,
To keep it builded, be the ram to batter
The fortress of it; for better might we
Have loved without this mean, if on both parts
This be not cherish'd.

Ant. Make me not offended
In your distrust.

Cæs. I have said.

Ant. You shall not find,
Though you be therein curious, the least cause
For what you seem to fear. So, the gods keep you,
And make the hearts of Romans serve your ends.
We will here part.

Cæs. Farewell, my dearest sister, fare thee well:
The elements be kind to thee, and make
Thy spirits all of comfort! fare thee well.

Oct. My noble brother!—

Ant. The April 's in her eyes; it is love's spring,
And these the showers to bring it on.—Be cheerful.

Oct. Sir, look well to my husband's house; and—

Cæs. What, Octavia?

Oct. I 'll tell you in your ear.

Ant. Her tongue will not obey her heart, nor can
Her heart inform her tongue; the swan's down feather,
That stands upon the swell at the full of tide,
And neither way inclines.

Eno. Will Cæsar weep? [*Aside to* AGRIPPA.

Agr. He has a cloud in 's face.

Eno. He were the worse for that, were he a horse;
So is he, being a man.

Agr. Why, Enobarbus,
When Antony found Julius Cæsar dead,
He cried almost to roaring; and he wept,
When at Philippi he found Brutus slain.

Eno. That year, indeed, he was troubled with a rheum;
What willingly he did confound, he wail'd:
Believe 't, till I weep too.

Cæs. No, sweet Octavia,
You shall hear from me still: the time shall not
Out-go my thinking on you.

Ant. Come, sir, come;
I 'll wrestle with you in my strength of love:
Look, here I have you; thus I let you go,
And give you to the gods.
Cæs. Adieu; be happy.
Lep. Let all the number of the stars give light
To thy fair way!
Cæs. Farewell, farewell. [*Kisses* OCTAVIA
Ant. Farewell. [*Trumpets sound. Exeunt.*

SCENE III.—Alexandria. A Room in the Palace.

Enter CLEOPATRA, CHARMIAN, IRAS, *and* ALEXAS.

Cleo. Where is the fellow?
Alex. Half afeard to come.
Cleo. Go to, go to.—Come hither, sir.

Enter ELIS, *the Messenger.*[1]

Alex. Good majesty,
Herod of Jewry dare not look upon you,
But when you are well pleas'd.
Cleo. That Herod's head
I 'll have: but how, when Antony is gone,
Through whom I might command it?—Come thou near.
Mess. Most gracious majesty,—
Cleo. Didst thou behold
Octavia?
Mess. Ay, dread queen.
Cleo. Where?
Mess. Madam, in Rome.
I look'd her in the face; and saw her led
Between her brother and Mark Antony.
Cleo. Is she as tall as me?
Mess. She is not, madam.
Cleo. Didst hear her speak? Is she shrill-tongu'd, or low?
Mess. Madam, I heard her speak: she is low-voic'd.
Cleo. That 's not so good: he cannot like her long.
Char. Like her? O Isis! 't is impossible.
Cleo. I think so, Charmian: dull of tongue, and dwarfish!—
What majesty is in her gait? Remember,
If e'er thou look'dst on majesty.
Mess. She creeps;
Her motion and her station are as one:

[1] *Enter a Messenger:* in f. e

She shows a body rather than a life;
A statue, than a breather.

Cleo. Is this certain?

Mess. Or I have no observance.

Char. Three in Egypt
Cannot make better note.

Cleo. He 's very knowing,
I do perceive 't.—There 's nothing in her yet.—
The fellow has good judgment.

Char. Excellent.

Cleo. Guess at her years, I pr'ythee.

Mess. Madam,
She was a widow.

Cleo. Widow?—Charmian, hark.

Mess. And I do think, she 's thirty.

Cleo. Bear'st thou her face in mind? is 't long, or round?

Mess. Round, even to faultiness.

Cleo. For the most part, too, they are foolish that are so.—
Her hair, what colour?

Mess. Brown, madam; and her forehead
As low as you could wish it.

Cleo. There 's gold for thee:
Thou must not take my former sharpness ill.
I will employ thee back again: I find thee
Most fit for business. Go, make thee ready;
Our letters are prepar'd. [*Exit Messenger.*

Char. A proper man.

Cleo. Indeed, he is so: I repent me much,
That I so harry'd[1] him. Why, methinks, by him,
This creature 's no such thing.

Char. Nothing, madam.

Cleo. The man hath seen some majesty, and should know.

Char. Hath he seen majesty? Isis else defend,
And serving you so long!

Cleo. I have one thing more to ask him yet, good Charmian:
But 't is no matter; thou shalt bring him to me
Where I will write. All may be well enough.

Char. I will warrant you, madam. [*Exeunt.*

[1] *Vexed.*

SCENE IV.—Athens. A Room in ANTONY'S House.

Enter ANTONY *and* OCTAVIA.

Ant. Nay, nay, Octavia, not only that,—
That were excusable, that, and thousands more
Of semblable import,—but he hath wag'd
New wars 'gainst Pompey; made his will, and read it
To public ear,
Spoke scantly of me: when perforce he could not
But pay me terms of honour, coldly and sickly
He vented them; most narrow measure lent me.
When the best hint was given him, he but look'd,[1]
Or did it from his teeth.

Oct. O, my good lord!
Believe not all; or, if you must believe,
Stomach not all. A more unhappy lady,
If this division chance, ne'er stood between,
Praying for both parts:
The good gods will mock me presently,
When I shall pray, "O, bless my lord and husband!"
Undo that prayer, by crying out as loud,
"O, bless my brother!" Husband win, win brother,
Prays, and destroys the prayer; no midway
'Twixt these extremes at all.

Ant. Gentle Octavia,
Let your best love draw to that point, which seeks
Best to preserve it. If I lose mine honour,
I lose myself; better I were not yours,
Than yours so branchless. But, as you requested,
Yourself shall go between us: the mean time, lady,
I'll raise the preparation of a war
Shall stay your brother. Make your soonest haste:
So, your desires are yours.

Oct. Thanks to my lord.
The Jove of power make me most weak, most weak,
Your reconciler! Wars 'twixt you twain would be,
As if the world should cleave, and that slain men
Should solder up the rift.

Ant. When it appears to you where this begins,
Turn your displeasure that way; for our faults
Can never be so equal, that your love
Can equally move with them. Provide your going;
Choose your own company, and command what cost
Your heart has mind to. [*Exeunt.*

[3] not took 't: in f. e.

SCENE V.—The Same. Another Room in the Same.

Enter ENOBARBUS *and* EROS, *meeting.*

Eno. How now, friend Eros?

Eros. There is strange news come, sir.

Eno. What, man?

Eros. Cæsar and Lepidus have made wars upon Pompey.

Eno. This is old: what is the success?

Eros. Cæsar, having made use of him in the wars 'gainst Pompey, presently denied him rivality, would not let him partake in the glory of the action; and not resting here, accuses him of letters he had formerly wrote to Pompey; upon his own appeal, seizes him: so the poor third is up till death enlarge his confine.

Eno. Then, world,[1] thou hast a pair of chaps, no more;
And throw between them all the food thou hast,
They 'll grind each other. Where is Antony?

Eros. He 's walking in the garden—thus; and spurns
The rush that lies before him; cries, "Fool, Lepidus!"
And threats the throat of that his officer,
That murder'd Pompey.

Eno. Our great navy 's rigg'd.

Eros. For Italy, and Cæsar. More, Domitius;
My lord desires you presently: my news
I might have told hereafter.

Eno. 'T will be naught;
But let it be.—Bring me to Antony.

Eros. Come, sir. [*Exeunt.*

SCENE VI.—Rome. A Room in CÆSAR'S House.

Enter CÆSAR, AGRIPPA, *and* MECÆNAS.

Cæs. Contemning Rome, he has done all this, and more,
In Alexandria: here 's the manner of it.
I' the market-place, on a tribunal silver'd,
Cleopatra and himself in chairs of gold
Were publicly enthron'd: at their feet sat
Cæsarion, whom they call my father's son,
And all the unlawful issue, that their lust
Since then hath made between them. Unto her
He gave the 'stablishment of Egypt; made her

[1] would: in folio. Johnson made the change

Of lower Syria, Cyprus, Lydia,
Absolute queen.
Mec. This in the public eye?
Cæs. I' the common show-place, where they exercise.
His sons he there[1] proclaim'd the kings of kings:
Great Media, Parthia, and Armenia,
He gave to Alexander; to Ptolemy he assign'd
Syria, Cilicia, and Phœnicia. She
In the habiliments of the goddess Isis
That day appear'd; and oft before gave audience,
As 'tis reported, so.
Mec. Let Rome be thus
Inform'd.
Agr. Who, queasy with his insolence
Already, will their good thoughts call from him.
Cæs. The people know it; and have now receiv'd
His accusations.
Agr. Whom does he accuse?
Cæs. Cæsar; and that, having in Sicily
Sextus Pompeius spoil'd, we had not rated him
His part o' the isle: then does he say, he lent me
Some shipping unrestor'd: lastly, he frets,
That Lepidus of the triumvirate
Should be depos'd; and, being, that we detain
All his revenue.
Agr. Sir, this should be answer'd.
Cæs. 'T is done already, and a messenger gone.
I have told him, Lepidus was grown too cruel;
That he his high authority abus'd,
And did deserve his change: for what I have conquer'd,
I grant him part; but then, in his Armenia,
And other of his conquer'd kingdoms, I
Demand the like.
Mec. He 'll never yield to that.
Cæs. Nor must not, then, be yielded to in this.
Enter OCTAVIA, *with her Train.*
Oct. Hail, Cæsar, and my lord! hail, most dear Cæsar!
Cæs. That ever I should call thee cast-away!
Oct. You have not call'd me so, nor have you cause.
Cæs. Why have you stol'n upon us thus? You come not
Like Cæsar's sister: the wife of Antony
Should have an army for an usher, and

[1] hither: in folio. Steevens made the change.

The neighs of horse to tell of her approach,
Long ere she did appear; the trees by the way,
Should have borne men, and expectation fainted,
Longing for what it had not; nay, the dust
Should have ascended to the roof of heaven,
Rais'd by your populous troops. But you are come
A market-maid to Rome, and have prevented
The ostentation of our love, which, left unshown,
Is often held[1] unlov'd: we should have met you
By sea and land, supplying every stage
With an augmented greeting.
Oct. Good my lord,
To come thus was I not constrain'd, but did it
Of my free-will. My lord, Mark Antony,
Hearing that you prepar'd for war, acquainted
My grieved ear withal; whereon, I begg'd
His pardon for return.
Cæs. Which soon he granted,
Being an obstruct[2] 'tween his lust and him.
Oct. Do not say so, my lord.
Cæs. I have eyes upon him,
And his affairs come to me on the wind.
Where is he now?
Oct. My lord, in Athens.
Cæs. No, my most wronged sister; Cleopatra
Hath nodded him to her: he hath given his empire
Up to a whore: they are now levying
The kings o' the earth for war. He hath assembled
Bocchus, the king of Lybia; Archelaus,
Of Cappadocia; Philadelphos, king
Of Paphlagonia; the Thracian king, Adallas:
King Malchas of Arabia; king of Pont;
Herod of Jewry; Mithridates, king
Of Comagene; Polemon and Amintas,
The kings of Mede, and Lycaonia,
With a more larger list of sceptres.
Oct. Ah me, most wretched,
That have my heart parted betwixt two friends,
That do afflict each other!
Cæs. Welcome hither.
Your letters did withhold our breaking forth,
Till we perceiv'd, both how you were wronged,[3]

[1] left: in f. e. [2] abstract: in folio. Warburton made the change.
[3] wrong led: in f. e.

And we in negligent danger. Cheer your heart:
Be you not troubled with the time, which drives
O'er your content these strong necessities;
But let determin'd things to destiny
Hold unbewail'd their way. Welcome to Rome;
Nothing more dear to me. You are abus'd
Beyond the mark of thought; and the high gods,
To do you justice, make his ministers
Of us and those that love you. Best of comfort;
And ever welcome to us.

Agr. Welcome, lady.

Mec. Welcome, dear madam.
Each heart in Rome does love and pity you:
Only the adulterous Antony, most large
In his abominations, turns you off,
And gives his potent regiment[1] to a trull,
That noises it against us.

Oct. Is it so, sir?

Cæs. Most certain. Sister, welcome: pray you,
Be ever known to patience. My dear'st sister! [*Exeunt.*

SCENE VII.—ANTONY'S Camp, near the Promontory of Actium.

Enter CLEOPATRA *and* ENOBARBUS.

Cleo. I will be even with thee, doubt it not.

Eno. But why, why, why?

Cleo. Thou hast forspoke[2] my being in these wars,
And say'st, it is not fit.

Eno. Well, is it, is it?

Cleo. If not denounc'd against us, why should not we
Be there in person?

Eno. [*Aside.*] Well, I could reply:—
If we should serve with horse and mares together,
The horse were merely lost; the mares would bear
A soldier, and his horse.

Cleo. What is 't you say?

Eno. Your presence needs must puzzle Antony;
Take from his heart, take from his brain, from 's time,
What should not then be spar'd. He is already
Traduc'd for levity; and 't is said in Rome,
That Photinus an eunuch, and your maids,
Manage this war.

Cleo. Sink Rome; and their tongues rot,

[1] *Government.* [2] *Spoken against.*

That speak against us! A charge we bear i' the war,
And as the president of my kingdom will
Appear there for a man. Speak not against it;
I will not stay behind.

Eno. Nay, I have done.
Here comes the emperor.

Enter ANTONY *and* CANIDIUS.

Ant. Is 't not strange, Canidius,
That from Tarentum, and Brundusium,
He could so quickly cut the Ionian sea,
And take in[1] Toryne?—You have heard on 't, sweet?

Cleo. Celerity is never more admir'd,
Than by the negligent.

Ant. A good rebuke,
Which might have well become the best of men,
To taunt at slackness.—Canidius, we
Will fight with him by sea.

Cleo. By sea! what else?

Can. Why will my lord do so?

Ant. For that he dares us to 't.

Eno. So hath my lord dar'd him to single fight.

Can. Ay, and to wage this battle at Pharsalia,
Where Cæsar fought with Pompey; but these offers,
Which serve not for his vantage, he shakes off,
And so should you.

Eno. Your ships are not well mann'd;
Your mariners are muliters, reapers, people
Ingross'd by swift impress: in Cæsar's fleet
Are those, that often have 'gainst Pompey fought.
Their ships are yare,[2] yours, heavy: no disgrace
Shall fall you for refusing him at sea,
Being prepar'd for land.

Ant. By sea, by sea.

Eno. Most worthy sir, you therein throw away
The absolute soldiership you have by land;
Distract your army, which doth most consist
Of war-mark'd footmen; leave unexecuted
Your own renowned knowledge; quite forego
The way which promises assurance, and
Give up yourself merely to chance and hazard,
From firm security.

Ant. I'll fight at sea.

Cleo. I have sixty sails, Cæsar none better.

[1] *Conquer.* [2] *Easily managed.*

Ant. Our overplus of shipping will we burn,
And with the rest, full-mann'd, from the head of Actium
Beat th' approaching Cæsar: but if we fail,

Enter a Messenger.

We then can do 't at land.—Thy business?
Mess. The news is true, my lord; he is descried;
Cæsar has taken Toryne.
Ant. Can he be there in person? 't is impossible;
Strange, that his power should be.—Canidius,
Our nineteen legions thou shalt hold by land,
And our twelve thousand horse: we 'll to our ship.

Enter a Soldier.

Away, my Thetis!—How now, worthy soldier!
Sold. O, noble emperor! do not fight by sea;
Trust not to rotten planks. Do you misdoubt
This sword, and these my wounds? Let the Egyptians,
And the Phœnicians, go a ducking; we
Have used to conquer standing on the earth,
And fighting foot to foot.
Ant. Well, well.—Away!
[*Exeunt* ANTONY, CLEOPATRA, *and* ENOBARBUS.
Sold. By Hercules, I think, I am i' the right.
Can. Soldier, thou art; but his whole action grows
Not in the power on 't: so our leader 's led,
And we are women's men.
Sold. You keep by land
The legions and the horse whole, do you not?
Can. Marcus Octavius, Marcus Justeius,
Publicola, and Cælius, are for sea;
But we keep whole by land. This speed of Cæsar's
Carries beyond belief.
Sold. While he was yet in Rome,
His power went out in such distractions, as
Beguil'd all spies.
Can. Who 's his lieutenant, hear you?
Sold. They say, one Taurus.
Can. Well I know the man.

Enter a Messenger.

Mess. The emperor calls Canidius.
Can. With news the time 's with labour; and throws forth
Each minute some. [*Exeunt.*

SCENE VIII.—A Plain near Actium.

Enter CÆSAR, TAURUS, *Officers, and others.*

Cæs. Taurus!
Taur. My lord.
Cæs. Strike not by land; keep whole:
Provoke not battle, till we have done at sea.
Do not exceed the prescript of this scroll: [*Giving it.*[1]
Our fortune lies upon this jump. [*Exeunt.*

Enter ANTONY *and* ENOBARBUS.

Ant. Set we our squadrons on yond' side o' the hill,
In eye of Cæsar's battle; from which place
We may the number of the ships behold,
And so proceed accordingly. [*Exeunt.*

Enter CANIDIUS, *marching with his Land Army one Way over the Stage; and* TAURUS, *the Lieutenant of* CÆSAR, *the other Way. After their going in is heard the Noise of a Sea-Fight.*

Alarum. Re-enter ENOBARBUS.

Eno. Naught, naught, all naught! I can behold no longer.
The Antoniad, the Egyptian admiral,
With all their sixty, fly, and turn the rudder:
To see 't, mine eyes are blasted.

Enter SCARUS.

Scar. Gods, and goddesses,
All the whole synod of them!
Eno. What 's thy passion?
Scar. The greater cantle[2] of the world is lost
With very ignorance: we have kiss'd away
Kingdoms and provinces.
Eno. How appears the fight?
Scar. On our side like the token'd pestilence,
Where death is sure. Yond' ribald hag[3] of Egypt,
Whom leprosy o'ertake! i' the midst o' the fight,—
When vantage, like a pair of twins, appear'd
Both as the same, or rather ours the elder;—
The brize[4] upon her like a cow in June,
Hoists sails, and flies.
Eno. That I beheld:
Mine eyes did sicken at the sight, and could not
Endure a further view.

[1] Not in f. e. [2] *Portion.* [3] ribald-rid nag: in f. e. [4] *Gad fly.*

Scar. She once being loof'd,
The noble ruin of her magic, Antony,
Claps on his sea-wing, and like a doting mallard,
Leaving the fight in height, flies after her.
I never saw an action of such shame:
Experience, manhood, honour, ne'er before
Did violate so itself.

Eno. Alack, alack!

Enter CANIDIUS.

Can. Our fortune on the sea is out of breath,
And sinks most lamentably. Had our general
Been what he knew himself, it had gone well:
O! he has given example for our flight,
Most grossly, by his own.

Eno. Ay, are you thereabouts? Why then, good night
Indeed.

Can. Towards Peloponnesus are they fled.

Scar. 'T is easy to 't; and there I will attend
What farther comes.

Can. To Cæsar will I render
My legions, and my horse: six kings already
Show me the way of yielding.

Eno. I'll yet follow
The wounded chance of Antony, though my reason
Sits in the wind against me. [*Exeunt.*

SCENE IX.—Alexandria. A Room in the Palace.

Enter ANTONY, *and Attendants.*

Ant. Hark! the land bids me tread no more upon 't;
It is asham'd to bear me.—Friends, come hither,
I am so lated in the world, that I
Have lost my way for ever.—I have a ship
Laden with gold; take that, divide it; fly,
And make your peace with Cæsar.

Att. Fly! not we.

Ant. I have fled myself, and have instructed cowards
To run, and show their shoulders.—Friends, be gone;
I have myself resolv'd upon a course,
Which has no need of you; be gone:
My treasure 's in the harbour, take it.—O!
I follow'd that I blush to look upon:
My very hairs do mutiny; for the white
Reprove the brown for rashness, and they them
For fear and doting.—Friends, be gone: you shall

Have letters from me to some friends, that will
Sweep your way for you. Pray you, look not sad,
Nor make replies of lothness: take the hint
Which my despair proclaims; let that be left
Which leaves itself: to the sea-side straightway:
I will possess you of that ship and treasure.
Leave me, I pray, a little; 'pray you now:
Nay, do so; for, indeed, I have lost command,
Therefore, I pray you. I'll see you by and by.
[*Sits down.*

Enter EROS, *and* CLEOPATRA, *led by* CHARMIAN, *and* IRAS.

Eros. Nay, gentle madam, to him; comfort him.
Iras. Do, most dear queen.
Char. Do! Why, what else?
Cleo. Let me sit down.—O Juno!
Ant. No, no, no, no, no.
Eros. See you here, sir?
Ant. O fie, fie, fie!
Char. Madam,—
Iras. Madam: O good empress!—
Eros. Sir, sir,—
Ant. Yes, my lord, yes.—He, at Philippi, kept
His sword e'en like a dancer, while I struck
The lean and wrinkled Cassius; and 't was I
That the mad Brutus ended: he alone
Dealt on lieutenantry, and no practice had
In the brave squares of war; yet now—No matter.
Cleo. Ah! stand by.
Eros. The queen, my lord, the queen.
Iras. Go to him, madam, speak to him:
He is unqualitied with very shame.
Cleo. Well then,—sustain me:—O!
Eros. Most noble sir, arise; the queen approaches
Her head 's declin'd, and death will seize her; but
Your comfort makes the rescue.
Ant. I have offended reputation
By most unnoble swerving.
Eros. Sir, the queen.
Ant. O! whither hast thou led me, Egypt? See,
How I convey my shame out of thine eyes,
By looking back what I have left behind
'Stroy'd in dishonour.
Cleo. O my lord, my lord!
Forgive my fearful sails: I little thought,

You would have follow'd.
Ant. Egypt, thou knew'st too well.
My heart was to thy rudder tied by the strings,
And thou shouldst tow me after: o'er my spirit
Thy full supremacy thou knew'st, and that
Thy beck might from the bidding of the gods
Command me.
Cleo. O, my pardon!
Ant. Now I must
To the young man send humble treaties, dodge
And palter in the shifts of lowness, who
With half the bulk o' the world play'd as I pleas'd,
Making, and marring fortunes. You did know,
How much you were my conqueror; and that
My sword, made weak by my affection, would
Obey it on all cause.
Cleo. Pardon, pardon!
Ant. Fall not a tear, I say: one of them rates
All that is won and lost. Give me a kiss;
Even this repays me.—We sent our schoolmaster;
Is he come back?—Love, I am full of lead.—
Some wine, within there, and our viands!—Fortune knows,
We scorn her most when most she offers blows. [*Exeunt.*

SCENE X.—CÆSAR'S Camp in Egypt.

Enter CÆSAR, DOLABELLA, THYREUS, *and others.*

Cæs. Let him appear that 's come from Antony.—
Know you him?
Dol. Cæsar, 't is his schoolmaster:
An argument that he is pluck'd, when hither
He sends so poor a pinion of his wing,
Which had superfluous kings for messengers,
Not many moons gone by.

Enter EUPHRONIUS.

Cæs. Approach, and speak.
Eup. Such as I am, I come from Antony:
I was of late as petty to his ends,
As is the morn-dew on the myrtle leaf
To his grand sea.
Cæs. Be it so. Declare thine office.
Eup. Lord of his fortunes he salutes thee, and
Requires to live in Egypt; which not granted,
He lessens his requests, and to thee sues

To let him breathe between the heavens and earth,
A private man in Athens: this for him.
Next, Cleopatra does confess thy greatness,
Submits her to thy might, and of thee craves
The circle of the Ptolemies for her heirs,
Now hazarded to thy grace.
Cæs. For Antony,
I have no ears to his request. The queen
Of audience, nor desire, shall fail; so she
From Egypt drive her all-disgraced friend,
Or take his life there: this if she perform,
She shall not sue unheard. So to them both.
Eup. Fortune pursue thee!
Cæs. Bring him through the bands.
[*Exit* EUPHRONIUS.
To try thy eloquence, now 't is time; despatch.
From Antony win Cleopatra: promise, [*To* THYREUS.
And in our name, what she requires; add more,
From thine invention, offers. Women are not
In their best fortunes strong, but want will perjure
The ne'er-touch'd vestal. Try thy cunning, Thyreus;
Make thine own edict for thy pains, which we
Will answer as a law.
Thyr. Cæsar, I go.
Cæs. Observe how Antony becomes his flaw,
And what thou think'st his very action speaks
In every power that moves.
Thyr. Cæsar, I shall. [*Exeunt.*

SCENE XI.—Alexandria. A Room in the Palace.

Enter CLEOPATRA, ENOBARBUS, CHARMIAN, *and* IRAS.

Cleo. What shall we do, Enobarbus?
Eno. Think, and die
Cleo. Is Antony, or we, in fault for this?
Eno. Antony only, that would make his will
Lord of his reason. What though you fled
From that great face of war, whose several ranges
Frighted each other, why should he follow?
The itch of his affection should not then
Have nick'd his captainship; at such a point,
When half to half the world oppos'd, he being
The mooted[1] question. 'T was a shame, no less
Than was his loss, to course your flying flags,

[1] mered: in f. e.

And leave his navy gazing.
Cleo. Pr'ythee, peace.

Enter ANTONY, *with* EUPHRONIUS.

Ant. Is that his answer?
Eup. Ay, my lord.
Ant. The queen shall then have courtesy, so she
Will yield us up.
Eup. He says so.
Ant. Let her know it.—
To the boy Cæsar send this grizled head
And he will fill thy wishes to the brim
With principalities.
Cleo. That head, my lord?
Ant. To him again. Tell him, he wears the rose
Of youth upon him, from which the world should note
Something particular: his coin, ships, legions,
May be a coward's; whose ministers would prevail
Under the service of a child, as soon
As i' the command of Cæsar: I dare him, therefore,
To lay his gay comparisons apart,
And answer me declin'd; sword against sword,
Ourselves alone. I 'll write it: follow me.

[*Exeunt* ANTONY *and* EUPHRONIUS.

Eno. Yes, like enough, high-battled Cæsar will
Unstate his happiness, and be stag'd t' the show
Against a sworder.—I see, men's judgments are
A parcel of their fortunes; and things outward
Do draw the inward qualities[1] after them,
To suffer all alike. That he should dream,
Knowing all miseries,[2] the full Cæsar will
Answer his emptiness!—Cæsar, thou hast subdu'd
His judgment too.

Enter an Attendant.

Ant. A messenger from Cæsar.
Cleo. What, no more ceremony?—See, my women!—
Against the blown rose may they stop their nose,
That kneel'd unto the bud.—Admit him, sir.
Eno. Mine honesty and I begin to square.[3] [*Aside*
The loyalty well held to fools does make
Our faith mere folly: yet he, that can endure
To follow with allegiance a fallen lord,
Does conquer him that did his master conquer,
And earns a place i' the story.

[1] quality: in f. e. [2] measures: in f. e. [3] *Quarrel*

Enter THYREUS.

Cleo. Cæsar's will?
Thyr. Hear it apart.
Cleo. None but friends: say boldly.
Thyr. So, haply, are they friends to Antony.
Eno. He needs as many, sir, as Cæsar has,
Or needs not us. If Cæsar please, our master
Will leap to be his friend: for us, you know,
Whose he is, we are, and that 's Cæsar's.
Thyr. So.—
Thus then, thou most renown'd: Cæsar entreats,
Not to consider in what case thou stand'st,
Farther then he is Cæsar.
Cleo. Go on: right royal.
Thyr. He knows, that you embrace not Antony
As you did love, but as you feard'd him.
Cleo. O!
Thyr. The scars upon your honour, therefore, he
Does pity, as constrained blemishes,
Not as deserv'd.
Cleo. He is a god, and knows
What is most right. Mine honour was not yielded,
But conquer'd merely.
Eno. [*Aside.*] To be sure of that,
I will ask Antony.—Sir, sir, thou 'rt so leaky,
That we must leave thee to thy sinking, for
Thy dearest quit thee. [*Exit* ENOBARBUS.
Thyr. Shall I say to Cæsar
What you require of him? for he partly begs
To be desir'd to give. It much would please him,
That of his fortunes you should make a staff
To lean upon; but it would warm his spirits,
To hear from me you had left Antony,
And put yourself under his shroud, who is[1]
The universal landlord.
Cleo. What 's your name?
Thyr. My name is Thyreus.
Cleo. Most kind messenger,
Say to great Cæsar, that[2] in deputation[3]
I kiss his conqu'ring hand: tell him, I am prompt
To lay my crown at 's feet, and there to kneel:
Tell him, from his all-obeying breath I hear

[1] The words "who is," are not in f. e. [2] this: in f. e. [3] disputation: in f. e.

The doom of Egypt.
Thyr. 'T is your noblest course.
Wisdom and fortune combating together,
If that the former dare but what it can,
No chance may shake it. Give me grace to lay
My duty on your hand.
Cleo. Your Cæsar's father oft,
When he hath mus'd of taking kingdoms in,
Bestow'd his lips on that unworthy place,
As it rain'd kisses. [THYR. *kisses her Hand.*[1]

Re-enter ANTONY *and* ENOBARBUS.

Ant. Favours, by Jove that thunders!—
What art thou, fellow?
Thyr. One, that but performs
The bidding of the fullest man, and worthiest
To have command obey'd.
Eno. You will be whipp'd.
Ant. Approach, there.—Ah, you kite!—Now gods and devils!
Authority melts from me: of late, when I cry'd, "ho!"
Like boys unto a muss, kings would start forth,
And cry, "Your will?" Have you no ears? I am

Enter Attendants.

Antony yet. Take hence this Jack, and whip him.
Eno. 'T is better playing with a lion's whelp,
Than with an old one dying.
Ant. Moon and stars!
Whip him.—Were 't twenty of the greatest tributaries
That do acknowledge Cæsar, should I find them
So saucy with the hand of—she here, what 's her name,
Since she was Cleopatra?—Whip him, fellows,
Till, like a boy, you see him cringe his face,
And whine aloud for mercy. Take him hence.
Thyr. Mark Antony,—
Ant. Tug him away: being whipp'd,
Bring him again.—The Jack of Cæsar shall
Bear us an errand to him.—

[*Exeunt Attend. with* THYREUS.

You were half blasted ere I knew you: ha!
Have I my pillow left unpress'd in Rome,
Forborne the getting of a lawful race,
And by a gem of women, to be abus'd
By one that looks on feeders?

[1] Not in f. e.

Cleo. Good my lord,—
Ant. You have been a boggler ever:—
But when we in our viciousness grow hard,
(O misery on 't!) the wise gods seel[1] our eyes,
In our own filth drop our clear judgments; make us
Adore our errors; laugh at us, while we strut
To our confusion.
Cleo. O! is it come to this?
Ant. I found you as a morsel, cold upon
Dead Cæsar's trencher: nay, you were a fragment
Of Cneius Pompey's; besides what hotter hours,
Unregister'd in vulgar fame, you have
Luxuriously pick'd out; for, I am sure,
Though you can guess what temperance should be,
You know not what it is.
Cleo. Wherefore is this?
Ant. To let a fellow that will take rewards,
And say, "God quit you!" be familiar with
My playfellow, your hand; that kingly seal,
And plighter of high hearts!—O! that I were
Upon the hill of Basan, to outroar
The horned herd, for I have savage cause;
And to proclaim it civilly were like
A halter'd neck, which does the hangman thank
For being yare about him.—
Re-enter Attendants, with THYREUS.
Is he whipp'd?
1 *Att.* Soundly, my lord.
Ant. Cry'd he? and begg'd he pardon?
1 *Att* He did ask favour.
Ant. If that thy father live, let him repent
Thou wast not made his daughter; and be thou sorry
To follow Cæsar in his triumph, since
Thou hast been whipp'd for following him: henceforth,
The white hand of a lady fever thee:
Shake but to look on 't. Get thee back to Cæsar,
Tell him thy entertainment: look, thou say,
He makes me angry with him; for he seems
Proud and disdainful, harping on what I am,
Not what he knew I was. He makes me angry,
And at this time most easy 't is to do 't,
When my good stars, that were my former guides,
Have empty left their orbs, and shot their fires

[1] *Blind.*

Into the abysm of hell. If he mislike
My speech, and what is done, tell him, he has
Hipparchus, my enfranchis'd bondman, whom
He may at pleasure whip, or hang, or torture,
As he shall like, to quit me. Urge it thou:
Hence, with thy stripes! begone! [*Exit* THYREUS.
Cleo. Have you done yet?
Ant. Alack! our terrene moon
Is now eclips'd, and it portends alone
The fall of Antony.
Cleo. I must stay his time.
Ant. To flatter Cæsar, would you mingle eyes
With one that ties his points?[1]
Cleo. Not know me yet?
Ant. Cold-hearted toward me?
Cleo. Ah, dear! if it be so,
From my cold heart let heaven engender hail,
And poison it in the source, and the first stone
Drop in my neck: as it determines, so
Dissolve my life! The next Cæsarion smite,
Till by degrees the memory of my womb,
Together with my brave Egyptians all,
By the discandying[2] of this pelleted storm,
Lie graveless, till the flies and gnats of Nile
Have buried them for prey!
Ant. I am satisfied.
Cæsar sits down in Alexandria, where
I will oppose his fate. Our force by land
Hath nobly held; our sever'd navy, too,
Have knit again, a fleet threat'ning most sealike.
Where hast thou been, my heart?—Dost thou hear,
lady?
If from the field I shall return once more
To kiss these lips, I will appear in blood;
I and my sword will earn our chronicle:
There 's hope in 't yet.
Cleo That 's my brave lord!
Ant. I will be treble-sinew'd, hearted, breath'd,
And fight maliciously: for when mine hours
Were nice and lucky, men did ransom lives
Of me for jests; but now I 'll set my teeth,
And send to darkness all that stop me.—Come,

[1] *Tags* to strings by which garments were fastened. [2] discandering: in folios.

Let's have one other gaudy[1] night.—Call to me
All my sad captains: fill our bowls; once more
Let's mock the midnight bell.
Cleo. It is my birthday:
I had thought to have held it poor; but since my lord
Is Antony again, I will be Cleopatra.
Ant. We will yet do well.
Cleo. Call all his noble captains to my lord.
Ant. Do so, we'll speak to them; and to-night I'll force
The wine peep through their scars.—Come on, my queen;
There's sap in 't yet. The next time I do fight,
I'll make death love me. for I will contend
Even with his pestilent scythe.
[*Exeunt* ANTONY, CLEOPATRA, *and Attendants.*
Eno. Now he'll outstare the lightning. To be furious,
Is to be frighted out of fear; and in that mood,
The dove will peck the estridge; and I see still,
A diminution in our captain's brain
Restores his heart. When valour preys on[2] reason,
It eats the sword it fights with. I will seek
Some way to leave him. [*Exit*

ACT IV.

SCENE I.—CÆSAR's Camp at Alexandria.

Enter CÆSAR, *reading a Letter;* AGRIPPA, MECÆNAS, *and others.*

Cæs. He calls me boy, and chides, as he had power
To beat me out of Egypt; my messenger
He hath whipp'd with rods, dares me to personal combat,
Cæsar to Antony: let the old ruffian know
I have many other ways to die; mean time,
Laugh at his challenge.
Mec. Cæsar must think,
When one so great begins to rage, he's hunted

[1] Latin, *gaudium;* festivity. [2] in: in folio.

Even to falling. Give him no breath, but now
Make boot of his distraction: never anger
Made good guard for itself.

Cæs. Let our best heads
Know, that to-morrow the last of many battles
We mean to fight. Within our files there are,
Of those that serv'd Mark Antony but late,
Enough to fetch him in. See it done;
And feast the army: we have store to do 't,
And they have earn'd the waste.—Poor Antony!
[*Exeunt.*

SCENE II.—Alexandria. A Room in the Palace.

Enter ANTONY, CLEOPATRA, ENOBARBUS, CHARMIAN, IRAS, ALEXAS, *and others.*

Ant. He will not fight with me, Domitius?

Eno. No.

Ant. Why should he not?

Eno. He thinks, being twenty times of better fortune,
He is twenty men to one.

Ant. To-morrow, soldier,
By sea and land I 'll fight: or I will live,
Or bathe my dying honour in the blood
Shall make it live again. Woo't thou fight well?

Eno. I 'll strike; and cry, "Take all."

Ant. Well said; come on.—
Call forth my household servants: let 's to-night

Enter Servants.

Be bounteous at our meal.—Give me thy hand,
Thou hast been rightly honest;—so hast thou;—
Thou,—and thou,—and thou:—you have serv'd me
And kings have been your fellows. [well,

Cleo. What means this?

Eno. 'T is one of those odd tricks, which sorrow shoots
Out of the mind.

Ant. And thou art honest too.
I wish I could be made so many men,
And all of you clapp'd up together in
An Antony, that I might do you service,
So good as you have done.

Serv. The gods forbid!

Ant. Well, my good fellows, wait on me to-night;
Scant not my cups, and make as much of me,
As when mine empire was your fellow too,

And suffer'd my command.
Cleo. What does he mean?
Eno. To make his followers weep.
Ant. Tend me to-night,
May be, it is the period of your duty:
Haply, you shall not see me more; or if,
A mangled shadow: perchance, to-morrow
You 'll serve another master. I look on you,
As one that takes his leave. Mine honest friends,
I turn you not away; but, like a master
Married to your good service, stay till death.
Tend me to-night two hours, I ask no more,
And the gods yield you for 't!
Eno. What mean you, sir,
To give them this discomfort? Look, they weep;
And I, an ass, am onion-ey'd: for shame,
Transform us not to women.
Ant. Ho, ho, ho!
Now, the witch take me, if I meant it thus.
Grace grow where those drops fall! My hearty friends,
You take me in too dolorous a sense,
For I spake to you for your comfort; did desire you
To burn this night with torches. Know, my hearts,
I hope well of to-morrow; and will lead you,
Where rather I 'll expect victorious life,
Than death and honour. Let 's to supper; come,
And drown consideration. [*Exeunt.*

SCENE III.—The Same. Before the Palace.

Enter Two Soldiers, to their Guard.

1 *Sold.* Brother, good night: to-morrow is the day.
2 *Sold.* It will determine one way: fare you well.
Heard you of nothing strange about the streets?
1 *Sold.* Nothing. What news?
2 *Sold.* Belike, 't is but a rumour. Good night to you.
1 *Sold.* Well, sir, good night.

Enter Two other Soldiers.

2 *Sold.* Soldiers, have careful watch.
3 *Sold.* And you. Good night, good night.
[*The first Two place themselves at their Posts.*
4 *Sold.* Here we: [*They take their Posts.*] and if to-morrow
Our navy thrive, I have an absolute hope
Our landmen will stand up.

3 *Sold.* 'T is a brave army,
And full of purpose.
[*Music of Hautboys under the Stage.*
4 *Sold.* Peace! what noise?
1 *Sold.* List, list!
2 *Sold.* Hark!
1 *Sold.* Music i' the air.
3 *Sold.* Under the earth.
4 *Sold.* It signs well, does it not?
3 *Sold.* No.
1 *Sold.* Peace! I say. What should this mean?
2 *Sold.* 'T is the god Hercules, who Antony lov'd,
Now leaves him.
1 *Sold.* Walk; let 's see if other watchmen
Do hear what we do. [*They advance to another Post.*
2 *Sold.* How now, masters!
Omnes. How now!
How now! do you hear this? [*Speaking together.*
1 *Sold.* Ay; Is 't not strange?
3 *Sold.* Do you hear, masters? do you hear?
1 *Sold.* Follow the noise so far as we have quarter;
Let 's see how it will give off.
Omnes. Content: 'T is strange. [*Exeunt.*

SCENE IV.—The Same. A Room in the Palace.

Enter ANTONY, *and* CLEOPATRA; CHARMIAN, *and others, attending.*

Ant. Eros! mine armour, Eros!
Cleo. Sleep a little.
Ant. No, my chuck.—Eros, come; mine armour, Eros!

Enter EROS, *with Armour.*

Come, good fellow, put mine[1] iron on:—
If fortune be not ours to-day, it is
Because we brave her.—Come.
Cleo. Nay, I 'll help too.
What 's this for?
Ant. Ah, let be, let be! thou art
The armourer of my heart:—false, false; this, this.
Cleo. Sooth, la! I 'll help.[2]
Ant. Thus it must be.[3] Well, well;
We shall thrive now.—Seest thou, my good fellow?

[1] thine: in f. e. [2] This and the previous speech, are printed as one in the folio. Hanmer made the change. [3] f. e. give these words to CLEOPATRA.

Go, put on thy defences.
Eros. Briefly, sir.
Cleo. Is not this buckled well?
Ant. Rarely, rarely:
He that unbuckles this, till we do please
To doff 't for our repose, shall bear[1] a storm.—
Thou fumblest, Eros; and my queen 's a squire
More tight at this, than thou. Despatch.—O, love!
That thou couldst see my wars to-day, and knew'st
The royal occupation! thou shouldst see

Enter an armed Soldier.

A workman in 't.—Good morrow to thee; welcome:
Thou look'st like him that knows a warlike charge.
To business that we love we rise betime,
And go to 't with delight.
Sold. A thousand, sir,
Early though 't be, have on their riveted trim,
And at the port expect you. [*Shout. Trumpets flourish.*

Enter Captains, and Soldiers.

Capt. The morn is fair.—Good morrow, general.
All. Good morrow, general.
Ant. 'T is well blown, lads.
This morning, like the spirit of a youth
That means to be of note, begins betimes.—
So so; come, give me that: this way; well said.
Fare thee well, dame: whate'er becomes of me,
This is a soldier's kiss. Rebukable, [*Kisses her.*
And worthy shameful check it were, to stand
On more mechanic compliment: I'll leave thee
Now, like a man of steel.—You, that will fight,
Follow me close; I'll bring you to 't.—Adieu.
[*Exeunt* ANTONY, EROS, *Officers, and Soldiers.*
Char. Please you, retire to your chamber.
Cleo. Lead me.
He goes forth gallantly. That he and Cæsar might
Determine this great war in single fight!
Then, Antony,—but now,—well, on. [*Exeunt.*

SCENE V.—ANTONY'S Camp near Alexandria.

Trumpets sound. Enter ANTONY *and* EROS; *a Soldier meeting them.*

Sold. The gods make this a happy day to Antony
Ant. Would thou, and those thy scars, had once prevail'd

[1] hear: in f. e.

To make me fight at land!
Sold. Hadst thou done so,
The kings that have revolted, and the soldier
That has this morning left thee, would have still
Follow'd thy heels.
Ant. Who 's gone this morning?
Sold. Who?
One ever near thee: call for Enobarbus,
He shall not hear thee; or from Cæsar's camp
Say, "I am none of thine."
Ant. What say'st thou?
Sold. Sir,
He is with Cæsar.
Eros. Sir, his chests and treasure
He has not with him.
Ant. Is he gone?
Sold. Most certain.
Ant. Go, Eros, send his treasure after; do it:
Detain no jot, I charge thee. Write to him
(I will subscribe) gentle adieus, and greetings:
Say, that I wish he never find more cause
To change a master.—O! my fortunes have
Corrupted honest men:—despatch.—Enobarbus!
[*Exeunt.*

SCENE VI.—CÆSAR's Camp before Alexandria.

Flourish. Enter CÆSAR, *with* AGRIPPA, ENOBARBUS, *and others.*

Cæs. Go forth, Agrippa, and begin the fight.
Our will is, Antony be took alive;
Make it so known.
Agr. Cæsar, I shall. [*Exit* AGRIPPA.
Cæs. The time of universal peace is near:
Prove this a prosperous day, the three-nook'd world
Shall bear the olive freely.

Enter a Messenger.

Mess. Antony
Is come into the field.
Cæs. Go; charge Agrippa
Plant those that have revolted in the van,
That Antony may seem to spend his fury
Upon himself. [*Exeunt all but* ENOBARBUS.[1]
Eno. Alexas did revolt, and went to Jewry on

[1] *Exeunt* CÆSAR *and Train:* in f. e.

Affairs of Antony; there did persuade
Great Herod to incline himself to Cæsar,
And leave his master Antony: for this pains
Cæsar hath hang'd him. Canidius, and the rest
That fell away, have entertainment, but
No honourable trust. I have done ill,
Of which I do accuse myself so sorely,
That I will joy no more.

Enter a Soldier of CÆSAR'S.

Sold. Enobarbus, Antony
Hath after thee sent all thy treasure, with
His bounty overplus: the messenger
Came on my guard, and at thy tent is now
Unloading of his mules.

Eno. I give it you.

Sold. Mock not, Enobarbus,
I tell you true: best you safed[1] the bringer
Out of the host; I must attend mine office,
Or would have done 't myself. Your emperor
Continues still a Jove. [*Exit Soldier.*

Eno. I am alone the villain of the earth,
And feel I am so most.—O Antony!
Thou mine of bounty, how wouldst thou have paid
My better service, when my turpitude
Thou dost so crown with gold! This blows my heart:
If swift thought break it not, a swifter mean
Shall outstrike thought: but thought will do 't, I feel.
I fight against thee?—No: I will go seek
Some ditch, wherein to die; the foul'st best fits
My latter part of life. [*Exit.*

SCENE VII.—Field of Battle between the Camps.

Alarum. Drums and Trumpets. Enter AGRIPPA, *and others.*

Agr. Retire; we have engag'd ourselves too far.
Cæsar himself has work, and our oppression
Exceeds what we expected. [*Exeunt.*

Alarum. Enter ANTONY, *and* SCARUS *wounded.*

Scar. O my brave emperor, this is fought indeed!
Had we done so at first, we had driven them home
With clouts about their heads. [*Shouts afar off.*[2]

Ant. Thou bleed'st apace.

Scar. I had a wound here that was like a T,

[1] *Made safe.* [2] Not in f. e.

But now 't is made an H.

Ant. They do retire.

Scar. We 'll beat 'em into bench-holes. I have yet
Room for six scotches more.

Enter EROS.

Eros. They are beaten, sir; and our advantage serves
For a fair victory.

Scar. Let us score their backs,
And snatch 'em up, as we take hares, behind:
'T is sport to maul a runner.

Ant. I will reward thee
Once for thy sprightly comfort, and ten-fold
For thy good valour. Come thee on.

Scar. I 'll halt after. [*Exeunt.*

SCENE VIII.—Under the Walls of Alexandria.

Alarum. Enter ANTONY, *marching;* SCARUS, *and Forces.*

Ant. We have beat him to his camp. Run one before,
And let the queen know of our gests.[1] To-morrow,
Before the sun shall see us, we 'll spill the blood
That has to-day escap'd. I thank you all,
For doughty-handed are you; and have fought
Not as you serv'd the cause, but as it had been
Each man's, like mine: you have shown all Hectors.
Enter the city, clip your wives, your friends,
Tell them your feats; whilst they with joyful tears
Wash the congealment from your wounds, and kiss
The honour'd gashes whole.—Give me thy hand:

Enter CLEOPATRA, *attended.*

To this great fairy I 'll commend thy acts,
Make her thanks bless thee.—O, thou day o' the world!
Chain mine arm'd neck; leap thou, attire and all,
Through proof of harness to my heart, and there
Ride on the pants triumphing.

Cleo. Lord of lords!
O infinite virtue! com'st thou smiling from
The world's great snare uncaught?

Ant. My nightingale,
We have beat them to their beds. What, girl! though grey
Do something mingle with our younger brown; yet have we
A brain that nourishes our nerves, and can

[2] *Deeds.* guests: in f. e.

Get goal for goal of youth. Behold this man;
[*Pointing to* SCARUS.[1]
Commend unto his lips thy favouring hand:—
Kiss it, my warrior:—he hath fought to-day,
As if a god, in hate of mankind, had
Destroy'd in such a shape.
Cleo. I 'll give thee, friend,
An armour all of gold; it was a king's.
Ant. He has deserv'd it, were it carbuncled
Like glowing Phœbus' car.—Give me thy hand:
Through Alexandria make a jolly march;
Bear our hack'd targets like the men that owe them.
Had our great palace the capacity
To camp this host, we all would sup together,
And drink carouses to the next day's fate,
Which promises royal peril.—Trumpeters,
With brazen din blast you the city's ear;
Make mingle with our rattling tabourines,
That heaven and earth may strike their sounds together,
Applauding our approach. [*Exeunt.*

SCENE IX.—CÆSAR's Camp.

Sentinels on their Post. Enter ENOBARBUS.

1 *Sold.* If we be not reliev'd within this hour,
We must return to the court of guard.[2] The night
Is shiny, and, they say, we shall embattle
By the second hour i' the morn.
2 *Sold.* This last day was
A shrewd one to us.
Eno. O! bear me witness, night,—
3 *Sold.* What man is this?
2 *Sold.* Stand close, and list him.
Eno. Be witness to me, O thou blessed moon!
When men revolted shall upon record
Bear hateful memory, poor Enobarbus did
Before thy face repent.—
1 *Sold.* Enobarbus!
3 *Sold.* Peace!
Hark farther.
Eno. O sovereign mistress of true melancholy!
The poisonous damp of night disponge upon me,
That life, a very rebel to my will, [*Lying down.*[3]
May hang no longer on me: throw my heart

[1] Not in f. e. [2] *Place of mustering the guard.* [3] Not in f. e.

Against the flint and hardness of my fault,
Which, being dried with grief, will break to powder,
And finish all foul thoughts. O Antony!
Nobler than my revolt is infamous,
Forgive me in thine own particular;
But let the world rank me in register
A master-leaver, and a fugitive.
O Antony! O Antony! [*Dies.*

2 *Sold.* Let 's speak to him.

1 *Sold.* Let 's hear him; for the things he speaks
May concern Cæsar.

3 *Sold.* Let 's do so. But he sleeps.

1 *Sold.* Swoons rather; for so bad a prayer as his
Was never yet 'fore[1] sleep.

2 *Sold.* Go we to him.

3 *Sold.* Awake, sir; awake! speak to us.

2 *Sold.* Hear you, sir?

1 *Sold.* The hand of death hath raught[2] him. Hark! the drums [*Drums afar off.*
Do early wake the sleepers. Let us bear him
To the court of guard; he is of note. Our hour
Is fully out.

3 *Sold.* Come on, then;
He may recover yet. [*Exeunt, with the Body.*

SCENE X.—Between the two Camps.

Enter ANTONY *and* SCARUS, *with Forces, marching.*

Ant. Their preparation is to-day by sea:
We please them not by land.

Scar. For both, my lord.

Ant. I would, they 'd fight i' the fire, or i' the air;
We 'd fight there too. But this it is: our foot
Upon the hills adjoining to the city
Shall stay with us (order for sea is given,
They have put forth the haven)
Where their appointment we may best discover,
And look on their endeavour. [*Exeunt.*

Enter CÆSAR, *and his Forces, marching.*

Cæs. But[3] being charg'd, we will be still by land,
Which, as I take 't, we shall; for his best force
Is forth to man his galleys. To the vales,
And hold our best advantage! [*Exeunt*

[1] for: in f. e [2] *Reached.* [3] *Unless.*

Re-enter ANTONY *and* SCARUS.

Ant. Yet they are not join'd. Where yond' pine does [stand,
I shall discover all: I'll bring thee word
Straight, how 't is like to go. [*Exit.*
Scar. Swallows have built
In Cleopatra's sails their nests: the augurers[1]
Say, they know not,—they cannot tell;—look grimly,
And dare not speak their knowledge. Antony
Is valiant, and dejected; and by starts
His fretted fortunes give him hope, and fear,
Of what he has, and has not.
[*Alarum afar off, as at a Sea-Fight.*

Re-enter ANTONY.

Ant. All is lost!
This foul Egyptian hath betray'd me:
My fleet hath yielded to the foe; and yonder
They cast their caps up, and carouse together
Like friends long lost.—Triple-turn'd whore! 't is thou
Hast sold me to this novice, and my heart
Makes only wars on thee.—Bid them all fly;
For when I am reveng'd upon my charm,
I have done all.—Bid them all fly; be gone.
[*Exit* SCARUS.
O sun! thy uprise shall I see no more:
Fortune and Antony part here; even here
Do we shake hands.—All come to this?—The hearts
That spaniel'd[2] me at heels, to whom I gave
Their wishes, do discandy, melt their sweets
On blossoming Cæsar; and this pine is bark'd,
That overtopp'd them all. Betray'd I am.
O this false spell[3] of Egypt! this great[4] charm,—
Whose eye beck'd forth my wars, and call'd them home
Whose bosom was my crownet, my chief end,
Like a right gipsy, hath, at fast and loose,[5]
Beguil'd me to the very heart of loss.—
What, Eros! Eros!

Enter CLEOPATRA.

Ah, thou spell! Avaunt!
Cleo. Why is my lord enrag'd against his love?
Ant. Vanish, or I shall give thee thy deserving,
And blemish Cæsar's triumph. Let him take thee,

[1] auguries: in folio. [2] pannelled: in folio. Hanmer made the change. [3] soul: in f. e. [4] grave: in f. e. [5] A *game*, now called "pricking in the garter," in vogue with gypsies.

And hoist thee up to the shouting plebeians:
Follow his chariot, like the greatest spot
Of all thy sex; most monster-like, be shown
For poor'st diminutives, for doits;[1] and let
Patient Octavia plough thy visage up
With her prepared nails. [*Exit* CLEO.
'T is well thou 'rt gone,
If it be well to live; but better 't were
Thou fell'st under my fury, for one death
Might have prevented many.—Eros, ho!—
The shirt of Nessus is upon me: teach me,
Alcides, thou mine ancestor, thy rage:
Let me lodge Lichas on the horns o' the moon;
And with those hands, that grasp'd the heaviest club,
Subdue my worthiest self. The witch shall die:
To the young Roman boy she hath sold me, and I fall
Under this plot; she dies for 't.—Eros, ho! [*Exit.*

SCENE XI.—Alexandria. A Room in the Palace.

Enter CLEOPATRA, CHARMIAN, IRAS, *and* MARDIAN.

Cleo. Help me, my women! O! he is more mad
Than Telamon for his shield; the boar of Thessaly
Was never so emboss'd.[2]

Char. To the monument!
There lock yourself, and send him word you are dead.
The soul and body rive not more in parting,
Than greatness going off.

Cleo. To the monument!
Mardian, go tell him I have slain myself;
Say, that the last I spoke was, Antony,
And word it, pr'ythee, piteously. Hence,
Mardian, and bring me how he takes my death.—
To the Monument! [*Exeunt.*

SCENE XII.—The Same. Another Room.

Enter ANTONY *and* EROS.

Ant. Eros, thou yet behold'st me.

Eros. Ay, noble lord.

Ant. Sometime, we see a cloud that 's dragonish,
A vapour, sometime, like a bear, or lion,
A tower'd citadel, a pendant rock,
A forked mountain, or blue promontory
With trees upon 't, that nod unto the world,

[1] dolts: in folio. [2] *Foaming at the mouth.*

And mock our eyes with air: thou hast seen these signs;
They are black vesper's pageants.
Eros. Ay, my lord.
Ant. That, which is now a horse, even with a thought,
The rack dislimns, and makes it indistinct,
As water is in water.
Eros. It does, my lord.
Ant. My good knave, Eros, now thy captain is
Even such a body: here I am Antony,
Yet cannot hold this visible shape, my knave.
I made these wars for Egypt, and the queen,
Whose heart, I thought, I had, for she had mine,
Which, whilst it was mine, had annex'd unto 't
A million more, now lost: she, Eros, has
Pack'd cards with Cæsar's, and false play'd my glory
Unto an enemy's triumph.—
Nay, weep not, gentle Eros; there is left us
Ourselves to end ourselves.—O, thy vile lady!

Enter MARDIAN.

She has robb'd me of my sword.
Mar. No, Antony:
My mistress lov'd thee, and her fortunes mingled
With thine entirely.
Ant. Hence, saucy eunuch: peace!
(She hath betray'd me, and shall die the death.)
Mar. Death of one person can be paid but once,
And that she has discharg'd. What thou wouldst do,
Is done unto thy hand: the last she spake
Was, Antony! most noble Antony!
Then, in the midst a tearing groan did break
The name of Antony; it was divided
Between her heart and lips. She render'd life,
Thy name so buried in her.
Ant. Dead, then?
Mar. Dead.
Ant. Unarm me, Eros: the long day's task is done,
And we must sleep.—That thou depart'st hence safe,
Does pay thy labour richly; go.—[*Exit* MARDIAN.
Off, pluck off:—
The seven-fold shield of Ajax cannot keep
The battery from my heart. O, cleave, my sides!
Heart, once be stronger than thy continent,
Crack thy frail case!—Apace, Eros, apace.—

No more a soldier:—bruised pieces, go;
You have been nobly borne.—From me a while.—
[*Exit* EROS.
I will o'ertake thee, Cleopatra, and
Weep for my pardon. So it must be, for now
All length is torture: since the torch is out,
Lie down, and stray no farther. Now all labour
Mars what it does; yea, very force entangles
Itself with strength: seal then, and all is done.—
Eros!—I come, my queen.—Eros!—Stay for me:
Where souls do couch on flowers, we'll hand in hand,
And with our sprightly port make the ghosts gaze:
Dido and her Æneas shall want troops,
And all the haunt be ours.—Come, Eros! Eros!

Re-enter EROS.

Eros. What would my lord?
Ant. Since Cleopatra died
I have liv'd in such dishonour, that the gods
Detest my baseness. I, that with my sword
Quarter'd the world, and o'er green Neptune's back
With ships made cities, condemn myself to lack
The courage of a woman; less noble minded
Than she, which by her death our Cæsar tells,
"I am conqueror of myself." Thou art sworn, Eros,
That when the exigent should come, (which now
Is come indeed) when I should see behind me
The inevitable prosecution of
Disgrace and horror, that on my command
Thou then wouldst kill me: do 't; the time is come.
Thou strik'st not me, 't is Cæsar thou defeatest.
Put colour in thy cheek.
Eros. The gods withhold me!
Shall I do that, which all the Parthian darts,
Though enemy, lost aim, and could not?
Ant. Eros,
Wouldst thou be window'd in great Rome, and see
Thy master thus with pleach'd[1] arms, bending down
His corrigible neck, his face subdued
To penetrative shame, whilst the wheel'd seat
Of fortunate Cæsar, drawn before him, branded
His baseness that ensued?
Eros. I would not see 't.
Ant. Come, then; for with a wound I must be cur'd.

[1] *Interwoven.*

Draw that thy honest sword, which thou hast worn
Most useful for thy country.
Eros. O, sir! pardon me.
Ant. When I did make thee free, swor'st thou not then
To do this when I bade thee? Do it at once,
Or thy precedent services are all
But accidents unpurpos'd. Draw, and come.
Eros. Turn from me, then, that noble countenance,
Wherein the worship of the whole world lies.
Ant. Lo thee! [*Turning his face from him.*
Eros. My sword is drawn.
Ant. Then, let it do at once
The thing why thou hast drawn it.
Eros. My dear master,
My captain, and my emperor, let me say,
Before I strike this bloody stroke, farewell.
Ant. 'T is said, man; and farewell.
Eros. Farewell, great chief. Shall I strike now?
Ant. Now, Eros.
Eros. Why, there then.—[*Falls on his Sword.*]
Thus do I escape the sorrow
Of Antony's death. [*Dies.*
Ant. Thrice nobler than myself!
Thou teachest me, O valiant Eros! what
I should, and thou couldst not. My queen and Eros
Have, by their brave instruction, got upon me
A nobleness in record: but I will be
A bridegroom in my death, and run into 't
As to a lover's bed. Come then; and, Eros,
Thy master dies thy scholar: to do thus
[*Falling on his Sword.*
I learn'd of thee.—How! not dead? not dead?—
The guard!—how?[1]—O, despatch me!

Enter DERCETAS *and Guard.*

1 *Guard.* What 's the noise?
Ant. I have done my work ill, friends: O! make an end
Of what I have begun.
2 *Guard.* The star is fallen.
1 *Guard.* And time is at his period.
All. Alas, and woe!
Ant. Let him that loves me, strike me dead.

[1] ho: in f. e.; often, says Dyce, printed, "how."

1 *Guard.* Not I.
2 *Guard.* Nor I.
3 *Guard.* Nor any one. [*Exeunt Guard.*
Der. Thy death and fortunes bid thy followers fly
This sword but shown to Cæsar, with this tidings,
Shall enter me with him.

Enter DIOMEDES.

Dio. Where 's Antony?
Der. There, Diomed; there.
Dio. Lives he?
Wilt thou not answer, man? [*Exit* DERCETAS.
Ant. Art thou there, Diomed? Draw thy sword, and give me
Sufficing strokes for death.
Dio. Most absolute lord,
My mistress, Cleopatra, sent me to thee.
Ant. When did she send thee?
Dio. Now, my lord.
Ant. Where is she?
Dio. Lock'd in her monument. She had a prophesying fear
Of what hath come to pass; for when she saw
(Which never shall be found) you did suspect
She had compos'd[1] with Cæsar, and that your rage
Would not be purg'd, she sent you word she was dead,
But, fearing since how it might work, hath sent
Me to proclaim the truth; and I am come,
I dread, too late.
Ant. Too late, good Diomed. Call my guard, I pr'ythee.
Dio. What, ho! the emperor's guard! The guard, what, ho!
Come; your lord calls.

Enter some of the Guard.

Ant. Bear me, good friends, where Cleopatra bides;
'T is the last service that I shall command you.
1 *Guard.* Woe, woe are we, sir, you may not live to wear
All your true followers out.
All. Most heavy day!
Ant. Nay, good my fellows, do not please sharp fate
To grace it with your sorrows: bid that welcome
Which comes to punish us, and we punish it,
Seeming to bear it lightly. Take me up:

[1] dispos'd: in f. e.

I have led you oft; carry me now, good friends,
And have my thanks for all. [*Exeunt, bearing* ANTONY.

SCENE XIII.—The Same. A Monument.

Enter, above, CLEOPATRA, CHARMIAN, *and* IRAS.

Cleo. O Charmian! I will never go from hence.
Char. Be comforted, dear madam.
Cleo. No, I will not.
All strange and terrible events are welcome,
But comforts we despise: our size of sorrow,
Proportion'd to our cause, must be as great

Enter, below, DIOMEDES.

As that which makes it.—How now! is he dead?
Dio. His death 's upon him, but not dead.
Look out o' the other side your monument,
His guard have brought him thither.

Enter, below, ANTONY, *borne by the Guard.*

Cleo. O sun,
Burn the great sphere thou mov'st in!—darkling stand,
Thou[1] varying shore o' th' world. O Antony, Antony,
Antony!
Help, Charmian, help, Iras, help: help, friends
Below; let 's draw him thither.
Ant. Peace!
Not Cæsar's valour hath o'erthrown Antony,
But Antony's hath triumph'd on itself.
Cleo. So it should be, that none but Antony
Should conquer Antony; but woe 't is so!
Ant. I am dying, Egypt, dying; only
I here importune death a while, until
Of many thousand kisses the poor last
I lay upon thy lips.—
Cleo. I dare not, dear,
(Dear my lord, pardon) I dare not,
Lest I be taken: not the imperious show
Of the full-fortun'd Cæsar ever shall
Be brooch'd with me; if knife, drugs, serpents, have
Edge, sting, or operation, I am safe.
Your wife Octavia, with her modest eyes,
And still condition,[2] shall acquire no honour
Demuring upon me.—But come, come, Antony,—
Help me, my women,—we must draw thee up.—
Assist, good friends.

[1] The: in f. e. [2] conclusion: in f. e.

Ant. O! quick, or I am gone.
Cleo. Here 's port,[1] indeed!—How heavy weighs my lord!
Our strength is all gone into heaviness,
That makes the weight: had I great Juno's power,
The strong-wing'd Mercury should fetch thee up,
And set thee by Jove's side. Yet come a little;—
Wishers were ever fools.—O! come, come, come;
[*They draw* ANTONY *up.*
And welcome, welcome! die, where[2] thou hast liv'd:
Quicken with kissing: had my lips that power,
Thus would I wear them out.
All. A heavy sight.
Ant. I am dying, Egypt, dying.
Give me some wine, and let me speak a little.
Cleo. No, let me speak; and let me rail so high,
That the false housewife Fortune break her wheel,
Provok'd by my offence.
Ant. One word, sweet queen.
Of Cæsar seek your honour with your safety.—O!
Cleo. They do not go together.
Ant. Gentle, hear me.
None about Cæsar trust, but Proculeius.
Cleo. My resolution, and my hands, I 'll trust;
None about Cæsar.
Ant. The miserable change now at my end
Lament nor sorrow at, but please your thoughts,
In feeding them with those my former fortunes,
Wherein I liv'd the greatest prince o' the world,
The noblest: and do now not basely die,
Nor cowardly put off my helmet to
My countryman, a Roman by a Roman
Valiantly vanquish'd. Now, my spirit is going;
I can no more. [*Dies*
Cleo. Noblest of men, woo't die?
Hast thou no care of me? shall I abide
In this dull world, which in thy absence is
No better than a stye?—O! see, my women,
The crown o' the earth doth melt.—My lord!—
O! wither'd is the garland of the war,
The soldier's pole is fallen: young boys, and girls,
Are level now with men; the odds is gone,
And there is nothing left remarkable

[1] sport: in f. e. [2] when: in folio. Pope made the change.

Beneath the visiting moon.
Char. O, quietness, lady!
Iras. She is dead too, our sovereign.
Char. Lady!—
Iras. Madam!—
Char. O madam, madam, madam!
Iras. Royal Egypt!
Empress!
Char. Peace, peace, Iras!
Cleo. No more, but e'en a woman; and commanded
By such poor passion as the maid that milks,
And does the meanest chares.[1]—It were for me
To throw my sceptre at the injurious gods;
To tell them, that this world did equal theirs,
Till they had stolen our jewel. All 's but naught;
Patience is sottish, and impatience does
Become a dog that 's mad: then is it sin,
To rush into the secret house of death,
Ere death dare come to us?—How do you, women?
What, what! good cheer! Why, how now, Charmian!
My noble girls!—Ah, women, women! look,
Our lamp is spent, it 's out.—Good sirs, take heart:
[*To the Guard below.*
We 'll bury him; and then, what 's brave, what 's noble,
Let 's do it after the high Roman fashion,
And make death proud to take us. Come, away:
This case of that huge spirit now is cold.
Ah, women, women! come; we have no friend
But resolution, and the briefest end.
[*Exeunt; those above bearing off* ANTONY'S *Body*

ACT V.

SCENE I.—CÆSAR'S Camp before Alexandria.

Enter CÆSAR, AGRIPPA, DOLABELLA, MECÆNAS, GALLUS, PROCULEIUS, *and others.*

Cæs. Go to him, Dolabella, bid him yield;
Being so frustrate, tell him, that he mocks

[1] *Chores.*

The pauses that he makes.[1]
Dol. Cæsar, I shall. [*Exit* DOLABELLA.
Enter DERCETAS, *with the Sword of* ANTONY.
Cæs. Wherefore is that? and what art thou, that dar'st
Appear thus to us?
Der. I am call'd Dercetas.
Mark Antony I serv'd, who best was worthy
Best to be serv'd: whilst he stood up, and spoke,
He was my master, and I wore my life,
To spend upon his haters. If thou please
To take me to thee, as I was to him
I 'll be to Cæsar; if thou pleasest not,
I yield thee up my life.
Cæs. What is 't thou say'st?
Der. I say, O Cæsar! Antony is dead.
Cæs. The breaking of so great a thing should make
A greater crack: the round world should have shook
Lions into civil streets,
And citizens to their dens. The death of Antony
Is not a single doom: in the name lay
A moiety of the world.
Der. He is dead, Cæsar;
Not by a public minister of justice,
Nor by a hired knife; but that self hand,
Which writ his honour in the acts it did,
Hath, with the courage which the heart did lend it,
Split that self noble heart.[2] This is his sword;
I robb'd his wound of it: behold it, stain'd
With his most noble blood.
Cæs. Look you sad, friends?
The gods rebuke me, but it is tidings
To wash the eyes of kings.
Agr. And strange it is,
That nature must compel us to lament
Our most persisted deeds.
Mec. His taints and honours
Weighed[3] equal with him.
Agr. A rarer spirit never
Did steer humanity; but you gods will give us
Some faults to make us men. Cæsar is touch'd.

[1] in f. e.:
Tell him
He mocks us by the pauses, &c.
[2] Splitted the heart: in f. e. [3] Waged: in folio, 1623.

Mec. When such a spacious mirror's set before him,
He needs must see himself.
Cæs. O Antony!
Have I follow'd thee to this?—but we do lance
Diseases in our bodies. I must perforce
Have shown to thee such a declining day,
Or look on thine: we could not stall together
In the whole world. But yet let me lament,
With tears as sovereign as the blood of hearts,
That thou, my brother, my competitor
In top of all design, my mate in empire,
Friend and companion in the front of war,
The arm of mine own body, and the heart
Where mine his thoughts did kindle, that our stars,
Unreconcileable should divide
Our equalness to this.—Hear me, good friends,—
But I will tell you at some meeter season:

Enter a Messenger.

The business of this man looks out of him;
We'll hear him what he says.—Whence are you?
Mess. A poor Egyptian yet. The queen my mistress,
Confin'd in all she has, her monument,
Of thy intents desires instruction,
That she preparedly may frame herself
To the way she's forced to.
Cæs. Bid her have good heart:
She soon shall know of us, by some of ours,
How honourable and how kindly we
Determine for her; for Cæsar cannot live[1]
To be ungentle.
Mess. So the gods preserve thee! [*Exit*
Cæs. Come hither, Proculeius. Go, and say,
We purpose her no shame: give her what comforts
The quality of her passion shall require,
Lest in her greatness by some mortal stroke
She do defeat us; for her life in Rome
Would be eternal in our triumph. Go,
And with your speediest bring us what she says,
And how you find of her.
Pro. Cæsar, I shall. [*Exit* PROCULEIUS
Cæs. Gallus, go you along.—Where's Dolabella,
To second Proculeius? [*Exit* GALLUS
All. Dolabella!

[1] leave: in folio. Pope made the change.

Cæs. Let him alone, for I remember now
How he 's employed: he shall in time be ready.
Go with me to my tent, where you shall see
How hardly I was drawn into this war,
How calm and gentle I proceeded still
In all my writings. Go with me, and see
What I can show in this. [*Exeunt.*

SCENE II.—Alexandria. A Room in the Monument.

Enter CLEOPATRA, CHARMIAN, *and* IRAS.

Cleo. My desolation does begin to make
A better life. 'T is paltry to be Cæsar:
Not being fortune, he 's but fortune's knave,
A minister of her will; and it is great
To do that thing that ends all other deeds,
Which shackles accidents, and bolts up change;
Which sleeps, and never palates more the dug,[1]
The beggar's nurse and Cæsar's.

Enter, to the Gates of the Monument, PROCULEIUS, GALLUS, *and Soldiers.*

Pro. Cæsar sends greeting to the queen of Egypt;
And bids thee study on what fair demands
Thou mean'st to have him grant thee.
Cleo. What 's thy name?
Pro. My name is Proculeius.
Cleo. Antony
Did tell me of you, bade me trust you; but
I do not greatly care to be deceiv'd,
That have no use for trusting. If your master
Would have a queen his beggar, you must tell him,
That majesty, to keep decorum, must
No less beg than a kingdom: if he please
To give me conquer'd Egypt for my son,
He gives me so much of mine own, as I
Will kneel to him with thanks.
Pro. Be of good cheer;
You are fallen into a princely hand, fear nothing.
Make your full reference freely to my lord,
Who is so full of grace, that it flows over
On all that need. Let me report to him
Your sweet dependancy, and you shall find
A conqueror, that will pray in aid for kindness,
Where he for grace is kneel'd to.

[1] dung: in f. e.

Cleo. Pray you, tell him
I am his fortune's vassal, and I send him
The greatness he has got. I hourly learn
A doctrine of obedience, and would gladly
Look him i' the face.
Pro. This I'll report, dear lady.
Have comfort; for, I know, your plight is pitied
Of him that caus'd it.
Gal. You see how easily she may be surpris'd.
[PROCULEIUS, *and two of the Guard, ascend the Monument by a Ladder, and come behind* CLEOPATRA. *Some of the Guard unbar and open the Gates.*
Guard her till Cæsar come.
[*To* PROCULEIUS *and the Guard.* *Exit* GALLUS.
Iras. Royal queen!
Char. O Cleopatra! thou art taken, queen!—
Cleo. Quick, quick, good hands. [*Drawing a Dagger.*
Pro. Hold, worthy lady, hold! [*Disarms her.*
Do not yourself such wrong, who are in this
Reliev'd, but not betray'd.
Cleo. What, of death, too,
That rids our dogs of languish?
Pro. Cleopatra,
Do not abuse my master's bounty, by
Th' undoing of yourself: let the world see
His nobleness well acted, which your death
Will never let come forth.
Cleo. Where art thou, death?
Come hither, come! come, come, and take a queen
Worth many babes and beggars!
Pro. O! temperance, lady
Cleo. Sir, I will eat no meat, I'll not drink, sir;
If idle talk will once be accessary,[1]
I'll not sleep neither. This mortal house I'll ruin,
Do Cæsar what he can. Know, sir, that I
Will not wait pinion'd at your master's court,
Nor once be chastis'd with the sober eye
Of dull Octavia. Shall they hoist me up,
And show me to the shouting varletry
Of censuring Rome? Rather a ditch in Egypt
Be gentle grave to me! rather on Nilus' mud
Lay me stark nak'd, and let the water flies

[1] necessary: in f e

Blow me into abhorring! rather make
My country's high pyramides my gibbet,
And hang me up in chains!

Pro. You do extend
These thoughts of horror farther, than you shall
Find cause in Cæsar.

Enter DOLABELLA.

Dol Proculeius,
What thou hast done thy master Cæsar knows,
And he hath sent for thee: for the queen,
I'll take her to my guard.

Pro. So, Dolabella,
It shall content me best: be gentle to her.—
To Cæsar I will speak what you shall please,
[*To* CLEOPATRA.
If you'll employ me to him.

Cleo. Say, I would die.
[*Exeunt* PROCULEIUS, *and Soldiers.*

Dol. Most noble empress, you have heard of me?

Cleo. I cannot tell.

Dol. Assuredly, you know me.

Cleo. No matter, sir, what I have heard or known.
You laugh, when boys, or women, tell their dreams;
Is't not your trick?

Dol. I understand not, madam.

Cleo. I dream'd, there was an emperor Antony:
O, such another sleep, that I might see
But such another man!

Dol. If it might please you,—

Cleo. His face was as the heavens: and therein stuck
A sun, and moon, which kept their course, and lighted
The little O, the earth.

Dol. Most sovereign creature,—

Cleo. His legs bestrid the ocean: his rear'd arm
Crested the world; his voice was propertied
As all the tuned spheres, and that to friends;
But when he meant to quail and shake the orb,
He was as rattling thunder. For his bounty,
There was no winter in't; an autumn[1] 't was,
That grew the more by reaping: his delights
Were dolphin-like; they show'd his back above
The element they liv'd in: in his livery
Walk'd crowns, and crownets; realms and islands were

[1] Antony: in folio. Theobald made the change.

As plates[1] dropp'd from his pocket.
Dol. Cleopatra,—
Cleo. Think you, there was, or might be, such a man
As this I dream'd of?
Dol. Gentle madam, no.
Cleo. You lie, up to the hearing of the gods:
But, if there be, or ever were one such,
It 's past the size of dreaming: nature wants stuff
To vie[2] strange forms with fancy; yet, to imagine
An Antony, were nature's piece 'gainst fancy,
Condemning shadows quite.
Dol. Hear me, good madam.
Your loss is as yourself, great; and you bear it
As answering to the weight: would I might never
O'ertake pursu'd success, but I do feel,
By the rebound of yours, a grief that smites[3]
My very heart at root.
Cleo. I thank you, sir.
Know you, what Cæsar means to do with me?
Dol. I am loath to tell you what I would you knew.
Cleo. Nay, pray you, sir,—
Dol. Though he be honourable,—
Cleo. He 'll lead me, then, in triumph?
Dol. Madam, he will; I know 't.
Within. Make way there!—Cæsar!

Enter CÆSAR, GALLUS, PROCULEIUS, MECÆNAS, SELEUCUS, *and Attendants.*

Cæs. Which is the queen of Egypt?
Dol. It is the emperor, madam. [CLEOPATRA *kneels*
Cæs. Arise, you shall not kneel.
I pray you, rise; rise, Egypt.
Cleo. Sir, the gods
Will have it thus: my master and my lord
I must obey.
Cæs. Take to you no hard thoughts:
The record of what injuries you did us,
Though written in our flesh, we shall remember
As things but done by chance.
Cleo. Sole sir o' the world,
I cannot project mine own cause so well
To make it clear; but do confess I have
Been laden with like frailties, which before
Have often sham'd our sex.

[1] *Silver coins.* [2] A term at cards, *to stake.* [3] suites: in folio.

Cæs. Cleopatra, know,
We will extenuate rather than enforce:
If you apply yourself to our intents,
(Which towards you are most gentle) you shall find
A benefit in this change: but if you seek
To lay on me a cruelty, by taking
Antony's course, you shall bereave yourself
Of my good purposes, and put your children
To that destruction which I'll guard them from,
If thereon you rely. I'll take my leave.
Cleo. And may through all the world: 't is yours; and we
Your scutcheons, and your signs of conquest, shall
Hang in what place you please. Here, my good lord.
Cæs. You shall advise me in all for Cleopatra.
Cleo. This is the brief of money, plate, and jewels,
I am possess'd of: 't is exactly valued;
[*Showing a Paper.*[1]
Not petty things admitted.—Where 's Seleucus?
Sel. Here, madam.
Cleo. This is my treasurer: let him speak, my lord,
Upon his peril, that I have reserv'd
To myself nothing.—Speak the truth, Seleucus.
Sel. Madam,
I had rather seal my lips, than to my peril
Speak that which is not.
Cleo. What have I kept back?
Sel. Enough to purchase what you have made known.
Cæs. Nay, blush not, Cleopatra; I approve
Your wisdom in the deed.
Cleo. See, Cæsar! O, behold,
How pomp is follow'd! mine will now be yours,
And should we shift estates, yours would be mine.
The ingratitude of this Seleucus does
Even make me wild.—O slave, of no more trust
Than love that 's hir'd!—What! goest thou back? thou shalt
Go back, I warrant thee; but I'll catch thine eyes,
Though they had wings. Slave, soul-less villain, dog!
O rarely base!
Cæs. Good queen, let us entreat you.
Cleo. O Cæsar! what a wounding shame is this;
That thou, vouchsafing here to visit me,

[1] Not in f. e.

Doing the honour of thy lordliness
To one so meek, that mine own servant should
Parcel the sum of my disgraces by
Addition of his envy! Say, good Cæsar,
That I some lady trifles have reserv'd,
Immoment toys, things of such dignity
As we greet modern[1] friends withal; and say,
Some nobler token I have kept apart
For Livia, and Octavia, to induce
Their mediation, must I be unfolded
With one that I have bred? Ye[2] gods! it smites me
Beneath the fall I have. Pr'ythee, go hence;
[*To* SELEUCUS.
Or I shall show the cinders of my spirit[3]
Through th' ashes of mischance.[4]—Wert thou a man,
Thou wouldst have mercy on me.

Cæs. Forbear, Seleucus. [*Exit* SELEUCUS.

Cleo. Be it known, that we, the greatest, are misthought
For things that others do; and when we fall,
We answer others' merits in our name,
And[5] therefore to be pitied.

Cæs. Cleopatra,
Not what you have reserv'd, nor what acknowledg'd,
Put we i' the roll of conquest: still be it yours,
Bestow it at your pleasure; and believe,
Cæsar's no merchant, to make prize with you
Of things that merchants sold. Therefore be cheer'd;
Make not your thoughts your prisons: no, dear queen;
For we intend so to dispose you, as
Yourself shall give us counsel. Feed, and sleep:
Our care and pity is so much upon you,
That we remain your friend; and so, adieu.

Cleo. My master, and my lord!

Cæs. Not so. Adieu.
[*Flourish. Exeunt* CÆSAR, *and his Train.*

Cleo. He words me, girls, he words me, that I should not
Be noble to myself: but hark thee, Charmian.
[*Whispers* CHARMIAN.

Iras. Finish, good lady; the bright day is done,
And we are for the dark.

[1] *Common.* [2] The: in f. e. [3] spirits: in f. e. [4] my change: in f. e. [5] Are: in f. e.

Cleo. Hie thee again:
I have spoken already, and it is provided;
Go, put it to the haste.
Char. Madam, I will.

Re-enter DOLABELLA.

Dol. Where is the queen?
Char. Behold, sir. [*Exit* CHARMIAN.
Cleo. Dolabella?
Dol. Madam, as thereto sworn by your command,
Which my love makes religion to obey,
I tell you this: Cæsar through Syria
Intends his journey, and within three days
You with your children will he send before.
Make your best use of this; I have perform'd
Your pleasure, and my promise.
Cleo. Dolabella,
I shall remain your debtor.
Dol. I your servant.
Adieu, good queen; I must attend on Cæsar.
Cleo. Farewell, and thanks. [*Exit* DOL.] Now, Iras, what think'st thou?
Thou, an Egyptian puppet, shalt be shown
In Rome, as well as I: mechanic slaves
With greasy aprons, rules, and hammers, shall
Uplift us to the view: in their thick breaths,
Rank of gross diet, shall we be enclouded,
And forc'd to drink their vapour.
Iras. The gods forbid!
Cleo. Nay, 't is most certain, Iras. Saucy lictors
Will catch at us, like strumpets; and scald rhymers
Ballad us out o' tune: the quick comedians
Extemporally will stage us, and present
Our Alexandrian revels: Antony
Shall be brought drunken forth, and I shall see
Some squeaking Cleopatra boy my greatness
I' the posture of a whore.
Iras. O, the good gods!
Cleo. Nay, that is certain.
Iras. I 'll never see it; for, I am sure, my nails
Are stronger than mine eyes.
Cleo. Why, that 's the way
To foil[1] their preparation, and to conquer
Their most assur'd[2] intents.—Now, Charmian?—

[1] fool: in f. e. [2] absurd: in f. e.

Re-enter CHARMIAN.

Show me, my women, like a queen :—go fetch
My best attires ;—I am again for Cydnus,
To meet Mark Antony.—Sirrah, Iras, go.—
Now, noble Charmian, we 'll despatch indeed ;
And, when thou hast done this chare, I 'll give thee leave
To play till dooms-day.—Bring our crown and all.
Wherefore 's this noise ? [*Exit* IRAS. *A noise within.*

Enter one of the Guard.

Guard. Here is a rural fellow,
That will not be denied your highness' presence :
He brings you figs.

Cleo. Let him come in.—How poor an instrument [*Exit Guard.*
May do a noble deed ! he brings me liberty.
My resolution's plac'd, and I have nothing
Of woman in me : now from head to foot
I am marble-constant ; now the fleeting moon
No planet is of mine.

Re-enter Guard, with a Clown bringing in a Basket.

Guard. This is the man.

Cleo. Avoid, and leave him.— [*Exit Guard.*
Hast thou the pretty worm of Nilus there,
That kills and pains not ?

Clown. Truly I have him ; but I would not be the party that should desire you to touch him, for his biting is immortal : those that do die of it do seldom or never recover.

Cleo. Remember'st thou any that have died on 't ?

Clown. Very many, men and women too. I heard of one of them no longer than yesterday : a very honest woman, but something given to lie, as a woman should not do but in the way of honesty, how she died of the biting of it, what pain she felt.—Truly, she makes a very good report o' the worm ; but he that will believe all that they say, shall never be saved by half that they do. But this is most fallible, the worm 's an adder-worm.

Cleo. Get thee hence : farewell.

Clown. I wish you all joy of the worm.

Cleo. Farewell. [*Clown sets down the Basket.*

Clown. You must think this, look you, that the worm will do his kind.

Cleo. Ay, ay; farewell.

Clown. Look you, the worm is not to be trusted but in the keeping of wise people; for, indeed, there is no goodness in the worm.

Cleo. Take thou no care: it shall be heeded.

Clown. Very good. Give it nothing, I pray you, for it is not worth the feeding.

Cleo. Will it eat me?

Clown. You must not think I am so simple, but I know the devil himself will not eat a woman: I know, that a woman is a dish for the gods, if the devil dress her not; but, truly, these same whoreson devils do the gods great harm in their women, for in every ten that they make, the devils mar nine.

Cleo. Well, get thee gone: farewell.

Clown. Yes, forsooth; I wish you joy of the worm. [*Exit.*

Re-enter IRAS, *with a Robe, Crown, &c.*

Cleo. Give me my robe, put on my crown; I have
Immortal longings in me. Now, no more
The juice of Egypt's grape shall moist this lip.—
Yare, yare, good Iras; quick.—Methinks, I hear
Antony call: I see him rouse himself
To praise my noble act; I hear him mock
The luck of Cæsar, which the gods give men
To excuse their after wrath. Husband, I come:
Now to that name my courage prove my title.
I am fire, and air; my other elements
I give to baser life.—So,—have you done?
Come then, and take the last warmth of my lips.
Farewell, kind Charmian:—Iras, long farewell.
[*Kisses them.* IRAS *falls, and dies*
Have I the aspick in my lips? Dost fall?
If thou and nature can so gently part,
The stroke of death is as a lover's pinch,
Which hurts, and is desir'd. Dost thou lie still?
If thus thou vanishest, thou tell'st the world
It is not worth leave-taking.

Char. Dissolve, thick cloud, and rain, that I may say
The gods themselves do weep.

Cleo. This proves me base:
If she first meet the curled Antony,
He'll make demand of her, and spend that kiss,

Which is my heaven to have. Come. thou mortal wretch,
[*She applies the Asp to her Breast.*
With thy sharp teeth this knot intrinsicate
Of life at once untie · poor venomous fool,
Be angry, and despatch. O! couldst thou speak,
That I might hear thee call great Cæsar ass
Unpolicied!

Char. O eastern star!

Cleo. Peace, peace!
Dost thou not see my baby at my breast,
That sucks the nurse asleep?

Char. O, break! O, break!

Cleo. As sweet as balm, as soft as air, as gentle.—
O Antony!—Nay, I will take thee too.—
[*Applying another Asp to her Arm.*
Why[1] should I stay— [*Falls, and dies.*

Char. In this wild[2] world?—So, fare thee well.—
Now boast thee, death, in thy possession lies
A lass unparallel'd.—Downy windows, close;
And golden Phœbus never be beheld
Of eyes again so royal! Your crown 's awry[3];
I 'll mend it, and then play—

Enter the Guard, rushing in.

1 *Guard.* Where is the queen?

Char. Speak softly; wake her not.

1 *Guard.* Cæsar hath sent—

Char. Too slow a messenger. [*Applies the Asp.*
O! come; apace; despatch: I partly feel thee.

1 *Guard.* Approach, ho! All 's not well: Cæsar 's beguil'd.

2 *Guard.* There 's Dolabella sent from Cæsar: call him.

1 *Guard.* What work is here?—Charmian, is this well done?

Char. It is well done, and fitting for a princess
Descended of so many royal kings.
Ah, soldier! [*Dies.*

Enter DOLABELLA.

Dol. How goes it here?

2 *Guard.* All dead.

Dol. Cæsar, thy thoughts
Touch their effects in this: thyself art coming

[1] What: in f. e. [2] Steevens reads: vild (the old form of vile).
[3] away: in folio. Pope made the change.

To see perform'd the dreaded act, which thou
So sought'st to hinder.
Within. A way there! a way for Cæsar!
Enter CÆSAR, *and all his Train.*
Dol. O, sir! you are too sure an augurer:
That you did fear, is done.
Cæs. Bravest at the last:
She levell'd at our purposes, and, being royal,
Took her own way.—The manner of their deaths?
I do not see them bleed.
Dol. Who was last with them?
1 *Guard.* A simple countryman that brought her figs:
This was his basket.
Cæs. Poison'd, then.
1 *Guard.* O Cæsar!
This Charmian lived but now; she stood, and spake.
I found her trimming up the diadem
On her dead mistress: tremblingly she stood,
And on the sudden dropp'd.
Cæs. O noble weakness!—
If they had swallow'd poison, 't would appear
By external swelling; but she looks like sleep,
As she would catch another Antony
In her strong toil of grace.
Dol. Here, on her breast,
There is a vent of blood, and something blown:
The like is on her arm.
1 *Guard.* This is an aspick's trail; and these fig-leaves
Have slime upon them, such as the aspick leaves
Upon the caves of Nile.
Cæs. Most probable,
That so she died; for her physician tells me,
She hath pursu'd conclusions infinite
Of easy ways to die.—Take up her bed,
And bear her women from the monument.
She shall be buried by her Antony;
No grave upon the earth shall clip in it
A pair so famous. High events as these
Strike those that make them; and their story is
No less in pity, than his glory, which
Brought them to be lamented. Our army shall,
In solemn show, attend this funeral,
And then to Rome.—Come, Dolabella, see
High order in this great solemnity. [*Exeunt.*

CYMBELINE.

"The Tragedie of Cymbeline" was first printed in the folio of 1623, where it stands last in the division of "Tragedies," and occupies thirty-one pages; viz. from p. 369 to p. 399, misprinted p. 993. There is another error in the pagination, as p. 379 is numbered p. 389. These errors are corrected in the three later folios.

INTRODUCTION.

The materials in Holinshed for the historical portion of "Cymbeline" are so imperfect and scanty, that a belief may be entertained that Shakespeare resorted to some other more fertile source, which the most diligent inquiries have yet failed to discover. The names of Cymbeline and of his sons, Guiderius and Arviragus, occur in the old Chronicle, and there we hear of the tribute demanded by the Roman emperor, but nothing is said of the stealing of the two young princes, nor of their residence with Bellarius among the mountains, and final restoration to their father.

All that relates to Posthumus, Imogen, and Iachimo is merely fabulous, and some of the chief incidents of this part of the plot are to be found in French, Italian, and English. We will speak of them separately.

They had been employed for a dramatic purpose in France at an early date, in a Miracle-play, printed in 1839 by Messrs. Monmerqué and Michel, in their *Theatre Francois au Moyen-age*, from a manuscript in the Bibliothèque du Roi. In that piece, mixed up with many romantic circumstances, we find the wager on the chastity of the heroine, her flight in the disguise of a page, the proof of her innocence, and her final restoration to her husband. There also we meet with two circumstances, introduced into Shakespeare's "Cymbeline," but not contained in any other version of the story with which we are acquainted: we allude to the boast of Berengier (the Iachimo of the French Drama), that if he were allowed the opportunity of speaking to the heroine but twice, he should be able to accomplish his design: Iachimo (Act i. sc. 5) makes the same declaration. Again, in the French Miracle-play, Berengier takes exactly Shakespeare's mode of assailing the virtue of Imogen, by exciting her anger and jealousy by pretending that her husband, in Rome, had set her the example of infidelity. Incidents somewhat similar are narrated in the French romances of *La Violette*, and *Flore et Jehanne:* in the latter, the villain, being secretly admitted by an old woman into the bed-room of the heroine, has the means of ascertaining a particular mark upon her person while she is bathing.

The novel by Boccaccio has many corresponding features: it is the ninth of *Giornata II.*, and bears the following title: "Bernabo da Genova, da Ambrogiuolo ingannato, perde il suo, e comanda che la moglie innocente sia uccisa. Ella scampa, et in habito di huomo serve il Soldano; ritrova l'ingannatore, e Bernabo conduce in Alessandria, dove l'ingannatore punito, ripreso habito feminile col marito ricchi si tornano a Genova." This tale includes one circumstance only found there and in Shakespeare's play: we allude to the mole which Iachimo saw on the breast of Imogen. The parties are all merchants in Boccaccio, excepting towards the close of his novel, where the Soldan is introduced: the villain, instead of being forgiven, is punished by being anointed with honey, and exposed in the sun to flies, wasps, and mosquitoes, which eat the flesh from his bones.

A modification of this production seems to have found its way into our language at the commencement of the seventeenth century. Steevens states that it was printed in 1603, and again in 1620, in a tract called "Westward for Smelts." If there be no error as to the date, the edition of 1603 has been lost, for no copy of that year now seems to exist in any public or private collection. Mr. Halliwell, in his reprint of The First Sketch of "The Merry Wives of Windsor," (for the Shakespeare Society) p. 135, has expressed his opinion that Steevens must have been mistaken, and that "Westward for Smelts" was not published until 1620: only one copy even of this impression is known[1]; and if, in fact, it were not, as Steevens supposes, a reprint, of course Shakespeare could not have resorted to it: however, he might, without much difficulty, have gone to the original; or some version may then have been in existence, of which he availed himself, but which has not come down to our day. The incidents in "Westward for Smelts" are completely anglicised, and the scene is laid in this country in the reigns of Henry VI. and Edward IV. In the French and Italian versions, Iachimo (or the person answering to him) is conveyed to Imogen's chamber in a chest, but in "Westward for Smelts," where the tale is in other respects vulgarised, he conceals himself under her bed.

Some German critics, whose opinions are often entitled to the most respectful consideration, have supposed that "Cymbeline" was written in 1614 or 1615, not adverting to the circumstance that Shakespeare had then relinquished all connection with the stage, and had retired from the metropolis. Malone thought that 1609 was the year which could be most probably fixed upon; and although we do not adopt his reasoning upon the point, we are strongly inclined to believe that this drama was not, at all events, written at an earlier period. Forman, the astrologer, was present when "Cymbeline" was acted—most likely, in 1610 or 1611—but he does not in his Diary insert the date when, nor the theatre where, he saw it. His brief account of the plot, in his "Booke of Plaies and Notes thereof" (MS. Ashmol. No. 208), is in the following terms:—

"Remember, also, the story of Cymbeline, king of England in Lucius' time: how Lucius came from Octavius Cæsar for tribute,

[1] Among Capell's books, which he gave to Trinity College, Cambridge, and which are there preserved with care proportionate to their value.

and being denied, after sent Lucius with a great army of soldiers, who landed at Milford Haven, and after were vanquished by Cymbeline, and Lucius taken prisoner; and all by means of three outlaws, of the which two of them were the sons of Cymbeline, stolen from him when they were but two years old, by an old man whom Cymbeline banished; and he kept them as his own sons twenty years with him in a cave. And how one of them slew Cloten, that was the queen's son, going to Milford Haven to seek the love of Imogen, the king's daughter, whom he had banished also for loving his daughter.

"And how the Italian that came from her love conveyed himself into a chest, and said it was a chest of plate, sent from her love and others to be presented to the king. And in the deepest of the night, she being asleep, he opened the chest and came forth of it, and viewed her in her bed, and the marks of her body, and took away her bracelet, and after accused her of adultery to her love, &c. And in the end, how he came with the Romans into England, and was taken prisoner, and after revealed to Imogen, who had turned herself into man's apparel, and fled to meet her love at Milford Haven; and chanced to fall on the cave in the woods where her two brothers were: and how by eating a sleeping dram they thought she had been dead, and laid her in the woods, and the body of Cloten by her, in her love's apparel that he left behind him, and how she was found by Lucius," &c.

We have certainly no right to conclude that "Cymbeline" was a new piece when Forman witnessed the performance of it; but various critics have concurred in the opinion (which we ourselves entertain) that in style and versification it resembles "The Winter's Tale," and that the two dramas belong to about the same period of the poet's life. Forman saw "The Winter's Tale" on 17th May, 1611, and, perhaps, he saw "Cymbeline" at the Globe in the spring of the preceding year. However, upon this point, we have no evidence to guide us, beyond the mere mention of the play and its incidents in Forman's Diary. That it was acted at court at an early date is more than probable, but we are without any record of such an event until 1st January, 1633 (Vide Hist. of Engl. Dram. Poetry and the Stage, vol. ii. p. 57); under which date Sir Henry Herbert, the Master of the Revels, registers that it was performed by the King's Players, and that it was "well liked by the King." The particular allusion in Act ii. sc. 4, to "proud Cleopatra" on the Cydnus, which "swell'd above his banks," might lead us to think that "Antony and Cleopatra" had preceded "Cymbeline."

It is the last of the "Tragedies" in the folio of 1623, and we have reason to suppose that it had not been printed at any earlier date. The divisions of acts and scenes are throughout regularly marked.

DRAMATIS PERSONÆ.

CYMBELINE, King of Britain.
CLOTEN, Son to the Queen by a former Husband.
LEONATUS POSTHUMUS, Husband to Imogen.
BELARIUS, a banished Lord, disguised under the name of Morgan.

GUIDERIUS, ARVIRAGUS, } Sons to Cymbeline, disguised under the names of Polydore and Cadwal, supposed Sons to Belarius.

PHILARIO, Friend to Posthumus, IACHIMO, Friend to Philario, } Italians.
A French Gentleman, Friend to Philario.
CAIUS LUCIUS, General of the Roman Forces.
A Roman Captain.
Two British Captains.
PISANIO, Servant to Posthumus.
CORNELIUS, a Physician.
Two Gentlemen.
Two Jailors.

QUEEN, Wife to Cymbeline.
IMOGEN, Daughter to Cymbeline by a former Queen.
HELEN, Woman to Imogen.

Lords, Ladies, Roman Senators, Tribunes, Apparitions, a Soothsayer, a Dutch Gentleman, a Spanish Gentleman, Muscians, Officers, Captains, Soldiers, Messengers, and other Attendants.

SCENE, sometimes in Britain, sometimes in Italy.

CYMBELINE.

ACT I.

SCENE I.—Britain. The Garden of CYMBELINE'S Palace.

Enter Two Gentlemen.

1 *Gent.* You do not meet a man, but frowns: our bloods
No more obey the heavens, than our courtiers
Still seem as does the king.
2 *Gent.* But what 's the matter?
1 *Gent.* His daughter, and the heir of 's kingdom, whom
He purpos'd to his wife's sole son, (a widow
That late he married) hath referr'd herself
Unto a poor but worthy gentleman. She 's wedded;
Her husband banish'd; she imprison'd: all
Is outward sorrow, though, I think, the king
Be touch'd at very heart.
2 *Gent.* None but the king?
1 *Gent.* He that hath lost her, too: so is the queen
That most desir'd the match; but not a courtier,
Although they wear their faces to the bent
Of the king's looks, hath a heart that is not
Glad at the thing they scowl at.
2 *Gent.* And why so?
1 *Gent.* He that hath miss'd the princess is a thing
Too bad for bad report; and he that hath her,
(I mean, that married her,—alack, good man!—
And therefore banish'd) is a creature such
As, to seek through the regions of the earth
For one his like, there would be something failing
In him that should compare. I do not think,

So fair an outward, and such stuff within,
Endows a man but he.
2 *Gent.* You speak him far.
1 *Gent.* I do extend him, sir, within himself;
Crush him together, rather than unfold
His measure duly.
2 *Gent.* What 's his name, and birth?
1 *Gent.* I cannot delve him to the root. His father
Was called Sicilius, who did join his honour
Against the Romans with Cassibelan,
But had his titles by Tenantius, whom
He serv'd with glory and admir'd success;
So gain'd the sur-addition, Leonatus:
And had, besides this gentleman in question,
Two other sons, who, in the wars o' the time,
Died with their swords in hand; for which their father
Then old and fond of 's[1] issue, took such sorrow,
That he quit being; and his gentle lady,
Big of this gentleman, our theme, deceas'd
As he was born. The king he takes the babe
To his protection; calls him Posthumus Leonatus;
Breeds him, and makes him of his bed-chamber,
Puts him to all the learnings that his time
Could make him the receiver of; which he took,
As we do air, fast as 't was minister'd; and
In his spring became a harvest; liv'd in court,
(Which rare it is to do) most prais'd, most lov'd;
A sample to the youngest, to the more mature,
A glass that feated[2] them; and to the graver,
A child that guided dotards: for his mistress,
For whom he now is banish'd, her own price
Proclaims how she esteem'd him and his virtue;
By her election may be truly read
What kind of man he is.
2 *Gent.* I honour him,
Even out of your report. But, pray you, tell me,
Is she sole child to the king?
1 *Gent.* His only child.
He had two sons, (if this be worth your hearing,
Mark it) the eldest of them at three years old,
I' the swathing clothes the other, from their nursery
Were stol'n; and to this hour no guess in knowledge
Which way they went.

[1] of: in f. e. [2] *Made them fine*

2 *Gent.* How long is this ago?
1 *Gent.* Some twenty years.
2 *Gent.* Strange a king's children should be so convey'd,
So slackly guarded, and the search so slow,
That could not trace them!
1 *Gent.* Howsoe'er 't is strange,
Or that the negligence may well be laugh'd at,
Yet is it true, sir.
2 *Gent.* I do well believe you.
1 *Gent.* We must forbear. Here comes the gentleman, the queen, and princess. [*Exeunt.*

SCENE II.—The Same.

Enter the QUEEN, POSTHUMUS, *and* IMOGEN.

Queen. No, be assur'd, you shall not find me, daughter,
After the slander of most step-mothers,
Evil-ey'd unto you: you are my prisoner, but
Your jailor shall deliver you the keys
That lock up your restraint. For you, Posthumus,
So soon as I can win th' offended king,
I will be known your advocate: marry, yet
The fire of rage is in him: and 't were good,
You lean'd unto his sentence, with what patience
Your wisdom may inform you.
Post. Please your highness,
I will from hence to-day.
Queen. You know the peril.
I 'll fetch a turn about the garden, pitying
The pangs of barr'd affections, though the king
Hath charg'd you should not speak together.
[*Exit* QUEEN.
Imo. O dissembling courtesy! How fine this tyrant
Can tickle where she wounds!—My dearest husband,
I something fear my father's wrath; but nothing
(Always reserv'd my holy duty) what
His rage can do on me. You must be gone;
And I shall here abide the hourly shot
Of angry eyes; not comforted to live,
But that there is this jewel in the world,
That I may see again.
Post. My queen! my mistress!
O, lady! weep no more, lest I give cause

To be suspected of more tenderness
Than doth become a man. I will remain
The loyal'st husband that did e'er plight troth:
My residence in Rome at one Philario's;
Who to my father was a friend, to me
Known but by letter. Thither write, my queen,
And with mine eyes I 'll drink the words you send,
Though ink be made of gall.

Re-enter QUEEN.

Queen. Be brief, I pray you:
If the king come, I shall incur I know not
How much of his displeasure. [*Aside.*] Yet I 'll move him
To walk this way. I never do him wrong,
But he does buy my injuries to be friends,
Pays dear for my offences. [*Exit.*

Post. Should we be taking leave
As long a term as yet we have to live,
The loathness to depart would grow. Adieu!

Imo. Nay, stay a little:
Were you but riding forth to air yourself,
Such parting were too petty. Look here, love:
This diamond was my mother's; take it, heart;
But keep it till you woo another wife,
When Imogen is dead.

Post. How! how! another?—
You gentle gods, give me but this I have,
And sear up my embracements from a next
With bonds of death!—Remain, remain thou here [*Putting on the Ring.*
While sense can keep it on. And sweetest, fairest,
As I my poor self did exchange for you,
To your so infinite loss, so in our trifles
I still win of you: for my sake, wear this:
It is a manacle of love; I 'll place it
Upon this fairest prisoner.
[*Putting a Bracelet on her Arm.*

Imo. O, the gods!
When shall we see again?

Enter CYMBELINE *and Lords.*

Post. Alack, the king!

Cym. Thou basest thing, avoid! hence, from my sight!
If after this command thou fraught the court
With thy unworthiness, thou diest. Away!

Thou 'rt poison to my blood.
Post. The gods protect you,
And bless the good remainders of the court!
I am gone. [*Exit.*
Imo. There cannot be a pinch in death
More sharp than this is.
Cym. O disloyal thing!
That shouldst repair my youth, thou heapest
A year's age on me.
Imo. I beseech you, sir,
Harm not yourself with your vexation;
I am senseless of your wrath: a touch more rare
Subdues all pangs, all fears.
Cym. Past grace? obedience?
Imo. Past hope, and in despair; that way, past grace.
Cym. That mightst have had the sole son of my queen.
Imo. O bless'd, that I might not! I chose an eagle,
And did avoid a puttock.[1]
Cym. Thou took'st a beggar would[2] have made my throne
A seat for baseness.
Imo. No; I rather added
A lustre to it.
Cym. O thou vile one!
Imo. Sir,
It is your fault that I have lov'd Posthumus.
You bred him as my play-fellow; and he is
A man worth any woman; overbuys me
Almost the sum he pays.
Cym. What! art thou mad?
Imo. Almost, sir: heaven restore me!—Would I were
A neatherd's daughter, and my Leonatus
Our neighbour shepherd's son!

Re-enter QUEEN.

Cym. Thou foolish thing!—
They were again together: you have done [*To the* QUEEN.
Not after our command. Away with her,
And pen her up.
Queen. Beseech your patience.—Peace!
Dear lady daughter, peace!—Sweet sovereign,
Leave us to ourselves; and make yourself some comfort
Out of your best advice.

[1] *Hawk* of a worthless breed. [2] a beggar; wouldst, &c.: in f. e.

Cym. Nay, let her languish
A drop of blood a day; and, being aged,
Die of this folly. [*Exit.*

Enter PISANIO.

Queen. Fie!—You must give way:
Here is your servant.—How now, sir! What news?
Pis. My lord your son drew on my master.
Queen. Ha!
No harm, I trust, is done?
Pis. There might have been,
But that my master rather play'd than fought,
And had no help of anger: they were parted
By gentlemen at hand.
Queen. I am very glad on 't.
Imo. Your son 's my father's friend; he takes his part.—
To draw upon an exile!—O brave sir!—
I would they were in Afric both together,
Myself by with a needle, that I might prick
The goer back.—Why came you from your master?
Pis. On his command. He would not suffer me
To bring him to the haven: left these notes
Of what commands I should be subject to,
When 't pleas'd you to employ me.
Queen. This hath been
Your faithful servant: I dare lay mine honour,
He will remain so.
Pis. I humbly thank your highness.
Queen. Pray, walk a while.
Imo. About some half hour hence,
Pray you, speak with me. You shall, at least,
Go see my lord aboard: for this time, leave me. [*Exeunt.*

SCENE III.—A Public Place.

Enter CLOTEN, *and Two Lords.*

1 *Lord.* Sir, I would advise you to shift a shirt: the violence of action hath made you reek as a sacrifice. Where air comes out, air comes in; there 's none abroad so wholesome as that you vent.

Clo. If my shirt were bloody, then to shift it—Have I hurt him?

2 *Lord.* [*Aside.*] No, faith; not so much as his patience.

1 *Lord.* Hurt him? his body 's a passable carcass, if he be not hurt: it is a thoroughfare for steel, if it be not hurt.

2 *Lord.* [*Aside.*] His steel was in debt; it went o' the backside the town.

Clo. The villain would not stand me.

2 *Lord.* [*Aside.*] No; but he fled forward still, toward your face.

1 *Lord* Stand you! You have land enough of your own: but he added to your having, gave you some ground.

2 *Lord.* [*Aside.*] As many inches as you have oceans. —Puppies!

Clo. I would they had not come between us.

2 *Lord.* [*Aside.*] So would I, till you had measured how long a fool you were upon the ground.

Clo. And that she should love this fellow, and refuse me!

2 *Lord.* [*Aside.*] If it be a sin to make a true election, she is damned.

1 *Lord.* Sir, as I told you always, her beauty and her brain go not together: she 's a good sign, but I have seen small reflection of her wit.

2 *Lord.* [*Aside.*] She shines not upon fools, lest the reflection should hurt her.

Clo. Come, I 'll to my chamber. Would there had been some hurt done!

2 *Lord.* [*Aside.*] I wish not so; unless it had been the fall of an ass, which is no great hurt.

Clo. You 'll go with us?

1 *Lord.* I 'll attend your lordship.

Clo. Nay, come, let 's go together.

2 *Lord.* Well, my lord. [*Exeunt*

SCENE IV.—A Room in CYMBELINE'S Palace.

Enter IMOGEN *and* PISANIO.

Imo. I would thou grew'st unto the shores o' the haven,
And question'dst every sail: if he should write,
And I not have it, 't were a paper lost
As offer'd mercy is. What was the last
That he spake to thee?

Pis. It was, his queen, his queen!

Imo. Then wav'd his handkerchief?

Pis. And kiss'd it, madam.

Imo. Senseless linen, happier therein than I!—
And that was all?
Pis. No, madam; for so long
As he could make me with this eye or ear
Distinguish him from others, he did keep
The deck, with glove, or hat, or handkerchief,
Still waving, as the fits and stirs of his mind
Could best express how slow his soul sail'd on,
How swift his ship.
Imo. Thou shouldst have made him
As little as a crow, or less, ere left
To after-eye him.
Pis. Madam, so I did.
Imo. I would have broke mine eye-strings, crack'd them, but
To look upon him, till the diminution
Of space had pointed him sharp as my needle;
Nay, follow'd him, till he had melted from
The smallness of a gnat to air; and then
Have turn'd mine eye, and wept.—But, good Pisanio,
When shall we hear from him?
Pis. Be assur'd, madam,
With his next vantage.
Imo. I did not take my leave of him, but had
Most pretty things to say: ere I could tell him,
How I would think on him, at certain hours,
Such thoughts, and such; or I could make him swear
The shes of Italy should not betray
Mine interest, and his honour; or have charg'd him,
At the sixth hour of morn, at noon, at midnight,
T' encounter me with orisons, for then
I am in heaven for him: or ere I could
Give him that parting kiss, which I had set
Betwixt two charming words, comes in my father,
And, like the tyrannous breathing of the north,
Shakes all our buds from growing.

Enter a Lady.

The queen, madam,
Desires your highness' company.
Imo. Those things I bid you do, get them despatch'd.—
I will attend the queen.
Pis. Madam, I shall. [*Exeunt.*

SCENE V.—Rome. An Apartment in PHILARIO'S House.

Enter PHILARIO, IACHIMO, *a Frenchman, a Dutchman, and a Spaniard.*

Iach. Believe it, sir, I have seen him in Britain: he was then of a crescent note; expected to prove so worthy, as since he hath been allowed the name of; but I could then have looked on him without the help of admiration, though the catalogue of his endowments had been tabled by his side, and I to peruse him by items.

Phi. You speak of him when he was less furnished, than now he is, with that which makes him both without and within.

French. I have seen him in France: we had very many there could behold the sun with as firm eyes as he.

Iach. This matter of marrying his king's daughter, (wherein he must be weighed rather by her value, than his own) words him, I doubt not, a great deal from the matter.

French. And, then, his banishment.—

Iach. Ay, and the approbations[1] of those that weep this lamentable divorce and her dolours,[2] are wont[3] wonderfully to extend him; be it but to fortify her judgment, which else an easy battery might lay flat, for taking a beggar without more[4] quality. But how comes it, he is to sojourn with you? How creeps acquaintance?

Phi. His father and I were soldiers together; to whom I have been often bound for no less than my life.—

Enter POSTHUMUS.

Here comes the Briton. Let him be so entertained amongst you, as suits with gentlemen of your knowing to a stranger of his quality.—I beseech you all, be better known to this gentleman, whom I commend to you, as a noble friend of mine: how worthy he is, I will leave to appear hereafter, rather than story him in his own hearing.

French. Sir, we have known together in Orleans.

Post. Since when I have been debtor to you for

[1] approbation: in f. e. [2] under her colours: in f. e. [3] This word is not in f. e. [4] less: in f. e.

courtesies, which I will be ever to pay, and yet pay still.

French. Sir, you o'er-rate my poor kindness. I was glad I did atone[1] my countryman and you: it had been pity, you should have been put together with so mortal a purpose, as then each bore, upon importance of so slight and trivial a nature.

Post. By your pardon, sir, I was then a young traveller; rather shunned to go even with what I heard, than in my every action to be guided by others' experiences: but, upon my mended judgment, (if I not[2] offend to say it is mended) my quarrel was not altogether slight.

French. Faith, yes, to be put to the arbitrement of swords; and by such two, that would, by all likelihood, have confounded one the other, or have fallen both.

Iach. Can we, with manners, ask what was the difference?

French. Safely, I think. 'T was a contention in public, which may, without contradiction, suffer the report. It was much like an argument that fell out last night, where each of us fell in praise of our country mistresses; this gentleman at that time vouching, (and upon warrant of bloody affirmation) his to be more fair, virtuous, wise, chaste, constant, qualified, and less attemptable, than any the rarest of our ladies in France.

Iach. That lady is not now living; or this gentleman's opinion, by this, worn out.

Post. She holds her virtue still, and I my mind.

Iach. You must not so far prefer her 'fore ours of Italy.

Post. Being so far provoked as I was in France, I would abate her nothing; though I profess myself her adorer, not her friend.

Iach. As fair, and as good, (a kind of hand-in-hand comparison) had been something too fair, and too good, for any lady in Britany. If she went before others I have seen, as that diamond of yours outlustres many I have beheld, I could not but believe[3] she excelled many; but I have not seen the most precious diamond that is, nor you the lady.

Post. I praised her as I rated her; so do I my stone.

[1] *Reconcile.* [2] Not in folio. [3] not believe: in folio. Malone made the change.

Iach. What do you esteem it at?

Post. More than the world enjoys.

Iach. Either your unparagoned mistress is dead, or she 's outprized by a trifle.

Post. You are mistaken: the one may be sold, or given; or if there were wealth enough for the purchase, or merit for the gift: the other is not a thing for sale, and only the gift of the gods.

Iach. Which the gods have given you?

Post. Which, by their graces, I will keep.

Iach. You may wear her in title yours; but, you know, strange fowl light upon neighbouring ponds. Your ring may be stolen, too: so, of your brace of unprizeable estimations, the one is but frail, and the other casual; a cunning thief, or a that way accomplished courtier, would hazard the winning both of first and last.

Post. Your Italy contains none so accomplished a courtier to convince[1] the honour of my mistress, if in the holding or loss of that you term her frail. I do nothing doubt, you have store of thieves; notwithstanding, I fear not my ring.

Phi. Let us leave here, gentlemen.

Post. Sir, with all my heart. This worthy signior, I thank him, makes no stranger of me; we are familiar at first.

Iach. With five times so much conversation, I should get ground of your fair mistress; make her go back, even to the yielding, had I admittance, and opportunity to friend.

Post. No, no.

Iach. I dare thereupon pawn the moiety of my estate to your ring, which, in my opinion, o'ervalues it something, but I make my wager rather against your confidence, than her reputation: and, to bar your offence herein too, I durst attempt it against any lady in the world.

Post. You are a great deal abused in too bold a persuasion: and I doubt not you 'll sustain what you 're worthy of by your attempt.

Iach. What 's that?

Post. A repulse; though your attempt, as you call it, deserve more,—a punishment too.

[1] *Overcome*

Phil. Gentlemen, enough of this; it came in too suddenly: let it die as it was born, and, I pray you, be better acquainted.

Iach. Would I had put my estate, and my neighbour's, on the approbation[1] of what I have spoke.

Po[illegible]at lady would you choose to assail?

[illegible] ours; whom in constancy, you think, stands so [illegible]te. I will lay you ten thousand ducats to your ring, that, commend me to the court where your lady is, with no more advantage than the opportunity of a second conference, and I will bring from thence that ho[illegible] of hers, which you imagine so reserved.

Post. I will wage against your gold, gold to it: my ring I hold dear as my finger; 't is part of it.

Iach. You are afeard,[2] and therein the wiser. If you buy ladies' flesh at a million a dram, you cannot preserve it from tainting. But I see, you have some religion in you, that you fear.

Post. This is but a custom in your tongue: you bear a graver purpose, I hope.

Iach. I am the master of my speeches; and would undergo what 's spoken, I swear.

Post. Will you?—I shall but lend my diamond till your return. Let there be covenants drawn between us. My mistress exceeds in goodness the hugeness of your unworthy thinking: I dare you to this match. Here 's my ring.

Phil. I will have it no lay.

Iach. By the gods, it is one.—If I bring you no sufficient testimony, that I have enjoyed the dearest bodily part of your mistress, my ten thousand ducats are yours; so is your diamond too: if I come off, and leave her in such honour as you have trust in, she your jewel, this your jewel, and my gold are yours;—provided, I have your commendation, for my more free entertainment.

Post. I embrace these conditions; let us have articles betwixt us.—Only, thus far you shall answer: if you make good[3] your vauntage[4] upon her, and give me directly to understand you have prevail'd, I am no farther your enemy; she is not worth our debate: if she remain unseduced, (you not making it appear otherwise) for your ill opinion, and the assault you

[1] *Proof.* [2] a friend: in f. e. [3] Not in f. e. [4] voyage: in f. e.

have made to her chastity, you shall answer me with your sword.

Iach. Your hand: a covenant. We will have these things set down by lawful counsel, and straight away for Britain, lest the bargain should catch cold, and starve. I will fetch my gold, and have our two wagers recorded.

Post. Agreed. [*Exeunt* POSTHUMUS *and* IACHIMO.

French. Will this hold, think you?

Phi. Signior Iachimo will not from it. Pray, let us follow 'em. [*Exeunt.*

SCENE VI.—Britain. A Room in CYMBELINE'S Palace.

Enter QUEEN, *Ladies, and* CORNELIUS.

Queen. Whiles yet the dew's on ground, gather those flowers:
Make haste. Who has the note of them?

1 *Lady.* I, madam.

Queen. Despatch.— [*Exeunt Ladies.*
Now, master doctor, have you brought those drugs?

Cor. Pleaseth your highness, ay: here they are, madam: [*Presenting a small Box.*
But I beseech your grace, without offence,
(My conscience bids me ask) wherefore you have
Commanded of me these most poisonous compounds,
Which are the movers of a languishing death;
But though slow, deadly?

Queen. I wonder, doctor,
Thou ask'st me such a question: have I not been
Thy pupil long? Hast thou not learn'd me how
To make perfumes? distil? preserve? yea, so,
That our great king himself doth woo me oft
For my confections? Having thus far proceeded,
(Unless thou think'st me devilish) is 't not meet
That I did amplify my judgment in
Other conclusions? I will try the forces
Of these thy compounds on such creatures as
We count not worth the hanging, (but none human)
To try the vigour of them, and apply
Allayments to their act; and by them gather
Their several virtues, and effects.

Cor. Your highness
Shall from this practice but make hard your heart:

Besides, the seeing these effects will be
Both noisome and infectious.
Queen. O! content thee.—
Enter PISANIO.
[*Aside.*][1] Here comes a flattering rascal; upon him
Will I first work: he 's for his master,
And enemy to my son.—How now, Pisanio!—
Doctor, your service for this time is ended:
Take your own way.
Cor. [*Aside.*] I do suspect you, madam;
But you shall do no harm.
Queen. Hark thee, a word.—
[*She talks apart to* PISANIO.
Cor. I do not like her. She doth think, she has
Strange lingering poisons: I do know her spirit,
And will not trust one of her malice with
A drug of such damn'd nature. Those she has
Will stupify and dull the sense awhile;
Which first, perchance, she 'll prove on cats, and dogs,
Then afterward up higher; but there is
No danger in what show of death it makes
More than the locking up the spirits a time,
To be more fresh, reviving. She is fool'd
With a most false effect; and I the truer,
So to be false with her.
Queen. No farther service, doctor,
Until I send for thee.
Cor. I humbly take my leave. [*Exit.*
Queen. Weeps she still, say'st thou? Dost thou think, in time
She will not quench, and let instruction enter
Where folly now possesses? Do thou work:
When thou shalt bring me word she loves my son,
I'll tell thee on the instant thou art, then,
As great as is thy master: greater; for
His fortunes all lie speechless, and his name
Is at last gasp: return he cannot, nor
Continue where he is: to shift his being,
Is to exchange one misery with another,
And every day that comes comes to decay
A day's work in him. What shalt thou expect,
To be depender on a thing that leans?

[1] *To* PISANIO: in f. e.

Who cannot be new-built; nor has no friends,
[*The* QUEEN *drops the Box:* PISANIO *takes it up and presents it.*
So much as but to prop him.—Thou tak'st up
Thou know'st not what; but take it for thy labour.
It is a thing I made, which hath the king
Five times redeem'd from death: I do not know
What is more cordial:—nay, I pr'ythee, take it;
It is an earnest of a farther good
That I mean to thee. Tell thy mistress how
The case stands with her: do 't as from thyself.
Think what a chance thou chancest on; but think
Thou hast thy mistress still; to boot, my son,
Who shall take notice of thee. I'll move the king
To any shape of thy preferment, such
As thou 'lt desire; and then myself, I chiefly,
That set thee on to this desert, am bound
To load thy merit richly. Call my women:
Think on my words. [*Exit* PIS.]—A sly and constant knave,
Not to be shak'd; the agent for his master,
And the remembrancer of her, to hold
The hand fast to her lord.—I have given him that,
Which, if he take, shall quite unpeople her
Of liegers for her suite; and which she after,
Except she bend her humour, shall be assur'd

Re-enter PISANIO, *and Ladies.*

To taste of too.—So, so;—well done, well done.
The violets, cowslips, and the primroses,
Bear to my closet.—Fare thee well, Pisanio;
Think on my words. [*Exeunt* QUEEN *and Ladies.*

Pis. And shall do;
But when to my good lord I prove untrue,
I'll choke myself: there's all I'll do for you. [*Exit.*

SCENE VII.—Another Room in the Same.

Enter IMOGEN.

Imo. A father cruel, and a step-dame false;
A foolish suitor to a wedded lady,
That hath her husband banish'd:—O, that husband!
My supreme crown of grief, and those repeated
Vexations of it! Had I been thief-stolen,
As my two brothers, happy! but most miserable

Is the desire that's glorious: blessed be those,
How mean soe'er, that have their honest wills,
Which seasons comfort.—Who may this be? Fie!

Enter PISANIO *and* IACHIMO.

Pis. Madam, a noble gentleman of Rome
Comes from my lord with letters.

Iach. Change you, madam?
The worthy Leonatus is in safety,
And greets your highness dearly. [*Gives a Letter.*

Imo. Thanks, good sir:
You are kindly welcome.

Iach. All of her, that is out of door, most rich! [*Aside.*
If she be furnish'd with a mind so rare,
She is alone the Arabian bird, and I
Have lost the wager. Boldness, be my friend:
Arm me, audacity, from head to foot,
Or, like the Parthian, I shall flying fight;
Rather, directly fly.

Imo. [*Reads.*] "He is one of the noblest note, to whose kindnesses I am most infinitely tied. Reflect upon him accordingly, as you value your truest—
"LEONATUS."

So far I read aloud;
But even the very middle of my heart
Is warm'd by the rest, and takes it thankfully.—
You are as welcome, worthy sir, as I
Have words to bid you; and shall find it so
In all that I can do.

Iach. Thanks, fairest lady.—
What! are men mad? Hath nature given them eyes
To see this vaulted arch, and the rich cope[1]
O'er[2] sea and land, which can distinguish 'twixt
The fiery orbs above, and the twinn'd stones
Upon th' unnumber'd[3] beach: and can we not
Partition make with spectacles so precious
'Twixt fair and foul?

Imo. What makes your admiration?

Iach. It cannot be i' the eye; for apes and monkeys,
'Twixt two such shes, would chatter this way, and
Contemn with mows the other: nor i' the judgment;
For idiots, in this case of favour, would
Be wisely definite: nor i' the appetite;

[1] crop: in f. e. [2] Of: in f. e. [3] the number'd: in f. e.

Sluttery, to such neat excellence oppos'd,
Should make desire vomit to emptiness,
Not so allur'd to feed.

Imo. What is the matter, trow?

Iach. The cloyed will,
(That satiate yet unsatisfied desire,
That tub both fill'd and running) ravening first
The lamb, longs after for the garbage.

Imo. What, dear sir,
Thus raps you? Are you well?

Iach. Thanks, madam, well.—Beseech you, sir, desire [*To* PISANIO.
My man's abode where I did leave him; he
Is strange and peevish.

Pis. I was going, sir,
To give him welcome. [*Exit* PISANIO.

Imo. Continues well my lord? His health, 'beseech you?

Iach. Well, madam.

Imo. Is he dispos'd to mirth? I hope, he is.

Iach. Exceeding pleasant; none, a stranger there,
So merry and so gamesome: he is call'd
The Briton reveller.

Imo. When he was here,
He did incline to sadness; and oft-times
Not knowing why.

Iach. I never saw him sad.
There is a Frenchman his companion, one,
An eminent monsieur, that, it seems, much loves
A Gallian girl at home; he furnaces
The thick sighs from him, whiles the jolly Briton
(Your lord, I mean) laughs from 's free lungs, cries, "O!
Can my sides hold, to think, that man,—who knows
By history, report, or his own proof,
What woman is, yea, what she cannot choose
But must be,—will his free hours languish
For assur'd bondage?"

Imo. Will my lord say so?

Iach. Ay, madam, with his eyes in flood with laughter:
It is a recreation to be by,
And hear him mock the Frenchman; but, heavens know,
Some men are much to blame.

Imo. Not he, I hope.

Iach. Not he; but yet heaven's bounty towards him might
Be us'd more thankfully. In himself, 't is much;
In you,—which I account beyond all talents,—
Whilst I am bound to wonder, I am bound
To pity too.
Imo. What do you pity, sir?
Iach. Two creatures, heartily.
Imo. Am I one, sir?
You look on me: what wreck discern you in me,
Deserves your pity?
Iach. Lamentable! What!
To hide me from the radiant sun, and solace
I' the dungeon by a snuff?
Imo. I pray you, sir,
Deliver with more openness your answers
To my demands. Why do you pity me?
Iach. That others do,
I was about to say, enjoy your—But
It is an office of the gods to venge it,
Not mine to speak on 't.
Imo. You do seem to know
Something of me, or what concerns me: pray you,
(Since doubting things go ill, often hurts more
Than to be sure they do; for certainties
Either are past remedies, or, timely knowing,
The remedy then born) discover to me
What both you spur and stop.
Iach. Had I this cheek
To bathe my lips upon; this hand, whose touch,
Whose every touch, would force the feeler's soul
To the oath of loyalty; this object, which
Takes prisoner the wild motion of mine eye,
Fixing it only here; should I (damn'd then)
Slaver with lips as common as the stairs
That mount the Capitol: join gripes with hands
Made hard with hourly falsehood (falsehood as
With labour), then bo-peeping[1] in an eye,
Base and illustrous as the smoky light
That 's fed with stinking tallow, it were fit,
That all the plagues of hell should at one time
Encounter such revolt.
Imo. My lord, I fear,

[1] by peeping: in f. e.

Has forgot Britain.

Iach. And himself. Not I,
Inclin'd to this intelligence, pronounce
The beggary of his change; but 't is your graces
That, from my mutest conscience, to my tongue
Charms this report out.

Imo. Let me hear no more.

Iach. O dearest soul! your cause doth strike my heart
With pity, that doth make me sick. A lady
So fair, and fasten'd to an empery
Would make the great'st king double, to be partner'd
With tomboys, hir'd with that self exhibition
Which your own coffers yield! with diseas'd ventures,
That pay[1] with all infirmities for gold
Which rottenness can lend nature! such boil'd stuff,
As well might poison poison! Be reveng'd,
Or she that bore you was no queen, and you
Recoil from your great stock.

Imo. Reveng'd!
How should I be reveng'd? If this be true,
(As I have such a heart, that both mine ears
Must not in haste abuse) if it be true,
How should I be reveng'd?

Iach. Should he make me
Live, like Diana's priest, betwixt cold sheets,
Whiles he is vaulting variable ramps,
In your despite, upon your purse? Revenge it.
I dedicate myself to your sweet pleasure,
More noble than that runagate to your bed,
And will continue fast to your affection,
Still close, as sure.

Imo. What ho, Pisanio!

Iach. Let me my service tender on your lips.

Imo. Away!—I do contemn[2] mine ears, that have
So long attended thee.—If thou wert honourable,
Thou wouldst have told this tale for virtue, not
For such an end thou seek'st, as base, as strange.
Thou wrong'st a gentleman, who is as far
From thy report, as thou from honour; and
Solicit'st here a lady, that disdains
Thee and the devil alike.—What ho, Pisanio!—
The king my father shall be made acquainted

[1] play: in f. e. [2] condemn: in f. e.

Of thy assault: if he shall think it fit,
A saucy stranger, in his court, to mart
As in a Romish stew, and to expound
His beastly mind to us, he hath a court
He little cares for, and a daughter whom
He not respects at all.—What ho, Pisanio!—

Iach. O happy Leonatus! I may say;
The credit, that thy lady hath of thee,
Deserves thy trust; and thy most perfect goodness
Her assur'd credit.—Blessed live you long!
A lady to the worthiest sir, that ever
Country call'd his: and you his mistress, only
For the most worthiest fit. Give me your pardon.
I have spoke this, to know if your affiance
Were deeply rooted; and shall make your lord,
That which he is, new o'er: and he is one
The truest manner'd; such a holy witch,
That he enchants societies unto him:
Half all men's hearts are his.

Imo. You make amends.

Iach. He sits 'mongst men, like a descended god:
He hath a kind of honour sets him off,
More than a mortal seeming. Be not angry,
Most mighty princess, that I have adventur'd
To try your taking of a false report; which hath
Honour'd with confirmation your great judgment
In the election of a sir so rare,
Which, you know, cannot err. The love I bear him
Made me to fan you thus; but the gods made you,
Unlike all others, chaffless. Pray, your pardon.

Imo. All 's well, sir. Take my power i' the court for yours.

Iach. My humble thanks. I had almost forgot
T' entreat your grace but in a small request,
And yet of moment too, for it concerns
Your lord; myself, and other noble friends,
Are partners in the business.

Imo. Pray, what is 't?

Iach. Some dozen Romans of us, and your lord,
(The best feather of our wing) have mingled sums,
To buy a present for the emperor;
Which I, the factor for the rest, have done
In France: 't is plate of rare device, and jewels
Of rich and exquisite form. Their value 's great,

And I am something curious, being strange,
To have them in safe stowage: may it please you
To take them in protection?
Imo. Willingly,
And pawn mine honour for their safety: since
My lord hath interest in them, I will keep them
In my bed-chamber.
Iach. They are in a trunk,
Attended by my men; I will make bold
To send them to you, only for this night,
I must aboard to-morrow.
Imo. O! no, no.
Iach. Yes, I beseech; or I shall short my word,
By lengthening my return. From Gallia
I cross'd the seas on purpose, and on promise
To see your grace.
Imo. I thank you for your pains;
But not away to-morrow.
Iach. O! I must, madam:
Therefore, I shall beseech you, if you please
To greet your lord with writing, do 't to-night:
I have outstay'd[1] my time, which is material
To the tender of our present.
Imo. I will write.
Send your trunk to me: It shall safe be kept,
And truly yielded you. You 're very welcome.
[*Exeunt.*

ACT II.

SCENE I.—Court before CYMBELINE's Palace.

Enter CLOTEN, *and Two Lords,*[2] *as from the Bowling-alley.*

Clo. Was there ever man had such luck! when I kissed the jack upon an up-cast, to be hit away! I had a hundred pound on 't: and then a whoreson jackanapes must take me up for swearing; as if I borrowed mine oaths of him, and might not spend them at my pleasure.

[1] outstood: in f. e. [2] The rest of this direction is not in f. e.

1 *Lord.* What got he by that? You have broke his pate with the bowl.

2 *Lord.* [*Aside.*] If his wit had been like him that broke it, it would have run all out.

Clo. When a gentleman is disposed to swear, it is not for any standers-by to curtail his oaths, ha?

2 *Lord.* No, my lord; [*Aside.*] nor crop the ears of them.

Clo. Whoreson dog! — I give him satisfaction? Would he had been one of my rank!

2 *Lord.* [*Aside.*] To have smelt like a fool.

Clo. I am not vexed more at any thing in the earth. —A pox on 't! I had rather not be so noble as I am: they dare not fight with me, because of the queen my mother. Every jack-slave hath his belly full of fighting, and I must go up and down like a cock that no body can match.

2 *Lord.* [*Aside.*] You are cock and capon too; and you crow, cock, with your comb on.

Clo. Sayest thou?

2 *Lord.* It is not fit your lordship should undertake every companion that you give offence to.

Clo. No, I know that; but it is fit I should commit offence to my inferiors.

2 *Lord.* Ay, it is fit for your lordship only.

Clo. Why, so I say.

1 *Lord.* Did you hear of a stranger, that 's come to court to-night?

Clo. A stranger! and I not know on 't?

2 *Lord.* [*Aside.*] He 's a strange fellow himself, and knows it not.

1 *Lord.* There 's an Italian come; and 't is thought, one of Leonatus' friends.

Clo. Leonatus! a banished rascal; and he 's another, whatsoever he be. Who told you of this stranger?

1 *Lord.* One of your lordship's pages.

Clo. Is it fit I went to look upon him? Is there no derogation in 't?

1 *Lord.* You cannot derogate, my lord.

Clo. Not easily, I think.

2 *Lord.* [*Aside.*] You are a fool granted; therefore, your issues being foolish do not derogate.

Clo. Come, I 'll go see this Italian. What I have lost to-day at bowls, I 'll win to-night of him. Come, go.

2 Lord. I 'll attend your lordship.

[*Exeunt* CLOTEN *and first Lord.*

That such a crafty devil as is his mother
Should yield the world this ass! a woman, that
Bears all down with her brain; and this her son
Cannot take two from twenty for his heart,
And leave eighteen. Alas, poor princess!
Thou divine Imogen, what thou endurest,
Betwixt a father by thy step-dame govern'd;
A mother hourly coining plots; a wooer,
More hateful than the foul expulsion is
Of thy dear husband, than that horrid act
Of the divorce he 'd make! The heavens hold firm
The walls of thy dear honour; keep unshak'd
That temple, thy fair mind; that thou may'st stand
T' enjoy thy banish'd lord, and this great land! [*Exit.*

SCENE II.—A Bed-Chamber; in one part of it, a great Trunk.

IMOGEN *reading in her Bed;* HELEN *attending.*

Imo. Who 's there? my woman, Helen?
Lady. Please you, madam.
Imo. What hour is it?
Lady. Almost midnight, madam.
Imo. I have read three hours, then. Mine eyes are weak;
Fold down the leaf where I have left: to bed.
Take not away the taper, leave it burning;
And if thou canst awake by four o' the clock,
I pr'ythee, call me. Sleep hath seiz'd me wholly.

[*Exit* HELEN.

To your protection I commend me, gods!
From fairies, and the tempters of the night,
Guard me, beseech ye! [*Sleeps.*

Enter IACHIMO *from the Trunk.*

Iach. The crickets sing, and man's o'er-labour'd sense
Repairs itself by rest: our Tarquin thus
Did softly press the rushes,[1] ere he waken'd
The chastity he wounded. Cytherea,
How bravely thou becom'st thy bed! fresh lily,
And whiter than the sheets! That I might touch!
But kiss; one kiss!—Rubies unparagon'd, [*Kissing her.*[2]
How dearly they do 't.—'T is her breathing that

[1] *The covering of floors.* [2] Not in f. e.

Perfumes the chamber thus: the flame o' the taper
Bows toward her, and would under-peep her lids,
To see the enclosed lights, now canopied
Under the windows; white and azure, lac'd
With blue of heaven's own tinct.—But my design,
To note the chamber: I will write all down:—
[*Takes out his tables.*[1]
Such, and such, pictures:—there the window;—such
Th' adornment of her bed:—the arras, figures,
Why, such, and such;—and the contents o' the story.—
Ah! but some natural notes about her body,
Above ten thousand meaner moveables
Would testify, t' enrich mine inventory:
O sleep, thou ape of death, lie dull upon her,
And be her sense but as a monument,
Thus in a chapel lying!—Come off, come off;—
[*Taking off her Bracelet.*
As slippery, as the Gordian knot was hard.—
'T is mine; and this will witness outwardly,
As strongly as the conscience does within,
To the madding of her lord.—On her left breast
A mole cinque-spotted, like the crimson drops
I' the bottom of a cowslip: here 's a voucher,
Stronger than ever law could make: this secret
Will force him think I have pick'd the lock, and ta'en
The treasure of her honour. No more.—To what end?
Why should I write this down, that 's riveted,
Screw'd to my memory? She hath been reading late
The tale of Tereus; here the leaf 's turn'd down,
Where Philomel gave up.—I have enough:
To the trunk again, and shut the spring of it.
Swift, swift, you dragons of the night, that dawning
May dare[2] the raven's eye: I lodge in fear;
Though this a heavenly angel, hell is here.
[*Clock strikes.*
One, two, three,—time, time! [*Exit into the Trunk.*

SCENE III.—An Ante-Chamber adjoining IMOGEN'S Apartment.

Enter CLOTEN *and Lords.*

1 *Lord.* Your lordship is the most patient man in loss, the most coldest that ever turned up ace.

Clo. It would make any man cold to lose.

[1] Not in f. e. [2] bare: in f. e.

1 *Lord.* But not every man patient, after the noble temper of your lordship. You are most hot, and furious, when you win.

Clo. Winning will put any man into courage. If I could get this foolish Imogen, I should have gold enough. It 's almost morning, is 't not?

1 *Lord.* Day, my lord.

Clo. I would this music would come. I am advised to give her music o' mornings; they say, it will penetrate.

Enter Musicians.

Come on; tune: if you can penetrate her with your fingering, so; we 'll try with tongue too: if none will do, let her remain; but I 'll never give o'er. First, a very excellent good conceited thing; after, a wonderful sweet air, with admirable rich words to it,—and then let her consider.

SONG.

Hark! hark! the lark at heaven's gate sings,
And Phœbus 'gins arise,
His steeds to water at those springs
On chalic'd flowers that lies;
And winking Mary-buds begin
To ope their golden eyes;
With every thing that pretty is,
My lady sweet, arise;
Arise, arise!

So, get you gone. If this penetrate, I will consider your music the better: if it do not, it is a fault[1] in her ears, which horse-hairs, and calves'-guts, nor the voice of an unpav'd eunuch to boot, can never amend.

[*Exeunt Musicians.*

Enter CYMBELINE *and* QUEEN.

2 *Lord.* Here comes the king.

Clo. I am glad I was up so late, for that 's the reason I was up so early: he cannot choose but take this service I have done, fatherly.—Good morrow to your majesty, and to my gracious mother.

Cym. Attend you here the door of our stern daughter? Will she not forth?

Clo. I have assailed her with music, but she vouchsafes no notice.

Cym. The exile of her minion is too new

[1] vice: in f. e.

She hath not yet forgot him: some more time
Must wear the print of his remembrance out,
And then she 's yours.

Queen. You are most bound to the king,
Who lets go by no vantages, that may
Prefer you to his daughter. Frame yourself
To orderly solicits, and be friended
With aptness of the season: make denials
Increase your services: so seem, as if
You were inspir'd to do those duties which
You tender to her; that you in all obey her,
Save when command to your dismission tends,
And therein you are senseless.

Clo. Senseless? not so.

Enter a Messenger.

Mess. So like you, sir, ambassadors from Rome:
The one is Caius Lucius.

Cym. A worthy fellow,
Albeit he comes on angry purpose now;
But that 's no fault of his: we must receive him
According to the honour of his sender;
And towards himself, his goodness forespent on us,
We must extend our notice.—Our dear son,
When you have given good morning to your mistress,
Attend the queen, and us; we shall have need
To employ you towards this Roman.—Come, our queen.
[*Exeunt* CYM., QUEEN, *Lords, and Mess.*

Clo. If she be up, I 'll speak with her; if not,
Let her lie still, and dream.—By your leave, ho!—
I know her women are about her: what [*Calls.*[1]
If I do line one of their hands? 'T is gold
Which buys admittance; oft it doth; and makes
Diana's rangers, false themselves, yield up
Their deer to the stand o' the stealer; and 't is gold
Which makes the true man kill'd, and saves the thief;
Nay, sometime, hangs both thief and true man: what
Can it not do, and undo? I will make
One of her women lawyer to me; for
I yet not understand the case myself.
By your leave. [*Knocks*

Enter a Lady.

Lady. Who 's there, that knocks?

Clo. A gentleman.

[1] *Knocks:* in f. e.

Lady. No more?
Clo. Yes, and a gentlewoman's son.
Lady. That 's more
Than some, whose tailors are as dear as yours,
Can justly boast of. What 's your lordship's pleasure?
Clo. Your lady's person: is she ready?
Lady. Ay,
To keep her chamber.
Clo. There 's gold for you: sell me your good report.
Lady. How! my good name? or to report of you
What I shall think is good?—the princess——

Enter IMOGEN.

Clo. Good morrow, fairest: sister, your sweet hand.
Imo. Good morrow, sir. You lay out too much pains
For purchasing but trouble: the thanks I give,
Is telling you that I am poor of thanks,
And scarce can spare them.
Clo. Still, I swear, I love you
Imo. If you but said so, 't were as deep with me:
If you swear still, your recompense is still
That I regard it not.
Clo. This is no answer.
Imo. But that you shall not say I yield, being silent,
I would not speak. I pray you, spare me: faith,
I shall unfold equal discourtesy
To your best kindness. One of your great knowing
Should learn, being taught, forbearance.
Clo. To leave you in your madness? 't were my sin
I will not.
Imo. Fools are not mad folks.
Clo. Do you call me fool?
Imo. As I am mad, I do:
If you 'll be patient, I 'll no more be mad;
That cures us both. I am much sorry, sir,
You put me to forget a lady's manners,
By being so verbal: and learn now, for all,
That I, which know my heart, do here pronounce,
By the very truth of it, I care not for you;
And am so near the lack of charity,
(To accuse myself) I hate you; which I had rather
You felt than make 't my boast.
Clo. You sin against
Obedience, which you owe your father. For
The contract you pretend with that base wretch,

(One, bred of alms, and foster'd with cold dishes,
With scraps o' the court) it is no contract, none:
And though it be allow'd in meaner parties,
(Yet who than he more mean?) to knit their souls
(On whom there is no more dependency
But brats and beggary) in self-figur'd knot,
Yet you are curb'd from that enlargement by
The consequence o' the crown, and must not foil[1]
The precious note of it with a base slave,
A hilding[2] for a livery, a squire's cloth,
A pantler, not so eminent.

Imo. Profane fellow!
Wert thou the son of Jupiter, and no more
But what thou art besides, thou wert too base
To be his groom: thou wert dignified enough,
Even to the point of envy, if 't were made
Comparative for your virtues, to be styl'd
The under hangman of his kingdom, and hated
For being preferr'd so well.

Clo. The south-fog rot him!

Imo. He never can meet more mischance, than come
To be but nam'd of thee. His meanest garment,
That ever hath but clipp'd his body, is dearer
In my respect than all the hairs above thee,
Were they all made such men.—How now, Pisanio!

Enter PISANIO.

Clo. His garment? Now, the devil—

Imo. To Dorothy my woman hie thee presently.—

Clo. His garment?

Imo. I am sprited with a fool;
Frighted, and anger'd worse.—Go, bid my woman
Search for a jewel, that too casually
Hath left mine arm: it was thy master's; 'shrew me,
If I would lose it for a revenue
Of any king's in Europe. I do think,
I saw 't this morning: confident I am,
Last night 't was on mine arm; I kiss'd it.
I hope, it be not gone to tell my lord
That I kiss aught but he.

Pis. 'T will not be lost.

Imo. I hope so: go, and search. [*Exit* PIS.

Clo. You have abus'd me.—
His meanest garment?

[1] Most mod. eds. read: soil. [2] *A low wretch.*

Imo. Ay; I said so, sir.
If you will make 't an action, call witness to 't.
Clo. I will inform your father.
Imo. Your mother too:
She 's my good lady; and will conceive, I hope,
But the worst of me. So I leave you, sir,
To the worst of discontent. [*Exit.*
Clo. I 'll be reveng'd.—
His meanest garment?—Well. [*Exit.*

SCENE IV.—Rome. An Apartment in PHILARIO's House.

Enter POSTHUMUS *and* PHILARIO.

Post. Fear it not, sir: I would, I were so sure
To win the king, as I am bold, her honour
Will remain hers.
Phi. What means do you make to him?
Post. Not any; but abide the change of time;
Quake in the present winter's state, and wish
That warmer days would come. In these fear'd hopes,
I barely gratify your love; they failing,
I must die much your debtor.
Phi. Your very goodness, and your company,
O'erpays all I can do. By this, your king
Hath heard of great Augustus: Caius Lucius
Will do 's commission throughly; and, I think,
He 'll grant the tribute, send the arrearages,
Or look upon our Romans, whose remembrance
Is yet fresh in their grief.
Post. I do believe,
(Statist though I am none, nor like to be)
That this will prove a war; and you shall hear
The legion, now in Gallia, sooner landed
In our not-fearing Britain, than have tidings
Of any penny tribute paid. Our countrymen
Are men more order'd, than when Julius Cæsar
Smil'd at their lack of skill, but found their courage
Worthy his frowning at: their discipline
(Now mingled[1] with their courages) will make known
To their approvers, they are people, such
That mend upon the world.

Enter IACHIMO.

Phi. See! Iachimo?

[1] wing-led: in first folio; second folio, as in text

Post. The swiftest harts have posted you by land,
And winds of all the corners kiss'd your sails,
To make your vessel nimble.

Phi. Welcome, sir.

Post. I hope, the briefness of your answer made
The speediness of your return.

Iach. Your lady
Is one of the fairest that I have look'd upon.

Post. And, therewithal, the best; or let her beauty
Look through a casement to allure false hearts,
And be false with them.

Iach. Here are letters for you.

Post. Their tenor good, I trust.

Iach. 'T is very like.

Phi. Was Caius Lucius in the Britain court,
When you were there?

Iach. He was expected then,
But not approach'd.

Post. All is well yet.—
Sparkles this stone as it was wont? or is 't not
Too dull for your good wearing?

Iach. If I had lost,[1]
I should have lost the worth of it in gold.
I 'll make a journey twice as far, t' enjoy
A second night of such sweet shortness, which
Was mine in Britain; for the ring is won.

Post. The stone 's too hard to come by.

Iach. Not a whit
Your lady being so easy.

Post. Make not, sir,
Your loss your sport: I hope, you know that we
Must not continue friends.

Iach. Good sir, we must,
If you keep covenant. Had I not brought
The knowledge of your mistress home, I grant
We were to question farther: but I now
Profess myself the winner of her honour,
Together with your ring; and not the wronger
Of her, or you, having proceeded but
By both your wills.

Post. If you can make 't apparent
That you have tasted her in bed, my hand
And ring are yours: if not, the foul opinion

[1] If I have lost it: in f. e.

You had of her pure honour, gains, or loses,
Your sword, or mine; or masterless leaves both
To who shall find them.
Iach. Sir, my circumstances,
Being so near the truth, as I will make them,
Must first induce you to believe: whose strength
I will confirm with oath; which, I doubt not,
You 'll give me leave to spare, when you shall find
You need it not.
Post. Proceed.
Iach. First, her bedchamber,
(Where, I confess, I slept not, but, profess,
Had that was well worth watching) it was hang'd
With tapestry of silk and silver; the story,
Proud Cleopatra, when she met her Roman,
And Cydnus swell'd above the banks, or for
The press of boats, or pride: a piece of work
So bravely done, so rich, that it did strive
In workmanship, and value; which, I wonder'd,
Could be so rarely and exactly wrought,
Since the true life on 't 'twas.[1]
Post. This is most[2] true;
And this you might have heard of here, by me,
Or by some other.
Iach. More particulars
Must justify my knowledge.
Post. So they must,
Or do your honour injury.
Iach. The chimney
Is south the chamber; and the chimney-piece,
Chaste Dian, bathing: never saw I figures
So likely to report themselves: the cutter
Was as another nature, dumb; outwent her,
Motion and breath left out.
Post. This is a thing,
Which you might from relation likewise reap,
Being, as it is, much spoke of.
Iach. The roof o' the chamber
With golden cherubins is fretted: her andirons
(I had forgot them) were two winged[3] Cupids
Of silver, each on one foot standing, nicely
Depending on their brands.
Post. This is her honour.—

[1] was: in f. e. [2] Not in f. e. [3] winking: in f. e.

Let it be granted, you have seen all this, (and praise
Be given to your remembrance) the description
Of what is in her chamber nothing saves
The wager you have laid.
Iach. Then, if you can,
Be pale: I beg but leave to air this jewel; see!—
[*Producing the Bracelet.*
And now 't is up again: it must be married
To that your diamond; I 'll keep them.
Post. Jove!—
Once more let me behold it. Is it that
Which I left with her?
Iach. Sir, (I thank her) that:
She stripp'd it from her arm; I see her yet;
Her pretty action did outsell her gift,
And yet enrich'd it too. She gave it me,
And said, she priz'd it once.
Post. May be, she pluck'd it off,
To send it me.
Iach. She writes so to you, doth she?
Post. O! no, no, no; 't is true. Here, take this too;
[*Giving the Ring.*
It is a basilisk unto mine eye,
Kills me to look on 't.—Let there be no honour,
Where there is beauty; truth, where semblance; love
Where there 's another man: the vows of women
Of no more bondage be, to where they are made,
Than they are to their virtues, which is nothing.—
O, above measure false!
Phi. Have patience, sir,
And take your ring again; 't is not yet won:
It may be probable she lost it; or,
Who knows, if one of her women, being corrupted,
Hath stolen it from her?
Post. Very true;
And so, I hope, he came by 't.—Back my ring.—
Render to me some corporal sign about her,
More evident than this, for this was stolen.
Iach. By Jupiter, I had it from her arm.
Post. Hark you, he swears; by Jupiter he swears.
'T is true;—nay, keep the ring—'t is true. I am sure
She would not lose it: her attendants are
All sworn, and honourable:—they induc'd to steal it!
And by a stranger!—No, he hath enjoy'd her:

The cognizance of her incontinency
Is this:—she hath bought the name of whore thus dearly.—
There, take thy hire; and all the fiends of hell
Divide themselves between you!

Phi. Sir, be patient.
This is not strong enough to be believ'd
Of one persuaded well of.

Post. Never talk on 't;
She hath been colted by him.

Iach. If you seek
For farther satisfying, under her breast
(Worthy the[1] pressing) lies a mole, right proud
Of that most delicate lodging: by my life,
I kiss'd it, and it gave me present hunger
To feed again, though full. You do remember
This stain upon her?

Post. Ay, and it doth confirm
Another stain, as big as hell can hold,
Were there no more but it.

Iach. Will you hear more?

Post. Spare your arithmetic: never count the turns
Once, and a million!

Iach. I 'll be sworn,——

Post. No swearing.
If you will swear you have not done 't, you lie;
And I will kill thee, if thou dost deny
Thou 'st made me cuckold.

Iach. I will deny nothing.

Post. O, that I had her here, to tear her limb-meal!
I will go there, and do 't; i' the court; before
Her father.—I 'll do something. [*Exit.*

Phi. Quite besides
The government of patience!—You have won:
Let 's follow him, and pervert the present wrath
He hath against himself.

Iach. With all my heart. [*Exeunt.*

SCENE V.—The Same. Another Room in the Same.

Enter POSTHUMUS.

Post. Is there no way for men to be, but women
Must be half-workers? We are all bastards;
And that most venerable man, which I

[1] her: in folio. Rowe made the change.

Did call my father, was I know not where
When I was stamped; some coiner with his tools
Made me a counterfeit: yet my mother seemed
The Dian of that time; so doth my wife
The nonpareil of this.—O vengeance, vengeance!
Me of my lawful pleasure she restrain'd,
And pray'd me oft forbearance; did it with
A pudency so rosy, the sweet view on 't
Might well have warm'd old Saturn; that I thought her
As chaste as unsunn'd snow:—O, all the devils!—
This yellow Iachimo, in an hour,—was 't not?—
Or less,—at first; perchance he spoke not, but,
Like a full-acorn'd boar, a foaming[1] one,
Cry'd "oh!" and mounted; found no opposition
But what he look'd for should oppose, and she
Should from encounter guard. Could I find out
The woman's part in me! For there 's no motion
That tends to vice in man, but I affirm
It is the woman's part: be it lying, note it,
The woman's; flattering, hers; deceiving, hers;
Lust and rank thoughts, hers, hers; revenges, hers;
Ambitions, covetings, change of prides, disdain,
Nice longings, slanders, mutability,
All faults that may be nam'd; nay, that hell knows,
Why, hers, in part, or all: but, rather, all;
For even to vice
They are not constant, but are changing still
One vice, but of a minute old, for one
Not half so old as that. I 'll write against them,
Detest them, curse them.—Yet 't is greater skill,
In a true hate, to pray they have their will:
The very devils cannot plague them better. [*Exit*

[1] German: in f. e.

ACT III.

SCENE I.—Britain. A Room of State in CYMBELINE'S Palace.

Enter CYMBELINE, QUEEN, CLOTEN, *and Lords, at one Door; at another,* CAIUS LUCIUS, *and Attendants.*

Cym. Now say, what would Augustus Cæsar with us?
Luc. When Julius Cæsar (whose remembrance yet
Lives in men's eyes, and will to ears, and tongues,
Be theme, and hearing ever) was in this Britain
And conquer'd it, Cassibelan, thine uncle,
(Famous in Cæsar's praises, no whit less
Than in his feats deserving it) for him
And his succession, granted Rome a tribute,
Yearly three thousand pounds; which by thee lately
Is left untender'd.
Queen. And, to kill the marvel,
Shall be so ever.
Clo. There be many Cæsars,
Ere such another Julius. Britain is
A world by itself; and we will nothing pay,
For wearing our own noses.
Queen. That opportunity,
Which then they had to take from us, to resume
We have again.—Remember, sir, my liege,
The kings your ancestors, together with
The natural bravery of your isle; which stands
As Neptune's park, ribbed and paled in
With rocks[1] unscaleable, and roaring waters;
With sands, that will not bear your enemies' boats,
But suck them up to the top-mast. A kind of conquest
Cæsar made here; but made not here his brag
Of "came," and "saw," and "overcame:" with shame
(The first that ever touch'd him) he was carried
From off our coast, twice beaten: and his shipping,
(Poor ignorant baubles!) on our terrible seas,
Like egg-shells mov'd upon their surges, crack'd
As easily 'gainst our rocks. For joy whereof
The fam'd Cassibelan, who was once at point
(O, giglot fortune!) to master Cæsar's sword,

[1] oaks: in folio. Hanmer made the change.

Made Lud's town with rejoicing fires bright,
And Britons strut with courage.

Clo. Come, there 's no more tribute to be paid. Our kingdom is stronger than it was at that time; and, as I said, there is no more such Cæsars: other of them may have crooked noses; but, to owe such straight arms, none.

Cym. Son, let your mother end.

Clo. We have yet many among us can gripe as hard as Cassibelan: I do not say, I am one; but I have a hand.—Why tribute? why should we pay tribute? If Cæsar can hide the sun from us with a blanket, or put the moon in his pocket, we will pay him tribute for light; else, sir, no more tribute, pray you now.

Cym. You must know,
Till the injurious Romans did extort
This tribute from us, we were free: Cæsar's ambition,
(Which swell'd so much, that it did almost stretch
The sides o' the world) against all colour, here
Did put the yoke upon us; which to shake off,
Becomes a warlike people, whom we reckon
Ourselves to be.

Clo. We do.[1]

Cym. Say, then, to Cæsar,
Our ancestor was that Mulmutius, which
Ordain'd our laws; whose use the sword of Cæsar
Hath too much mangled; whose repair, and franchise,
Shall, by the power we hold, be our good deed,
Though Rome be therefore angry. Mulmutius made our laws,
Who was the first of Britain which did put
His brows within a golden crown, and call'd
Himself a king.

Luc. I am sorry, Cymbeline,
That I am to pronounce Augustus Cæsar
(Cæsar, that hath more kings his servants, than
Thyself domestic officers) thine enemy.
Receive it from me, then.—War, and confusion,
In Cæsar's name pronounce I 'gainst thee: look
For fury not to be resisted.—Thus defied,
I thank thee for myself.

Cym. Thou art welcome, Caius.
Thy Cæsar knighted me; my youth I spent

[1] *i. e.* make these two words part of CYMBELINE'S speech.

Much under him; of him I gather'd honour:
Which he, to seek of me again, perforce,
Behoves me keep at utterance.[1] I am perfect,
That the Pannonians and Dalmatians, for
Their liberties, are now in arms; a precedent
Which not to read would show the Britons cold:
So Cæsar shall not find them.

Luc. Let proof speak.

Clo. His majesty bids you welcome. Make pastime with us a day or two, or longer: if you seek us afterwards in other terms, you shall find us in our salt-water girdle: if you beat us out of it, it is yours. If you fall in the adventure, our crows shall fare the better for you; and there 's an end.

Luc. So, sir.

Cym. I know your master's pleasure, and he mine:
All the remain is, welcome. [*Exeunt.*

SCENE II.—Another Room in the Same.

Enter PISANIO.

Pis. How! of adultery? Wherefore write you not
What monsters her accuse?—Leonatus!
O, master! what a strange infection
Is fallen into thy ear! What false Italian
(As poisonous tongued, as handed) hath prevail'd
On thy too ready hearing?—Disloyal? No:
She 's punish'd for her truth; and undergoes,
More goddess-like than wife-like, such assaults
As would take in[2] some virtue.—O, my master!
Thy mind to her is now as low, as were
Thy fortunes.—How! that I should murder her?
Upon the love, and truth, and vows, which I
Have made to thy command?—I, her?—her blood?
If it be so to do good service, never
Let me be counted serviceable. How look I,
That I should seem to lack humanity,
So much as this fact comes to? "Do 't. The letter [*Reading*
That I have sent her, by her own command
Shall give thee opportunity:"—O, damn'd paper!
Black as the ink that 's on thee. Senseless bauble,
Art thou a feodary[3] for this act, and look'st
So virgin-like without? Lo! here she comes.

[1] *Fight to extremity.* [2] *Conquer.* [3] *Accomplice.*

Enter IMOGEN.

I am ignorant in what I am commanded.
Imo. How now, Pisanio!
Pis. Madam, here is a letter from my lord.
Imo. Who? thy lord? that is my lord: Leonatus.
O! learn'd indeed were that astronomer,
That knew the stars, as I his characters;
He'd lay the future open.—You good gods,
Let what is here contain'd relish of love,
Of my lord's health, of his content,—yet not,
That we two are asunder,—let that grieve him:
Some griefs are medicinable; that is one of them,
For it doth physic love;—of his content,
All but in that!—Good wax, thy leave.—Bless'd be,
You bees, that make these locks of counsel! Lovers,
And men in dangerous bonds, pray not alike:
Though forfeiters you cast in prison, yet
You clasp young Cupid's tables.—Good news, gods!
[*Reads.*

"Justice, and your father's wrath, should he take me in his dominion, could not be so cruel to me, as you, O the dearest of creatures, would even renew me with your eyes. Take notice, that I am in Cambria, at Milford-Haven: what your own love will out of this advise you follow. So, he wishes you all happiness, that remains loyal to his vow, and your, increasing in love,

"LEONATUS POSTHUMUS."

O, for a horse with wings!—Hear'st thou, Pisanio?
He is at Milford-Haven: read, and tell me
How far 't is thither. If one of mean affairs
May plod it in a week, why may not I
Glide thither in a day?—Then, true Pisanio,
(Who long'st, like me, to see thy lord; who long'st,—
O, let me 'bate!—but not like me;—yet long'st,—
But in a fainter kind:—O! not like me,
For mine 's beyond beyond) say, and speak thick,[1]
(Love's counsellor should fill the bores of hearing,
To the smothering of the sense) how far it is
To this same blessed Milford: and, by the way,
Tell me how Wales was made so happy, as
T' inherit such a haven: but, first of all,
How we may steal from hence; and, for the gap

[1] *Rapidly.*

That we shall make in time, from our hence-going,
And our return, to excuse:—but first, how get hence.
Why should excuse be born, or e'er begot?
We 'll talk of that hereafter. Pr'ythee, speak,
How many score of miles may we well ride
'Twixt hour and hour?

Pis. One score 'twixt sun and sun,
Madam, 's enough for you, and too much, too.

Imo. Why, one that rode to 's execution, man,
Could never go so slow: I have heard of riding wagers,
Where horses have been nimbler than the sands
That run i' the clocks by half.[1]—But this is foolery.—
Go, bid my woman feign a sickness; say
She 'll home to her father; and provide me, presently,
A riding suit, no costlier than would fit
A franklin's housewife.

Pis. Madam, you 're best consider.

Imo. I see before me, man: nor here, nor here,
Nor what ensues, but have a fog in them,
That I cannot look through. Away, I pr'ythee:
Do as I bid thee. There 's no more to say;
Accessible is none but Milford way. [*Exeunt.*

SCENE III.—Wales. A mountainous Country, with a Cave.

Enter BELARIUS, GUIDERIUS, *and* ARVIRAGUS.

Bel. A goodly day not to keep house, with such
Whose roof 's as low as ours. Stoop,[2] boys: this gate
Instructs you how t' adore the heavens, and bows you
To a morning's holy office: the gates of monarchs
Are arch'd so high, that giants may jet[3] through
And keep their impious turbands on, without
Good-morrow to the sun.—Hail, thou fair heaven!
We house i' the rock, yet use thee not so hardly
As prouder livers do.

Gui. Hail, heaven!

Arv. Hail, heaven!

Bel. Now, for our mountain sport. Up to yond' hill:
Your legs are young; I 'll tread these flats. Consider,
When you above perceive me like a crow,
That it is place which lessens and sets off;

[1] the clock's behalf: in f. e. [2] Sleep: in folio. Hanmer made the change. [3] *Strut.*

And you may then revolve what tales I have told you,
Of courts, of princes, of the tricks in war:
That service is not service, so being done,
But being so allow'd: to apprehend thus,
Draws us a profit from all things we see;
And often, to our comfort, shall we find
The sharded beetle in a safer hold
Than is the full-wing'd eagle. O! this life
Is nobler, than attending for a check;
Richer, than doing nothing for a bob;[1]
Prouder, than rustling in unpaid-for silk:
Such gain the cap of him, that makes him fine,
Yet keeps his book uncross'd.[2] No life to ours.
Gui. Out of your proof you speak: we, poor unfledg'd,
Have never wing'd from view o' the nest; nor know not
What air 's from home. Haply this life is best,
If quiet life be best; sweeter to you,
That have a sharper known, well corresponding
With your stiff age; but unto us it is
A cell of ignorance, travelling abed,
A prison for[3] a debtor, that not dares
To stride a limit.
Arv. What should we speak of,
When we are old as you? when we shall hear
The rain and wind beat dark December, how
In this our pinching cave shall we discourse
The freezing hours away?—We have seen nothing.
We are beastly: subtle as the fox for prey;
Like warlike as the wolf for what we eat:
Our valour is to chase what flies; our cage
We make a quire, as doth the prison'd bird,
And sing our bondage freely.
Bel. How you speak!
Did you but know the city's usuries,
And felt them knowingly: the art o' the court,
As hard to leave, as keep; whose top to climb
Is certain falling, or so slippery, that
The fear 's as bad as falling: the toil of the war,
A pain that only seems to seek out danger

[1] bribe: in f. e. Dyce reads: *brabe*, an expression of contempt
[2] *His accounts unpaid.* [3] or: in folio. Pope made the change.

I' the name of fame, and honour; which dies i' the search,
And hath as oft a slanderous epitaph,
As record of fair act; nay, many times,
Doth ill deserve by doing well; what 's worse,
Must court'sy at the censure.—O, boys! this story
The world may read in me: my body 's mark'd
With Roman swords, and my report was once
First with the best of note. Cymbeline lov'd me;
And when a soldier was the theme, my name
Was not far off: then, was I as a tree,
Whose boughs did bend with fruit; but, in one night,
A storm, or robbery, call it what you will,
Shook down my mellow hangings, nay, my leaves,
And left me bare to weather.

Gui. Uncertain favour!

Bel. My fault being nothing (as I have told you oft)
But that two villains, whose false oaths prevail'd
Before my perfect honour, swore to Cymbeline,
I was confederate with the Romans: so,
Follow'd my banishment; and this twenty years
This rock, and these demesnes, have been my world;
Where I have liv'd at honest freedom, paid
More pious debts to heaven, than in all
The fore-end of my time.—But, up to the mountains!
This is not hunter's language.—He that strikes
The venison first shall be the lord o' the feast;
To him the other two shall minister,
And we will fear no poison, which attends
In place of greater state. I 'll meet you in the valleys.
[*Exeunt* GUI. *and* ARV.
How hard it is, to hide the sparks of nature!
These boys know little, they are sons to the king;
Nor Cymbeline dreams that they are alive.
They think, they are mine; and, though train'd up thus meanly
I' the cave wherein they bow,[1] their thoughts do hit
The roofs of palaces; and nature prompts them,
In simple and low things, to prince it, much
Beyond the trick of others. This Polydore,—
The heir of Cymbeline and Britain, whom
The king his father call'd Guiderius,—Jove!
When on my three-foot stool I sit, and tell

[1] where on the bow: in folio. Warburton made the change.

The warlike feats I have done, his spirits fly out
Into my story: say,—"Thus mine enemy fell;
And thus I set my foot on 's neck;" even then
The princely blood flows in his cheek, he sweats,
Strains his young nerves, and puts himself in posture
That acts my words. The younger brother, Cadwal,
(Once Arviragus) in as like a vigour,[1]
Strikes life into my speech, and shows much more
His own conceiving. Hark! the game is rous'd.—
[*Horns wind.*[2]
O Cymbeline! heaven, and my conscience, knows,
Thou didst unjustly banish me; whereon
At three, and two years-old, I stole these babes,
Thinking to bar thee of succession, as
Thou reft'st me of my lands. Euriphile,
Thou wast their nurse; they took thee for their mother,
And every day do honour to her grave:
Myself, Belarius, that am Morgan call'd,
They take for natural father. [*Horn.*]—The game is up. [*Exit.*

SCENE IV.—Near Milford-Haven.

Enter Pisanio *and* Imogen.

Imo. Thou told'st me, when we came from horse, the place
Was near at hand.—Ne'er long'd my mother so
To see me first, as I have now. Pisanio! Man!
Where is Posthumus? What is in thy mind
That makes thee stare thus? Wherefore breaks that sigh
From th' inward of thee? One, but painted thus,
Would be interpreted a thing perplex'd
Beyond self-explication: put thyself
Into a haviour of less fear, ere wildness
Vanquish my staider senses. What 's the matter?
Why tender'st thou that paper to me, with
[Pis. *offers a Letter.*[3]
A look untender? If it be summer news,
Smile to 't before; if winterly, thou need'st
But keep that countenance still.—My husband's hand!
That drug-damn'd Italy hath out-craftied him,
And he 's at some hard point.—Speak, man: thy tongue

[1] figure: in f. e. [2] [3] Not in f. e.

May take off some extremity, which to read
Would be even mortal to me.

Pis. Please you, read ; [*Giving it.*[1]
And you shall find me, wretched man, a thing
The most disdain'd of fortune.

Imo. [*Reads.*] "Thy mistress, Pisanio, hath played the strumpet in my bed ; the testimonies whereof lie bleeding in me. I speak not out of weak surmises, but from proof as strong as my grief, and as certain as I expect my revenge. That part, thou, Pisanio, must act for me, if thy faith be not tainted with the breach of hers. Let thine own hands take away her life ; I shall give thee opportunity at Milford-Haven ; she hath my letter for the purpose : where, if thou fear to strike, and to make me certain it is done, thou art the pander to her dishonour, and equally to me disloyal."

Pis. What shall I need to draw my sword ? the paper
Hath cut her throat already.—No ; 't is slander,
Whose edge is sharper than the sword ; whose tongue
Outvenoms all the worms of Nile ; whose breath
Rides on the posting winds, and doth belie
All corners of the world : kings, queens, and states,
Maids, matrons, nay, the secrets of the grave
This viperous slander enters.—What cheer, madam ?

Imo. False to his bed ! What is it to be false ?
To lie in watch there, and to think on him ?
To weep 'twixt clock and clock ? if sleep charge nature,
To break it with a fearful dream of him,
And cry myself awake ? that 's false to his bed,
Is it ?

Pis. Alas, good lady !

Imo. I false ? Thy conscience witness.—Iachimo,
Thou didst accuse him of incontinency ;
Thou then look'dst like a villain ; now, methinks,
Thy favour 's good enough. Some jay of Italy,
Who smothers her with painting,[2] hath betray'd him :
Poor I am stale, a garment out of fashion ;
And, for I am richer than to hang by the walls,
I must be ripp'd :—to pieces with me !—O !
Men's vows are women's traitors. All good seeming,
By thy revolt, O husband ! shall be thought
Put on for villainy ; not born where 't grows
But worn a bait for ladies.

[1] Not in f. e. [2] Whose mother was her painting : in f. e.

Pis. Good madam, hear me.
Imo. True honest men being heard, like false Æneas
Were in his time thought false; and Sinon's weeping
Did scandal many a holy tear; took pity
From most true wretchedness: so thou, Posthumus,
Wilt lay the leaven on all proper men:
Goodly, and gallant, shall be false, and perjur'd,
From thy great fall.—Come, fellow, be thou honest:
Do thou thy master's bidding. When thou seest him,
A little witness my obedience: look!
I draw the sword myself: take it; and hit
The innocent mansion of my love, my heart.
Fear not; 't is empty of all things, but grief:
Thy master is not there, who was, indeed,
The riches of it. Do his bidding; strike.
Thou may'st be valiant in a better cause,
But now thou seem'st a coward.
Pis. Hence, vile instrument!
Thou shalt not damn my hand.
Imo. Why, I must die;
And if I do not by thy hand, thou art
No servant of thy master's. Against self-slaughter
There is a prohibition so divine,
That cravens my weak hand. Come, here 's my heart:
Something 's afore 't:[1]—Soft, soft! we 'll no defence;
Obedient as the scabbard.—What is here?
The scriptures of the loyal Leonatus,
All turn'd to heresy? Away, away,
Corrupters of my faith! you shall no more
Be stomachers to my heart. Thus may poor fools
Believe false teachers: though those that are betray'd
Do feel the treason sharply, yet the traitor
Stands in worse case of woe.
And thou, Posthumus, that didst set up
My disobedience 'gainst the king my father,
And make me put into contempt the suits
Of princely followers,[2] shalt hereafter find
It is no act of common passage, but
A strain of rareness: and I grieve myself,
To think, when thou shalt be disedg'd by her
That now thou tir'st[3] on, how thy memory
Will then be pang'd by me.—Pr'ythee, despatch:

[1] a-foot: in folio. Rowe made the change. [2] fellows: in f. e.
[3] *Feed on*, like a bird of prey.

The lamb entreats the butcher: where 's thy knife?
Thou art too slow to do thy master's bidding,
When I desire it too.
  Pis. O gracious lady!
Since I receiv'd command to do this business,
I have not slept one wink.
  Imo. Do 't, and to bed, then.
  Pis. I 'll crack mine eye-balls first.[1]
  Imo. And[2] wherefore, then,
Didst undertake it? Why hast thou abus'd
So many miles with a pretence? this place?
Mine action, and thine own? our horses' labour?
The time inviting thee? the perturb'd court,
For my being absent; whereunto I never
Purpose return? Why hast thou gone so far,
To be unbent, when thou hast ta'en thy stand,
Th' elected deer before thee?
  Pis. But to win time,
To lose so bad employment; in the which
I have consider'd of a course. Good lady,
Hear me with patience.
  Imo. Talk thy tongue weary; speak:
I have heard I am a strumpet, and mine ear,
Therein false struck, can take no greater wound,
Nor tent to bottom that. But speak.
  Pis. Then, madam,
I thought you would not back again.
  Imo. Most like,
Bringing me here to kill me.
  Pis. Not so, neither:
But if I were as wise as honest, then
My purpose would prove well. It cannot be,
But that my master is abus'd:
Some villain, ay, and singular in his art,
Hath done you both this cursed injury.
  Imo. Some Roman courtezan.
  Pis. No, on my life.
I 'll give but notice you are dead, and send him
Some bloody sign of it; for 't is commanded
I should do so: you shall be miss'd at court,
And that will well confirm it.
  Imo. Why, good fellow,

[1] I 'll wake mine eye-balls blind first: in f. e. [2] This word is not in f. e

What shall I do the while? where bide? how live?
Or in my life what comfort, when I am
Dead to my husband?
  Pis. If you 'll back to the court,—
  Imo. No court, no father; nor no more ado
With that harsh, noble, simple, empty[1] nothing,
That Cloten, whose love-suit hath been to me
As fearful as a siege.
  Pis. If not at court,
Then not in Britain must you bide.
  Imo. Where then?
Hath Britain all the sun that shines? Day, night,
Are they not but in Britain? I' the world's volume
Our Britain seems as of it, but not in it;
In a great pool, a swan's nest: pr'ythee, think
There 's livers out of Britain.
  Pis. I am most glad
You think of other place. Th' ambassador,
Lucius the Roman, comes to Milford-Haven
To-morrow: now, if you could wear a mind
Dark as your fortune is, and but disguise
That, which, t' appear itself, must not yet be,
But by self-danger, you should tread a course
Privy, yet[2] full of view: yea, haply, near
The residence of Posthumus; so nigh, at least,
That though his actions were not visible, yet
Report should render him hourly to your ear,
As truly as he moves.
  Imo. O, for such means!
Though peril to my modesty, not death on 't,
I would adventure.
  Pis. Well then, here 's the point.
You must forget to be a woman; change
Command into obedience; fear, and niceness,
(The handmaids of all women, or more truly,
Woman it pretty self) into a waggish carriage:[3]
Ready in gibes, quick-answer'd, saucy, and
As quarrelous as the weasel: nay, you must
Forget that rarest treasure of your cheek,
Exposing it (but, O, the harder heart!
Alack, no remedy!) to the greedy touch
Of common-kissing Titan; and forget

[1] This word is not in f. e. [2] Pretty, and full, &c : in f. e. courage : in f. e.

Your laboursome and dainty trims, wherein
You made great Juno angry.
Imo. Nay, be brief:
I see into thy end, and am almost
A man already.
Pis. First, make yourself but like one.
Forethinking this, I have already fit
('T is in my cloak-bag) doublet, hat, hose, all
That answer to them: would you, in their serving,
And with what imitation you can borrow
From youth of such a season, 'fore noble Lucius
Present yourself, desire his service, tell him
Wherein you are happy, (which you[1] will make him know,
If that his head have ear in music) doubtless,
With joy he will embrace you; for he 's honourable,
And, doubling that, most holy. Your means abroad,
You have me, rich; and I will never fail
Beginning nor supplyment.
Imo. Thou art all the comfort
The gods will diet me with. Pr'ythee, away:
There 's more to be consider'd, but we 'll even
All that good time will give us. This attempt
I 'm soldier to, and will abide it with
A prince's courage. Away, I pr'ythee.
Pis. Well, madam, we must take a short farewell,
Lest, being miss'd, I be suspected of
Your carriage from the court. My noble mistress,
Here is a box; I had it from the queen:
What 's in 't is precious; if you are sick at sea,
Or stomach-qualm'd at land, a dram of this
Will drive away distemper.—To some shade,
And fit you to your manhood.—May the gods
Direct you to the best!
Imo. Amen. I thank thee. [*Exeunt*

SCENE V.—A Room in CYMBELINE's Palace.

Enter CYMBELINE, QUEEN, CLOTEN, LUCIUS, *and Lords*.

Cym. Thus far; and so farewell.
Luc. Thanks, royal sir
My emperor hath wrote, I must from hence;
And am right sorry that I must report ye
My master's enemy.
Cym. Our subjects, sir,

[1] Not in folio

Will not endure his yoke: and for ourself,
To show less sovereignty than they, must needs
Appear unkinglike.
Luc. So, sir. I desire of you
A conduct over land to Milford-Haven.—
Madam, all joy befall your grace, and you!
Cym. My lords, you are appointed for that office;
The due of honour in no point omit.
So, farewell, noble Lucius.
Luc. Your hand, my lord.
Clo. Receive it friendly; but from this time forth
I wear it as your enemy.
Luc. Sir, the event
Is yet to name the winner. Fare you well.
Cym. Leave not the worthy Lucius, good my lords,
Till he have cross'd the Severn.—Happiness!
[*Exeunt* LUCIUS *and Lords*
Queen. He goes hence frowning; but it honours us,
That we have given him cause.
Clo. 'T is all the better:
Your valiant Britons have their wishes in it.
Cym. Lucius hath wrote already to the emperor
How it goes here. It fits us, therefore, ripely,
Our chariots and our horsemen be in readiness:
The powers that he already hath in Gallia
Will soon be drawn to head, from whence he moves
His war for Britain.
Queen. 'T is not sleepy business,
But must be look'd to speedily, and strongly.
Cym. Our expectation that it would be thus
Hath made us forward. But, my gentle queen,
Where is our daughter? She hath not appear'd
Before the Roman, nor to us hath tender'd
The duty of the day. She looks us like
A thing more made of malice, than of duty:
We have noted it.—Call her before us, for
We have been too slight in sufferance. [*Exit an Attendant*
Queen. Royal sir,
Since the exile of Posthumus, most retir'd
Hath her life been; the cure whereof, my lord,
'T is time must do. Beseech your majesty,
Forbear sharp speeches to her: she 's a lady
So tender of rebuke, that words are strokes,
And strokes death to her.

Re-enter an Attendant.

Cym. Where is she, sir? How
Can her contempt be answer'd?

Atten. Please you, sir,
Her chambers are all lock'd; and there 's no answer
That will be given to the loud'st[1] noise we make.

Queen. My lord, when last I went to visit her,
She pray'd me to excuse her keeping close;
Whereto constrain'd by her infirmity,
She should that duty leave unpaid to you,
Which daily she was bound to proffer: this
She wish'd me to make known, but our great court
Made me to blame in memory.

Cym. Her doors lock'd?
Not seen of late? Grant, heavens, that which I
Fear prove false! [*Exit.*

Queen. Son, I say, follow the king.

Clo. That man of hers, Pisanio, her old servant,
I have not seen these two days.

Queen. Go, look after.— [*Exit* CLOTEN.
Pisanio, thou that stand'st so for Posthumus,
He hath a drug of mine: I pray, his absence
Proceed by swallowing that, for he believes
It is a thing most precious. But for her,
Where is she gone? Haply, despair hath seiz'd her;
Or, wing'd with fervour of her love, she 's flown
To her desir'd Posthumus. Gone she is
To death, or to dishonour; and my end
Can make good use of either: she being down,
I have the placing of the British crown.

Re-enter CLOTEN.

How now, my son!

Clo. 'T is certain, she is fled.
Go in, and cheer the king: he rages; none
Dare come about him.

Queen. All the better: may
This night forestal him of the coming day! [*Exit* QUEEN

Clo. I love, and hate her, for she 's fair and royal;
And that she hath all courtly parts, more exquisite
Than lady, ladies, woman: from every one
The best she hath, and she, of all compounded,
Outsells them all. I love her therefore; but,
Disdaining me, and throwing favours on

[1] loud of: in folio.

The low Posthumus, slanders so her judgment,
That what 's else rare is chok'd; and in that point
I will conclude to hate her; nay, indeed,
To be reveng'd upon her: for, when fools shall—

Enter PISANIO.

Who is here?—What! are you packing, sirrah?
Come hither. Ah, you precious pandar! Villain,
Where is thy lady? In a word, or else
Thou art straightway with the fiends.

Pis. O, good my lord

Clo. Where is thy lady? or, by Jupiter—
I will not ask again. Close villain,
I 'll have this secret from thy heart, or rip
Thy heart to find it. Is she with Posthumus?
From whose so many weights of baseness cannot
A dram of worth be drawn.

Pis. Alas, my lord!
How can she be with him? When was she miss'd?
He is in Rome.

Clo. Where is she, sir? Come nearer;
No farther halting: satisfy me home
What is become of her?

Pis. O, my all-worthy lord!

Clo. All-worthy villain!
Discover where thy mistress is, at once,
At the next word.—No more of worthy lord,—
Speak, or thy silence on the instant is
Thy condemnation and thy death.

Pis. Then sir,
This paper is the history of my knowledge
Touching her flight. [*Presenting a Letter.*

Clo. Let 's see 't.—I will pursue her
Even to Augustus' throne.

Pis. [*Aside.*] Or this, or perish.
She 's far enough; and what he learns by this,
May prove his travel, not her danger.

Clo. Humph!

Pis. [*Aside.*] I 'll write to my lord she 's dead. O Imogen,
Safe may'st thou wander, safe return again!

Clo. Sirrah, is this letter true?

Pis. Sir, as I think.

Clo. It is Posthumus' hand; I know 't.—Sirrah, if thou wouldst not be a villain, but do me true service, undergo those employments, wherein I should have cause to use thee, with a serious industry,—that is, what villany so'er I bid thee do, to perform it directly and truly. I would think thee an honest man: thou shouldst neither want my means for thy relief, nor my voice for thy preferment.

Pis. Well, my good lord.

Clo. Wilt thou serve me? For since patiently and constantly thou hast stuck to the bare fortune of that beggar Posthumus, thou canst not, in the course of gratitude, but be a diligent follower of mine. Wilt thou serve me?

Pis. Sir, I will.

Clo. Give me thy hand: here 's my purse. Hast any of thy late master's garments in thy possession?

Pis. I have, my lord, at my lodging, the same suit he wore when he took leave of my lady and mistress.

Clo. The first service thou dost me, fetch that suit hither: let it be thy first service; go.

Pis. I shall, my lord. [*Exit.*

Clo. Meet thee at Milford-Haven.—I forgot to ask him one thing; I 'll remember 't anon.—Even there thou villain, Posthumus, will I kill thee.—I would, these garments were come. She said upon a time (the bitterness of it I now belch from my heart) that she held the very garment of Posthumus in more respect than my noble and natural person, together with the adornment of my qualities. With that suit upon my back, will I ravish her: first kill him, and in her eyes; there shall she see my valour, which will then be a torment to her contempt. He on the ground, my speech of insultment ended on his dead body,—and when my lust hath dined, (which, as I say, to vex her, I will execute in the clothes that she so praised) to the court I 'll knock her back, foot her home again. She hath despised me rejoicingly, and I 'll be merry in my revenge.

Re-enter PISANIO, *with the Clothes.*

Be those the garments?

Pis. Ay, my noble lord.

Clo. How long is 't since she went to Milford-Haven?

Pis. She can scarce be there yet.

Clo. Bring this apparel to my chamber; that is the second thing that I have commanded thee; the third is, that thou wilt be a voluntary mute to my design. Be but duteous, and true preferment shall tender itself to thee.—My revenge is now at Milford: would I had wings to follow it.—Come, and be true. [*Exit.*

Pis. Thou bidd'st me to thy loss: for true to thee
Were to prove false, which I will never be
To him that is most true.—To Milford go,
And find not her whom thou pursuest. Flow, flow,
You heavenly blessings, on her! This fool's speed
Be cross'd with slowness: labour be his meed! [*Exit.*

SCENE VI.—Before the Cave of BELARIUS.

Enter IMOGEN, *attired like a Boy.*

Imo. I see a man's life is a tedious one:
I have 'tir'd'[1] myself, and for two nights together
Have made the ground my bed: I should be sick,
But that my resolution helps me.—Milford,
When from the mouutain-top Pisanio show'd thee,
Thou wast within a ken. O Jove! I think,
Foundations fly the wretched; such, I mean,
Where they should be reliev'd. Two beggars told me
I could not miss my way: will poor folks lie,
That have afflictions on them, knowing 't is
A punishment, or trial? Yes; no wonder,
When rich ones scarce tell true: to lapse in fulness
Is sorer, than to lie for need; and falsehood
Is worse in kings, than beggars.—My dear lord!
Thou art one o' the false ones: now I think on thee,
My hunger 's gone; but even before, I was
At point to sink for food.—But what is this?
[*Seeing the Cave*
Here is a path to it: 't is some savage hold:
I were best not call; I dare not call; yet famine,
Ere clean it o'erthrow nature, makes it valiant.
Plenty, and peace, breed cowards; hardness ever
Of hardiness is mother.—Ho! Who 's here?
If any thing that 's civil, speak; if savage,
Take, or lend.—Ho!—No answer? then, I 'll enter.
Best draw my sword; and if mine enemy
But fear the sword like me, he 'll scarcely look on 't.
Such a foe, good heavens! [*Exit into the Cave.*

Enter BELARIUS, GUIDERIUS, *and* ARVIRAGUS.

Bel. You, Polydore, have prov'd best woodman, and

[1] tired: in f. e. [2] Not in f. e

Are master of the feast: Cadwal, and I,
Will play the cook and servant; 't is our match:
The sweat of industry would dry, and die,
But for the end it works to. Come; our stomachs
Will make what 's homely, savoury: weariness
Can snore upon the flint, when resty[1] sloth
Finds the down pillow hard.—Now, peace be here,
Poor house, that keep'st thyself!

Gui. I am thoroughly weary.

Arv. I am weak with toil, yet strong in appetite.

Gui. There is cold meat i' the cave: we 'll browze on that,
Whilst what we have kill'd be cook'd.

Bel. Stay: come not in. [*Looking in.*
But that it eats our victuals, I should think
Here were a fairy.

Gui. What 's the matter, sir?

Bel. By Jupiter, an angel! or, if not,
An earthly paragon!—Behold divineness
No elder than a boy!

Enter IMOGEN.

Imo. Good masters, harm me not:
Before I enter'd here, I call'd; and thought
To have begg'd, or bought, what I have took. Good troth,
I have stolen nought; nor would not, though I had found
Gold strew'd i' the floor. Here 's money for my meat.
I would have left it on the board, so soon
As I had made my meal, and parted
With prayers for the provider.

Gui. Money, youth?

Arv. All gold and silver rather turn to dirt;
As 't is no better reckon'd, but of those
Who worship dirty gods.

Imo. I see, you are angry.
Know, if you kill me for my fault, I should
Have died, had I not made it.

Bel. Whither bound?

Imo. To Milford-Haven.

Bel. What 's your name?

Imo. Fidele, sir. I have a kinsman, who
Is bound for Italy: he embark'd at Milford;
To whom being going, almost spent with hunger

[1] *Rusty.*

I am fallen in this offence.
Bel. Pr'ythee, fair youth,
Think us no churls, nor measure our good minds
By this rude place we live in. Well encounter'd.
'T is almost night: you shall have better cheer
Ere you depart; and thanks, to stay and eat it.—
Boys, bid him welcome.
Gui. Were you a woman, youth,
I should woo hard, but be your groom.—In honesty,
I bid for you, as I do buy.
Arv. I 'll make 't my comfort,
He is a man: I 'll love him as my brother;
And such a welcome as I 'd give to him
After long absence, such is yours.—Most welcome.
Be sprightly, for you fall 'mongst friends.
Imo. 'Mongst friends!
If brothers?—[*Aside.*] Would it had been so, that they
Had been my father's sons: then, had my prize
Been less; and so more equal ballasting
To thee, Posthumus.
Bel. He wrings at some distress.
Gui. Would I could free 't!
Arv. Or I; what'er it be,
What pain it cost, what danger. Gods!
Bel. Hark, boys. [*Whispering.*
Imo. Great men,
That had a court no bigger than this cave,
That did attend themselves, and had the virtue
Which their own conscience seal'd them, (laying by
That nothing gift of differing[1] multitudes)
Could not out-peer these twain. Pardon me, gods!
I 'd change my sex to be companion with them,
Since Leonatus false.
Bel. It shall be so.
Boys, we 'll go dress our hunt.—Fair youth, come in:
Discourse is heavy, fasting; when we have supp'd,
We 'll mannerly demand thee of thy story,
So far as thou wilt speak it.
Gui. Pray, draw near.
Arv. The night to the owl, and morn to the lark, less welcome.
Imo. Thanks, sir.
Arv. I pray, draw near. [*Exeunt,*[2] *into the Cave.*

1 *Discordant.* 2 The rest of this direction is not in f. e.

SCENE VII.—Rome.

Enter Two Senators and Tribunes.

1 *Sen.* This is the tenour of the emperor's writ
That since the common men are now in action
'Gainst the Pannonians and Dalmatians;
And that the legions now in Gallia are
Full weak to undertake our wars against
The fallen-off Britons, that we do incite
The gentry to this business. He creates
Lucius pro-consul; and to you, the tribunes,
For this immediate levy he commends
His absolute commission. Long live Cæsar!
Tri. Is Lucius general of the forces?
2 *Sen.* Ay.
Tri. Remaining now in Gallia?
1 *Sen.* With those legions
Which I have spoke of, whereunto your levy
Must be suppliant: the words of your commission
Will tie you to the numbers, and the time
Of their despatch.
Tri. We will discharge our duty. [*Exeunt.*

ACT IV.

SCENE I.—The Forest, near the Cave.

Enter CLOTEN.

Clo. I am near to the place where they should meet, if Pisanio have mapped it truly. How fit his garments serve me! Why should his mistress, who was made by him that made the tailor, not be fit too? the rather (saving reverence of the word) for 't is said, a woman's fitness comes by fits. Therein I must play the workman. I dare speak it to myself, (for it is not vain-glory for a man and his glass to confer in his own chamber) I mean, the lines of my body are as well-drawn as his; no less young, more strong, not beneath him in fortunes, beyond him in the advantage of the time, above him in birth, alike conversant in general services, and more remarkable in single oppositions: yet this perverse errant[1] thing loves him in my despite. What mortality is! Posthumus, thy head, which now is growing upon thy shoulders, shall within this hour be off, thy mistress enforced, thy garments cut to pieces before thy face; and all this done, spurn her home to her father, who may, haply, be a little angry for my so rough usage, but my mother, having power of his testiness, shall turn all into my commendations. My horse is tied up safe: out, sword, and to a sore purpose. Fortune, put them into my hand! This is the very description of their meeting-place, and the fellow dares not deceive me. [*Exit.*

SCENE II.—Before the Cave.

Enter, from the Cave, BELARIUS, GUIDERIUS, ARVIRAGUS, *and* IMOGEN.

Bel. You are not well: [*To* IMOGEN.] remain here in the cave:
We'll come to you after hunting.
Arv. Brother, stay here: [*To* IMOGEN
Are we not brothers?
Imo. So man and man should be;
But clay and clay differs in dignity,
Whose dust is both alike. I am very sick.
Gui. Go you to hunting; I'll abide with him.
Imo. So sick I am not,—yet I am not well;
But not so citizen a wanton, as
To seem to die, ere sick. So please you, leave me;
Stick to your journal course: the breach of custom
Is breach of all. I am ill; but your being by me
Cannot amend me: society is no comfort
To one not sociable. I am not very sick,
Since I can reason of it: pray you, trust me here;
I'll rob none but myself, and let me die,
Stealing so poorly.
Gui. I love thee; I have spoke it:
How much the quantity, the weight as much,
As I do love my father.
Bel. What! how? how?
Arv. If it be sin to say so, sir, I yoke me
In my good brother's fault: I know not why

[1] this imperseverant thing: in f. e.

I love this youth ; and I have heard you say,
Love's reason's without reason : the bier at door,
And a demand who is 't shall die, I'd say,
My father, not this youth.
Bel. [*Aside.*] O noble strain !
O worthiness of nature ! breed of greatness !
Cowards father cowards, and base things sire base:
Nature hath meal and bran : contempt and grace.
I am not their father ; yet who this should be
Doth miracle itself, lov'd before me.—
'T is the ninth hour o' the morn.
Arv. Brother, farewell.
Imo. I wish ye sport.
Arv. You health.—So please you, sir.
Imo. [*Aside.*] These are kind creatures. Gods, what lies I have heard !
Our courtiers say, all 's savage but at court :
Experience, O ! thou disprov'st report.
Th' imperious seas breed monsters ; for the dish,
Poor tributary rivers as sweet fish.
I am sick still ; heart-sick.—Pisanio,
I 'll now taste of thy drug.
Gui. I could not stir him :
He said, he was gentle, but unfortunate ;
Dishonestly afflicted, but yet honest.
Arv. Thus did he answer me ; yet said, hereafter
I might know more.
Bel. To the field, to the field !—
We 'll leave you for this time ; go in, and rest.
Arv. We'll not be long away.
Bel. Pray, be not sick,
For you must be our house-wife.
Imo. Well, or ill,
I am bound to you.
Bel. And shalt be ever. [*Exit* IMOGEN
This youth, howe'er distress'd, appears he hath had
ood ancestors.
Arv. How angel-like he sings.
Gui. But his neat cookery : he cut our roots in characters ;
And sauc'd our broths, as Juno had been sick,
And he her dieter.
Arv. Nobly he yokes
A smiling with a sigh, as if the sigh
Was that it was, for not being such a smile ;

The smile mocking the sigh, that it would fly
From so divine a temple, to commix
With winds that sailors rail at.
Gui. I do note,
That grief and patience, rooted in him[1] both,
Mingle their spurs[2] together.
Arv. Grow, patience!
And let the stinking elder, grief, untwine
His perishing root with the increasing vine!
Bel. It is great morning. Come; away!—Who's there? [*They stand back.*[3]

Enter CLOTEN.

Clo. I cannot find those runagates: that villain
Hath mock'd me.—I am faint.
Bel. Those runagates!
Means he not us? I partly know him; 't is
Cloten, the son o' the queen. I fear some ambush.
I saw him not these many years, and yet
I know 't is he.—We are held as outlaws: hence!
Gui. He is but one. You and my brother search
What companies are near: pray you, away;
Let me alone with him.
[*Exeunt* BELARIUS *and* ARVIRAGUS.
Clo. Soft! what are you
That fly me thus? some villain mountaineers?
I have heard of such.—What slave art thou?
Gui. A thing
More slavish did I ne'er, than answering
A slave without a knock.
Clo. Thou art a robber,
A law-breaker, a villain. Yield thee, thief.
Gui. To whom? to thee? What art thou? Have not I
An arm as big as thine? a heart as big?
Thy words, I grant, are bigger; for I wear not
My dagger in my mouth. Say, what thou art,
Why I should yield to thee.
Clo. Thou villain base,
Know'st me not by my clothes?
Gui. No, nor thy tailor, rascal,
Who is thy grandfather: he made those clothes,
Which, as it seems, make thee.
Clo. Thou precious varlet,
My tailor made them not.

[1] them: in folio. [2] *Projecting roots.* [3] Not in f. e.

Gui. Hence then, and thank
The man that gave them thee. Thou art some fool;
I am loath to beat thee.
Clo. Thou injurious thief,
Hear but my name, and tremble.
Gui. What 's thy name?
Clo. Cloten, thou villain.
Gui. Cloten, thou double villain, be thy name,
I cannot tremble at it: were it toad, or adder, spider,
'T would move me sooner.
Clo. To thy farther fear,
Nay, to thy mere confusion, thou shalt know
I 'm son to the queen.
Gui. I am sorry for 't, not seeming
So worthy as thy birth.
Clo. Art not afear'd?
Gui. Those that I reverence, those I fear, the wise:
At fools I laugh, not fear them.
Clo. Die the death.
When I have slain thee with my proper hand,
I 'll follow those that even now fled hence,
And on the gates of Lud's town set your heads.
Yield, rustic, mountaineer. [*Exeunt, fighting.*

Enter BELARIUS *and* ARVIRAGUS.

Bel. No company 's abroad.
Arv. None in the world. You did mistake him, sure.
Bel. I cannot tell: long is it since I saw him,
But time hath nothing blurr'd those lines of favour
Which then he wore: the snatches in his voice,
And burst of speaking, were as his. I am absolute
'T was very Cloten.
Arv. In this place we left them:
I wish my brother make good time with him,
You say he is so fell.
Bel. Being scarce made up,
I mean, to man, he had not apprehension
Of roaring terrors; for th' effect[1] of judgment
Is oft the cause of fear. But see, thy brother.

Re-enter GUIDERIUS, *with* CLOTEN'S *Head.*

Gui. This Cloten was a fool, an empty purse,
There was no money in 't. Not Hercules
Could have knock'd out his brains, for he had none;
Yet I not doing this, the fool had borne

[1] for defect: in folio. Theobald made the change.

My head, as I do his.
Bel. What hast thou done?
Gui. I am perfect what: cut off one Cloten's head,
Son to the queen after his own report;
Who call'd me traitor, mountaineer; and swore,
With his own single hand he 'd take us in,
Displace our heads, where (thank the gods!) they grow
And set them on Lud's town.
Bel. We are all undone.
Gui. Why, worthy father, what have we to lose,
But that he swore to take, our lives? The law
Protects not us; then, why should we be tender,
To let an arrogant piece of flesh threat us;
Play judge, and executioner, all himself,
For we do fear the law? What company
Discover you abroad?
Bel. No single soul
Can we set eye on, but in all safe reason
He must have some attendants. Though his humour[1]
Was nothing but mutation; ay, and that
From one bad thing to worse; not frenzy, not
Absolute madness, could so far have rav'd,
To bring him here alone. Although, perhaps,
It may be heard at court, that such as we
Cave here, hunt here, are outlaws, and in time
May make some stronger head; the which he hearing
(As it is like him) might break out, and swear
He 'd fetch us in, yet is 't not probable
To come alone, either he so undertaking,
Or they so suffering: then, on good ground we fear,
If we do fear this body hath a tail
More perilous than the head.
Arv. Let ordinance
Come as the gods foresay it: howsoe'er,
My brother hath done well.
Bel. I had no mind
To hunt this day: the boy Fidele's sickness
Did make my way long forth.
Gui. With his own sword,
Which he did wave against my throat, I have ta'en
His head from him: I 'll throw 't into the creek
Behind our rock; and let it to the sea,
And tell the fishes he 's the queen's son, Cloten:

[1] honour: in folio. Theobald made the change.

That 's all I reck. [*Exit*
Bel. I fear, 't will be reveng'd.
Would, Polydore, thou hadst not done 't, though valour
Becomes thee well enough.
Arv. 'Would I had done 't,
So the revenge alone pursued me.—Polydore,
I love thee brotherly, but envy much,
Thou hast robb'd me of this deed : I would revenges,
That possible strength might meet, would seek us through,
And put us to our answer.
Bel. Well, 't is done.
We 'll hunt no more to-day, nor seek for danger
Where there's no profit. I pr'ythee, to our rock :
You and Fidele play the cooks ; I 'll stay
Till hasty Polydore return, and bring him
To dinner presently.
Arv. Poor sick Fidele !
I 'll willingly to him : to gain his colour,
I 'd let a parish of such Clotens blood,
And praise myself for charity. [*Exit*
Bel. O thou goddess,
Thou divine Nature, how[1] thyself thou blazon'st
In these two princely boys ! They are as gentle
As zephyrs blowing below the violet,
Not wagging his sweet head ; and yet as rough,
Their royal blood enchaf'd, as the rud'st wind,
That by the top doth take the mountain pine,
And make him stoop to the vale. 'T is wonder,
That an invisible instinct should frame them
To royalty unlearn'd, honour untaught,
Civility not seen from other, valour
That wildly grows in them, but yields a crop
As if it had been sow'd ! Yet still it's strange,
What Cloten's being here to us portends,
Or what his death will bring us.

Re-enter GUIDERIUS.

Gui. Where 's my brother ?
I have sent Cloten's clotpoll down the stream
In embassy to his mother : his body 's hostage
For his return. [*Solemn Music.*
Bel. My ingenious instrument !
Hark, Polydore, it sounds ; but what occasion

[1] thou : in folio. Malone made the change

Hath Cadwal now to give it motion? Hark!
Gui. Is he at home?
Bel. He went hence even now.
Gui. What does he mean? since death of my dear'st mother
It did not speak before. All solemn things
Should answer solemn accidents. The matter?
Triumphs for nothing, and lamenting toys,
Is jollity for apes, and grief for boys.
Is Cadwal mad?

Re-enter ARVIRAGUS, *bearing in his Arms* IMOGEN, *as dead.*

Bel. Look! here he comes,
And brings the dire occasion in his arms
Of what we blame him for.
Arv. The bird is dead,
That we have made so much on. I had rather
Have skipp'd from sixteen years of age to sixty,
To have turn'd my leaping time into a crutch,
Than have seen this.
Gui. O sweetest, fairest lily!
My brother wears thee not the one half so well,
As when thou grew'st thyself.
Bel. O, melancholy!
Who ever yet could sound thy bottom? find
The ooze, to show what coast thy sluggish crare[1]
Might easiliest harbour in?—Thou blessed thing!
Jove knows what man thou mightst have made; but I,
Thou diedst a most rare boy, of melancholy.—
How found you him?
Arv. Stark, as you see:
Thus smiling, as some fly had tickled slumber,
Not as death's dart, being laugh'd at; his right cheek
Reposing on a cushion.
Gui. Where?
Arv. O' the floor;
His arms thus leagu'd: I thought he slept, and put
My clouted brogues[2] from off my feet, whose rudeness
Answer'd my steps too loud.
Gui. Why, he but sleeps;
If he be gone, he 'll make his grave a bed:
With female fairies will his tomb be haunted,
And worms will not come to thee.

[1] *A small vessel.* [2] Irish, *brog*, a shoe.

Arv. With fairest flowers,
Whilst summer lasts, and I live here, Fidele,
I 'll sweeten thy sad grave: thou shalt not lack
The flower, that 's like thy face, pale primrose; nor
The azur'd hare-bell, like thy veins; no, nor
The leafy eglantine,[1] whom not to slander,
Out-sweeten'd not thy breath: the ruddock[2] would,
With charitable bill (O bill, sore-shaming
Those rich-left heirs, that let their fathers lie
Without a monument!) bring thee all this;
Yea, and furr'd moss besides, when flowers are none,
To winter-guard[3] thy corse.
Gui. Pr'ythee, have done;
And do not play in wench-like words with that
Which is so serious. Let us bury him,
And not protract with admiration what
Is now due debt.—To the grave!
Arv. Say, where shall 's lay him?
Gui. By good Euriphile, our mother.
Arv. Be 't so:
And let us, Polydore, though now our voices
Have got the mannish crack, sing him to the ground,
As once[4] our mother: use like note, and words,
Save that Euriphile must be Fidele.
Gui. Cadwal,
I cannot sing: I 'll weep, and word it with thee
For notes of sorrow, out of tune, are worse
Than priests and fanes that lie.
Arv. We 'll speak it, then.
Bel. Great griefs, I see, medicine the less; for Cloten
Is quite forgot. He was a queen's son, boys;
And, though he came our enemy, remember,
He was paid for that: though mean and mighty, rotting
Together, have one dust, yet reverence,
(That angel of the world) doth make distinction
Of place 'twixt high and low. Our foe was princely,
And though you took his life, as being our foe,
Yet bury him as a prince.
Gui. Pray you, fetch him hither.
Thersites' body is as good as Ajax,
When neither is alive.
Arv. If you 'll go fetch him.

[1] leaf of eglantine: in f. e. [2] *Red-breast.* [3] winter-ground: in f. e. [4] to our: in folio.

We 'll say our song the whilst.—Brother, begin.
[*Exit* BELARIUS.

Gui. Nay, Cadwal, we must lay his head to the east:
My father hath a reason for 't.

Arv. 'T is true.

Gui. Come on then, and remove him.

Arv. So.—Begin.

SONG.

Gui. *Fear no more the heat o' the sun,*
Nor the furious winter's rages;
Thou thy worldly task hast done,
Home art gone, and ta'en thy wages:
Golden lads and lasses must,[1]
As chimney-sweepers, come to dust.

Arv. *Fear no more the frown o' the great,*
Thou art past the tyrant's stroke;
Care no more to clothe, and eat;
To thee the reed is as the oak:
The sceptre, learning, physic, must
All follow this, and come to dust.

Gui. *Fear no more the lightning-flash,*
Arv. *Nor th' all-dreaded thunder-stone;*
Gui. *Fear not slander, censure rash;*
Arv. *Thou hast finish'd joy and moan:*
Both. *All lovers young, all lovers must*
Consign to thee, and come to dust.

Gui. *No exorciser harm thee!*
Arv. *Nor no witchcraft charm thee!*
Gui. *Ghost unlaid forbear thee!*
Arv. *Nothing ill come near thee!*
Both. *Quiet consummation have;*
And renowned be thy grave!

Re-enter BELARIUS, *with the Body of* CLOTEN.

Gui. We have done our obsequies. Come, lay him down. [*They place him beside* IMOGEN.

Bel. Here 's a few flowers, but about midnight more:
The herbs that have on them cold dew o' the night,
Are strewings fitt'st for graves.—Upon their faces.—
You were as flowers, now wither'd; even so
These herb'lets shall, which we upon you strew.—
Come on, away; apart upon our knees.

[1] *and girls all must:* in f. e. [2] Not in f. e.

The ground that gave them first has them again:
Their pleasures here are past, so is their pain.
[*Exeunt* BELARIUS, GUIDERIUS, *and* AR GUS.
Imo. [*Awaking.*] Yes, sir, to Milford-Have hich
is the way?—
I thank you.—By yond' bush?—Pray, how far hi r?
'Ods pittikins!—can it be six miles yet?—
I have gone all night:—'faith, I 'll lie down and sleep.
But, soft! no bedfellow.—O, gods and goddesses!
[*Seeing the Body.*
These flowers are like the pleasures of the world;
This bloody man, the care on 't.—I hope I drea
For lo[1]! I thought I was a cave-keeper,
And cook to honest creatures; but 't is not so:
'T was but a bolt of nothing, shot at nothing,
Which the brain makes of fumes. Our very eyes
Are sometimes like our judgments, blind. Good faith,
I tremble still with fear; but if there be
Yet left in heaven as small a drop of pity
As a wren's eye, fear'd gods, a part of it!
The dream 's here still: even when I wake, it is
Without me, as within me; not imagin'd, felt.
A headless man!—The garment of Posthumus!
I know the shape of 's leg: this is his hand;
His foot Mercurial; his Martial thigh;
The brawns of Hercules: but his Jovial[2] face—
Murder in heaven!—How?—'T is gone.—Pisanio,
All curses madded Hecuba gave the Greeks,
And mine to boot, be darted on thee! Thou,
Conspir'd with that irregulous devil, Cloten,
Hast here cut off my lord.—To write, and read,
Be henceforth treacherous!—Damn'd Pisanio
Hath with his forged letters,—damn'd Pisanio—
From this most bravest vessel of the world
Struck the main-top!—O, Posthumus! alas!
Where is thy head? where's that? Ah me! where's that?
Pisanio might have kill'd thee at the heart,
And left thy head on.—How should this be? Pisanio!
'T is he, and Cloten: malice and lucre in them
Have laid this woe here. O! 't is pregnant, pregnant.
The drug he gave me, which, he said, was precious
And cordial to me, have I not found it
Murderous to the senses? That confirms it home:

[1] so: in f. e. [2] *Like Jove*

This is Pisanio's deed, and Cloten's: O!—
Give colour to my pale cheek with thy blood,
That we the horrider may seem to those
Which chance to find us. O, my lord, my lord!

Enter Lucius, *a Captain, and other Officers, and a Soothsayer.*

Cap. To them the legions garrison'd in Gallia,
After your will, have cross'd the sea; attending
You here at Milford-Haven, with your ships:
They are in readiness.

Luc. But what from Rome?

Cap. The senate hath stirr'd up the confiners,
And gentlemen of Italy; most willing spirits,
That promise noble service, and they come
Under the conduct of bold Iachimo,
Sienna's brother.

Luc. When expect you them?

Cap. With the next benefit o' the wind.

Luc. This forwardness
Makes our hopes fair. Command, our present numbers
Be muster'd; bid the captains look to 't.—Now, sir,
What have you dream'd of late of this war's purpose?

Sooth. Last night the very gods show'd me a vision,
(I fast, and pray'd, for their intelligence) thus:—
I saw Jove's bird, the Roman eagle, wing'd
From the spungy south to this part of the west,
There vanish'd in the sunbeams: which portends,
(Unless my sins abuse my divination)
Success to the Roman host.

Luc. Dream often so,
And never false.—Soft, ho? what trunk is here,
Without his top? The ruin speaks, that sometime
It was a worthy building.—How? a page!—
Or dead, or sleeping on him? But dead rather;
For nature doth abhor to make his bed
With the defunct, or sleep upon the dead.—
Let 's see the boy's face.

Cap. He is alive, my lord.

Luc. He 'll then instruct us of this body.—Young one,
Inform us of thy fortunes; for, it seems,
They crave to be demanded. Who is this,
Thou mak'st thy bloody pillow? Or who was he,
That, otherwise than noble nature did,

Hath alter'd that good picture? What 's thy interest
In this sad wreck? How came it? Who is it?
What art thou?

Imo. I am nothing: or if not,
Nothing to be were better. This was my master,
A very valiant Briton, and a good,
That here by mountaineers lies slain.—Alas!
There are no more such masters: I may wander
From east to occident, cry out for service,
Try many, all good, serve truly, never
Find such another master.

Luc. 'Lack, good youth!
Thou mov'st no less with thy complaining, than
Thy master in bleeding. Say his name, good friend.

Imo. Richard du Champ [*Aside.*] If I do lie, and do
No harm by it, though the gods hear, I hope
They 'll pardon.—Say you, sir?

Luc. Thy name?

Imo Fidele, sir.

Luc. Thou dost approve thyself the very same:
Thy name well fits thy faith; thy faith, thy name.
Wilt take thy chance with me? I will not say,
Thou shalt be so well master'd, but, be sure,
No less belov'd. The Roman emperor's letters,
Sent by a consul to me, should not sooner
Than thine own worth, prefer thee: go with me.

Imo. I 'll follow, sir. But first, an 't please the gods,
I 'll hide my master from the flies, as deep
As these poor pickaxes can dig: and when
With wild wood-leaves and weeds I have strew'd his grave,
And on it said a century of prayers,
Such as I can, twice o'er, I 'll weep, and sigh;
And, leaving so his service, follow you,
So please you entertain me.

Luc. Ay, good youth;
And rather father thee, than master thee.—My friends
The boy hath taught us manly duties: let us
Find out the prettiest daisied plot we can,
And make him with our pikes and partisans
A grave: come, arm him.—Boy, he is preferr'd
By thee to us, and he shall be interr'd,
As soldiers can. Be cheerful; wipe thine eyes:
Some falls are means the happier to arise. [*Exeunt.*

SCENE III.—A Room in CYMBELINE'S Palace.

Enter CYMBELINE, *Lords, and* PISANIO.

Cym. Again: and bring me word how 't is with her.
A fever with the absence of her son;
A madness, of which her life 's in danger.—Heavens,
How deeply you at once do touch me! Imogen,
The great part of my comfort, gone: my queen
Upon a desperate bed, and in a time
When fearful wars point at me: her son gone,
So needful for this present: it strikes me past
The hope of comfort.—But for thee, fellow,
Who needs must know of her departure, and
Dost seem so ignorant, we 'll enforce it from thee
By a sharp torture.

Pis. Sir, my life is yours,
I humbly set it at your will; but, for my mistress,
I nothing know where she remains, why gone,
Nor when she purposes to return. Beseech your highness,
Hold me your loyal servant.

1 *Lord.* Good my liege,
The day that she was missing he was here:
I dare be bound he 's true, and shall perform
All parts of his subjection loyally. For Cloten,
There wants no diligence in seeking him,
And will, no doubt, be found.

Cym. The time is troublesome:
We 'll slip you for a season; but with jealousy
[*To* PISANIO.
You yet depend.

1 *Lord.* So please your majesty,
The Roman legions, all from Gallia drawn,
Are landed on your coast, with a supply
Of Roman gentlemen by the senate sent.

Cym. Now for the counsel of my son and queen!—
I am amaz'd with matter.

1 *Lord.* Good my liege,
Your preparation can affront no less
Than what you hear of: come more, for more you 're ready.
The want is, but to put these powers in motion,
That long to move.

Cym. I thank you. Let 's withdraw,
And meet the time, as it seeks us: we fear not

What can from Italy annoy us, but
We grieve at chances here.—Away! [*Exeunt.*

Pis. I had no letter from my master, since
I wrote him Imogen was slain. 'T is strange:
Nor hear I from my mistress, who did promise
To yield me often tidings; neither know I
What is betid to Cloten, but remain
Perplex'd in all: the heavens still must work.
Wherein I am false, I am honest; not true, to be true
These present wars shall find I love my country,
Even to the note o' the king, or I 'll fall in them.
All other doubts by time let them be clear'd;
Fortune brings in some boats that are not steer'd. [*Exit.*

SCENE IV.—Before the Cave.

Enter BELARIUS, GUIDERIUS, *and* ARVIRAGUS.

Gui. The noise is round about us.
Bel. Let us from it.
Arv. What pleasure, sir, find we in life, to lock it
From action and adventure?
Gui. Nay, what hope
Have we in hiding us? this way the Romans
Must or for Britons slay us, or receive us
For barbarous and unnatural revolts
During their use, and slay us after.
Bel. Sons,
We 'll higher to the mountains; there secure us.
To the king's party there 's no going: newness
Of Cloten's death (we being not known, not muster'd
Among the bands) may drive us to a render
Where we have liv'd; and so extort from 's that
Which we have done, whose answer would be death
Drawn on with torture.
Gui. This is, sir, a doubt,
In such a time nothing becoming you,
Nor satisfying us.
Arv. It is not likely,
That when they hear the[1] Roman horses neigh.
Behold their quarter'd fires, have both their eyes
And ears so cloy'd importantly as now,
That they will waste their time upon our note,
To know from whence we are.
Bel. O! I am known

[1] their: in folio

Of many in the army: many years,
Though Cloten then but young, you see, not wore him
From my remembrance: and, besides, the king
Hath not deserv'd my service, nor your loves,
Who find in my exile the want of breeding,
The certainty of this hard life; aye, hopeless
To have the courtesy your cradle promis'd,
But to be still hot summer's tanlings, and
The shrinking slaves of winter.

Gui. Than be so,
Better to cease to be. Pray, sir, to the army:
I and my brother are not known; yourself,
So out of thought, and thereto so o'ergrown,
Cannot be question'd.

Arv. By this sun that shines,
I'll thither. What thing is 't, that I never
Did see man die? scarce ever look'd on blood,
But that of coward hares, hot goats, and venison?
Never bestrid a horse, save one that had
A rider like myself, who ne'er wore rowel,
Nor, iron, on his heel? I am asham'd
To look upon the holy sun, to have
The benefit of his bless'd beams, remaining
So long a poor unknown.

Gui. By heavens, I'll go.
If you will bless me, sir, and give me leave,
I'll take the better care; but if you will not,
The hazard therefore due fall on me by
The hands of Romans.

Arv. So say I. Amen.

Bel. No reason I, since of your lives you set
So slight a valuation, should reserve
My crack'd one to more care. Have with you, boys.
If in your country wars you chance to die,
That is my bed too, lads, and there I'll lie:
Lead, lead! The time seems long; their blood thinks scorn,
Till it fly out, and show them princes born. [*Exeunt*

ACT V.

SCENE I.—A Field between the British and Roman Camps.

Enter Posthumus, *with a bloody Handkerchief.*

Post. Yea, bloody cloth, I 'll keep thee ; for I wish'd[1]
Thou shouldst be colour'd thus. You married ones,
If each of you should take this course, how many
Must murder wives much better than themselves
For wrying but a little ?—O, Pisanio !
Every good servant does not all commands ;
No bond, but to do just ones.—Gods ! if you
Should have ta'en vengeance on my faults, I never
Had liv'd to put on[2] this : so had you saved
The noble Imogen to repent, and struck
Me, wretch, more worth your vengeance. But, alack !
You snatch some hence for little faults ; that 's love,
To have them fall no more : you some permit
To second ills with ills, each later[3] worse,
And make men[4] dread it, to the doer's thrift.
But Imogen is your own : do your best wills,
And make me bless'd to obey !—I am brought hither
Among the Italian gentry, and to fight
Against my lady's kingdom : 't is enough
That, Britain, I have kill'd thy mistress ; peace !
I 'll give no wound to thee. Therefore, good heavens,
Hear patiently my purpose. I 'll disrobe me
Of these Italian weeds, and suit myself
As does a Briton peasant : so I 'll fight
Against the part I come with ; so I 'll die
For thee, O Imogen ! even for whom my life
Is, every breath, a death : and thus unknown,
Pitied nor hated, to the face of peril
Myself I 'll dedicate. Let me make men know
More valour in me, than my habits show.
Gods, put the strength o' the Leonati in me !
To shame the guise o' the world, I will begin
The fashion, less without, and more within. [*Exit.*

[1] am wish'd : in folio Pope made the change. [2] *Instigate*
[3] elder : in f e. [4] them : in f e.

SCENE II.—The Same.

Trumpets and Drums. Enter at one Side, LUCIUS, IACHIMO, *and the Roman Army: at the other Side, the British Army;* LEONATUS POSTHUMUS *following like a poor Soldier. They march over and go out. Alarums. Then enter again in skirmish,* IACHIMO *and* POSTHUMUS: *he vanquisheth and disarmeth* IACHIMO, *and then leaves him. Alarums on both sides.*

Iach. The heaviness and guilt within my bosom
Takes off my manhood: I have belied a lady,
The princess of this country, and the air on 't
Revengingly enfeebles me; or could this carl,[1]
A very drudge of nature's, have subdu'd me
In my profession? Knighthoods and honours, borne
As I wear mine, are titles but of scorn.
If that thy gentry, Britain, go before
This lout, as he exceeds our lords, the odds
Is, that we scarce are men, and you are gods. [*Exit.*

Alarums. The Battle continues: the Britons fly; CYMBELINE *is taken: then enter, to his rescue,* BELARIUS, GUIDERIUS, *and* ARVIRAGUS.

Bel. Stand, stand! We have the advantage of the ground.
The lane is guarded: nothing routs us, but
The villainy of our fears.

Gui. Arv. Stand, stand, and fight!

Alarums. Enter POSTHUMUS, *and seconds the Britons, they rescue* CYMBELINE, *and exeunt: then, enter* LUCIUS, IACHIMO, *and* IMOGEN.

Luc. Away, boy, from the troops, and save thyself;
For friends kill friends, and the disorder 's such
As war were hood-wink'd.

Iach. 'T is their fresh supplies.

Luc. It is a day turn'd strangely: or betimes
Let 's re-enforce, or fly. [*Exeunt.*

SCENE III.—Another Part of the Field.

Enter POSTHUMUS *and a Briton Lord.*

Lord. Cam'st thou from where they made the stand?

Post. I did;
Though you, it seems, come from the fliers.

Lord. I did.

[1] *Churl.*

Post. No blame be to you, sir; for all was lost,
But that the heavens fought. The king himself
Of his wings destitute, the army broken,
And but the backs of Britons seen, all flying
Through a strait lane: the enemy full-hearted,
Lolling the tongue with slaughtering, having work
More plentiful than tools to do 't, struck down
Some mortally, some slightly touch'd, some falling
Merely through fear; that the strait pass was damm'd
With dead men hurt behind, and cowards living
To die with lengthen'd shame.

Lord. Where was this lane?

Post. Close by the battle, ditch'd, and wall'd with turf;
Which gave advantage to an ancient soldier,
An honest one, I warrant; who deserv'd
So long a breeding, as his white beard came to,
In doing this for 's country: athwart the lane,
He, with two striplings, (lads more like to run
The country base,[1] than to commit such slaughter;
With faces fit for masks, or, rather, fairer
Than those for preservation cas'd, or shame)
Made good the passage; cried to those that fled,
"Our Britain's harts die flying, not our men:
To darkness fleet souls that fly backwards! Stand;
Or we are Romans, and will give you that
Like beasts, which you shun beastly, and may save,
But to look back in frown: stand, stand!"—These three,
Three thousand confident, in act as many,
(For three performers are the file, when all
The rest do nothing) with this word, "stand, stand!"
Accommodated by the place, more charming
With their own nobleness (which could have turn'd
A distaff to a lance) gilded pale looks,
Part shame, part spirit renew'd; that some, turn'd coward
But by example (O, a sin in war,
Damn'd in the first beginners!) 'gan to look
The way that they did, and to grin like lions
Upon the pikes o' the hunters. Then began
A stop i' the chaser, a retire; anon,
A rout, confusion thick: forthwith they fly,
Chickens, the way which they stopp'd eagles; slaves,

[1] The rustic game of *prison base*, or *bars*, consisting of a race.

The strides they victors made. And now our cowards
(Like fragments in hard voyages) became
The life o' the need: having found the back-door open
Of the unguarded hearts, Heavens, how they wound!
Some slain before; some dying; some, their friends,
O'er-borne i' the former wave: ten chac'd by one,
Are now each one the slaughter-man of twenty:
Those that would die or ere resist are grown
The mortal bugs[1] o' the field.
Lord. This was strange chance:
A narrow lane, an old man, and two boys?
Post. Nay, do not wonder at it: you are made
Rather to wonder at the things you hear
Than to work any. Will you rhyme upon 't,
And vent it for a mockery? Here is one:
"Two boys, an old man twice a boy, a lane,
Preserv'd the Britons, was the Romans' bane."
Lord. Nay, be not angry, sir.
Post. 'Lack! to what end?
Who dares not stand his foe, I 'll be his friend;
For if he 'll do, as he is made to do,
I know, he 'll quickly fly my friendship too.
You have put me into rhyme.
Lord. Farewell; you are angry. [*Exit.*
Post. Still going?—This is a lord. O noble misery!
To be i' the field, and ask, what news, of me.
To-day, how many would have given their honours
To have sav'd their carcasses? took heel to do 't,
And yet died too? I, in mine own woe charm'd,
Could not find death where I did hear him groan,
Nor feel him where he struck: being an ugly monster,
'T is strange he hides him in fresh cups, soft beds,
Sweet words; or hath more ministers than we
That draw his knives i' the war.—Well, I will find him;
For being now a favourer to the Briton,
No more a Briton, I have resum'd again
The part I came in. Fight I will no more,
But yield me to the veriest hind, that shall
Once touch my shoulder. Great the slaughter is
Here made by the Roman; great the answer be
Britons must take; for me, my ransom 's death:
On either side I come to spend my breath,
Which neither here I 'll keep, nor bear again,

[1] *Terrors.*

But end it by some means for Imogen.

Enter two Briton Captains, and Soldiers.

1 *Cap.* Great Jupiter be prais'd! Lucius is taken.
'T is thought, the old man and his sons were angels.

2 *Cap.* There was a fourth man, in a silly habit,
That gave th' affront with them.

1 *Cap.* So 't is reported;
But none of them can be found.—Stand! who is there?

Post. A Roman,
Who had not now been drooping here, if seconds
Had answer'd him.

2 *Cap.* Lay hands on him; a dog!
A leg of Rome shall not return to tell
What crows have peck'd them here. He brags his service,
As if he were of note. Bring him to the king.

Enter CYMBELINE, *attended;* BELARIUS, GUIDERIUS, ARVIRAGUS, PISANIO, *and Roman Captives. The Captains present* POSTHUMUS *to* CYMBELINE, *who delivers him over to a Jailor; after which, all go out.*

SCENE IV.—A Prison.

Enter POSTHUMUS, *and Two Jailors.*

1 *Jail.* You shall not now be stolen; you have locks upon you:
So, graze as you find pasture.

2 *Jail.* Ay, or a stomach. [*Exeunt Jailors.*

Post. Most welcome, bondage, for thou art a way,
I think, to liberty. Yet am I better
Than one that 's sick o' the gout; since he had rather
Groan so in perpetuity, than be cur'd
By the sure physician, death, who is the key
T' unbar these locks. My conscience, thou art fetter'd
More than my shanks, and wrists: you good gods, give me
The penitent instrument to pick that bolt,
Then, free for ever! Is 't enough, I am sorry?
So children temporal fathers do appease;
Gods are more full of mercy. Must I repent?
I cannot do it better than in gyves,
Desir'd, more than constrain'd: to satisfy,
If of my freedom 't is the main part, take
No stricter render of me than my all.
I know, you are more clement than vile men,

Who of their broken debtors take a third,
A sixth, a tenth, letting them thrive again
On their abatement: that 's not my desire.
For Imogen's dear life, take mine; and though
'T is not so dear, yet 't is a life; you coin'd it:
'Tween man and man they weigh not every stamp,
Though light, take pieces for the figure's sake:
You rather mine, being yours; and so, great powers,
If you will take this audit, take this life,
And cancel these cold bonds. O Imogen!
I 'll speak to thee in silence. [*He sleeps.*

Solemn Music. Enter, as an Apparition, SICILIUS LEONATUS, *Father to* POSTHUMUS, *an old Man attired like a Warrior; leading in his Hand an ancient Matron, his Wife and Mother to* POSTHUMUS, *with Music before them: then, after other Music, follow the Two young Leonati, Brothers to* POSTHUMUS, *with Wounds as they died in the Wars. They circle* POSTHUMUS *round as he lies sleeping.*

Sici. No more, thou thunder-master, show
Thy spite on mortal flies:
With Mars fall out, with Juno chide,
That thy adulteries
Rates and revenges.

Hath my poor boy done aught but well?
Whose face I never saw;
I died, whilst in the womb he stay'd
Attending nature's law.
Whose father, then, (as men report,
Thou orphans' father art)
Thou shouldst have been, and shielded him
From this earth-vexing smart.

Moth. Lucina lent not me her aid,
But took me in my throes;
That from me was Posthumus ript,
Came crying 'mongst his foes,
A thing of pity.

Sici. Great nature, like his ancestry,
Moulded the stuff so fair,
That he deserv'd the praise o' the world,
As great Sicilius' heir.

1 *Bro.* When once he was mature for man,
In Britain where was he,
That could stand up his parallel,
Or fruitful object be
In eye of Imogen, that best
Could deem his dignity?

Moth. With marriage wherefore was he mock'd,
To be exil'd, and thrown
From Leonati' seat, and cast
From her his dearest one,
Sweet Imogen?

Sici. Why did you suffer Iachimo,
Slight thing of Italy,
To taint his nobler heart and brain
With needless jealousy;
And to become the geck[1] and scorn
O' the other's villainy?

2 *Bro.* For this from stiller seats we came,
Our parents, and we twain,
That striking in our country's cause
Fell bravely, and were slain;
Our fealty, and Tenantius' right,
With honour to maintain.

1 *Bro.* Like hardiment Posthumus hath
To Cymbeline perform'd:
Then, Jupiter, thou king of gods,
Why hast thou thus adjourn'd
The graces for his merits due,
Being all to dolours turn'd?

Sici. Thy crystal window ope; look[2] out:
No longer exercise,
Upon a valiant race, thy harsh
And potent injuries.

Moth. Since, Jupiter, our son is good,
Take off his miseries.

Sici. Peep through thy marble mansion; help.
Or we poor ghosts will cry,
To the shining synod of the rest,
Against thy deity.

2 *Bro.* Help, Jupiter! or we appeal,
And from thy justice fly.

[1] *Fool.* [2] look, look: in folio.

JUPITER *descends in Thunder and Lightning, sitting upon an Eagle: he throws a Thunderbolt; the Ghosts fall on their Knees.*

Jup. No more, you petty spirits of regions low,
Offend our hearing: hush!—How dare you ghosts
Accuse the thunderer, whose bolt you know,
Sky-planted, batters all rebelling coasts?
Poor shadows of Elysium, hence; and rest
Upon your never-withering banks of flowers:
Be not with mortal accidents opprest;
No care of yours it is; you know, 'tis ours.
Whom best I love, I cross; to make my gift,
The more delay'd, delighted. Be content;
Your low-laid son our godhead will uplift:
His comforts thrive, his trials well are spent.
Our Jovial star reign'd at his birth, and in
Our temple was he married.—Rise, and fade!—
He shall be lord of lady Imogen,
And happier much by his affliction made.
This tablet lay upon his breast, wherein
Our pleasure his full fortune doth confine;
And so, away: no farther with your din
Express impatience, lest you stir up mine.—
Mount, eagle, to my palace crystalline. [*Ascends.*

Sici. He came in thunder; his celestial breath
Was sulphurous to smell: the holy eagle
Stoop'd, as to foot us: his ascension is
More sweet than our bless'd fields. His royal bird
Prunes the immortal wing, and cloys his beak,
As when his god is pleas'd.

All. Thanks, Jupiter.

Sici. The marble pavement closes; he is enter'd
His radiant roof.—Away! and, to be blest,
Let us with care perform his great behest. [*Ghosts vanish.*

Post. [*Waking.*] Sleep, thou hast been a grandsire, and begot
A father to me; and thou hast created
A mother, and two brothers. But (O scorn!)
Gone! they went hence so soon as they were born,
And so I am awake.—Poor wretches, that depend
On greatness' favour, dream as I have done;
Wake, and find nothing.—But, alas, I swerve:
Many dream not to find, neither deserve,
And yet are steep'd in favours; so am I,

That have this golden chance, and know not why.
[*Finding the Tablet*
What fairies haunt this ground? A book? O, rare one!
Be not, as in our fangled world, a garment
Nobler than that it covers: let thy effects
So follow, to be most unlike our courtiers,
As good as promise.

[*Reads.*] "When as a lion's whelp shall, to himself unknown, without seeking find, and be embraced by a piece of tender air; and when from a stately cedar shall be lopp'd branches, which, being dead many years, shall after revive, be jointed to the old stock, and freshly grow, then shall Posthumus end his miseries, Britain be fortunate, and flourish in peace and plenty."

'T is still a dream, or else such stuff as madmen
Tongue, and brain not; either both, or nothing:
Or senseless speaking, or a speaking such
As sense cannot untie. Be what it is,
The action of my life is like it, which
I'll keep, if but for sympathy.

Re-enter Jailors.

Jail. Come, sir, are you ready for death?

Post. Over-roasted, rather; ready long ago.

Jail. Hanging is the word, sir: if you be ready for that, you are well cooked.

Post. So, if I prove a good repast to the spectators, the dish pays the shot.

Jail. A heavy reckoning for you, sir; but the comfort is, you shall be called to no more payments, fear no more tavern bills, which are often the sadness of parting, as the procuring of mirth. You come in faint for want of meat, depart reeling with too much drink; sorry that you have paid too much, and sorry that you are paid too much; purse and brain both empty: the brain the heavier for being too light, the purse too light, being drawn of heaviness. O! of this contradiction you shall now be quit.—O, the charity of a penny cord! it sums up thousands in a trice: you have no true debitor and creditor but it; of what's past, is, and to come, the discharge.—Your neck, sir, is pen, book, and counters; so the acquittance follows.

Post. I am merrier to die, than thou art to live.

Jail. Indeed, sir, he that sleeps feels not the toothache; but a man that were to sleep your sleep, and a hangman to help him to bed, I think, he would change places with his officer; for, look you, sir, you know not which way you shall go.

Post. Yes, indeed do I, fellow.

Jail. Your death has eyes in 's head, then; I have not seen him so pictured: you must either be directed by some that take upon them to know, or take upon yourself that, which I am sure you do not know, or jump[1] the after-inquiry on your own peril: and how you shall speed in your journey's end, I think, you 'll never return to tell one.

Post. I tell thee, fellow, there are none want eyes to direct them the way I am going, but such as wink, and will not use them.

Jail. What an infinite mock is this, that a man should have the best use of eyes to see the way of blindness! I am sure, hanging 's the way of winking.

Enter a Messenger.

Mess. Knock off his manacles: bring your prisoner to the king.

Post. Thou bring'st good news. I am called to be made free.

Jail. I'll be hang'd, then.

Post. Thou shalt be then freer than a jailor; no bolts for the dead. [*Exeunt* POSTHUMUS *and Messenger.*

Jail. Unless a man would marry a gallows, and beget young gibbets, I never saw one so prone. Yet, on my conscience, there are verier knaves desire to live, for all he be a Roman; and there be some of them too, that die against their wills: so should I, if I were one. I would we were all of one mind, and one mind good: O, there were desolation of jailors, and gallowses! I speak against my present profit, but my wish hath a preferment in 't. [*Exeunt.*

SCENE V.—CYMBELINE'S Tent.

Enter CYMBELINE, BELARIUS, GUIDERIUS, ARVIRAGUS, PISANIO, *Lords, Officers, and Attendants.*

Cym. Stand by my side you, whom the gods have made
Preservers of my throne. Woe is my heart,
That the poor soldier, that so richly fought,
Whose rags sham'd gilded arms, whose naked breast

[1] *Risk.*

Stepp'd before targe of proof, cannot be found:
He shall be happy that can find him, if
Our grace can make him so.
  Bel. I never saw
Such noble fury in so poor a thing;
Such precious deeds in one, that promis'd nought
But beggary and poor looks.
  Cym. No tidings of him?
  Pis. He hath been search'd among the dead and living,
But no trace of him.
  Cym. To my grief, I am
The heir of his reward; which I will add
To you, the liver, heart, and brain of Britain,
By whom, I grant, she lives. 'T is now the time
To ask of whence you are: report it.
  Bel. Sir,
In Cambria are we born, and gentlemen.
Farther to boast, were neither true nor modest,
Unless I add, we are honest.
  Cym. Bow your knees.—
Arise, my knights o' the battle: I create you
Companions to our person, and will fit you
With dignities becoming your estates.

Enter CORNELIUS *and Ladies.*

There's business in these faces.—Why so sadly
Greet you our victory? you look like Romans,
And not o' the court of Britain.
  Cor. Hail, great king!
To sour your happiness, I must report
The queen is dead.
  Cym. Whom worse than a physician
Would this report become? But I consider,
By medicine life may be prolong'd, yet death
Will seize the doctor too.—How ended she?
  Cor. With horror, madly dying, like her life;
Which, being cruel to the world, concluded
Most cruel to herself. What she confess'd,
I will report, so please you: these her women
Can trip me, if I err, who, with wet cheeks,
Were present when she finish'd.
  Cym. Pr'ythee, say.
  Cor. First, she confess'd she never lov'd you; only
Affected greatness got by you, not you:
Married your royalty, was wife to your place,

Abhorr'd your person.
Cym. She alone knew this;
And, but she spoke it dying, I would not
Believe her lips in opening it. Proceed.
Cor. Your daughter, whom she bore in hand[1] to love
With such integrity, she did confess
Was as a scorpion to her sight; whose life,
But that her flight prevented it, she had
Ta'en off by poison.
Cym. O most delicate fiend!
Who is 't can read a woman?—Is there more?
Cor. More, sir, and worse. She did confess, she had
For you a mortal mineral; which, being took,
Should by the minute feed on life, and lingering
By inches waste you: in which time she purpos'd,
By watching, weeping, tendance, kissing, to
O'ercome you with her show; and in time
(When she had fitted you with her craft) to work
Her son into th' adoption of the crown:
But failing of her end by his strange absence,
Grew shameless-desperate; open'd, in despite
Of heaven and men, her purposes; repented
The evils she hatch'd were not effected; so,
Despairing died.
Cym. Heard you all this, her women?
Lady. We did so, please your highness.
Cym. Mine eyes
Were not in fault, for she was beautiful;
Mine ears, that heard her flattery; nor my heart,
That thought her like her seeming; it had been vicious,
To have mistrusted her: yet, O my daughter!
That it was folly in me, thou may'st say,
And prove it in thy feeling. Heaven mend all!
Enter Lucius, Iachimo, *the Soothsayer, and other Roman Prisoners, guarded;* Posthumus *behind, and* Imogen.
Thou com'st not, Caius, now for tribute: that
The Britons have raz'd out, though with the loss
Of many a bold one; whose kinsmen have made suit,
That their good souls may be appeas'd with slaughter
Of you their captives, which ourself have granted.
So, think of your estate.
Luc. Consider, sir, the chance of war: the day
Was yours by accident; had it gone with us,

[1] *Pretended.*

We should not, when the blood was cool, have threaten'd
Our prisoners with the sword. But since the gods
Will have it thus, that nothing but our lives
May be call'd ransom, let it come: sufficeth,
A Roman with a Roman's heart can suffer.
Augustus lives to think on 't; and so much
For my peculiar care. This one thing only
I will entreat: my boy, a Briton born,
Let him be ransom'd: never master had
A page so kind, so duteous, diligent,
So tender over his occasions, true,
So feat,[1] so nurse-like. Let his virtue join
With my request, which, I 'll make bold, your highness
Cannot deny: he hath done no Briton harm,
Though he have serv'd a Roman. Save him, sir,
And spare no blood beside.

Cym. I have surely seen him:
His favour[2] is familiar to me.—Boy,
Thou hast look'd thyself into my grace,
And art mine own.—I know not why, nor[3] wherefore,
To say, live, boy: ne'er thank thy master; live,
And ask of Cymbeline what boon thou wilt,
Fitting my bounty and thy state, I 'll give it;
Yea, though thou do demand a prisoner,
The noblest ta'en.

Imo. I humbly thank your highness.

Luc. I do not bid thee beg my life, good lad,
And yet I know thou wilt.

Imo. No, no; alack!
There 's other work in hand.—I see a thing
Bitter to me as death.—Your life, good master,
Must shuffle for itself.

Luc. The boy disdains me,
He leaves me, scorns me: briefly die their joys,
That place them on the truth of girls and boys.—
Why stands he so perplex'd?

Cym. What wouldst thou, boy?
I love thee more and more: think more and more
What 's best to ask. Know'st him thou look'st on? speak;
Wilt have him live? Is he thy kin? thy friend?

Imo. He is a Roman; no more kin to me,
Than I to your highness, who, being born your vassal,

[1] *Ready.* [2] *Countenance.* [3] Not in folio. Added by Rowe

Am something nearer.

Cym. Wherefore ey'st him so?

Imo. I 'll tell you, sir, in private, if you please
To give me hearing.

Cym. Ay, with all my heart,
And lend my best attention. What 's thy name?

Imo. Fidele, sir.

Cym. Thou art my good youth, my page;
I 'll be thy master: walk with me; speak freely.

[CYMBELINE *and* IMOGEN *converse apart.*

Bel. Is not this boy reviv'd from death?

Arv. One sand another
Not more resembles: that sweet rosy lad,
Who died, and was Fidele.—What think you?

Gui. The same dead thing alive.

Bel. Peace, peace! see farther; he eyes us not: forbear.
Creatures may be alike: were 't he, I am sure
He would have spoke to us.

Gui. But we saw him dead.

Bel. Be silent; let 's see farther.

Pis. [*Aside.*] It is my mistress!
Since she is living, let the time run on,
To good, or bad.

[CYMBELINE *and* IMOGEN *come forward.*

Cym. Come, stand thou by our side:
Make thy demand aloud.—Sir, [*To* IACHIMO.] step you forth;
Give answer to this boy, and do it freely,
Or, by our greatness, and the grace of it,
Which is our honour, bitter torture shall
Winnow the truth from falsehood.—On, speak to him.

Imo. My boon is, that this gentleman may render
Of whom he had this ring.

Post. [*Aside.*] What 's that to him?

Cym. That diamond upon your finger, say,
How came it yours?

Iach. Thou 'lt torture me to leave unspoken that
Which, to be spoke, would torture thee.

Cym. How! me?

Iach. I am glad to be constrain'd to utter that, which
Torments me to conceal. By villainy
I got this ring: 't was Leonatus' jewel;

Whom thou didst banish; and (which more may grieve thee,
As it doth me) a nobler sir ne'er liv'd
'Twixt sky and ground. Wilt thou hear more, my lord?

Cym. All that belongs to this.

Iach. That paragon, thy daughter,
For whom my heart drops blood, and my false spirits
Quail to remember,—Give me leave; I faint.

Cym. My daughter! what of her? renew thy strength:
I had rather thou shouldst live while nature will,
Than die ere I hear more. Strive, man, and speak.

Iach. Upon a time, (unhappy was the clock
That struck the hour) it was in Rome, (accurs'd
The mansion where) 't was at a feast, (O! would
Our viands had been poison'd, or at least
Those which I heav'd to head) the good Posthumus,
(What should I say? he was too good to be
Where ill men were, and was the best of all
Amongst the rar'st of good ones) sitting sadly,
Hearing us praise our loves of Italy
For beauty, that made barren the swell'd boast
Of him that best could speak: for feature, laming
The shrine of Venus, or straight-pight[1] Minerva,
Postures beyond brief nature; for condition,
A shop of all the qualities that man
Loves woman for; besides, that hook of wiving,
Fairness, which strikes the eye:——

Cym. I stand on fire.
Come to the matter.

Iach. All too soon I shall,
Unless thou wouldst grieve quickly.—This Posthumus,
(Most like a noble lord in love, and one
That had a royal lover) took his hint;
And, not dispraising whom we prais'd, (therein
He was as calm as virtue) he began
His mistress' picture; which by his tongue being made,
And then a mind put in 't, either our brags
Were crack'd of kitchen trulls, or his description
Prov'd us unspeaking sots.

Cym. Nay, nay, to the purpose.

Iach. Your daughter's chastity—there it begins

[1] *Placed upright.*

He spake of her as Dian had hot dreams,
And she alone were cold: whereat, I, wretch,
Made scruple of his praise; and wager'd with him
Pieces of gold 'gainst this, which then he wore
Upon his honour'd finger, to attain
In suit the place of his bed, and win this ring
By hers and mine adultery. He, true knight,
No lesser of her honour confident
Than I did truly find her, stakes this ring;
And would so, had it been a carbuncle
Of Phœbus' wheel; and might so safely, had it
Been all the worth of his car. Away to Britain
Post I in this design: well may you, sir,
Remember me at court, where I was taught
Of your chaste daughter the wide difference
'Twixt amorous and villainous. Being thus quench'd
Of hope, not longing, mine Italian brain
'Gan in your duller Britain operate
Most vilely; for my vantage, excellent;
And, to be brief, my practice so prevail'd,
That I return'd with simular proof, enough
To make the noble Leonatus mad,
By wounding his belief in her renown
With tokens thus, and thus; averring notes
Of chamber-hanging, pictures, this her bracelet,
(O cunning, how I got it!) nay, some marks
Of secret on her person, that he could not
But think her bond of chastity quite crack'd,
I having ta'en the forfeit. Whereupon,—
Methinks, I see him now,—

Post. Ay, so thou dost, [*Coming forward*

Italian fiend!—Ah me! most credulous fool,
Egregious murderer, thief, any thing
That 's due to all the villains past, in being,
To come!—O, give me cord, or knife, or poison,
Some upright justicer! Thou, king, send out
For torturers ingenious: it is I
That all the abhorred things o' the earth amend,
By being worse than they. I am Posthumus,
That kill'd thy daughter:—villain-like, I lie;
That caus'd a lesser villain than myself,
A sacrilegious thief, to do 't.—The temple
Of virtue was she:—yea, and she herself

Spit, and throw stones, cast mire upon me; set
The dogs o' the street to bay me: every villain
Be call'd Posthumus Leonatus, and
Be villainy less than 't was!—O Imogen!
My queen, my life, my wife! O Imogen,
Imogen, Imogen!

Imo. Peace, my lord! hear, hear!—

Post. Shall 's have a play of this? Thou scornful page,
There lie thy part. [*Striking her: she falls.*

Pis. O, gentlemen! help
Mine, and your mistress.—O, my lord Posthumus!
You ne'er kill'd Imogen till now.—Help, help!—
Mine honour'd lady!

Cym. Does the world go round?

Post. How come these staggers on me?

Pis. Wake, my mistress!

Cym. If this be so, the gods do mean to strike me
To death with mortal joy.

Pis. How fares my mistress?

Imo. O! get thee from my sight;
Thou gav'st me poison: dangerous fellow, hence!
Breathe not where princes are.

Cym. The tune of Imogen!

Pis. Lady,
The gods throw stones of sulphur on me, if
That box I gave you was not thought by me
A precious thing: I had it from the queen

Cym. New matter still?

Imo. It poison'd me.

Cor. O gods!
I left out one thing which the queen confess'd,
Which must approve thee honest: if Pisanio
Have, said she, given his mistress that confection
Which I gave him for a cordial, she is serv'd
As I would serve a rat.

Cym. What 's this, Cornelius?

Cor. The queen, sir, very oft importun'd me
To temper poisons for her; still pretending
The satisfaction of her knowledge, only
In killing creatures vile, as cats and dogs
Of no esteem: I, dreading that her purpose
Was of more danger, did compound for her
A certain stuff, which, being ta'en, would cease

The present power of life: but, in short time,
All offices of nature should again
Do their due functions.—Have you ta'en of it?

Imo. Most like I did, for I was dead.

Bel. My boys,
There was our error.

Gui. This is, sure, Fidele.

Imo. Why did you throw your wedded lady from you?
Think, that you are upon a rock; and now
Throw me again. [*Embracing* POSTHUMUS.

Post. Hang there like fruit, my soul,
Till the tree die!

Cym. How now! my flesh, my child?
What! mak'st thou me a dullard in this act?
Wilt thou not speak to me?

Imo. Your blessing, sir. [*Kneeling.*

Bel. Though you did love this youth, I blame ye not;
You had a motive for 't. [*To* GUIDERIUS *and* ARVIRAGUS.

Cym. My tears that fall,
Prove holy water on thee! Imogen,
Thy mother 's dead.

Imo I am sorry for 't, my lord.

Cym. O! she was naught; and 'long of her it was,
That we meet here so strangely: but her son
Is gone, we know not how, nor where.

Pis. My lord,
Now fear is from me, I 'll speak troth. Lord Cloten,
Upon my lady's missing, came to me
With his sword drawn: foam'd at the mouth, and swore,
If I discover'd not which way she was gone,
It was my instant death. By accident,
I had a feigned letter of my master's
Then in my pocket, which directed him
To seek her on the mountains near to Milford;
Where, in a frenzy, in my master's garments
Which he inforc'd from me away he posts
With unchaste purpose, and with oath to violate
My lady's honour: what became of him,
I farther know not.

Gui. Let me end the story.
I slew him there.

Cym. Marry, the gods forefend!
I would not thy good deeds should from my lips
Pluck a hard sentence: pr'ythee, valiant youth,

Deny 't again.

Gui. I have spoke it, and I did it.

Cym. He was a prince.

Gui. A most uncivil one. The wrongs he did me
Were nothing prince-like; for he did provoke me
With language that would make me spurn the sea
If it could so roar to me. I cut off 's head;
And am right glad, he is not standing here
To tell this tale of mine.

Cym. I am sorry for thee:
By thine own tongue thou art condemn'd, and must
Endure our law. Thou art dead.

Imo. That headless man
I thought had been my lord.

Cym. Bind the offender,
And take him from our presence.

Bel. Stay, sir king.
This man is better than the man he slew,
As well descended as thyself; and hath
More of thee merited, than a band of Clotens
Had ever scar for.—Let his arms alone;
[*To the Guard.*
They were not born for bondage.

Cym. Why, old soldier,
Wilt thou undo the worth thou art unpaid for,
By tasting of our wrath? How of descent
As good as we?

Arv. In that he spake too far.

Cym. And thou shalt die for 't.

Bel. We will die all three;
But I will prove that two on 's are as good
As I have given out him.—My sons, I must
For mine own part unfold a dangerous speech,
Though, haply, well for you.

Arv. Your danger 's ours.

Gui. And our good his.

Bel. Have at it, then, by leave
Thou hadst, great king, a subject, who was call'd
Belarius.

Cym. What of him? he is
A banish'd traitor.

Bel. He it is that hath
Assum'd this age: indeed, a banish'd man,
I know not how, a traitor.

Cym. Take him hence.
The whole world shall not save him.
Bel. Not too hot:
First pay me for the nursing of thy sons;
And let it be confiscate all, so soon
As I have receiv'd it.
Cym. Nursing of my sons?
Bel. I am too blunt, and saucy; here 's my knee:
Ere I arise, I will prefer my sons;
Then, spare not the old father. Mighty sir,
These two young gentlemen, that call me father,
And think they are my sons, are none of mine:
They are the issue of your loins, my liege,
And blood of your begetting.
Cym. How! my issue?
Bel. So sure as you your father's. I, old Morgan,
Am that Belarius whom you sometime banish'd:
Your pleasure was my mere offence, my punishment
Itself, and all my treason: that I suffer'd
Was all the harm I did. These gentle princes
(For such, and so they are) these twenty years
Have I train'd up; those arts they have, as I
Could put into them: my breeding was, sir, as
Your highness knows. Their nurse, Euriphile,
Whom for the theft I wedded, stole these children
Upon my banishment: I mov'd her to 't;
Having receiv'd the punishment before,
For that which I did then: beaten for loyalty
Excited me to treason. Their dear loss,
The more of you 't was felt, the more it shap'd
Unto my end of stealing them. But, gracious sir,
Here are your sons again; and I must lose
Two of the sweet'st companions in the world.—
The benediction of these covering heavens
Fall on their heads like dew! for they are worthy
To inlay heaven with stars.
Cym. Thou weep'st, and speak'st.
The service, that you three have done, is more
Unlike than this thou tell'st. I lost my children:
If these be they, I know not how to wish
A pair of worthier sons.
Bel. Be pleas'd a while.—
This gentleman, whom I call Polydore,
Most worthy prince, as yours is true Guiderius,

This gentleman, my Cadwal, Arviragus,
Your younger princely son: he, sir, was lapp'd
In a most curious mantle, wrought by the hand
Of his queen mother, which, for more probation,
I can with ease produce.

Cym. Guiderius had
Upon his neck a mole, a sanguine star:
It was a mark of wonder.

Bel. This is he,
Who hath upon him still that natural stamp.
It was wise nature's end in the donation,
To be his evidence now.

Cym. O! what am I
A mother to the birth of three? Ne'er mother
Rejoic'd deliverance more.—Bless'd pray you be,
That after this strange starting from your orbs,
You may reign in them now.—O Imogen!
Thou hast lost by this a kingdom.

Imo. No, my lord;
I have got two worlds by 't.—O, my gentle brothers!
Have we thus met? O! never say hereafter,
But I am truest speaker: you call'd me brother,
When I was but your sister; I you brothers,
When you[1] were so indeed.

Cym. Did you e'er meet?

Arv. Ay, my good lord.

Gui. And at first meeting lov'd;
Continued so, until we thought he died.

Cor. By the queen's dram she swallow'd.

Cym. O rare instinct!
When shall I hear all through? This fierce abridgment
Hath to it circumstantial branches, which
Distinction should be rich in.—Where? how liv'd you?
And when came you to serve our Roman captive?
How parted with your brothers? how first met them?
Why fled you from the court, and whither? These,
And your three motives to the battle, with
I know not how much more, should be demanded,
And all the other by-dependencies,
From chance to chance; but nor the time, nor place,
Will serve our long inter'gatories. See,
Posthumus anchors upon Imogen;
And she, like harmless lightning, throws her eye

[1] we: in folio. Rowe made the change.

On him, her brothers, me, her master, hitting
Each object with a joy: the counterchange
Is severally in all. Let 's quit this ground,
And smoke the temple with our sacrifices.—
Thou art my brother: so we 'll hold thee ever.
[*To* BELARIUS.

Imo. You are my father, too; and did relieve me,
To see this gracious season.

Cym. All o'erjoy'd,
Save these in bonds: let them be joyful too,
For they shall taste our comfort.

Imo. My good master,
I will yet do you service.

Luc. Happy be you!

Cym. The forlorn soldier, that so nobly fought,
He would have well become[1] this place, and grac'd
The thankings of a king.

Post. I am, sir,
The soldier that did company these three
In poor beseeming: 't was a fitment for
The purpose I then follow'd.—That I was he,
Speak, Iachimo: I had you down, and might
Have made you finish.

Iach. I am down again; [*Kneeling*
But now my heavy conscience sinks my knee,
As then your force did. Take that life, beseech you,
Which I so often owe; but your ring first,
And here the bracelet of the truest princess
That ever swore her faith.

Post. Kneel not to me:
The power that I have on you is to spare you;
The malice towards you to forgive you. Live,
And deal with others better.

Cym. Nobly doom'd.
We 'll learn our freeness of a son-in-law:
Pardon 's the word to all.

Arv. You holp us, sir,
As you did mean indeed to be our brother;
Joy'd are we, that you are.

Post. Your servant, princes.—Good my lord of
Rome,
Call forth your soothsayer. As I slept, methought,
Great Jupiter, upon his eagle back'd,

[1] becom'd: in folio.

Appear'd to me, with other spritely shows
Of mine own kindred: when I wak'd, I found
This label on my bosom; whose containing
Is so from sense in hardness, that I can
Make no collection of it: let him show
His skill in the construction.

Luc. Philarmonus!

Sooth. Here, my good lord. [*Coming forward.*

Luc. Read, and declare the meaning.

Sooth. [*Reads.*] "When as a lion's whelp shall, to himself unknown, without seeking find, and be embraced by a piece of tender air; and when from a stately cedar shall be lopped branches, which being dead many years shall after revive, be jointed to the old stock, and freshly grow, then shall Posthumus end his miseries, Britain be fortunate, and flourish in peace and plenty."
Thou, Leonatus, art the lion's whelp;
The fit and apt construction of thy name,
Being Leo-natus, doth import so much.
The piece of tender air, thy virtuous daughter,
[*To* CYMBELINE
Which we call *mollis aer;* and *mollis aer*
We term it *mulier:* which *mulier*, I divine,
Is this most constant wife; who, even now,
Answering the letter of the oracle,
Unknown to you, unsought, were clipp'd about
With this most tender air.

Cym. This hath some seeming.

Sooth. The lofty cedar, royal Cymbeline,
Personates thee; and thy lopp'd branches point
Thy two sons forth; who, by Belarius stolen,
For many years thought dead, are now reviv'd.
To the majestic cedar join'd, whose issue
Promises Britain peace and plenty.

Cym. Well;
My peace we will begin.—And, Caius Lucius,
Although the victor, we submit to Cæsar,
And to the Roman empire; promising
To pay our wonted tribute, from the which
We were dissuaded by our wicked queen;
Whom heavens, in justice, both on her and hers
Have laid most heavy hand.

Sooth. The fingers of the powers above do tune

The harmony of this peace. The vision,
Which I made known to Lucius ere the stroke
Of this yet scarce-cold battle, at this instant
Is full accomplish'd; for the Roman eagle,
Fror [illegible] outh to west on wing soaring aloft,
Less [illegible] herself, and in the beams o' the sun
So [illegible] h'd: which foreshow'd our princely eagle,
Th' [illegible] perial Cæsar, should again unite
H' [illegible] vour with the radiant Cymbeline,
Which shines here in the west.

Cym. Laud we the gods;
And let our crooked smokes climb to their nostrils
From our bless'd altars. Publish we this peace
To all our subjects. Set we forward. Let
A Roman and a British ensign wave
Friendly together; so through Lud's town march,
And in the temple of great Jupiter
Our peace we 'll ratify; seal it with feasts.—
Set on there!—Never was a war did cease,
Ere bloody hands were wash'd, with such a peace.

[*Exeunt.*

PERICLES, PRINCE OF TYRE.

"The late, And much admired Play, called Pericles, Prince of Tyre. With the true Relation of the whole Historie, aduentures, and fortunes of the said Prince: As also, The no lesse strange, and worthy accidents, in the Birth and Life, of his Daughter Mariana. As it hath been diuers and sundry times acted by his Maiesties Seruants, at the Globe on the Banck-side. By William Shakespeare. Imprinted at London for Henry Gosson, and are to be sold at the signe of the Sunne in Pater-noster row, &c. 1609." 4to. 35 leaves.

"The late, And much admired Play, called Pericles, Prince of Tyre. With the true Relation of the whole History, aduentures, and fortunes of the saide Prince. Written by W. Shakespeare. Printed for T. P. 1619." 4to. 34 leaves.

"The late, And much admired Play, called Pericles, Prince of Tyre. With the true Relation of the whole History, aduentures, and fortunes of the sayd Prince: Written by Will. Shakespeare: London, Printed by I. N. for R. B. and are to be sould at his shop in Cheapside, at the signe of the Bible. 1630." 4to. 34 leaves.

In the folio of 1664, the following is the heading of the page on which the play begins: "The much admired Play, called, Pericles, Prince of Tyre. With the true Relation of the whole History, Adventures, and Fortunes of the said Prince. Written by W. Shakespeare, and published in his life time." It occupies twenty-pages; viz. from p. 1 to p. 20, inclusive, a new pagination of the volume commencing with "Pericles." It is there divided into Acts, but irregularly, and the Scenes are not marked.

INTRODUCTION.

THE first question to be settled in relation to "Pericles," is its title to a place among the collected works of Shakespeare.

There is so marked a character about every thing that proceeded from the pen of our great dramatist,—his mode of thought, and his style of expression, are so unlike those of any of his contemporaries, that they can never be mistaken. They are clearly visible in all the later portion of the play; and so indisputable does this fact appear to us, that, we confidently assert, however strong may be the external evidence to the same point, the internal evidence is infinitely stronger: to those who have studied his works it will seem incontrovertible. As we do not rely merely upon particular expressions, nor upon separate passages, but upon the general complexion of whole scenes and acts, it is obvious, that we cannot here enter into proofs, which would require the re-impression of many of the succeeding pages.

An opinion has long prevailed, and we have no doubt it is well founded, that two hands are to be traced in the composition of "Pericles." The larger part of the first three Acts were in all probability the work of an inferior dramatist: to these Shakespeare added comparatively little; but he found it necessary, as the story advanced and as the interest increased, to insert more of his own composition. His hand begins to be distinctly seen in the third Act, and afterwards we feel persuaded that we could extract nearly every line that was not dictated by his great intellect. We apprehend that Shakespeare found a drama on the story in the possession of one of the companies performing in London, and that, in accordance with the ordinary practice of the time, he made additions to and improvements in it, and procured it to be represented at the Globe theatre[1]. Who might be the author of the original piece, it would be in vain to conjecture. Although we have no decisive proof that Shakespeare ever worked in immediate concert with any of his contemporaries, it was the custom with nearly all the dramatists of his day, and it is not impossible that such was the case with "Pericles."

The circumstance that it was a joint production, may partly account for the non-appearance of "Pericles" in the folio of 1623. Ben Jonson, when printing the volume of his Works,

[1] By a list of theatrical apparel, formerly belonging to Alleyn, and preserved at Dulwich College, it appears that he had probably acted in a play called "Pericles." See "Memoirs of Edward Alleyn," printed for the Shakespeare Society, p. 21. This might be the play which Shakespeare altered and improved.

in 1616, excluded for this reason "The Case is Altered," and "Eastward Ho!" in the composition of which he had been engaged with others; and when the player-editors of the folio of 1623 were collecting their materials, they perhaps omitted "Pericles" because some living author might have an interest in it. Of course we only advance this point as a mere speculation; and the fact that the publishers of the folio of 1623 could not purchase the right of the bookseller, who had then the property in "Pericles," may have been the real cause of its non-insertion.

The Registers of the Stationers' Company show that on the 20th May, 1608, Edward Blount (one of the proprietors of the folio of 1623) entered "The booke of Pericles, Prynce of Tyre," with one of the undoubted works of Shakespeare, "Antony and Cleopatra." Nevertheless, "Pericles" was not published by Blount, but by Gosson in the following year; and we may infer, either that Blount sold his interest to Gosson, or that Gosson anticipated Blount in procuring a manuscript of the play. Gosson may have subsequently parted with "Pericles" to Thomas Pavier, and hence the re-impression by the latter in 1619.

Having thus spoken of the internal evidence of authorship, and of the possible reason why "Pericles" was not included in the folio of 1623, we will now advert briefly to the external evidence, that it was the work of our great dramatist. In the first place it was printed in 1609, with his name at full length[2], and rendered unusually obvious, on the title-page. The answer, of course, may be that this was a fraud, and that it had been previously committed in the cases of the first part of "Sir John Oldcastle," 1600, and of "The Yorkshire Tragedy," 1608. It is undoubtedly true, that Shakespeare's name is upon those title-pages; but we know, with regard to "Sir John Oldcastle," that the original title-page, stating it to have been "Written by William Shakespeare" was cancelled, no doubt at the instance of the author to whom it was falsely imputed; and as to "The Yorkshire Tragedy," many persons have entertained the belief, in which we join, that Shakespeare had a share in its composition. We are not to forget that, in the year preceding, Nathaniel Butter had made very prominent use of Shakespeare's name, for the sale of three impressions of "King Lear;" and that in the very year when "Pericles" came out, Thorpe had printed a collection of scattered poems, recommending them to notice in very large capitals, by stating emphatically that they were "Shakespeare's Sonnets."

Confirmatory of what precedes, it may be mentioned, that previously to the insertion of "Pericles" in the folio of 1664, it had been imputed to Shakespeare by S. Shepherd, in his

[2] It seems that "Pericles" was reprinted under the same circumstances in 1611. I have never been able to meet with a copy of this edition, and doubted its existence, until Mr. Halliwell pointed it out to me, in a sale catalogue in 1804: it purported to have been "printed for S. S." This fact would show, that Shakespeare did not then contradict the reiterated assertion, that he was the author of the play.

"Times displayed in Six Sestiads," 1646; and in lines by J. Tatham, prefixed to R. Brome's "Jovial Crew," 1652. Dryden gave it to Shakespeare in 1675, in the Prologue to C. Davenant's "Circe." Thus, as far as stage tradition is of value, it is uniformly in favour of our position; and it is moreover to be observed, that until comparatively modern times it has never been contradicted.

The incidents of "Pericles" are found in Lawrence Twine's translation from the *Gesta Romanorum*, first published in 1576, under the title of "The Patterne of Painfull Adventures," in which the three chief characters are not named as in Shakespeare, but are called Apollonius, Lucina, and Tharsia[3]. This novel was several times reprinted, and an edition of it came out in 1607, which perhaps was the year in which "Pericles" was first represented "at the Globe on the Bank-side," as is stated on the title-page of the earliest edition in 1609. The drama seems to have been extremely popular, but the usual difficulty being experienced by booksellers in obtaining a copy of it, Nathaniel Butter probably employed some person to attend the performance at the theatre, and with the aid of notes there taken, and of Twine's version of the story, (which, as we remarked, had just before been reprinted) to compose a novel out of the incidents of the play under the following title: "The Painfull Adventures of Pericles Prince of Tyre. Being the true History of the Play of Pericles, as it was lately presented by the worthy and ancient Poet Iohn Gower. At London. Printed by T. P. for Nat. Butter. 1608." It has also a wood-cut of Gower, no doubt, in the costume he wore at the Globe.

This publication is valuable, not merely because it is the only known specimen of the kind of that date in our language, but because though in prose, (with the exception of a song) it gives some of the speeches more at length, than in the play as it has come down to us, and explains several obscure and disputed passages. For this latter purpose it will be seen that we have availed ourselves of it in our notes; but it will not be out of place here to speak of the strong presumptive evidence it affords, that the drama has not reached us by any means in the shape in which it was originally represented. The subsequent is given, in the novel of 1608, as the speech of Marina, when she is visited in the brothel by Lysimachus, the governor of Mitylene, whom, by her virtue, beauty, and eloquence, she diverts from the purpose for which he came.

[3] The novel is contained in a work called "Shakespeare's Library," as well as Gower's poetical version of the same incidents, extracted from his *Confessio Amantis*. Hence the propriety of making Gower the speaker of the various interlocutions in "Pericles." The origin of the story, as we find it in the *Gesta Romanorum*, is a matter of dispute: Belleforest asserts that the version in his *Histoires Tragiques* was from a manuscript *tiré du Grec*. Not long since, Mr. Thorpe printed an Anglo Saxon narrative of the same incidents; and it is stated to exist in Latin manuscripts of as early a date as the tenth century.—"Shakespeare's Library," part v. p. ii.

"If as you say, my lord, you are the governor, let not your authority which should teach you to rule others, be the means to make you misgovern yourself. If the eminence of your place came unto you by descent, and the royalty of your blood, let not your life prove your birth bastard: if it were thrown upon you by opinion, make good that opinion was the cause to make you great. What reason is there in your justice, who hath power over all, to undo any? If you take from me mine honour, you are like him that makes a gap into forbidden ground, after whom many enter, and you are guilty of all their evils. My life is yet unspotted, my chastity unstained in thought: then, if your violence deface this building, the workmanship of heaven, made up for good, and not to be the exercise of sin's intemperance, you do kill your own honour, abuse your own justice, and impoverish me."

Of this speech in the printed play we only meet with the following emphatic germ:—

"If you were born to honour, show it now:
If put upon you, make the judgment good,
That thought you worthy of it."—(A. iv. sc. 6.)

It will hardly be required of us to argue, that the powerful address, copied from the novel founded upon "Pericles," could not be the mere enlargement of a short-hand writer, who had taken notes at the theatre, who from the very difficulty of the operation, and from the haste with which he must afterwards have compounded the history, would be much more likely to abridge than to expand. In some parts of the novel it is evident that the prose, there used, was made up from the blank-verse composition of the drama, as acted at the Globe. In the latter we meet with no passage similar to what succeeds, but still the ease with which it may be re-converted into blank-verse renders it almost certain that it was so originally. Pericles tells Simonides, in the novel, that

"His blood was yet untainted, but with the heat got by the wrong the king had offered him, and that he boldly durst and did defy himself, his subjects, and the proudest danger that either tyranny or treason could inflict upon him."

To leave out only two or three expletives renders the sentence perfect dramatic blank-verse:—

"His blood was yet untainted, but with heat
Got by the wrong the king had offer'd him;
And that he boldly durst and did defy him,
His subjects, and the proudest danger that
Or tyranny or treason could inflict."

Many other passages to the same end might be produced from the novel of which there is no trace in the play. We shall not, however, dwell farther upon the point, than to mention a peculiarly Shakespearean expression, which occurs in the novel, and is omitted in the drama. Lychorida brings the new-born infant to Pericles, who in the printed play (Act iii. sc. 1) says to it,

——— "thou'rt the rudeliest welcome to this world
That e'er was prince's child. Happy what follows!
Thou hast as chiding a nativity,
As fire, air, water, earth, and heaven can make."

In the novel founded upon the play, the speech is thus given, and we have printed the expression, which, we think, must have come from the pen of Shakespeare, in italic type:

"*Poor inch of nature!* (quoth he) thou art as rudely welcome to the world, as ever princess' babe was, and hast as chiding a nativity as fire, air, earth and water can afford thee."

The existence of such a singular production was not known to any of the commentators; but several copies of it have been preserved, and one of them was sold in the library of the late Mr. Heber.

It will have been remarked, that the novel printed in 1608 states that "Pericles" had been "*lately* presented," and on the title-page of the edition of the play in 1609 it is termed "the *late* and much-admired Play called Pericles:" it is, besides, spoken of as "a new play," in a poetical tract called "Pimlico or Run Red-cap," printed in 1609. Another piece, called "Shore," is mentioned in "Pimlico," under exactly similar circumstances: there was an older drama upon the story of Jane Shore, and this, like "Pericles," had, in all probability, about the same date been revived at one of the theatres, with additions.

"Pericles" was five times printed before it was inserted in the folio of 1664, viz. in 1609, 1611, 1619, 1630, and 1635. The folio seems to have been copied from the last of these, with a multiplication of errors, but with some corrections. The first edition of 1609 was obviously brought out in haste, and there are many corruptions in it; but more pains were taken with it than Malone, Steevens, and others imagined: they never compared different copies of the same edition, or they would have seen that the impressions vary importantly, and that several mistakes, discovered as the play went through the press, were carefully set right: these will be found pointed out in our notes. The commentators dwelt upon the blunders of the old copies, in order to warrant their own extraordinary innovations; but wherever we could do so, with due regard to the sense of the author, we have restored the text to that of the earliest impression.

DRAMATIS PERSONÆ.

ANTIOCHUS, King of Antioch.
PERICLES, Prince of Tyre.
HELICANUS, } two Lords of Tyre.
ESCANES, }
SIMONIDES, King of Pentapolis.
CLEON, Governor of Tharsus.
LYSIMACHUS, Governor of Mitylene.
CERIMON, a Lord of Ephesus.
THALIARD, a Lord of Antioch.
PHILEMON, Servant to Cerimon.
LEONINE, Servant to Dionyza.
Marshal.
A Pander, and his Wife.
BOULT, their Servant.
GOWER, as Chorus.

The Daughter of Antiochus.
DIONYZA, Wife to Cleon.
THAISA, Daughter to Simonides.
MARINA, Daughter to Pericles and Thaisa.
LYCHORIDA, Nurse to Marina.
DIANA.

Lords, Ladies, Knights, Gentlemen, Sailors, Pirates, Fishermen, Messengers, &c.

SCENE, dispersedly in various Countries.

PERICLES, PRINCE OF TYRE.

ACT I.

Enter GOWER.

Before the Palace of Antioch.

To sing a song that old was sung,
From ashes ancient Gower is come;
Assuming man's infirmities,
To glad your ear, and please your eyes.
It hath been sung at festivals,
On ember-eves, and holy ales,[1]
And lords and ladies in their lives
Have read it for restoratives:
The purpose[2] is to make men glorious;
Et bonum quo antiquius, eo melius.
If you, born in these latter times,
When wit 's more ripe, accept my rhymes,
And that to hear an old man sing,
May to your wishes pleasure bring,
I life would wish, and that I might
Waste it for you, like taper-light.—
This Antioch, then: Antiochus the great
Built up this city for his chiefest seat,
The fairest in all Syria;
I tell you what my authors say:
This king unto him took a feere,[3]
Who died and left a female heir,
So buxom, blithe, and full of face,
As heaven had lent her all his grace;
With whom the father liking took,

[1] *Festivals;* days: in old copies. Farmer made the change
[2] purchase: in old copies. [3] *Mate.*

And her to incest did provoke.
Bad child, worse father, to entice his own
To evil, should be done by none.
By[1] custom what they did begin
Was with long use account no sin.
The beauty of this sinful dame
Made many princes thither frame,
To seek her as a bed-fellow,
In marriage pleasures play-fellow:
Which to prevent he made a law,
To keep her still and men in awe,
That whoso ask'd her for his wife,
His riddle told not, lost his life:
So, for her many a wight did die,
As yond' grim looks[2] do testify.
What now ensues, to the judgment of your eye
I give, my cause who best can justify. [*Exit.*

SCENE I.—Antioch. A Room in the Palace.

Enter ANTIOCHUS, PERICLES, *and Attendants.*

Ant. Young prince of Tyre, you have at large receiv'd
The danger of the task you undertake.

Per. I have, Antiochus, and with a soul
Embolden'd with the glory of her praise,
Think death no hazard in this enterprise. [*Music.*

Ant. Bring in our daughter, clothed like a bride,
For the embracements even of Jove himself;
At whose conception, (till Lucina reign'd)
Nature this dowry gave, to glad her presence,
The senate-house of planets all did sit,
To knit in her their best perfections.

Enter the Daughter of ANTIOCHUS.

Per. See, where she comes, apparell'd like the spring,
Graces her subjects, and her thoughts the king
Of every virtue gives renown to men!
Her face, the book of praises, where is read
Nothing but curious pleasures, as from thence
Sorrow were ever ras'd,[3] and testy wrath
Could never be her mild companion.
Ye gods, that made me man, and sway in love,
That have inflam'd desire in my breast,
To taste the fruit of yon celestial tree,

[1] But: in old copies. [2] Of the decapitated heads over the city gate
[3] rack'd: in old copies.

Or die in the adventure, be my helps,
As I am son and servant to your will,
To compass such a boundless[1] happiness!

Ant. Prince Pericles,—

Per. That would be son to great Antiochus.

Ant. Before thee stands this fair Hesperides,
With golden fruit, but dangerous to be touch'd;
For death-like dragons here affright thee hard:
Her face, like heaven, enticeth thee to view
Her countless glory, which desert must gain:
And which, without desert, because thine eye
Presumes to reach, all thy whole heap must die.
Yond' sometime famous princes, like thyself,
Drawn by report, adventurous by desire,
Tell thee with speechless tongues, and semblance pale,
That, without covering, save yond' field of stars,
They here stand martyrs, slain in Cupid's wars;
And with dead cheeks advise thee to desist,
For going on death's net, whom none resist.

Per. Antiochus, I thank thee, who hath taught
My frail mortality to know itself,
And by those fearful objects to prepare
This body, like to them, to what I must:
For death remember'd should be like a mirror,
Who tells us, life 's but breath; to trust it, error.
I 'll make my will, then; and as sick men do,
Who know the world, see heaven, but feeling woe,
Gripe not at earthly joys, as erst they did:
So, I bequeath a happy peace to you,
And all good men, as every prince should do:
My riches to the earth from whence they came,
But my unspotted fire of love to you.
[*To the Daughter of* ANTIOCHUS.
Thus, ready for the way of life or death,
I wait the sharpest blow.

Ant. Scorning advice, read the conclusion, then;
Which read and not expounded, 't is decreed,
As these before thee, thou thyself shalt bleed.

Daugh. Of all, 'say'd yet, may'st thou prove prosperous!
Of all, 'say'd yet, I wish thee happiness.

Per. Like a bold champion, I assume the lists,
Nor ask advice of any other thought

[1] bondless: in old copies. Rowe made the change.

But faithfulness, and courage.

THE RIDDLE.

I am no viper, yet I feed
On mother's flesh, which did me breed;
I sought a husband, in which labour,
I found that kindness in a father:
He 's father, son, and husband mild,
I mother, wife, and yet his child.
How they may be, and yet in two,
As you will live, resolve it you.

Sharp physick is the last: but, O! you powers,
That give heaven countless eyes to view men's acts,
Why cloud they not their sights perpetually,
If this be true, which makes me pale to read it?
Fair glass of light, I lov'd you, and could still,
Were not this glorious casket stor'd with ill;
But I must tell you,—now, my thoughts revolt,
For he 's no man on whom perfections wait,
That, knowing sin within, will touch the gate.
You 're a fair viol, and your sense the strings,
Who, finger'd to make man his lawful music,
Would draw heaven down and all the gods to hearken;
But being play'd upon before your time,
Hell only danceth to so harsh a chime.
Good sooth, I care not for you.

Ant. Prince Pericles, touch not, upon thy life,
For that 's an article within our law,
As dangerous as the rest. Your time 's expir'd:
Either expound now, or receive your sentence.

Per. Great king,
Few love to hear the sins they love to act;
'T would 'braid yourself too near for me to tell it.
Who has a book of all that monarchs do,
He 's more secure to keep it shut, than shown;
For vice repeated is like the wandering wind,
Blows dust in others' eyes, to spread itself;
And yet the end of all is bought thus dear,
The breath is gone, and the sore eyes see clear:
To stop the air would hurt them. The blind mole casts
Copp'd hills towards heaven, to tell the earth is throng'd
By man's oppression; and the poor worm doth die for 't.
Kings are earth's gods; in vice their law 's their will,
And if Jove stray, who dares say Jove doth ill?
It is enough you know; and it is fit,

What being more known grows worse, to smother it.
All love the womb that their first beings bred,
Then, give my tongue like leave to love my head.
Ant. [*Aside.*] Heaven, that I had thy head! he has found the meaning;
But I will gloze with him. [*To him.*] Young prince of Tyre,
Though by the tenour of our strict edict,
Your exposition misinterpreting,
We might proceed to cancel of your days;
Yet hope, succeeding from so fair a tree
As your fair self, doth tune us otherwise.
Forty days longer we do respite you;
If by which time our secret be undone,
This mercy shows, we 'll joy in such a son:
And until then your entertain shall be,
As doth befit our honour, and your worth.
[*Exeunt* ANTIOCHUS, *his Daughter, and Attendants.*
Per. How courtesy would seem to cover sin,
When what is done is like an hypocrite,
The which is good in nothing but in sight.
If it be true that I interpret false,
Then were it certain, you were not so bad,
As with foul incest to abuse your soul;
Where now you 're both a father and a son,
By your untimely claspings with your child,
(Which pleasure fits a husband, not a father)
And she an eater of her mother's flesh,
By the defiling of her parent's bed;
And both like serpents are, who though they feed
On sweetest flowers, yet they poison breed.
Antioch, farewell! for wisdom sees, those men
Blush not in actions blacker than the night,
Will shun' no course to keep them from the light:
One sin, I know, another doth provoke;
Murder 's as near to lust, as flame to smoke.
Poison and treason are the hands of sin,
Ay, and the targets, to put off the shame:
Then, lest my life be cropp'd to keep you clear,
By flight I 'll shun the danger which I fear. [*Exit.*

Re-enter ANTIOCHUS.

Ant. He hath found the meaning, for the which we mean

' show: in old copies. Malone made the change.

To have his head.
He must not live to trumpet forth my infamy,
Nor tell the world, Antiochus doth sin
In such a loathed manner:
And therefore instantly this prince must die;
For by his fall my honour must keep high.
Who attends us there?

Enter THALIARD.

Thal. Doth your highness call?
Ant. Thaliard,
You 're of our chamber, and our mind partakes
Her private actions to your secrecy;
And for your faithfulness we will advance you.
Thaliard, behold, here 's poison, and here 's gold;
We hate the prince of Tyre, and thou must kill him:
It fits thee not to ask the reason why,
Because we bid it. Say, is it done?
Thal. My lord,
'T is done.

Enter a Messenger.

Ant. Enough.—
Let your breath cool yourself, telling your haste.
Mess. My lord, prince Pericles is fled.
[*Exit Messenger.*
Ant. As thou
Wilt live, fly after: and, as[1] an arrow, shot
From a well-experienc'd archer, hits the mark
His eye doth level at, so ne'er return,
Unless thou say Prince Pericles is dead.
Thal. My lord, if I
Can get him once within my pistol's length,
I 'll make him sure: so, farewell to your highness. [*Exit.*
Ant. Thaliard, adieu.—Till Pericles be dead,
My heart can lend no succour to my head. [*Exit.*

SCENE II.—Tyre. A Room in the Palace.

Enter PERICLES, HELICANUS, *and other Lords.*

Per. Let none disturb us: why should this change of thoughts?
The sad companion, dull-ey'd melancholy,
By me so us'd a guest is, not an hour,
In the day's glorious walk, or peaceful night,
The tomb where grief should sleep, can breed me quiet.

[1] like: in quartos.

Here pleasures court mine eyes, and mine eyes shun
them,
And danger, which I fear'd, is at Antioch,
Whose arm seems far too short to hit me here;
Yet neither pleasure's art can joy my spirits,
Nor yet the other's distance comfort me.
Then, it is thus: that passions of the mind,
That have their first conception by mis-dread,
Have after-nourishment and life by care;
And what was first but fear what might be done,
Grows elder now, and cares it be not done:
And so with me:—the great Antiochus
('Gainst whom I am too little to contend,
Since he 's so great, can make his will his act)
Will think me speaking, though I swear to silence:
Nor boots it me to say, I honour,
If he suspect I may dishonour him:
And what may make him blush in being known,
He 'll stop the course by which it might be known.
With hostile forces he 'll o'erspread the land,
And with the ostent[1] of war will look so huge,
Amazement shall drive courage from the state;
Our men be vanquish'd ere they do resist,
And subjects punish'd that ne'er thought offence:
Which care of them, not pity of myself,
(Who am[2] no more but as the tops of trees,
Which fence the roots they grow by, and defend them)
Makes both my body pine, and soul to languish,
And punish that before, that he would punish.

1 *Lord.* Joy and all comfort in your sacred breast.

2 *Lord.* And keep your mind, till you return to us,
Peaceful and comfortable.

Hel. Peace, peace! and give experience tongue.
They do abuse the king, that flatter him:
For flattery is the bellows blows up sin;
The thing the which is flatter'd, but a spark,
To which that blast[3] gives heat[4] and stronger glowing;
Whereas reproof, obedient and in order,
Fits kings, as they are men, for they may err:
When signior Sooth, here, does proclaim a peace,
He flatters you, makes war upon your life.

[1] stint: in old copies. Tyrwhitt made the change. [2] once: in old copies. Steevens made the change. [3] spark: in old copies. Mason made the change. [4] heart: in old copies.

Prince, pardon me, or strike me, if you please;
I cannot be much lower than my knees.
Per. All leave us else; but let your cares o'er-look
What shipping, and what lading 's in our haven,
And then return to us. [*Exeunt Lords.*] Helicanus, thou
Hast moved us: what seest thou in our looks?
Hel. An angry brow, dread lord.
Per. If there be such a dart in prince's frowns,
How durst thy tongue move anger to our face?
Hel. How dare the plants look up to heaven, from whence
They have their nourishment?
Per. Thou know'st I have power
To take thy life from thee.
Hel. I have ground the axe myself;
Do you but strike the blow.
Per. Rise, pr'ythee rise.
Sit down; thou art no flatterer:
I thank thee for it; and heaven forbid,
That kings should let their ears hear their faults hid.
Fit counsellor, and servant for a prince,
Who by thy wisdom mak'st a prince thy servant,
What wouldst thou have me do?
Hel. To bear with patience
Such griefs as you yourself do lay upon yourself.
Per. Thou speak'st like a physician, Helicanus,
That ministers a potion unto me,
That thou wouldst tremble to receive thyself.
Attend me, then: I went to Antioch,
Where, as thou know'st, against the face of death
I sought the purchase of a glorious beauty,
From whence an issue I might propagate,
Are arms to princes, and bring joys to subjects.
Her face was to mine eye beyond all wonder;
The rest (hark in thine ear) as black as incest:
Which by my knowledge found, the sinful father
Seem'd not to strike, but smooth: but thou know'st this
'T is time to fear, when tyrants seem to kiss.
Which fear so grew in me, I hither fled
Under the covering of a careful night,
Who seem'd my good protector; and being here,
Bethought me what was past, what might succeed
I knew him tyrannous; and tyrants' fears

Decrease not, but grow faster than the years.
And should he doubt[1] it, (as no doubt he doth)
That I should open to the listening air,
How many worthy princes' bloods were shed,
To keep his bed of blackness unlaid ope,
To lop that doubt he'll fill this land with arms,
And make pretence of wrong that I have done him;
When all, for mine, if I may call 't, offence,
Must feel war's blow, who spares not innocence:
Which love to all, of which thyself art one,
Who now reprov'st me for it—

Hel. Alas, sir!

Per. Drew sleep out of mine eyes, blood from my cheeks,
Musings into my mind, a thousand doubts
How I might stop this tempest ere it came;
And finding little comfort to relieve them,
I thought it princely charity to grieve them.

Hel. Well, my lord, since you have given me leave to speak,
Freely will I speak. Antiochus you fear,
And justly too, I think, you fear the tyrant,
Who either by public war, or private treason,
Will take away your life.
Therefore, my lord, go travel for a while,
Till that his rage and anger be forgot,
Or till the Destinies do cut his thread of life.
Your rule direct to any; if to me,
Day serves not light more faithful than I'll be.

Per. I do not doubt thy faith;
But should he wrong my liberties in my absence?

Hel. We'll mingle our bloods together in the earth,
From whence we had our being and our birth.

Per. Tyre, I now look from thee, then; and to Tharsus
Intend my travel, where I'll hear from thee,
And by whose letters I'll dispose myself.
The care I had, and have, of subjects' good,
On thee I lay, whose wisdom's strength can bear it.
I'll take thy word for faith, not ask thine oath;
Who shuns not to break one, will sure[2] crack both.
But in our orbs we live so round and safe,

[1] doo 't: in old copies. Malone made the change. [2] Not in quartos.

That time of both this truth shall ne'er convince,[1]
Thou show'dst a subject's shine, I a true prince.
[*Exeunt.*

SCENE III.—Tyre. An Ante-chamber in the Palace.

Enter THALIARD.

Thal So, this is Tyre, and this is the court. Here must I kill king Pericles; and if I do not, I am sure to be hang'd at home: 't is dangerous.—Well, I perceive he was a wise fellow, and had good discretion, that being bid to ask what he would of the king, desired he might know none of his secrets: now do I see he had some reason for it; for if a king bid a man be a villain, he is bound by the indenture of his oath to be one.—Hush! here come the lords of Tyre.

Enter HELICANUS, ESCANES, *and other Lords.*

Hel. You shall not need, my fellow peers of Tyre,
Farther to question me of your king's departure:
His seal'd commission, left in trust with me,
Doth speak sufficiently, he 's gone to travel.

Thal. [*Aside.*] How! the king gone?

Hel. If farther yet you will be satisfied,
Why, as it were unlicens'd of your loves,
He would depart, I 'll give some light unto you.
Being at Antioch—

Thal. [*Aside.*] What from Antioch?

Hel. Royal Antiochus (on what cause I know not)
Took some displeasure at him: at least, he judg'd so;
And doubting lest that he had err'd or sinn'd,
To show his sorrow he 'd correct himself;
So puts himself unto the shipman's toil,
With whom each minute threatens life or death.

Thal. [*Aside.*] Well, I perceive
I shall not be hang'd now, although I would;
But since he 's gone, the king's seas must please
He 'scap'd the land, to perish at the sea.—
I 'll present myself.—[*To them.*] Peace to the lords of Tyre.

Hel. Lord Thaliard from Antiochus is welcome.

Thal. From him I come,
With message unto princely Pericles:
But since my landing I have understood,

[1] *Overcome.*

Your lord hath betook himself to unknown travels,
My message must return from whence it came.
Hel. We have no reason to desire it,
Commended to our master, not to us:
Yet, ere you shall depart, this we desire,
As friends to Antioch we may feast in Tyre. [*Exeunt.*

SCENE IV.—Tharsus. A Room in the Governor's House.

Enter CLEON, DIONYZA, *and Attendants.*

Cle. My Dionyza, shall we rest us here,
And by relating tales of other's griefs,
See if 't will teach us to forget our own?
Dio. That were to blow at fire in hope to quench it;
For who digs hills because they do aspire,
Throws down one mountain to cast up a higher.
O my distressed lord! even such our griefs;
Here they 're but felt, and seen with mischief's eyes,
But like to groves, being topp'd, they higher rise.
Cle. O Dionyza,
Who wanteth food, and will not say he wants it,
Or can conceal his hunger, till he famish?
Our tongues and sorrows do sound deep
Our woes into the air; our eyes do weep,
Till tongues fetch breath that may proclaim them louder;
That if heaven slumber, while their creatures want,
They may awake their helps to comfort them.
I 'll then discourse our woes, felt several years
And, wanting breath to speak, help me with tears.
Dio. I 'll do my best, sir.
Cle. This Tharsus, o'er which I have the government,
A city, on whom plenty held full hand,
For riches strew'd herself even in the streets,
Whose towers bore heads so high, they kiss'd the clouds
And strangers ne'er beheld, but wonder'd at;
Whose men and dames so jetted[1] and adorn'd,
Like one another's glass to trim them by:
Their tables were stor'd full to glad the sight,
And not so much to feed on as delight;
All poverty was scorn'd, and pride so great,
The name of help grew odious to repeat.
Dio. O! 't is too true.
Cle. But see what heaven can do! By this our change,

[1] *Strutted.*

These mouths, whom but of late, earth, sea, and air,
Were all too little to content and please,
Although they gave their creatures in abundance,
As houses are defil'd for want of use,
They are now starv'd for want of exercise:
Those palates, who not yet two summers[1] younger,
Must have inventions to delight the taste,
Would now be glad of bread, and beg for it:
Those mothers who to nousle up their babes
Thought nought too curious, are ready now
To eat those little darlings whom they lov'd.
So sharp are hunger's teeth, that man and wife
Draw lots, who first shall die to lengthen life.
Here stands a lord, and there a lady weeping;
Here many sink, yet those which see them fall,
Have scarce strength left to give them burial.
Is not this true?

Dio. Our cheeks and hollow eyes do witness it.

Cle. O! let those cities, that of plenty's cup
And her prosperities so largely taste,
With their superfluous riots, hear these tears:
The misery of Tharsus may be theirs.

Enter a Lord.

Lord. Where 's the lord governor?

Cle. Here.
Speak out thy sorrows which thou bring'st in haste,
For comfort is too far for us to expect.

Lord. We have descried, upon our neighbouring shore,
A portly sail of ships make hitherward.

Cle. I thought as much.
One sorrow never comes, but brings an heir
That may succeed as his inheritor;
And so in ours. Some neighbouring nation,
Taking advantage of our misery,
Hath[2] stuff'd these hollow vessels with their power,
To beat us down, the which are down already;
And make a conquest of unhappy me,
Whereas no glory 's got to overcome.

Lord. That 's the least fear; for by the semblance
Of their white flags display'd, they bring us peace,
And come to us as favourers, not as foes.

Cle. Thou speak'st like him 's[3] untutor'd to repeat;

[1] savers: in old copies. Steevens made the change. [2] That: in old copies. [3] Him who is.

Who makes the fairest show means most deceit.
But bring they what they will, and what they can,
What need we fear?
The ground 's the low'st, and we are half way there.
Go, tell their general we attend him here,
To know for what he comes, and whence he comes,
And what he craves.

Lord. I go, my lord. [*Exit.*

Cle. Welcome is peace, if he on peace consist;[1]
If wars, we are unable to resist.

Enter PERICLES, *with Attendants.*

Per. Lord governor, for so we hear you are,
Let not our ships and number of our men,
Be, like a beacon fir'd, to amaze your eyes.
We have heard your miseries as far as Tyre,
And seen the desolation of your streets;
Nor come we to add sorrow to your tears,
But to relieve them of their heavy load:
And these our ships you happily may think
Are like the Trojan horse, was stuff'd within
With bloody veins, expecting overthrow,
Are stor'd with corn to make your needy bread,
And give them life whom hunger starv'd half dead.

All. The gods of Greece protect you!
And we 'll pray for you.

Per. Arise, I pray you, arise:
We do not look for reverence, but for love,
And harbourage for ourself, our ships, and men.

Cle. The which when any shall not gratify,
Or pay you with unthankfulness in thought,
Be it our wives, our children, or ourselves,
The curse of heaven and men succeed their evils!
Till when, (the which, I hope, shall ne'er be seen)
Your grace is welcome to our town and us.

Per. Which welcome we 'll accept; feast here a while,
Until our stars that frown lend us a smile. [*Exeunt.*

[1] Stand.

ACT II.

Enter GOWER.

Gow. Here have you seen a mighty king
His child, I wis, to incest bring;
A better prince, and benign lord,
That will prove awful both in deed and word.
Be quiet, then, as men should be,
Till he hath pass'd necessity.
I 'll show you those in trouble's reign,
Losing a mite, a mountain gain
The good in conversation
(To whom I give my benizon)
Is still at Tharsus, where each man
Thinks all is writ he spoken can:
And to remember what he does,
Build his statue to make him glorious:
But tidings to the contrary
Are brought your eyes; what need speak I?

Dumb show.

Enter at one door PERICLES, *talking with* CLEON; *all the Train with them. Enter at another door, a Gentleman, with a Letter to* PERICLES: PERICLES *shows the Letter to* CLEON; *then gives the Messenger a reward, and knights him. Exeunt* PERICLES, CLEON, *&c. severally.*

Gow. Good Helicane hath[1] stay'd at home,
Not to eat honey like a drone,
From others' labours; for though he strive
To killen bad, keep good alive;
And, to fulfil his prince' desire,
Sends word of all that haps in Tyre:
How Thaliard came full bent with sin,
And hid intent, to murder him;
And that in Tharsus was not best
Longer for him to make his rest.
He knowing so,[2] put forth to seas,
Where when men been, there 's seldom ease,
For now the wind begins to blow;
Thunder above, and deeps below,

[1] that: in old copies. [2] doing so: in old copies. Steevens made the change.

Make such unquiet, that the ship,
Should house him safe, is wreck'd and split;
And he, good prince, having all lost,
By waves from coast to coast is tost.
All perishen of man, of pelf,
Ne aught escapen but himself;
Till fortune, tired with doing bad,
Threw him ashore, to give him glad:
And here he comes. What shall be next,
Pardon old Gower; this 'longs[1] the text. [*Exit.*

SCENE I.—Pentapolis. An open Place by the Sea-side.

Enter PERICLES, *wet.*

Per. Yet cease your ire, you angry stars of heaven!
Wind, rain, and thunder, remember, earthly man
Is but a substance that must yield to you;
And I, as fits my nature, do obey you.
Alas! the sea hath cast me on the rocks,
Wash'd me from shore to shore, and left me breath
Nothing to think on, but ensuing death:
Let it suffice the greatness of your powers,
To have bereft a prince of all his fortunes;
And having thrown him from your watery grave,
Here to have death in peace is all he'll crave.

Enter three Fishermen.

1 *Fish.* What, ho, Pilch![2]

2 *Fish.* Ho! come, and bring away the nets.

1 *Fish.* What, Patch-breech, I say!

3 *Fish.* What say you, master?

1 *Fish.* Look how thou stirrest now. Come away, or I'll fetch thee with a wannion.

3 *Fish.* 'Faith, master, I am thinking of the poor men, that were cast away before us even now.

1 *Fish.* Alas, poor souls! it grieved my heart to hear what pitiful cries they made to us to help them, when, well-a-day, we could scarce help ourselves.

3 *Fish.* Nay, master, said not I as much, when I saw the porpus, how he bounced and tumbled? they say, they are half fish, half flesh: a plague on them! they ne'er come, but I look to be washed. Master, I marvel how the fishes live in the sea.

1 *Fish.* Why as men do a-land: the great ones eat

[1] *Belongs to.* [2] *A leather*, or *covering.*

up the little ones. I can compare our rich misers to nothing so fitly as to a whale; a' plays and tumbles, driving the poor fry before him, and at last devours them all at a mouthful. Such whales have I heard on the land, who never leave gaping, till they 've swallowed the [illegible] parish, church, steeple, bells and all.

[illegible] A pretty moral.

3 *Fish.* But, master, if I had been the sexton, I would have been that day in the belfry.

2 *Fish.* Why, man?

3 *Fish.* Because he should have swallowed me too: and when I had been in his belly, I would have kept such a jangling of the bells, that he should never have left, till he cast bells, steeple, church, and parish, up again. But if the good king Simonides were of my mind——

Per. Simonides?

3 *Fish.* We would purge the land of these drones, that rob the bee of her honey.

Per. How from the finny[1] subject of the sea
These fishers tell the infirmities of men;
And from their watery empire recollect
All that may men approve, or men detect!—
Peace be at your labour, honest fishermen.

2 *Fish.* Honest! good fellow, what 's that? if it be a day fits you, search out of the calendar, and no body look after it.

Per. Y' may see, the sea hath cast me upon your
coast——

2 *Fish.* What a drunken knave was the sea, to cast thee in our way.

Per. A man whom both the waters and the wind,
In that vast tennis-court, hath made the ball
For them to play upon, entreats you pity him;
He asks of you, that never us'd to beg.

1 *Fish.* No, friend, cannot you beg? here 's them in our country of Greece, gets more with begging, than we can do with working.

2 *Fish.* Canst thou catch any fishes, then?

Per. I never practis'd it.

2 *Fish.* Nay, then thou wilt starve, sure; for here 's nothing to be got now a-days, unless thou canst fish for 't.

1 fenny: in old copies. Steevens made the change.

Per. What I have been I have forgot to know,
But what I am want teaches me to think on;
A man throng'd up with cold: my veins are chill,
And have no more of life, than may suffice
To give my tongue that heat to ask your help;
Which if you shall refuse, when I am dead,
For that I am a man, pray see me buried.

1 *Fish.* Die quoth-a? Now, gods forbid it! I have a gown here; come, put it on; keep thee warm. Now, afore me, a handsome fellow! Come, thou shalt go home, and we 'll have flesh for holidays, fish for fasting-days, and moreo'er puddings and flap-jacks;[1] and thou shalt be welcome.

Per. I thank you, sir.

2 *Fish.* Hark you, my friend, you said you could not beg.

Per. I did but crave.

2 *Fish.* But crave? Then I 'll turn craver too, and so I shall 'scape whipping.

Per. Why, are all your beggars whipped, then?

2 *Fish.* O! not all, my friend, not all; for if all your beggars were whipped, I would wish no better office than to be beadle. But, master, I 'll go draw up the net. [*Exeunt Two of the Fishermen.*

Per. How well this honest mirth becomes their labour!

1 *Fish.* Hark you, sir; do you know where you are?

Per. Not well.

1 *Fish.* Why, I 'll tell you: this is called Pentapolis, and our king the good Simonides.

Per. The good king Simonides, do you call him?

1 *Fish.* Ay, sir; and he deserves to be so called, for his peaceable reign, and good government.

Per. He is a happy king, since he gains from his subjects the name of good by his government. How far is his court distant from this shore?

1 *Fish.* Marry, sir, half a day's journey: and I 'll tell you, he hath a fair daughter, and to-morrow is her birth-day; and there are princes and knights come from all parts of the world, to joust and tourney for her love.

Per. Were my fortunes equal to my desires, I could wish to make one there.

[1] *Pancakes*, or *fritters*.

1 *Fish.* O, sir! things must be as they may; and what a man cannot get, he may lawfully deal for. His wife's soul—

Re-enter the Two Fishermen, drawing up a Net.

2 *Fish.* Help, master, help! here 's a fish hangs in the net, like a poor man's right in the law; 't will hardly come out. Ha! bots on 't; 't is come at last, and 't is turned to a rusty armour.

Per. An armour, friends! I pray you, let me see it.
Thanks, fortune, yet, that after all crosses
Thou giv'st me somewhat to repair myself:
And though it was mine own, part of mine heritage,
Which my dear father did bequeath to me,
With this strict charge (even as he left his life)
"Keep it, my Pericles, it hath been a shield
'Twixt me and death;" (and pointed to this brace)
"For that it sav'd me, keep it; in like necessity,
The which the gods protect thee from, it may defend
thee."
It kept where I kept, I so dearly lov'd it,
Till the rough seas, that spare nôt any man,
Took it in rage, though calm'd, have given 't again.
I thank thee for 't: my shipwreck now 's no ill,
Since I have here my father's gift in 's will.

1 *Fish.* What mean you, sir?

Per. To beg of you, kind friends, this coat of worth,
For it was sometime target to a king;
I know it by this mark. He lov'd me dearly,
And for his sake I wish the having of it;
And that you 'd guide me to your sovereign's court
Where with it I may appear a gentleman:
And if that ever my low fortunes better,
I 'll pay your bounties; till then, rest your debtor.

1 *Fish.* Why, wilt thou tourney for the lady?

Per. I 'll show the virtue I have borne in arms.

1 *Fish.* Why, do ye take it; and the gods give thee good on 't!

2 *Fish.* Ay, but hark you, my friend; 't was we that made up this garment through the rough seams of the waters: there are certain condolements, certain vails. I hope, sir, if you thrive, you 'll remember from whence you had it.

Per. Believe it, I will.
By your furtherance I am cloth'd in steel;

And spite of all the rapture[1] of the sea,
This jewel holds his biding[2] on my arm:
Unto thy value will I mount myself
Upon a courser, whose delightful steps
Shall make the gazer joy to see him tread —
Only, my friend, I yet am unprovided
Of a pair of bases.[3]

2 *Fish.* We 'll sure provide: thou shalt have my best gown to make thee a pair, and I 'll bring thee to the court myself.

Per. Then honour be but a goal to my will!
This day I 'll rise, or else add ill to ill. [*Exeunt.*

SCENE II.—The Same. A Platform leading to the Lists. A Pavilion near it, for the reception of the King, Princess, Ladies, Lords, &c.

Enter SIMONIDES. THAISA, *Lords, and Attendants.*

Sim. Are the knights ready to begin the triumph?

1 *Lord.* They are, my liege;
And stay your coming to present themselves.

Sim. Return them, we are ready; and our daughter,
In honour of whose birth these triumphs are,
Sits here, like beauty's child, whom nature gat
For men to see, and seeing wonder at. [*Exit a Lord*

Thai. It pleaseth you, my royal father, to express
My commendations great, whose merit 's less.

Sim. 'T is fit it should be so; for princes are
A model, which heaven makes like to itself:
As jewels lose their glory if neglected,
So princes their renown, if not respected.
'T is now your honour, daughter, to explain[4]
The labour of each knight in his device.

Thai. Which, to preserve mine honour, I 'll perform.

Enter a Knight: he passes over the Stage, and his Squire presents his Shield to the Princess.

Sim. Who is the first that doth prefer himself?

Thai. A knight of Sparta, my renowned father;
And the device he bears upon his shield
Is a black Æthiop, reaching at the sun;
The word, *Lux tua vita mihi.*

[1] rupture: in old copies. [2] building: in old copies. [3] A *mantle*, hanging from the middle to the knees. [4] entertain: in old copies. Steevens made the change

Sim. He loves you well that holds his life of you.
[*The second Knight passes over.*
Who is the second that presents himself?
Thai. A prince of Macedon, my royal father;
And the device he bears upon his shield
Is an arm'd knight, that 's conquer'd by a lady:
The motto thus, in Spanish, *Piu per dulzura que per fuerza.* [*The third Knight passes over.*
Sim. And what the third?
Thai. The third of Antioch;
And his device, a wreath of chivalry:
The word, *Me pompæ provexit apex.*
[*The fourth Knight passes over.*
Sim. What is the fourth?
Thai. A burning torch, that 's turned upside down;
The word, *Quod me alit, me extinguit.*
Sim. Which shows that beauty hath his power and will,
Which can as well inflame, as it can kill.
[*The fifth Knight passes over.*
Thai. The fifth, a hand environed with clouds,
Holding out gold that 's by the touchstone tried;
The motto thus, *Sic spectanda fides.*
[*The sixth Knight passes over.*
Sim. And what 's the sixth and last, the which the knight himself
With such a graceful courtesy deliver'd?
Thai. He seems to be a stranger; but his present is
A wither'd branch, that 's only green at top:
The motto, *In hac spe vivo.*
Sim. A pretty moral:
From the dejected state wherein he is,
He hopes by you his fortunes yet may flourish.
1 *Lord.* He had need mean better, than his outward show
Can any way speak in his just commend;
For by his rusty outside he appears
To have practis'd more the whipstock,[1] than the lance
2 *Lord.* He well may be a stranger, for he comes
To an honour'd triumph strangely furnished.
3 *Lord.* And on set purpose let his armour rust
Until this day, to scour it in the dust.
Sim. Opinion 's but a fool, that makes us scan

[1] *Whip handle*

The outward habit by the inward man.
But stay, the knights are coming: we 'll withdraw
Into the gallery. [*Exeunt.*
[*Great Shouts, and all cry,* The mean knight!

SCENE III.—The Same. A Hall of State. A Banquet prepared.

Enter SIMONIDES, THAISA, *Ladies, Lords, Knights, and Attendants.*

Sim. Knights,
To say you are welcome were superfluous.
To place upon the volume of your deeds,
As in a title-page, your worth in arms,
Were more than you expect, or more than 's fit,
Since every worth in show commends itself.
Prepare for mirth. for mirth becomes a feast
You are princes, and my guests.
Thai. But you, [*To* PER.] my knight and guest;
To whom this wreath of victory I give,
And crown you king of this day's happiness.
Per. 'T is more by fortune, lady, than my merit.
Sim. Call it by what you will, the day is yours;
And here, I hope, is none that envies it.
In framing an artist art hath thus decreed,
To make some good, but others to exceed;
And you 're her labour'd scholar. Come, queen o' the feast,
(For, daughter, so you are) here take your place:
Marshal the rest, as they deserve their grace.
Knights. We are honour'd much by good Simonides.
Sim. Your presence glads our days: honour we love,
For who hates honour hates the gods above.
Marshal. Sir, yond 's your place.
Per. Some other is more fit
1 *Knight.* Contend not, sir; for we are gentlemen,
That neither in our hearts, nor outward eyes,
Envy the great, nor do the low despise.
Per. You are right courteous knights.
Sim. Sit, sir; sit.
By Jove, I wonder, that is king of thoughts,
These cates resist me, he not thought upon.
Thai. By Juno, that is queen
Of marriage, all the viands that I eat
Do seem unsavoury, wishing him my meat.

Sure, he 's a gallant gentleman.
Sim. He 's but a country gentleman:
He has done no more than other knights have done,
He has broken a staff, or so: so, let it pass.
Thai. To me he seems like diamond to glass.
Per. Yond' king 's to me like to my father's picture,
Which tells me in that glory once he was;
Had princes sit, like stars, about his throne,
And he the sun for them to reverence.
None that beheld him, but like lesser lights
Did vail their crowns to his supremacy;
Where now his son, like a glow-worm in the night,
The which hath fire in darkness, none in light:
Whereby I see that Time 's the king of men;
He 's both their parent, and he is their grave,
And gives them what he will, not what they crave.
Sim. What! are you merry, knights?
1 *Knight.* Who can be other, in this royal presence?
Sim. Here, with a cup that 's stor'd unto the brim,
(As you do love, fill to your mistress' lips)
We drink this health to you.
Knights. We thank your grace.
Sim. Yet pause a while;
Yond' knight doth sit too melancholy,
As if the entertainment in our court,
Had not a show might countervail his worth.
Note it not you, Thaisa?
Thai. What is it
To me, my father?
Sim. O! attend, my daughter:
Princes, in this, should live like gods above,
Who freely give to every one that comes
To honour them; and princes, not doing so,
Are like to gnats, which make a sound, but kill'd
Are wonder'd at. Therefore,
To make his entrance more sweet, here say,
We drink this standing-bowl of wine to him.
Thai. Alas, my father! it befits not me
Unto a stranger knight to be so bold:
He may my proffer take for an offence,
Since men take women's gifts for impudence.
Sim. How!
Do as I bid you, or you 'll move me else.

Thai. [*Aside.*] Now, by the gods, he could not please me better.

Sim. And farther tell him, we desire to know,
Of whence he is, his name, and parentage.

Thai. The king my father, sir, has drunk to you.

Per. I thank him.

Thai. Wishing it so much blood unto your life.

Per. I thank both him and you, and pledge him freely.

Thai. And, farther, he desires to know of you,
Of whence you are, your name and parentage.

Per. A gentleman of Tyre (my name, Pericles,
My education been in arts and arms)
Who looking for adventures in the world,
Was by the rough seas reft of ships and men,
And after shipwreck driven upon this shore.

Thai. He thanks your grace; names himself Pericles,
A gentleman of Tyre,
Who only by misfortune of the seas
Bereft of ships and men, cast on the shore.

Sim. Now by the gods, I pity his misfortune,
And will awake him from his melancholy.
Come, gentlemen, we sit too long on trifles,
And waste the time which looks for other revels
Even in your armours, as you are address'd,
Will very well become a soldier's dance.
I will not have excuse, with saying, this
Loud music is too harsh for ladies' heads,
Since they love men in arms, as well as beds
[*The Knights dance*
So, this was well ask'd, 't was so well perform'd.
Come, sir;
Here is a lady that wants breathing too:
And I have often heard, you knights of Tyre
Are excellent in making ladies trip,
And that their measures are as excellent.

Per. In those that practise them, they are, my lord.

Sim. O! that 's as much, as you would be denied
[*The Knights and Ladies dance.*
Of your fair courtesy.—Unclasp, unclasp:
Thanks, gentlemen, to all; all have done well, [duct
But you the best. [*To* PERICLES.] Pages and lights, to con-
These knights unto their several lodgings!—Yours, sir,
We have given order to be next our own.

Per. I am at your grace's pleasure.

Sim. Princes, it is too late to talk of love,
And that 's the mark I know you level at:
Therefore, each one betake him to his rest;
To-morrow all for speeding do their best. [*Exeunt.*

SCENE IV.—Tyre. A Room in the Governor's House.

Enter HELICANUS *and* ESCANES.

Hel. No, Escanes; know this of me,
Antiochus from incest liv'd not free:
For which the most high gods, not minding longer
To withhold the vengeance, that they had in store,
Due to this heinous capital offence,
Even in the height and pride of all his glory,
When he was seated, and his daughter with him,
In a chariot of inestimable value,
A fire from heaven came, and shrivell'd up
Those bodies, even to loathing; for they so stunk,
That all those eyes ador'd them ere their fall,
Scorn now their hand should give them burial.
Esca. 'T was very strange.
Hel. And yet but just; for though
This king were great, his greatness was no guard
To bar heaven's shaft, but sin had his reward.
Esca. 'T is very true.

Enter Three Lords.

1 *Lord.* See! not a man, in private conference
Or council, has respect with him but he.
2 *Lord.* It shall no longer grieve without reproof.
3 *Lord.* And curs'd be he that will not second it.
1 *Lord.* Follow me, then.—Lord Helicane, a word.
Hel. With me? and welcome.—Happy day, my lords.
1 *Lord.* Know, that our griefs are risen to the top,
And now at length they overflow their banks.
Hel. Your griefs! for what? wrong not the prince you love.
1 *Lord.* Wrong not yourself, then, noble Helicane;
But if the prince do live, let us salute him,
Or know what ground 's made happy by his breath.
If in the world he live, we 'll seek him out;
If in his grave he rest, we 'll find him there;
And be resolved, he lives to govern us,
Or dead, gives cause to mourn his funeral,
And leaves us to our free election.

2 *Lord.* Whose death 's, indeed, the strongest in our censure:
And knowing this kingdom is without a head,
Like goodly buildings left without a roof,
Soon fall to ruin, your noble self,
That best know'st how to rule, and how to reign,
We thus submit unto, our sovereign.

All. Live, noble Helicane!

Hel. Try[1] honour's cause; forbear your suffrages:
If that you love prince Pericles, forbear.
Take I your wish, I leap into the seas,
Where 's hourly trouble for a minute's ease.
A twelvemonth longer, let me entreat you
To forbear the absence of your king;
If in which time expir'd he not return,
I shall with aged patience bear your yoke.
But if I cannot win you to this love,
Go search like nobles, like noble subjects,
And in your search spend your adventurous worth;
Whom if you find, and win unto return,
You shall like diamonds sit about his crown.

1 *Lord.* To wisdom he 's a fool that will not yield:
And since lord Helicane enjoineth us,
We with our travels will endeavour.

Hel. Then, you love us, we you, and we 'll clasp hands:
When peers thus knit a kingdom ever stands. [*Exeunt.*

SCENE V.—Pentapolis. A Room in the Palace.

Enter SIMONIDES, *reading a Letter: the Knights meet him.*

1 *Knight.* Good morrow to the good Simonides.

Sim. Knights, from my daughter this I let you know:
That for this twelvemonth she 'll not undertake
A married life.
Her reason to herself is only known,
Which yet from her by no means can I get.

2 *Knight.* May we not get access to her, my lord?

Sim. 'Faith, by no means: she hath so strictly tied her
To her chamber, that it is impossible.
One twelve moons more she 'll wear Diana's livery;
This by the eye of Cynthia hath she vow'd,
And on her virgin honour will not break it.

[1] Dyce reads: For.

3 *Knight.* Though loath to bid farewell, we take our
leaves. [*Exeunt.*
Sim. So,
They 're well despatch'd ; now to my daughter's letter.
She tells me here, she 'll wed the stranger knight,
Or never more to view nor day nor light.
'T is well, mistress ; your choice agrees with mine ;
I like that well :—nay, how absolute she 's in 't,
Not minding whether I dislike or no.
Well, I commend her choice,
And will no longer have it be delay'd.
Soft ! here he comes : I must dissemble it.

Enter PERICLES.

Per. All fortune to the good Simonides !
Sim. To you as much, sir. I am beholding to you
For your sweet music this last night : I do
Protest, my ears were never better fed
With such delightful pleasing harmony.
Per. It is your grace's pleasure to commend,
Not my desert.
Sim. Sir, you are music's master.
Per. The worst of all her scholars, my good lord.
Sim. Let me ask one thing.
What do you think of my daughter, sir ?
Per. As of a most virtuous princess.
Sim. And she is fair too, is she not ?
Per. As a fair day in summer ; wondrous fair.
Sim. My daughter, sir, thinks very well of you ;
Ay, so well, sir, that you must be her master,
And she 'll your scholar be : therefore, look to it.
Per. I am unworthy for her schoolmaster.
Sim. She thinks not so ; peruse this writing else.
Per. [*Aside.*] What 's here ?
A letter, that she loves the knight of Tyre ?
'T is the king's subtilty, to have my life.
[*To him.*] O ! seek not to entrap me, gracious lord,
A stranger and distressed gentleman.
That never aim'd so high to love your daughter,
But bent all offices to honour her.
Sim. Thou hast bewitch'd my daughter, and thou art
A villain.
Per. By the gods, I have not.
Never did thought of mine levy offence ;
Nor never did my actions yet commence
A deed might gain her love, or your displeasure.

Sim. Traitor, thou liest.
Per. Traitor!
Sim. Ay, traitor.
Per. Even in his throat, unless it be the king,
That calls me traitor, I return the lie.
Sim. [*Aside.*] Now, by the gods, I do applaud his courage.
Per. My actions are as noble as my thoughts,
That never relish'd of a base descent.
I came unto your court for honour's cause,
And not to be a rebel to her state;
And he that otherwise accounts of me,
This sword shall prove he 's honour's enemy.
Sim. No!—
Here comes my daughter, she can witness it.

Enter THAISA.

Per. Then, as you are as virtuous as fair,
Resolve your angry father, if my tongue
Did e'er solicit, or my hand subscribe
To any syllable that made love to you?
Thai. Why, sir, if you had,
Who takes offence at that would make me glad?
Sim. Yea, mistress, are you so peremptory?—
[*Aside.*] I am glad on 't with all my heart.
[*To her.*] I 'll tame you; I 'll bring you in subjection.
Will you, not having my consent,
Bestow your love and your affections
Upon a stranger? [*Aside.*] who, for aught I know,
May be, (nor can I think the contrary)
As great in blood as I myself.
[*To her.*] Therefore, hear you, mistress; either frame
Your will to mine; and you, sir, hear you,
Either be rul'd by me, or I will make you—
Man and wife.—Nay, come; your hands,
And lips must seal it too;
And being join'd, I 'll thus your hopes destroy,
And for farther grief,—God give you joy!—
What, are you both pleas'd?
Thai. Yes, if you love me, sir
Per. Even as my life, my blood that fosters it.
Sim. What! are you both agreed?
Both. Yes, if 't please your majesty.
Sim. It pleaseth me so well I 'll see you wed;
Then, with what haste you can, get you to bed.
[*Exeunt.*

ACT III.

Enter GOWER.

Gow. Now sleep yslaked hath the rout;
No din but snores the house about,
Made louder by the o'er-fed breast
Of this most pompous marriage feast.
The cat with eyne of burning coal,
Now couches 'fore the mouse's hole:
And crickets sing at the oven's mouth,
Are the blither for their drouth.
Hymen hath brought the bride to bed,
Where, by the loss of maidenhead,
A babe is moulded.—Be attent,
And time that is so briefly spent,
With your fine fancies quaintly eche[1];
What 's dumb in show, I 'll plain with speech.

Dumb Show.

Enter PERICLES *and* SIMONIDES *at one door, with Attendants; a Messenger meets them, kneels, and gives* PERICLES *a Letter:* PERICLES *shows it to* SIMONIDES; *the Lords kneel to* PERICLES. *Then, enter* THAISA *with child, and* LYCHORIDA: SIMONIDES *shows his Daughter the Letter; she rejoices: she and* PERICLES *take leave of her Father, and all depart.*

Gow. By many a dern and painful perch
Of Pericles the careful search
By the four opposing coignes,
Which the world together joins,
Is made, with all due diligence,
That horse, and sail, and high expence,
Can stand the quest. At last from Tyre
(Fame answering the most strange inquire,)
To the court of king Simonides
Are letters brought, the tenour these:—
Antiochus and his daughter dead.
The men of Tyrus on the head
Of Helicanus would set on
The crown of Tyre but he will none:
The mutiny he there hastes t' oppress;

[1] *Eke*

Says to them, if king Pericles
Come not home in twice six moons,
He, obedient to their dooms,
Will take the crown. The sum of this,
Brought hither to Pentapolis,
Yravished the regions round,
And every one with claps 'gan sound,
"Our heir apparent is a king!
Who dream'd, who thought of such a thing?"
Brief, he must hence depart to Tyre:
His queen, with child, makes her desire
(Which who shall cross?) along to go.
Omit we all their dole and woe:
Lychorida, her nurse, she takes,
And so to sea. Then, vessel shakes
On Neptune's billow; half the flood
Hath their keel cut; but fortune's mood
Varies again: the grizzly north
Disgorges such a tempest forth
That, as a duck for life that dives,
So up and down the poor ship drives.
The lady shrieks, and well-a-near,
Does fall in travail with her fear:
And what ensues in this self storm
Shall for itself itself perform.
I nill relate, action may
Conveniently the rest convey,
Which might not what by me is told.
In your imagination hold
This stage the ship, upon whose deck
The seas-tost Pericles appears to speak. [*Exit.*

SCENE I.

Enter PERICLES, *on shipboard.*

Per. Thou God of this great vast, rebuke these surges,
Which wash both heaven and hell; and thou, that hast
Upon the winds command, bind them in brass,
Having call'd them from the deep. O! still
Thy deafening, dreadful thunders; duly[1] quench
Thy nimble, sulphurous flashes!—O! how, Lychorida,
How does my queen?—Thou storm, venomously
Wilt thou spit all thyself?—The seaman's whistle

[1] daily: in old copies.

Is as a whisper in the ears of death,
Unheard.—Lychorida!—Lucina, O!
Divinest patroness and midwife, gentle
To those that cry by night, convey thy deity
Aboard our dancing boat; make swift the pangs
Of my queen's travails!—Now, Lychorida——

Enter LYCHORIDA, *with an Infant.*

Lyc. Here is a thing too young for such a place,
Who, if it had conceit, would die as I
Am like to do. Take in your arms this piece
Of your dead queen.

Per. How! how, Lychorida!

Lyc. Patience, good sir; do not assist the storm.
Here 's all that is left living of your queen,
A little daughter: for the sake of it,
Be manly, and take comfort.

Per. O you gods!
Why do you make us love your goodly gifts,
And snatch them straight away? We, here below,
Recall not what we give, and therein may
Use honour with you.

Lyc. Patience, good sir,
Even for this charge.

Per. Now, mild may be thy life;
For a more blust'rous birth had never babe:
Quiet and gentle thy conditions;
For thou 'rt the rudeliest welcome to this world,
That e'er was prince's child. Happy what follows!
Thou hast as chiding a nativity,
As fire, air, water, earth, and heaven can make,
To herald thee from the womb: even at the first,
Thy loss is more than can thy portage quit,
With all thou canst find here.—Now the good gods
Throw their best eyes upon it!

Enter Two Sailors.

1 *Sail.* What, courage, sir! God save you.

Per. Courage enough. I do not fear the flaw[1];
It hath done to me the worst: yet, for the love
Of this poor infant, this fresh new sea-farer,
I would it would be quiet.

1 *Sail.* Slack the bowlines there; thou wilt not wilt thou?—Blow, and split thyself.

[1] *Blast.*

2 *Sail.* But sea-room, an the brine and cloudy billow kiss the moon, I care not.

1 *Sail.* Sir, your queen must overboard; the sea works high, the wind is loud, and will not lie till the ship be cleared of the dead.

Per. That 's your superstition.

1 *Sail.* Pardon us, sir; with us at sea it hath been still observed, and we are strong in earnest.[1] Therefore briefly yield her, for she must overboard straight.

Per. As you think meet.—Most wretched queen!

Lyc. Here she lies, sir.

Per. A terrible child-bed hast thou had, my dear;
No light, no fire: the unfriendly elements
Forgot thee utterly; nor have I time
To give thee hallow'd to thy grave, but straight
Must cast thee, scarcely coffin'd, in the ooze;
Where, for a monument upon thy bones,
And aye[2]-remaining lamps, the belching whale,
And humming water must o'erwhelm thy corpse,
Lying with simple shells.—O Lychorida!
Bid Nestor bring me spices, ink and paper,
My casket and my jewels; and bid Nicander
Bring me the satin coffer[3]: lay the babe
Upon the pillow. Hie thee, whiles I say
A priestly farewell to her: suddenly, woman.
[*Exit* LYCHORIDA.

2 *Sail.* Sir, we have a chest beneath the hatches, caulk'd and bitumed ready.

Per. I thank thee. Mariner, say what coast is this?

2 *Sail.* We are near Tharsus.

Per. Thither, gentle mariner,
Alter thy course for Tyre. When canst thou reach it?

2 *Sail.* By break of day, if the wind cease.

Per. O! make for Tharsus.—
There will I visit Cleon, for the babe
Cannot hold out to Tyrus: there I 'll leave it
At careful nursing.—Go thy ways, good mariner:
I'll bring the body presently. [*Exeunt.*

[1] eastern: in old copies. M. Mason made the change Boswell reads: custom. [2] ayre: in old copies. Malone made the change. [3] coffin: in old copies.

SCENE II.—Ephesus. A Room in CERIMON'S House.

Enter CERIMON, *a Servant, and some Persons who have been Shipwrecked.*

Cer. Philemon, ho!

Enter PHILEMON.

Phil. Doth my lord call?

Cer. Get fire and meat for these poor men:
It has been a turbulent and stormy night.

Serv. I have been in many; but such a night as this,
Till now I ne'er endur'd.

Cer. Your master will be dead ere you return:
There 's nothing can be minister'd to nature,
That can recover him. Give this to the 'pothecary,
And tell me how it works. [*To* PHILEMON.

[*Exeunt* PHILEMON, *Servant, and the rest.*

Enter Two Gentlemen.

1 *Gent.* Good morrow, sir.

2 *Gent.* Good morrow to your lordship.

Cer. Gentlemen,
Why do you stir so early?

1 *Gent.* Sir,
Our lodgings, standing bleak upon the sea,
Shook, as the earth did quake;
The very principals did seem to rend,
And all to topple. Pure surprise and fear
Made me to quit the house.

2 *Gent.* This is the cause we trouble you so early;
'T is not our husbandry.

Cer. O! you say well.

1 *Gent.* But I much marvel that your lordship, having
Rich tire about you, should at these early hours
Shake off the golden slumber of repose.
'T is most strange,
Nature should be so conversant with pain,
Being thereto not compell'd.

Cer. I hold it ever,
Virtue and cunning[1] were endowments greater
Than nobleness and riches: careless heirs
May the two latter darken and expend;
But immortality attends the former,
Making a man a god. 'T is known, I ever

[1] *Knowledge.*

Have studied physic, through which secret art,
By turning o'er authorities, I have
(Together with my practice) made familiar
To me and to my aid, the blest infusions
That dwell in vegetives, in metals, stones;
And can speak of the disturbances that nature
Works, and of her cures; which doth give me
A more content, in course of true delight,
Than to be thirsty after tottering honour,
Or tie my treasure up in silken bags,
To please the fool and death.

2 *Gent.* Your honour has through Ephesus pour'd forth
Your charity, and hundreds call themselves
Your creatures, who by you have been restor'd:
And not your knowledge, your personal pain, but even
Your purse, still open, hath built lord Cerimon
Such strong renown as time shall never—

Enter Two Servants with a Chest.

Serv. So; lift there.

Cer. What is that?

Serv. Sir, even now
Did the sea toss upon our shores this chest:
'T is of some wreck.

Cer. Set it down; let's look upon 't.

2 *Gent.* 'T is like a coffin, sir.

Cer. Whate'er it be,
'T is wondrous heavy. Wrench it open straight:
If the sea's stomach be o'ercharg'd with gold,
'T is a good constraint of fortune it belches upon us.

2 *Gent.* 'T is so, my lord.

Cer. How close 't is caulk'd and bitum'd.
Did the sea cast it up?

Serv. I never saw so huge a billow, sir,
As toss'd it upon shore.

Cer. Come, wrench it open.
Soft, soft! it smells most sweetly in my sense.

2 *Gent.* A delicate odour.

Cer. As ever hit my nostril. So, up with it.
O, you most potent gods! what 's here? a corse?

1 *Gent.* Most strange!

Cer. Shrouded in cloth of state; balm'd and entreasured
With full bags of spices! A passport too:

Apollo, perfect me i' the characters! [*Unfolds a Scroll.*
"Here I give to understand, [Reads.
(If e'er this coffin drive a-land)
I, king Pericles, have lost
This queen, worth all our mundane cost.
Who finds her, give her burying;
She was the daughter of a king:
Besides this treasure for a fee,
The gods requite his charity!"
If thou liv'st, Pericles, thou hast a heart
That even cracks for woe!—This chanc'd to-night.

2 *Gent.* Most likely, sir.

Cer. Nay, certainly to-night;
For look, how fresh she looks.—They were too rough,
That threw her in the sea. Make fire within:
Fetch hither all the boxes in my closet.
Death may usurp on nature many hours,
And yet the fire of life kindle again
The overpressed spirits. I heard
Of an Egyptian, that had nine hours lien dead,
Who was by good appliance recovered.

Enter a Servant, with Boxes, Napkins, and Fire.

Well said, well said; the fire and the cloths.—
The rough and woful music that we have,
Cause it to sound, 'beseech you.
The vial once more:—how thou stirr'st, thou block!—
The music there!—I pray you, give her air.
Gentlemen,
This queen will live: nature awakes a warm
Breath out of her: she hath not been entranc'd
Above five hours. See, how she 'gins to blow
Into life's flower again!

1 *Gent.* The heavens
Through you increase our wonder, and set up
Your fame for ever.

Cer. She is alive! behold,
Her eyelids, cases to those heavenly jewels
Which Pericles hath lost,
Begin to part their fringes of bright gold:
The diamonds of a most praised water
Do appear to make the world twice rich. Live,
And make us weep to hear your fate, fair creature,
Rare as you seem to be! [*She moves*

Thai. O dear Diana!

Where am I? Where 's my lord? What world is this?
2 *Gent.* Is not this strange?
1 *Gent.* Most rare.
Cer. Hush, gentle neighbours!
Lend me your hands; to the next chamber bear her.
Get linen: now this matter must be look'd to,
For her relapse is mortal. Come, come;
And Æsculapius guide us!
[*Exeunt, carrying* THAISA *out.*

SCENE III.—Tharsus. A Room in CLEON'S House.

Enter PERICLES, CLEON, DIONYZA, LYCHORIDA, *and* MARINA.

Per. Most honour'd Cleon, I must needs be gone:
My twelve months are expir'd, and Tyrus stands
In a litigious peace. You, and your lady,
Take from my heart all thankfulness; the gods
Make up the rest upon you!
Cle. Your shafts[1] of fortune, though they hurt[2] you [mortally,
Yet glance full wanderingly[3] on us.
Dion. O, your sweet queen!
That the strict fates had pleas'd you had brought her [hither,
To have bless'd mine eyes!
Per. We cannot but obey
The powers above us. Could I rage and roar
As doth the sea she lies in, yet the end
Must be as 't is. My gentle babe Marina (whom,
For she was born at sea, I have nam'd so) here
I charge your charity withal, and leave her
The infant of your care; beseeching you
To give her princely training, that she may
Be manner'd as she is born.
Cle. Fear not, my lord, but think
Your grace, that fed my country with your corn,
(For which the people's prayers still fall upon you)
Must in your child be thought on. If neglection
Should therein make me vile, the common body,
By you reliev'd, would force me to my duty;
But if to that my nature need a spur,
The gods revenge it upon me and mine,
To the end of generation.
Per. I believe you;

[1] shakes: [2] haunt: [3] wondringly: in old copies. Steevens made the changes.

Your honour and your goodness teach me to 't,
Without your vows. Till she be married, madam,
By bright Diana, whom we honour all,
Unscissar'd shall this hair of mine remain,
Though I show will[1] in 't. So I take my leave.
Good madam, make me blessed in your care
In bringing up my child.

Dion. I have one myself,
Who shall not be more dear to my respect,
Than yours, my lord.

Per. Madam, my thanks and prayers.

Cle. We 'll bring your grace even to the edge o' the shore;
Then give you up to the mask'd Neptune, and
The gentlest winds of heaven.

Per. I will embrace
Your offer. Come, dear'st madam.—O! no tears,
Lychorida, no tears:
Look to your little mistress, on whose grace
You may depend hereafter.—Come, my lord. [*Exeunt.*

SCENE IV.—Ephesus. A Room in CERIMON's House.

Enter CERIMON *and* THAISA.

Cer. Madam, this letter, and some certain jewels,
Lay with you in your coffer, which are
At your command. Know you the character?

Thai. It is my lord's.
That I was shipp'd at sea, I well remember,
Even on my yearning time; but whether there
Delivered or no, by the holy gods,
I cannot rightly say. But since king Pericles,
My wedded lord, I ne'er shall see again,
A vestal livery will I take me to,
And never more have joy.

Cer. Madam, if this you purpose as you speak,
Diana's temple is not distant far,
Where you may abide till your date expire.
Moreover, if you please, a niece of mine
Shall there attend you.

Thai. My recompense is thanks, that 's all;
Yet my good will is great, though the gift small. [*Exeunt.*

[1] Dyce reads: ill.

ACT IV.

Enter GOWER.

Gow. Imagine Pericles arriv'd at Tyre,
Welcom'd and settled to his own desire·
His woful queen we leave at Ephesus,
Unto Diana there a votaress.
Now to Marina bend your mind,
Whom our fast-growing scene must find
At Tharsus, and by Cleon train'd
In music, letters; who hath gain'd
Of education all the grace,
Which makes her both the heart and place
Of general wonder. But alack!
That monster envy, oft the wrack
Of earnest praise, Marina's life
Seeks to take off by treason's knife.
And in this kind hath our Cleon
One daughter, and a wench full grown,
Even ripe for marriage rite:[1] this maid
Hight Philoten; and it is said
For certain in our story, she
Would ever with Marina be:
Be 't when she weav'd the sleided[2] silk
With fingers, long, small, white as milk;
Or when she would with sharp needle wound
The cambric, which she made more sound
By hurting it; or when to the lute
She sung, and made the night-bird mute,
That still records with moan; or when
She would with rich and constant pen
Vail to her mistress Dian; still
This Philoten contends in skill
With absolute Marina: so
With the dove of Paphos might the crow
Vie feathers white. Marina gets
All praises, which are paid as debts,
And not as given. This so darks
In Philoten all graceful marks,
That Cleon's wife, with envy rare,
A present murderer does prepare

[1] sight: in old copies. [2] *Raw.*

For good Marina, that her daughter
Might stand peerless by this slaughter.
The sooner her vile thoughts to stead,
Lychorida, our nurse, is dead:
And cursed Dionyza hath
The pregnant instrument of wrath
Prest[1] for this blow. The unborn event
I do commend to your content:
Only I carried winged time
Post on the lame feet of my rhyme;
Which never could I so convey,
Unless your thoughts went on my way.—
Dionyza doth appear,
With Leonine, a murderer. [*Exit.*

SCENE I.—Tharsus. An open Place near the Sea-shore.

Enter DIONYZA *and* LEONINE.

Dion. Thy oath remember; thou hast sworn to do 't:
'T is but a blow, which never shall be known.
Thou canst not do a thing i' the world so soon,
To yield thee so much profit. Let not conscience,
Which is but cold, inflaming love in thy bosom,
Inflame too nicely; nor let pity, which
Even women have cast off, melt thee, but be
A soldier to thy purpose.

Leon. I 'll do 't: but yet she is a goodly creature.

Dion. The fitter then the gods should have her. Here
She comes weeping for her old nurse's[2] death.
Thou art resolv'd?

Leon. I am resolv'd.

Enter MARINA, *with a Basket of Flowers.*

Mar. No, I will rob Tellus of her weed,
To strew thy grave[3] with flowers: the yellows, blues,
The purple violets, and marigolds,
Shall, as a carpet, hang upon thy grave,
While summer days do last. Ah me, poor maid!
Born in a tempest, when my mother died,
This world to me is like a lasting storm,
Whirring me from my friends.

Dion. How now, Marina! why do you weep[4] alone?
How chance my daughter is not with you? Do not

[1] *Ready.* [2] onely mistresse: in old copies. [3] green: in old copies.
[4] Some editions read: keep.

Consume your blood with sorrowing: you have
A nurse of me. Lord! how your favour 's[1] chang'd
With this unprofitable woe. Come, come;
Give me your flowers, ere the sea mar it.
Walk with Leonine; the air is quick there,
And it pierces and sharpens the stomach. Come,
Leonine, take her by the arm, walk with her.

Mar. No, I pray you;
I 'll not bereave you of your servant.

Dion. Come, come;
I love the king your father, and yourself,
With more than foreign heart. We every day
Expect him here: when he shall come, and find
Our paragon to all reports thus blasted,
He will repent the breadth of his great voyage;
Blame both my lord and me, that we have taken
No care to your best courses. Go, I pray you;
Walk, and be cheerful once again: reserve
That excellent complexion, which did steal
The eyes of young and old. Care not for me;
I can go home alone.

Mar. Well, I will go;
But yet I have no desire to it.

Dion. Come, come, I know 't is good for you.—
Walk half an hour, Leonine, at least.
Remember what I have said.

Leon. I warrant you, madam.

Dion. I 'll leave you, my sweet lady, for a while.
Pray you walk softly, do not heat your blood:
What! I must have care of you.

Mar. Thanks, sweet madam.—[*Exit* DIONYZA.
Is the wind westerly that blows?

Leon. South-west.

Mar. When I was born, the wind was north.

Leon. Was 't so?

Mar. My father, as nurse said, did never fear,
But cry'd "good seamen!" to the sailors, galling
His kingly hands hauling ropes;
And, clasping to the mast, endur'd a sea
That almost burst the deck.

Leon. When was this?

Mar. When I was born:
Never were waves nor wind more violent;

[1] *Face*

And from the ladder-tackle washes off
A canvass-climber. "Ha!" says one, "wilt out?"
And with a dropping industry they skip
From stem to stern: the boatswain whistles, and
The master calls, and trebles their confusion.

Leon. Come; say your prayers.

Mar. What mean you?

Leon. If you require a little space for prayer,
I grant it. Pray; but be not tedious,
For the gods are quick of ear, and I am sworn
To do my work with haste.

Mar. Why will you kill me?

Leon. To satisfy my lady.

Mar. Why would she have me kill'd?
Now as I can remember, by my troth
I never did her hurt in all my life.
I never spake bad word, nor did ill turn
To any living creature: believe me, la,
I never kill'd a mouse, nor hurt a fly:
I trod upon a worm against my will,
But I wept for it. How have I offended,
Wherein my death might yield her profit, or
My life imply her any danger?

Leon. My commission
Is not to reason of the deed, but do it.

Mar. You will not do 't for all the world, I hope.
You are well favour'd, and your looks foreshow
You have a gentle heart. I saw you lately,
When you caught hurt in parting two that fought:
Good sooth, it show'd well in you: do so now:
Your lady seeks my life; come you between,
And save poor me, the weaker.

Leon. I am sworn,
And will despatch.

Enter Pirates, whilst MARINA *is struggling.*

1 *Pirate.* Hold, villain! [LEONINE *runs away.*

2 *Pirate.* A prize! a prize!

3 *Pirate.* Half-part, mates, half-part. Come, let's have her aboard suddenly. [*Exeunt Pirates with* MARINA.

SCENE II.—Near the Same.

Enter LEONINE.

Leon. These roguing thieves serve the great pirate
Valdes;
And they have seiz'd Marina. Let her go:
There 's no hope she 'll return. I 'll swear she 's dead,
And thrown into the sea.—But I 'll see farther;
Perhaps they will but please themselves upon her,
Not carry her aboard. If she remain,
Whom they have ravish'd must by me be slain. [*Exit.*

SCENE III.—Mitylene. A Room in a Brothel.

Enter Pander, Bawd, and BOULT.

Pand. Boult.

Boult. Sir.

Pand. Search the market narrowly; Mitylene is full of gallants: we lost too much money this mart, by being too wenchless.

Bawd. We were never so much out of creatures. We have but poor three, and they can do no more than they can do; and they with continual action are even as good as rotten.

Pand. Therefore, let 's have fresh ones, whate'er we pay for them. If there be not a conscience to be used in every trade, we shall never prosper.

Bawd. Thou say'st true: 't is not the bringing up of poor bastards, as I think, I have brought up some eleven——

Boult. Ay, to eleven; and brought them down again. But shall I search the market?

Bawd. What else, man? The stuff we have, a strong wind will blow it to pieces, they are so pitifully sodden.

Pand. Thou say'st true; they 're too unwholesome o' conscience The poor Transilvanian is dead, that lay with the little baggage.

Boult. Ay, she quickly pooped him; she made him roast-meat for worms. But I 'll go search the market. [*Exit* BOULT.

Pand. Three or four thousand chequins were as pretty a proportion to live quietly, and so give over.

Bawd. Why, to give over, I pray you? is it a shame to get when we are old?

Pand. O! our credit comes not in like the commodity; nor the commodity wages not with the danger: therefore, if in our youths we could pick up some pretty estate, 't were not amiss to keep our door hatched. Besides, the sore terms we stand upon with the gods will be strong with us for giving over.

Bawd. Come; other sorts offend as well as we.

Pand. As well as we? ay, and better too; we offend worse. Neither is our profession any trade; it 's no calling. But here comes Boult.

Enter BOULT, *and the Pirates with* MARINA.

Boult. Come your ways. My masters, you say she 's a virgin?

1 *Pirate.* O, sir! we doubt it not.

Boult. Master, I have gone thorough for this piece, you see: if you like her, so; if not, I have lost my earnest.

Bawd. Boult, has she any qualities?

Boult. She has a good face, speaks well, and has excellent good clothes: there 's no farther necessity of qualities can make her be refused.

Bawd. What 's her price, Boult?

Boult. I cannot be bated one doit of a thousand pieces.

Pand. Well, follow me, my masters, you shall have your money presently. Wife, take her in: instruct her what she has to do, that she may not be raw in her entertainment. [*Exeunt Pander and Pirates.*

Bawd. Boult, take you the marks of her: the colour of her hair, complexion, height, her age, with warrant of her virginity, and cry, "He that will give most, shall have her first." Such a maidenhead were no cheap thing, if men were as they have been. Get this done as I command you.

Boult. Performance shall follow. [*Exit* BOULT.

Mar. Alack, that Leonine was so slack, so slow!
He should have struck, not spoke; or that these pirates,
(Not enough barbarous) had not o'erboard thrown me
For to seek my mother!

Bawd. Why lament you, pretty one?

Mar. That I am pretty.

Bawd. Come, the gods have done their part in you.

Mar. I accuse them not.

Bawd. You are lit into my hands, where you are like to live.

Mar. The more my fault,[1]
To 'scape his hands where I was like to die.

Bawd. Ay, and you shall live in pleasure.

Mar. No.

Bawd. Yes, indeed, shall you, and taste gentlemen of all fashions. You shall fare well: you shall have the difference of all complexions. What! do you stop your ears?

Mar. Are you a woman?

Bawd. What would you have me be, an I be not a woman?

Mar. An honest woman, or not a woman.

Bawd. Marry, whip thee, gosling: I think I shall have something to do with you. Come, you are a young foolish sapling, and must be bowed as I would have you.

Mar. The gods defend me!

Bawd. If it please the gods to defend you by men, then men must comfort you, men must feed you, men stir you up.—Boult 's returned.

Re-enter BOULT.

Now, sir, hast thou cried her through the market?

Boult. I have cried her almost to the number of her hairs: I have drawn her picture with my voice.

Bawd. And I pr'ythee, tell me, how dost thou find the inclination of the people, especially of the younger sort?

Boult. Faith, they listened to me, as they would have hearkened to their father's testament. There was a Spaniard's mouth so watered, that he went to bed to her very description.

Bawd. We shall have him here to-morrow with his best ruff on.

Boult. To-night, to-night. But, mistress, do you know the French knight that cowers i' the hams?

Bawd. Who? monsieur Veroles?

Boult. Ay: he offered to cut a caper at the proclamation; but he made a groan at it, and swore he would see her to-morrow.

Bawd. Well, well; as for him, he brought his disease hither: here he does but repair it. I know, he will come in our shadow, to scatter his crowns in the sun.

[1] *Misfortune*

Boult. Well, if we had of every nation a traveller, we should lodge them with this sign.

Bawd Pray you, come hither awhile. You have fortunes coming upon you. Mark me: you must seem to do that fearfully, which you commit willingly; to despise profit, where you have most gain. To weep that you live as you do makes pity in your lovers: seldom, but that pity begets you a good opinion, and that opinion a mere[1] profit.

Mar. I understand you not.

Boult. O! take her home, mistress, take her home. these blushes of hers must be quenched with some present practice.

Bawd. Thou say'st true, i' faith, so they must; for your bride goes to that with shame, which is her wa to go with warrant.

Boult. Faith, some do, and some do not. But, mistress, if I have bargained for the joint,—

Bawd. Thou may'st cut a morsel off the spit

Boult. I may so?

Bawd. Who should deny it? Come, young one, I like the manner of your garments well.

Boult. Ay, by my faith, they shall not be changed yet.

Bawd. Boult, spend thou that in the town: report what a sojourner we have; you 'll lose nothing by custom. When nature framed this piece, she meant thee a good turn: therefore, say what a paragon she is, and thou hast the harvest out of thine own report.

Boult. I warrant you, mistress, thunder shall not so awake the beds of eels, as my giving out her beauty stir up the lewdly inclined. I 'll bring home some to-night.

Bawd. Come your ways; follow me.

Mar. If fires be hot, knives sharp, or waters deep,
Untied I still my virgin knot will keep.
Diana, aid my purpose!

Bawd. What have we to do with Diana? Pray you, will you go with us? [*Exeunt.*

SCENE IV.—Tharsus. A Room in CLEON'S House

Enter CLEON *and* DIONYZA.

Dion. Why, are you foolish? Can it be undone?

Cle. O Dionyza! such a piece of slaughter
The sun and moon ne'er look'd upon.

[2] *Absolute.*

Dion. I think,
You 'll turn a child again.
Cle. Were I chief lord of all this spacious world,
I 'd give it to undo the deed. O lady!
Much less in blood than virtue, yet a princess
To equal any single crown o' the earth,
I' the justice of compare! O villain Leonine!
Whom thou hast poison'd too.
If thou hadst drunk to him, it had been a kindness
Becoming well thy face:[1] what canst thou say,
When noble Pericles shall demand his child?
Dion. That she is dead. Nurses are not the fates,
To foster it, nor ever to preserve.
She died at night; I 'll say so. Who can cross it,
Unless you play the pious innocent,
And for an honest attribute, cry out,
"She died by foul play?"
Cle. O! go to. Well, well;
Of all the faults beneath the heavens, the gods
Do like this worst.
Dion. Be one of those, that think
The pretty wrens of Tharsus will fly hence,
And open this to Pericles. I do shame
To think of what a noble strain you are,
And of how coward a spirit.
Cle. To such proceeding
Who ever but his approbation added,
Though not his pre[2]-consent, he did not flow
From honourable courses.
Dion. Be it so, then;
Yet none does know, but you, how she came dead,
Nor none can know, Leonine being gone.
She did disdain[3] my child, and stood between
Her and her fortunes: none would look on her,
But cast their gazes on Marina's face;
Whilst ours was blurted at, and held a malkin,[4]
Not worth the time of day. It pierc'd me thorough;
And though you call my course unnatural,
You not your child well loving, yet I find,
It greets me as an enterprise of kindness,
Perform'd to your sole daughter.
Cle. Heavens forgive it!

[1] Dyce reads: fact. [2] prince: in old copies. [3] Steevens reads: distain. (Sully by contrast.—*Dyce.*) [4] A *low wench.*

Dion. And as for Pericles,
What should he say? We wept after her hearse,
And even yet we mourn: her monument
Is almost finish'd, and her epitaphs
In glittering golden characters express
A general praise to her, and care in us
At whose expense 't is done.
Cle. Thou art like the harpy,
Which, to betray, doth with thine angel's face,
Seize with thine eagle's talons.
Dion. You are like one, that superstitiously
Doth swear to the gods, that winter kills the flies:
But yet, I know, you 'll do as I advise. [*Exeunt.*

Enter GOWER, *before the Monument of* MARINA *at Tharsus.*[1]

Gow. Thus time we waste, and longest leagues make short;
Sail seas in cockles, have, and wish but for 't;
Making (to take your imagination)
From bourn to bourn, region to region.
By you being pardon'd, we commit no crime
To use one language, in each several clime,
Where our scenes seem to live. I do beseech you,
To learn of me, who stand i' the gaps to teach you,
The stages of our story. Pericles
Is now again thwarting the wayward seas,
Attended on by many a lord and knight,
To see his daughter, all his life's delight.
Old Escanes, whom Helicanus late
Advanc'd in time to great and high estate,
Is left to govern. Bear you it in mind,
Old Helicanus goes along behind.
Well-sailing ships, and bounteous winds, have brought
This king to Tharsus, (think this pilot thought,
So with his steerage shall your thoughts grow on)
To fetch his daughter home, who first is gone.
Like motes and shadows see them move awhile;
Your ears unto your eyes I 'll reconcile.

Dumb show.

Enter PERICLES *with his Train, at one door;* CLEON *and* DIONYZA *at the other.* CLEON *shows* PERICLES

[1] In folio, 1664, in which the Acts are first marked, Act IV. commences

the Tomb of MARINA; *whereat* PERICLES *makes lamentation, puts on Sackcloth, and in a mighty passion departs.*

Gow. See, how belief may suffer by foul show.
The borrow'd passion stands for true old woe;
And Pericles, in sorrow all devour'd,
With sighs shot through, and biggest tears o'er-
show'r'd,
Leaves Tharsus, and again embarks. He swears
Never to wash his face, nor cut his hairs;
He puts on sackcloth, and to sea. He bears
A tempest, which his mortal vessel tears,
And yet he rides it out. Now, please you, wit
The epitaph is for Marina writ
By wicked Dionyza.
"*The fairest, sweet'st, and best, lies here,*
Who wither'd in her spring of year:
She was of Tyrus, the king's daughter,
On whom foul death hath made this slaughter.
Marina was she call'd; and at her birth,
Thetis, being proud, swallow'd some part o' the earth.
Therefore the earth, fearing to be o'erflow'd,
Hath Thetis' birth-child on the heavens bestow'd:
Wherefore she does (and swears she 'll never stint)
Make raging battery upon shores of flint."
No visor does become black villainy,
So well as soft and tender flattery.
Let Pericles believe his daughter 's dead,
And bear his courses to be ordered
By lady fortune; while our scene must play
His daughter's woe and heavy well-a-day,
In her unholy service. Patience then,
And think you now are all in Mitylen. [*Exit.*

SCENE V.—Mitylene. A Street before the Brothel.

Enter from the Brothel, two Gentlemen.

1 *Gent.* Did you ever hear the like?

2 *Gent.* No: nor never shall do in such a place as this, she being once gone.

1 *Gent.* But to have divinity preach'd there, did you ever dream of such a thing?

2 *Gent.* No, no. Come. I am for no more bawdy-houses. Shall we go hear the vestals sing?

1 *Gent.* I 'll do any thing now that is virtuous; but I am out of the road of rutting for ever. [*Exeunt.*

SCENE VI.—The Same. A Room in the Brothel.

Enter Pander, Bawd, and BOULT.

Pand. Well, I had rather than twice the worth of her, she had ne'er come here.

Bawd. Fie, fie upon her! she is able to freeze the god Priapus, and undo a whole generation: we must either get her ravished, or be rid of her. When she should do for clients her fitment, and do me the kindness of our profession, she has me her quirks, her reasons, her master reasons, her prayers, her knees, that she would make a puritan of the devil, if he should cheapen a kiss of her.

Boult. Faith, I must ravish her, or she 'll disfurnish us of all our cavaliers, and make all our swearers priests.

Pand. Now, the pox upon her green-sickness for me!

Bawd. 'Faith, there 's no way to be rid on 't, but by the way to the pox. Here comes the lord Lysimachus, disguised.

Boult. We should have both lord and lown, if the peevish baggage would but give way to customers.

Enter LYSIMACHUS.

Lys. How now! How a dozen of virginities?

Bawd. Now, the gods to-bless your honour!

Boult. I am glad to see your honour in good health.

Lys. You may so; 't is the better for you that your resorters stand upon sound legs. How now, wholesome iniquity! have you that a man may deal withal, and defy the surgeon?

Bawd. We have here one, sir, if she would—but there never came her like in Mitylene.

Lys. If she 'd do the deeds of darkness, thou wouldst say.

Bawd. Your honour knows what 't is to say, well enough.

Lys. Well; call forth, call forth.

Boult. For flesh and blood, sir, white and red, you shall see a rose; and she were a rose indeed, if she had but—

Lys. What, pr'ythee?

Boult. O, sir! I can be modest.

Lys. That dignifies the renown of a bawd, no less than it gives a good report to a number to be chaste.

Enter MARINA.

Bawd. Here comes that which grows to the stalk;—never pluck'd yet, I can assure you.—Is she not a fair creature?

Lys. Faith, she would serve after a long voyage at sea. Well, there 's for you: leave us.

Bawd. I beseech your honour, give me leave: a word, and I 'll have done presently.

Lys. I beseech you, do.

Bawd. First, I would have you note, this is an honourable man. [*To* MARINA.

Mar. I desire to find him so, that I may worthily note him.

Bawd. Next, he 's the governor of this country, and a man whom I am bound to.

Mar. If he govern the country, you are bound to him indeed; but how honourable he is in that, I know not.

Bawd. 'Pray you, without any more virginal fencing, will you use him kindly? He will line your apron with gold.

Mar. What he will do graciously, I will thankfully receive.

Lys. Have you done?

Bawd. My lord, she 's not paced yet; you must take some pains to work her to your manage.—Come, we will leave his honour and her together. Go thy ways.

[*Exeunt Bawd, Pander, and* BOULT.

Lys. Now, pretty one, how long have you been at this trade?

Mar. What trade, sir?

Lys. Why, I cannot name but I shall offend.

Mar. I cannot be offended with my trade. Please you to name it.

Lys. How long have you been of this profession?

Mar. Ever since I can remember.

Lys. Did you go to it so young? Were you a gamester at five, or at seven?

Mar. Earlier too, sir, if now I be one.

Lys. Why, the house you dwell in proclaims you to be a creature of sale.

Mar. Do you know this house to be a place of such resort, and will come into it? I hear say, you are of honourable parts, and are the governor of this place.

Lys. Why, hath your principal made known unto you who I am?

Mar. Who is my principal?

Lys. Why, your herb-woman; she that sets seed and roots of shame and iniquity. O! you have heard something of my power, and so stand aloof for more serious wooing. But I protest to thee, pretty one, my authority shall not see thee, or else, look friendly upon thee. Come, bring me to some private place: come, come.

Mar. If you were born to honour, show it now;
If put upon you, make the judgment good
That thought you worthy of it.

Lys. How 's this? how 's this?—Some more;—be sage.

Mar. For me,
That am a maid, though most ungentle fortune
Hath plac'd me in this sty, where, since I came,
Diseases have been sold dearer than physic,—
That the gods
Would set me free from this unhallow'd place,
Though they did change me to the meanest bird
That flies i' the purer air!

Lys. I did not think
Thou couldst have spoke so well; ne'er dream'd thou couldst.
Had I brought hither a corrupted mind,
Thy speech had alter'd it. Hold, here 's gold for thee:
Persevere in that clear way thou goest,
And the gods strengthen thee.

Mar. The gods preserve you!

Lys. For me, be you thoughten
That I came with no ill intent; for to me
The very doors and windows savour vilely.
Farewell. Thou art a piece of virtue, and
I doubt not but thy training hath been noble.
Hold, here 's more gold for thee.
A curse upon him, die he like a thief,
That robs thee of thy goodness! If thou dost hear
From me, it shall be for thy good.

Enter BOULT.

Boult. I beseech your honour, one piece for me.

Lys. Avaunt, thou damned door-keeper! Your house
But for this virgin that doth prop it, would
Sink, and overwhelm you. Away!

[*Exit* LYSIMACHUS

Boult. How's this? We must take another course with you. If your peevish chastity, which is not worth a breakfast in the cheapest country under the cope,[1] shall undo a whole household, let me be gelded like a spaniel. Come your ways.

Mar. Whither would you have me?

Boult. I must have your maidenhead taken off, or the common hangman shall execute it. Come your way. We'll have no more gentlemen driven away. Come your ways, I say.

Re-enter Bawd.

Bawd. How now! what's the matter?

Boult. Worse and worse, mistress: she has here spoken holy words to the lord Lysimachus.

Bawd. O, abominable!

Boult. She makes our profession as it were to stink afore the face of the gods.

Bawd. Marry, hang her up for ever!

Boult. The nobleman would have dealt with her like a nobleman, and she sent him away as cold as a snowball; saying his prayers, too.

Bawd. Boult, take her away; use her at thy pleasure: crack the glass of her virginity, and make the rest malleable.

Boult. An if she were a thornier piece of ground than she is, she shall be ploughed.

Mar. Hark, hark, you gods!

Bawd. She conjures: away with her. Would she had never come within my doors.—Marry, hang you!—She's born to undo us.—Will you not go the way of women-kind? Marry come up, my dish of chastity with rosemary and bays! [*Exit Bawd.*

Boult. Come, mistress; come your way with me.

Mar. Whither wilt thou have me?

Boult. To take from you the jewel you hold so dear.

Mar. Pr'ythee, tell me one thing first.

Boult. Come now, your one thing.

Mar. What canst thou wish thine enemy to be?

Boult. Why, I could wish him to be my master; or rather, my mistress.

Mar. Neither of these are so bad as thou art,
Since they do better thee in their command.
Thou hold'st a place, for which the pained'st fiend

[1] Cope, or covering of the sky.

Of hell would not in reputation change:
Thou 'rt the damn'd door-keeper to every coystrel[1]
That hither comes inquiring for his Tib;
To the cholerick fisting of each rogue thy ear
Is liable; thy food is such
As hath been belch'd on by infected lungs.

Boult. What would you have me do? go to the wars, would you? where a man may serve seven years for the loss of a leg, and have not money enough in the end to buy him a wooden one?

Mar. Do any thing but this thou doest. Empty
Old receptacles, or common sewers, of filth;
Serve by indenture to the common hangman:
Any of these ways are yet better than this;
For what thou professest, a baboon, could he speak,
Would own a name too dear. That the gods
Would safely deliver me from this place!
Here, here 's gold for thee.
If that thy master would gain by me,
Proclaim that I can sing, weave, sew, and dance,
With other virtues, which I 'll keep from boast;
And I will undertake all these to teach.
I doubt not but this populous city will
Yield many scholars.

Boult. But can you teach all this you speak of?

Mar. Prove that I cannot, take me home again,
And prostitute me to the basest groom
That doth frequent your house.

Boult. Well, I will see what I can do for thee: if I can place thee, I will.

Mar. But, amongst honest women?

Boult. Faith, my acquaintance lies little amongst them. But since my master and mistress have bought you, there 's no going but by their consent; therefore, I will make them acquainted with your purpose, and I doubt not but I shall find them tractable enough. Come; I 'll do for thee what I can: come your ways. [*Exeunt.*

[1] *Low groom.—Dyce.*

ACT V.

Enter GOWER.

Gow. Marina thus the brothel scapes, and chances
Into an honest house, our story says.
She sings like one immortal, and she dances,
As goddess-like, to her admired lays.
Deep clerks she dumbs, and with her needle composes
Nature's own shape, of bud, bird, branch, or berry,
That even her art sisters the natural roses;
Her inkle[1] silk, twin with the rubied cherry:
That pupils lacks she none of noble race,
Who pour their bounty on her; and her gain
She gives the cursed bawd. Here we her place,
And to her father turn our thoughts again,
Where we left him on the sea, tumbled and tost;
And, driven before the winds, he is arriv'd
Here where his daughter dwells: and on this coast
Suppose him now at anchor. The city striv'd
God Neptune's annual feast to keep: from whence
Lysimachus our Tyrian ship espies,
His banners sable, trimm'd with rich expense;
And to him in his barge with fervour hies.
In your supposing once more put your sight;
Of heavy Pericles think this the bark:
Where, what is done in action, more, if might,
Shall be discover'd; please you, sit, and hark. [*Exit.*

SCENE I.—On board PERICLES' Ship, off Mitylene. A Pavilion on deck, with a Curtain before it; PERICLES within it, reclining on a Couch. A Barge lying beside the Tyrian Vessel.

Enter Two Sailors, one belonging to the Tyrian Vessel, the other to the Barge; to them HELICANUS.

Tyr. Sail. Where 's the lord Helicanus? he can resolve you. [*To the Sailor of Mitylene.*
O here he is.—
Sir, there 's a barge put off from Mitylene,
And in it is Lysimachus, the governor,
Who craves to come aboard. What is your will?
Hel. That he have his. Call up some gentlemen.

[1] *Thread.*

Tyr. Sail. Ho, gentlemen! my lord calls.

Enter Two or Three Gentlemen.

1 *Gent.* Doth your lordship call?

Hel. Gentlemen,
There is some of worth would come aboard: I pray
Greet them fairly.

[*Gentlemen and Sailors descend, and go on board the Barge.*

Enter, from thence, LYSIMACHUS *and Lords; the Tyrian Gentlemen, and the Two Sailors.*

Tyr. Sail. Sir,
This is the man that can in aught you would
Resolve you.

Lys. Hail, reverend sir! The gods preserve you!

Hel. And you, sir, to outlive the age I am,
And die as I would do.

Lys. You wish me well.
Being on shore, honouring of Neptune's triumphs,
Seeing this goodly vessel ride before us,
I made to it to know of whence you are.

Hel. First, what is your place?

Lys. I am the governor of this place you lie before.

Hel. Sir,
Our vessel is of Tyre, in it the king;
A man, who for this three months hath not spoken
To any one, nor taken sustenance,
But to prorogue his grief.

Lys. Upon what ground is his distemperature?

Hel. It would be too tedious to repeat;
But the main grief of all springs from the loss
Of a beloved daughter and a wife.

Lys. May we not see him, then?

Hel. You may,
But bootless is your sight; he will not speak
To any.

Lys. Yet, let me obtain my wish.

Hel. Behold him. [PERICLES *discovered.*] This was a goodly person,
Till the disaster that one mortal night
Drove him to this.

Lys. Sir king, all hail! the gods preserve you!
Hail, royal sir!

Hel. It is in vain; he will not speak to you.

1 *Lord.* Sir, we have a maid in Mitylene, I durst wager,
Would win some words of him.

Lys. 'T is well bethought
She, questionless, with her sweet harmony,
And other choice attractions, would allure,
And make a battery through his deafen'd[1] parts,
Which now are midway stopp'd:
She is all happy as the fair'st of all,
And with her fellow maids is now upon
The leafy shelter that abuts against
The island's side.

[*He whispers one of the attendant Lords.—Exit Lord.*

Hel. Sure, all effectless; yet nothing we 'll omit,
That bears recovery's name.
But, since your kindness we have stretch'd thus far,
Let us beseech you,
That for our gold we may provision have,
Wherein we are not destitute for want,
But weary for the staleness.

Lys. O, sir! a courtesy,
Which, if we should deny, the most just God
For every graff would send a caterpillar,
And so afflict[2] our province.—Yet once more
Let me entreat to know at large the cause
Of your king's sorrow.

Hel. Sit, sir, I will recount it to you.—
But see, I am prevented.

Enter Lord, MARINA, *and a young Lady.*

Lys. O! here is
The lady that I sent for. Welcome, fair one!
Is 't not a goodly presence?

Hel. She 's a gallant lady.

Lys. She 's such a one, that were I well assur'd she came
Of gentle kind, and noble stock, I 'd wish
No better choice, and think me rarely wed.—
Fair one, all goodness that consists in bounty
Expect even here, where is a kingly patient:
If that thy prosperous and artificial feat
Can draw him but to answer thee in aught,
Thy sacred physic shall receive such pay
As thy desires can wish.

[1] defended: in old copies. [2] inflict: in old copies.

Mar. Sir, I will use
My utmost skill in his recovery,
Provided none but I and my companion
Be suffer'd to come near him.
Lys. Come, let us leave her;
And the gods make her prosperous! [MARINA *sings.*
Lys. Mark'd he your music?
Mar. No, nor look'd on us
Lys. See, she will speak to him.
Mar. Hail, sir! my lord, lend ear.—
Per. Hum! ha!
Mar. I am a maid,
My lord, that ne'er before invited eyes,
But have been gaz'd on like a comet: she speaks,
My lord, that may be, hath endur'd a grief
Might equal yours, if both were justly weigh'd.
Though wayward fortune did malign my state,
My derivation was from ancestors
Who stood equivalent with mighty kings;
But time hath rooted out my parentage,
And to the world and awkward casualties
Bound me in servitude.—I will desist;
But there is something glows upon my cheek,
And whispers in mine ear, "Go not till he speak."
Per. My fortunes—parentage—good parentage—
To equal mine!—was it not thus? what say you?
Mar. I said, my lord, if you did know my parentage,
You would not do me violence.
Per. I do think so.
I pray you, turn your eyes again upon me.—
You are like something that—What countrywoman?
Here of these shores?
Mar. No, nor of any shores;
Yet I was mortally brought forth, and am
No other than I appear.
Per. I am great with woe, and shall deliver weeping.
My dearest wife was like this maid, and such a one
My daughter might have been: my queen's square brows;
Her stature to an inch; as wand-like straight;
As silver-voic'd; her eyes as jewel-like,
And cas'd as richly: in pace another Juno;
Who starves the ears she feeds, and makes them hungry,
The more she gives them speech.—Where do you live?

Mar. Where I am but a stranger: from the deck
You may discern the place.
Per. Where were you bred?
And how achiev'd you these endowments, which
You make more rich to owe.[1]
Mar. Should I tell my history,
'T would seem like lies, disdain'd in the reporting.
Per. Pr'ythee, speak:
Falseness cannot come from thee, for thou look'st
Modest as justice, and thou seem'st a palace
For the crown'd truth to dwell in. I 'll believe thee,
And make my senses credit thy relation
To points that seem impossible; for thou look'st
Like one I lov'd indeed. What were thy friends?
Didst thou not say, when I did push thee back,
(Which was when I perceiv'd thee) that thou cam'st
From good descending?
Mar. So indeed I did.
Per. Report thy parentage. I think thou saidst
Thou hadst been toss'd from wrong to injury,
And that thou thought'st thy griefs might equal mine,
If both were open'd.
Mar. Some such thing
I said, and said no more but what my thoughts
Did warrant me was likely.
Per. Tell thy story;
If thine consider'd prove the thousandth part
Of my endurance, thou art a man, and I
Have suffer'd like a girl: yet thou dost look
Like Patience, gazing on kings' graves, and smiling
Extremity out of act. What were thy friends?
How lost thou them? Thy name, my most kind virgin?
Recount, I do beseech thee. Come, sit by me.
Mar. My name is Marina.
Per. O! I am mock'd,
And thou by some incensed god sent hither
To make the world to laugh at me.
Mar. Patience, good sir
Or here I'll cease.
Per. Nay, I 'll be patient.
Thou little know'st how thou dost startle me,
To call thyself Marina.
Mar. The name

[1] *Own.*

Was given me by one that had some power;
My father, and a king.

Per. How! a king's daughter?
And call'd Marina?

Mar. You said you would believe me;
But, not to be a troubler of your peace,
I will end here.

Per. But are you flesh and blood?
Have you a working pulse? and are no fairy
Motion?—Well: speak on. Where were you born,
And wherefore call'd Marina?

Mar. Call'd Marina,
For I was born at sea.

Per. At sea! what mother?

Mar. My mother was the daughter of a king;
Who died the minute I was born,
As my good nurse Lychorida hath oft
Deliver'd weeping.

Per. O! stop there a little.
This is the rarest dream that e'er dull'd sleep
Did mock sad fools withal; this cannot be.
My daughter 's buried.—Well:—where were you bred?
I 'll hear you more, to the bottom of your story,
And never interrupt you.

Mar. You scorn: believe me, 't were best I did give o'er.

Per. I will believe you by the syllable
Of what you shall deliver. Yet, give me leave:
How came you in these parts? where were you bred?

Mar. The king, my father, did in Tharsus leave me,
Till cruel Cleon, with his wicked wife,
Did seek to murder me; and having woo'd
A villain to attempt it, who having drawn to do 't,
A crew of pirates came and rescued me;
Brought me to Mitylene. But, good sir,
Whither will you have me? Why do you weep? It may be,
You think me an impostor: no, good faith;
I am the daughter to king Pericles,
If good king Pericles be.

Per. Ho, Helicanus!

Hel. Calls my gracious lord?

Per. Thou art a grave and noble counsellor,
Most wise in general: tell me, if thou canst,
What this maid is, or what is like to be,

That thus hath made me weep?
Hel. I know not; but
Here is the regent, sir, of Mitylene,
Speaks nobly of her.
Lys. She would never tell
Her parentage; being demanded that,
She would sit still and weep.
Per. O Helicanus! strike me, honour'd sir;
Give me a gash, put me to present pain,
Lest this great sea of joys rushing upon me,
O'erbear the shores of my mortality,
And drown me with their sweetness. O! come hither,
Thou that beget'st him that did thee beget;
Thou that wast born at sea, buried at Tharsus,
And found at sea again.—O Helicanus!
Down on thy knees, thank the holy gods as loud
As thunder threatens us: this is Marina!—
What was thy mother's name? tell me but that,
For truth can never be confirm'd enough,
Though doubts did ever sleep.
Mar. First, sir, I pray,
What is your title?
Per. I am Pericles of Tyre: but tell me, now,
My drown'd queen's name, (as in the rest you said
Thou hast been godlike perfect) the heir of kingdoms,
And another like to Pericles thy father.
Mar. Is it no more to be your daughter, than
To say, my mother's name was Thaisa?
Thaisa was my mother, who did end
The minute I began.
Per. Now, blessing on thee! rise; thou art my child.
Give me fresh garments! Mine own, Helicanus,
She is not dead at Tharsus, as she should have been,
By savage Cleon: she shall tell thee all;
When thou shalt kneel and justify in knowledge,
She is thy very princess.—Who is this?
Hel. Sir, 't is the governor of Mitylene,
Who, hearing of your melancholy state,
Did come to see you.
Per. I embrace you,
Give me my robes! I am wild in my beholding.
O heavens, bless my girl! But hark! what music?—

Tell Helicanus, my Marina, tell him
O'er, point by point, for yet he seems to doubt,
How sure you are my daughter.—But what music?
Hel. My lord I hear none.
Per. None?
The music of the spheres! list, my Marina.
Lys. It is not good to cross him: give him way.
Per. Rarest sounds! Do ye not hear?
Lys. Music? My lord, I hear—
Per. Most heavenly music:
It nips me unto list'ning, and thick slumber
Hangs upon mine eyes: let me rest. [*He sleeps.*
Lys. A pillow for his head.
[*The Curtain before the Pavilion of* PERICLES *is closed.*
So, leave him all.—Well, my companion-friends,
If this but answer to my just belief,
I'll well remember you.
[*Exeunt* LYSIMACHUS, HELICANUS, MARINA, *and Lady.*

SCENE II.—The Same.

PERICLES *on the Deck asleep;* DIANA *appearing to him in a vision.*

Dia. My temple stands in Ephesus: hie thee thither,
And do upon mine altar sacrifice.
There, when my maiden priests are met together,
Before the people all,
Reveal how thou at sea didst lose thy wife:
To mourn thy crosses, with thy daughter's, call,
And give them repetition to the life.
Or perform my bidding, or thou liv'st in woe:
Do't, and be[1] happy, by my silver bow.
Awake, and tell thy dream. [DIANA *disappears*
Per. Celestial Dian, goddess argentine,
I will obey thee.—Helicanus!
Enter LYSIMACHUS, HELICANUS, *and* MARINA.
Hel. Sir.
Per. My purpose was for Tharsus, there to strike
The inhospitable Cleon; but I am
For other service first: toward Ephesus
Turn our blown sails; eftsoons I'll tell thee why.—
Shall we refresh us, sir, upon your shore,
And give you gold for such provision

[1] Not in old copies.

As our intents will need?

Lys. Sir, with all my heart, and when you come ashore,
I have another suit.

Per. You shall prevail,
Were it to woo my daughter; for, it seems,
You have been noble towards her.

Lys. Sir, lend your arm.

Per. Come, my Marina. [*Exeunt.*

Enter GOWER, *before the Temple of* DIANA *at Ephesus.*

Gow. Now our sands are almost run;
More a little, and then dumb.
This, as[1] my last boon, give me,
For such kindness must relieve me,
That you aptly will suppose
What pageantry, what feats, what shows,
What minstrelsy, and pretty din,
The regent made in Mitylen,
To greet the king. So he thriv'd,
That he is promis'd to be wiv'd
To fair Marina; but in no wise
Till he had done his sacrifice,
As Dian bade: whereto being bound,
The interim, pray you, all confound.
In feather'd briefness sails are fill'd,
And wishes fall out as they're will'd.
At Ephesus, the temple see,
Our king, and all his company.
That he can hither come so soon,
Is by your fancy's thankful doom. [*Exit.*

SCENE III.—The Temple of DIANA at Ephesus: THAISA standing near the Altar, as high Priestess, a number of Virgins on each side: CERIMON and other Inhabitants of Ephesus attending.

Enter PERICLES, *with his Train;* LYSIMACHUS, HELICANUS, MARINA, *and a Lady.*

Per. Hail Dian! to perform thy just command,
I here confess myself the king of Tyre;
Who, frighted from my country, did wed
At Pentapolis, the fair Thaisa.
At sea in childbed died she, but brought forth

[1] Not in old copies.

A maid-child call'd Marina; who, O goddess!
Wears yet thy silver livery. She at Tharsus
Was nurs'd with Cleon, whom at fourteen years
He sought to murder, but her better stars
Brought her to Mitylene; against whose shore
Riding, her fortunes brought the maid aboard us,
Where, by her own most clear remembrance, she
Made known herself my daughter.

Thai. Voice and favour[1]! —
You are, you are—O royal Pericles!— [*She faints*

Per. What means the woman[2]? she dies; help gentlemen!

Cer. Noble sir,
If you have told Diana's altar true,
This is your wife.

Per. Reverend appearer, no:
I threw her overboard with these very arms.

Cer. Upon this coast, I warrant you.

Per. 'T is most certain

Cer. Look to the lady.—O! she 's but o'erjoy'd.
Early in blust'ring morn this lady was
Thrown on this shore. I op'd the coffin,
Found there rich jewels; recover'd her, and plac'd her
Here, in Diana's temple.

Per. May we see them?

Cer. Great sir, they shall be brought you to my house,
Whither I invite you. Look! Thaisa is recover'd.

Thai. O! let me look.
If he be none of mine, my sanctity
Will to my sense bend no licentious ear,
But curb it, spite of seeing. O, my lord!
Are you not Pericles? Like him you speak,
Like him you are. Did you not name a tempest,
A birth, and death?

Per. The voice of dead Thaisa!

Thai. That Thaisa am I, supposed dead, and drown'd.

Per. Immortal Dian!

Thai. Now I know you better.—
When we with tears parted Pentapolis,
The king, my father, gave you such a ring. [*Shows a Ring.*

Per. This, this: no more, you gods! your present kindness

[1] *Countenance.* [2] the mum: in old copies

Makes my past miseries sports: you shall do well,
That on the touching of her lips I may
Melt, and no more be seen. O! come, be buried
A second time within these arms.

Mar. My heart
Leaps to be gone into my mother's bosom.
[*Kneels to* THAISA

Per. Look, who kneels here. Flesh of thy flesh, Thaisa;
Thy burden at the sea, and call'd Marina,
For she was yielded there.

Thai. Bless'd, and mine own!

Hel. Hail, madam, and my queen!

Thai. I know you not.

Per. You have heard me say, when I did fly from Tyre,
I left behind an ancient substitute:
Can you remember what I call'd the man?
I have nam'd him oft.

Thai. 'T was Helicanus, then.

Per. Still confirmation!
Embrace him, dear Thaisa; this is he.
Now do I long to hear how you were found,
How possibly preserv'd, and whom to thank,
Besides the gods, for this great miracle.

Thai. Lord Cerimon, my lord; this man
Through whom the gods have shown their power, that can
From first to last resolve you.

Per. Reverend sir,
The gods can have no mortal officer
More like a god than you. Will you deliver
How this dead queen re-lives?

Cer. I will, my lord:
Beseech you, first go with me to my house,
Where shall be shown you all was found with her;
How she came placed here in the temple,
No needful thing omitted.

Per. Pure Dian! bless thee for thy vision,
I will offer night oblations to thee. Thaisa,
This prince, the fair-betrothed of your daughter,
Shall marry her at Pentapolis. And now,
This ornament,
Makes me look dismal, will I clip to form;
And what this fourteen years no razor touch'd,

To grace thy marriage-day, I 'll beautify.
Thai. Lord Cerimon hath letters of good credit:
Sir, my father 's dead.
Per. Heavens, make a star of him! Yet there, my queen,
We 'll celebrate their nuptials, and ourselves
Will in that kingdom spend our following days:
Our son and daughter shall in Tyrus reign.
Lord Cerimon, we do our longing stay,
To hear the rest untold.—Sir, lead 's the way.
[*Exeunt.*

Enter GOWER.

Gow. In Antiochus, and his daughter, you have heard
Of monstrous lust the due and just reward:
In Pericles, his queen, and daughter, seen,
Although assail'd with fortune fierce and keen,
Virtue preserv'd[1] from fell destruction's blast,
Led on by heaven, and crown'd with joy at last.
In Helicanus may you well descry
A figure of truth, of faith, and loyalty:
In reverend Cerimon there well appears,
The worth that learned charity aye wears.
For wicked Cleon and his wife, when fame
Had spread their cursed deed, the honour'd name
Of Pericles, to rage the city turn;
That him and his they in his palace burn.
The gods for murder seemed so content
To punish them,[2] although not done, but meant.
So on your patience evermore attending,
New joy wait on you! Here our play has ending

[1] preferred: in old copies. [2] Not in old copies; added by Malone.

END OF THE PLAYS.

POEMS.

VENUS AND ADONIS.

TO THE RIGHT HONOURABLE

HENRY WRIOTHESLY,

EARL OF SOUTHAMPTON, AND BARON OF TICHFIELD

RIGHT HONOURABLE,

I KNOW not how I shall offend in dedicating my unpolished lines to your lordship, nor how the world will censure me for choosing so strong a prop to support so weak a burden: only, if your honour seem but pleased, I account myself highly praised, and vow to take advantage of all idle hours, till I have honoured you with some graver labour. But if the first heir of my invention prove deformed, I shall be sorry it had so noble a god-father, and never after ear so barren a land, for fear it yield me still so bad a harvest. I leave it to your honourable survey, and your honour to your heart's content; which I wish may always answer your own wish, and the world's hopeful expectation.

Your honour's in all duty,

WILLIAM SHAKESPEARE.

INTRODUCTION.

We are told by Shakespeare, in his dedication of this poem to the Earl of Southampton, in 1593, that it was "the first heir of his invention;" and as it was the earliest printed, so probably, it was the earliest written of his known productions. At what time it is likely that he commenced the composition of it, is a question which we have considered in the biography of the poet.

The popularity of it is indisputable: having been originally printed by Richard Field, in 1593, 4to., that edition[1] seems to have been soon exhausted, and it was republished by the same printer in 1594, 4to., before 25th June, because on that day, according to the Stationers' Registers, he assigned over his interest in it to John Harrison, for whom Field printed an octavo impression in 1596. Field's second edition of 1594 was unknown to Malone and his contemporaries; and as it was not a re-issue of some remaining copies of 1593 with a new title-page, but a distinct re-impression, it affords some various readings, and not a few important confirmations of the correctness of the older text, corrupted more or less in all subsequent editions. Harrison published his second edition in 1600, which was the fourth time "Venus and Adonis" had been printed in seven years. It had been entered at Stationers' Hall by W. Leake, in 1596. After this date it went through the press many times, and copies in 1602, 1616, 1620, &c. are known: in 1627 it was printed by John Wreittoun, at Edinburgh.

The popularity of "Venus and Adonis" is established also by the frequent mention of it in early writers[2]. It is probable that Peele died in 1597, and very soon afterwards his "Merry Conceited Jests" must have been published, although no

[1] The memorandum of it in the Stationers' Registers runs thus:—

"18 April 1593.

"Richd Field] Entered as his Copy, licensed by the Archbishop of Canterbury, and the Wardens, a book intitled Venus and Adonis."

[2] Malone adverts to Richard Barnfield's notice of "Venus and Adonis," and "Lucrece." in 1598, (reprinted in 1605; see Bridgewater Catalogue, 4to, 1837. p. 23) as well as to William Barksted's allusion to it in 1607, in his "Myrrha the Mother of Adonis." To these may be added the praise of Shakespeare, and of his "Venus and Adonis," and "Lucrece," in the play of "The Return from Parnassus," which was certainly produced before the death of Queen Elizabeth.

edition of them is known older than that of 1607. In one of these, a tapster, "much given to poetry," is represented as having in his possession "the Knight of the Sun, Venus and Adonis, and other pamphlets." Thomas Heywood's "Fair Maid of the Exchange," was printed in 1607, but written some few years before, and there a young lover is recommended to court his mistress by the aid of "Venus and Adonis." How long this reputation, and for the same purpose, was maintained, may be seen from a passage in Lewis Sharpe's "Noble Stranger," 1640, where Pupillus exclaims, "Oh, for the book of Venus and Adonis, to court my mistress by!" Thomas Cranley, in his "Amanda," 1635, makes "Venus and Adonis" part of the library of a courtesan:

——— "amorous pamphlets, that best like thine eyes,
And songs of love, and sonnets exquisite;
Among these Venus and Adonis lies,
With Salmacis and her Hermaphrodite;
Pigmalion's there with his transform'd delight."

"Salmacis and her Hermaphrodite" refers to the poem imputed (perhaps falsely) to Beaumont, printed in 1604; and the third poem is "Pygmalion's Image," by Marston, published in 1598.

S. Nicholson, in his "Acolastus his Afterwitte," 1600, committed the most impudent plagiarisms from "Venus and Adonis;" and R. S., the author of "Phillis and Flora," 1598, did not scruple to copy, almost with verbal exactness, part of the description Shakespeare gives of the horse of Adonis: we extract the following lines, that the reader may be able to make a comparison (See p. 366):—

"His mayne thin hair'd, his neck high crested,
Small eare, short head, and burly breasted. * * *
Strait legg'd, large thigh'd, and hollow hoved,
All nature's skill in him was proved."

Our text of "Venus and Adonis," is that of the earliest quarto, 1593, which, for the time, is very correctly printed, and we will illustrate by a single quotation the importance of resorting to it: the line which there stands,

"He cheers the morn, and all the earth relieveth,"

is misprinted in all modern editions,

"He cheers the morn, and all the *world* relieveth."

The corruption was introduced in the quarto, 1594, and it has ever since been repeated. The same remark will apply to other changes; such as "all swoln with *chasing*," instead of "chafing;" "to love's *alarm*," instead of "alarms;" "from morn *to* night," instead of "till night," &c.; all which show strange carelessness of collation, but it is not necessary here to dwell upon them, as they are pointed out in the notes.

VENUS AND ADONIS.

Even as the sun with purple-colour'd face
Had ta'en his last leave of the weeping morn,
Rose-cheek'd Adonis hied him to the chase;
Hunting he lov'd, but love he laugh'd to scorn:
  Sick-thoughted Venus makes amain unto him,
  And like a bold-fac'd suitor 'gins to woo him.

Thrice fairer than myself, (thus she began)
The field's chief flower, sweet above compare,
Stain to all nymphs, more lovely than a man,
More white and red than doves or roses are;
  Nature that made thee, with herself at strife,
  Saith, that the world hath ending with thy life.

Vouchsafe, thou wonder, to alight thy steed,
And rein his proud head to the saddle-bow;
If thou wilt deign this favour, for thy meed
A thousand honey secrets shalt thou know:
  Here come and sit, where never serpent hisses,
  And being set, I 'll smother thee with kisses:

And yet not cloy thy lips with loath'd satiety,
But rather famish them amid their plenty,
Making them red and pale with fresh variety;
Ten kisses short as one, one long as twenty:
  A summer's day will seem an hour but short,
  Being wasted in such time-beguiling sport.

With this she seizeth on his sweating palm,
The precedent of pith and livelihood,
And, trembling in her passion, calls it balm,
Earth's sovereign salve to do a goddess good:
  Being so enrag'd, desire doth lend her force
  Courageously to pluck him from his horse.

Over one arm the lusty courser's rein,
Under her other was the tender boy,
Who blush'd and pouted in a dull disdain,
With leaden appetite, unapt to toy;
  She red and hot as coals of glowing fire,
  He red for shame, but frosty in desire.

The studded bridle on a ragged bough
Nimbly she fastens; (O, how quick is love!)
The steed is stalled up, and even now
To tie the rider she begins to prove:
  Backward she push'd him, as she would be thrust,
  And govern'd him in strength, though not in lust.

So soon was she along, as he was down,
Each leaning on their elbows and their hips:
Now doth she stroke his cheek, now doth he frown,
And 'gins to chide, but soon she stops his lips;
  And kissing speaks, with lustful language broken,
  If thou wilt chide, thy lips shall never open.

He burns with bashful shame, she with her tears
Doth quench the maiden burning of his cheeks;
Then with her windy sighs, and golden hairs,
To fan and blow them dry again she seeks:
  He saith she is immodest, blames her 'miss;[1]
  What follows more she murders[2] with a kiss.

Even as an empty eagle, sharp by fast,
Tires[3] with her beak on feathers, flesh, and bone,
Shaking her wings, devouring all in haste,
Till either gorge be stuff'd, or prey be gone;
  Even so she kiss'd his brow, his cheek, his chin,
  And where she ends she doth anew begin.

Forc'd to content,[4] but never to obey,
Panting he lies, and breatheth in her face;
She feedeth on the steam, as on a prey,
And calls it heavenly moisture, air of grace,
  Wishing her cheeks were gardens full of flowers
  So they were dew'd with such distilling showers.

[1] amiss, *fault*. [2] smothers: in eds., 1600, 1620. [3] *Preys*. [4] To be contented.

Look how a bird lies tangled in a net,
So fasten'd in her arms Adonis lies;
Pure shame and aw'd resistance made him fret,
Which bred more beauty in his angry eyes:
  Rain added to a river that is rank,[1]
  Perforce will force it overflow the bank.

Still she entreats, and prettily entreats,
For to a pretty ear she tunes her tale;
Still is he sullen, still he lowers and frets,
'Twixt crimson shame, and anger ashy-pale,
  Being red, she loves him best; and being white,
  Her best is better'd with a more delight.

Look how he can, she cannot choose but love;
And by her fair immortal hand she swears
From his soft bosom never to remove,
Till he take truce with her contending tears,
  Which long have rain'd, making her cheeks all wet
  And one sweet kiss shall pay this countless debt.

Upon this promise did he raise his chin,
Like a dive-dapper[2] peering through a wave,
Who being look'd on ducks as quickly in;
So offers he to give what she did crave,
  But when her lips were ready for his pay,
  He winks, and turns his lips another way.

Never did passenger in summer's heat,
More thirst for drink than she for this good turn.
Her help she sees, but help she cannot get;
She bathes in water, yet her fire must burn.
  O, pity, 'gan she cry, flint-hearted boy!
  'T is but a kiss I beg; why art thou coy?

I have been woo'd as I entreat thee now,
Even by the stern and direful god of war,
Whose sinewy neck in battle ne'er did bow,
Who conquers where he comes, in every jar;
  Yet hath he been my captive and my slave,
  And begg'd for that which thou unask'd shalt have

Over my altars hath he hung his lance,
His batter'd shield, his uncontrolled crest,
And for my sake hath learn'd to sport and dance,
To toy,[3] to wanton, dally, smile, and jest;

[1] *Full.* [6] di-dapper: old cop. [7] coy: old eds.

Scorning his churlish drum, and ensign red,
Making my arms his field, his tent my bed.

Thus he that over-rul'd, I oversway'd,
Leading him prisoner in a red rose chain:
Strong-temper'd steel his stronger strength obey'd,
Yet was he servile to my coy disdain.
O! be not proud, nor brag not of thy might,
For mastering her that foil'd the god of fight.

Touch but my lips with those fair lips of thine,
Though mine be not so fair, yet are they red,
The kiss shall be thine own as well as mine.
What seest thou in the ground? hold up thy head:
Look in mine eye-balls, there thy beauty lies;
Then, why not lips on lips, since eyes in eyes?

Art thou asham'd to kiss? then, wink again,
And I will wink; so shall the day seem night;
Love keeps his revels where there are but twain;
Be bold to play, our sport is not in sight:
These blue-vein'd violets whereon we lean,
Never can blab, nor know not what we mean.

The tender spring upon thy tempting lip
Shows thee unripe, yet may'st thou well be tasted.
Make use of time, let not advantage slip;
Beauty within itself should not be wasted:
Fair flowers that are not gather'd in their prime,
Rot and consume themselves in little time.

Were I hard-favour'd, foul, or wrinkled old,
Ill-nurtur'd, crooked, churlish, harsh in voice,
O'er-worn, despised, rheumatic, and cold,
Thick-sighted, barren, lean, and lacking juice,
Then mightst thou pause, for then I were not for thee
But having no defects, why dost abhor me?

Thou canst not see one wrinkle in my brow;
Mine eyes are grey[1] and bright, and quick in turning·
My beauty as the spring doth yearly grow,
My flesh is soft and plump, my marrow burning:
My smooth moist hand, were it with thy hand felt,
Would in thy palm dissolve, or seem to melt.

[1] Blue eyes were sometimes called grey.

Bid me discourse, I will enchant thine ear,
Or like a fairy trip upon the green,
Or like a nymph with long dishevelled hair,
Dance on the sands, and yet no footing seen:
  Love is a spirit, all compact of fire,
  Not gross to sink, but light, and will aspire.

Witness this primrose bank whereon I lie;
These forceless flowers like sturdy trees support me;
Two strengthless doves will draw me through the sky,
From morn till night, even where I list to sport me:
  Is love so light, sweet boy, and may it be
  That thou shouldst think it heavy unto thee?

Is thine own heart to thine own face affected?
Can thy right hand seize love upon thy left?
Then woo thyself, be of thyself rejected,
Steal thine own freedom, and complain on theft.
  Narcissus so himself himself forsook,
  And died to kiss his shadow in the brook.

Torches are made to light, jewels to wear,
Dainties to taste, fresh beauty for the use;
Herbs for their smell, and sappy plants to bear;
Things growing to themselves are growth's abuse:
  Seeds spring from seeds, and beauty breedeth beauty
  Thou wast begot, to get it is thy duty.

Upon the earth's increase why shouldst thou feed,
Unless the earth in thy increase be fed?
By law of nature thou art bound to breed,
That thine may live, when thou thyself art dead;
  And so in spite of death thou dost survive,
  In that thy likeness still is left alive.

By this, the love-sick queen began to sweat,
For where they lay the shadow had forsook them,
And Titan, 'tired in the mid-day heat,
With burning eye did hotly overlook them;
  Wishing Adonis had his team to guide,
  So he were like him, and by Venus' side.

And now Adonis, with a lazy sprite,
And with a heavy, dark, disliking eye,
His lowering brows o'er-whelming his fair sight,
Like misty vapours, when they blot the sky,

Souring his cheeks, cries, Fie ! no more of love :
The sun doth burn my face ; I must remove.

Ah me ! (quoth Venus,) young, and so unkind ?
What bare excuses mak'st thou to be gone !
I 'll sigh celestial breath, whose gentle wind
Shall cool the heat of this descending sun :
I 'll make a shadow for thee of my hairs ;
If they burn too, I 'll quench them with my tears.

The sun that shines from heaven shines but warm,
And lo ! I lie between that sun and thee :
The heat I have from thence doth little harm,
Thine eye darts forth the fire that burneth me ;
And were I not immortal, life were done,
Between this heavenly and earthly sun.

Art thou obdurate, flinty, hard as steel ?
Nay more than flint, for stone at rain relenteth ;
Art thou a woman's son, and canst not feel,
What 't is to love ? how want of love tormenteth ?
O ! had thy mother borne so hard a mind,
She had not brought forth thee, but died unkind.

What am I, that thou shouldst contemn me this ?
Or what great danger dwells upon my suit ?
What were thy lips the worse for one poor kiss ?
Speak fair ; but speak fair words, or else be mute :
Give me one kiss, I 'll give it thee again,
And one for interest, if thou wilt have twain.

Fie ! lifeless picture, cold and senseless stone,
Well-painted idol, image dull and dead,
Statue, contenting but the eye alone,
Thing like a man, but of no woman bred :
Thou art no man, though of a man's complexion,
For men will kiss even by their own direction.

This said, impatience chokes her pleading tongue,
And swelling passion doth provoke a pause ;
Red cheeks and fiery eyes blaze forth her wrong :
Being judge in love, she cannot right her cause ;
And now she weeps, and now she fain would speak,
And now her sobs do her intendments break.

Sometimes she shakes her head, and then his hand,
Now gazeth she on him, now on the ground;
Sometimes her arms infold him like a band:
She would, he will not in her arms be bound;
  And when from thence he struggles to be gone,
  She locks her lily fingers one in one.

Fondling, she saith, since I have hemm'd thee here,
Within the circuit of this ivory pale,
I 'll be a park, and thou shalt be my deer;
Feed where thou wilt, on mountain or in dale:
  Graze on my lips, and if those hills be dry,
  Stray lower, where the pleasant fountains lie.

Within this limit is relief enough,
Sweet bottom-grass, and high delightful plain,
Round rising hillocks, brakes obscure and rough,
To shelter thee from tempest, and from rain:
  Then, be my deer, since I am such a park;
  No dog shall rouse thee, though a thousand bark.

At this Adonis smiles, as in disdain,
That in each cheek appears a pretty dimple:
Love made those hollows, if himself were slain,
He might be buried in a tomb so simple;
  Fore-knowing well, if there he came to lie,
  Why, there Love liv'd, and there he could not die.

These lovely caves, the round enchanting pits,
Open'd their mouths to swallow Venus' liking.
Being mad before, how doth she now for wits?
Struck dead at first, what needs a second striking?
  Poor queen of love, in thine own law forlorn,
  To love a cheek that smiles at thee in scorn!

Now which way shall she turn? what shall she say?
Her words are done, her woes the more increasing;
The time is spent, her object will away,
And from her twining arms doth urge releasing.
  Pity! she cries, some favour, some remorse!
  Away he springs, and hasteth to his horse!

But lo! from forth a copse that neighbours by,
A breeding jennet, lusty, young, and proud,
Adonis' trampling courser doth espy,
And forth she rushes, snorts, and neighs aloud:

The strong-neck'd steed, being tied unto a tree,
Breaketh his rein, and to her straight goes he.

Imperiously he leaps, he neighs, he bounds,
And now his woven girths he breaks asunder;
The bearing earth with his hard hoof he wounds,
Whose hollow womb resounds like heaven's thunder:
The iron bit he crusheth 'tween his teeth,
Controlling what he was controlled with.

His ears up prick'd, his braided hanging mane
Upon his compass'd crest now stands on end;
His nostrils drink the air, and forth again,
As from a furnace, vapours doth he send:
His eye, which scornfully glisters like fire,
Shows his hot courage, and his high desire.

Sometime he trots, as if he told the steps
With gentle majesty, and modest pride;
Anon he rears upright, curvets and leaps,
As who should say, lo! thus my strength is tried,
And this I do, to captivate the eye
Of the fair breeder that is standing by.

What recketh he his rider's angry stir,
His flattering holla, or his "Stand, I say?"
What cares he now for curbs, or pricking spur,
For rich caparisons, or trapping gay?
He sees his love, and nothing else he sees,
For nothing else with his proud sight agrees.

Look, when a painter would surpass the life,
In limning out a well-proportion'd steed,
His art with nature's workmanship at strife,
As if the dead the living should exceed;
So did his horse excel a common one,
In shape, in courage, colour, pace, and bone

Round-hoof'd, short-jointed, the fetlocks shag and long,
Broad breast, full eye, small head, and nostril wide,
High crest, short ears, straight legs, and passing strong
Thin mane, thick tail, broad buttock, tender hide:
Look, what a horse should have he did not lack,
Save a proud rider on so proud a back.

Sometime he scuds far off, and there he stares;
Anon he starts at stirring of a feather:
To bid the wind a base[1] he now prepares,
And whe'r he run, or fly, they know not whether;
For through his mane and tail the high wind sings,
Fanning the hairs, who wave like feather'd wings.

He looks upon his love, and neighs unto her;
She answers him, as if she knew his mind:
Being proud, as females are, to see him woo her,
She puts on outward strangeness, seems unkind;
Spurns at his love, and scorns the heat he feels,
Beating his kind embracements with her heels.

Then, like a melancholy malcontent,
He vails his tail, that, like a falling plume,
Cool shadow to his melting buttock lent:
He stamps, and bites the poor flies in his fume.
His love, perceiving how he is enrag'd,
Grew kinder, and his fury was assuag'd.

His testy master goeth about to take him,
When lo! the unback'd breeder, full of fear,
Jealous of catching, swiftly doth forsake him,
With her the horse, and left Adonis there.
As they were mad, unto the wood they hie them,
Out-stripping crows that strive to over-fly them.

All swoln with chafing,[2] down Adonis sits,
Banning his boisterous and unruly beast:
And now the happy season once more fits,
That love-sick love by pleading may be blest;
For lovers say, the heart hath treble wrong,
When it is barr'd the aidance of the tongue.

An oven that is stopp'd, or river stay'd,
Burneth more hotly, swelleth with more rage:
So of concealed sorrow may be said,
Free vent of words love's fire doth assuage;
But when the heart's attorney once is mute,
The client breaks, as desperate in his suit.

He sees her coming, and begins to glow,
Even as a dying coal revives with wind,
And with his bonnet hides his angry brow;
Looks on the dull earth with disturbed mind,

[1] A *race*, *or game* of prison-base, or prison-bars [2] chasing: in ed 1600.

Taking no notice that she is so nigh,
For all askaunce he holds her in his eye.

O! what a sight it was, wistly to view
How she came stealing to the wayward boy;
To note the fighting conflict of her hue,
How white and red each other did destroy:
But now her cheek was pale, and by and by
It flash'd forth fire, as lightning from the sky.

Now was she just before him as he sat,
And like a lowly lover down she kneels;
With one fair hand she heaveth up his hat,
Her other tender hand his fair cheek feels:
His tenderer cheek receives her soft hand's print,
As apt as new-fall'n snow takes any dint.

O, what a war of looks was then between them!
Her eyes, petitioners, to his eyes suing;
His eyes saw her eyes as they had not seen them;
Her eyes woo'd still, his eyes disdain'd the wooing:
And all this dumb play had his acts made plain
With tears, which, chorus-like, her eyes did rain.

Full gently now she takes him by the hand,
A lily prison'd in a jail of snow,
Or ivory in an alabaster band;
So white a friend engirts so white a foe:
This beauteous combat, wilful and unwilling,
Show'd like two silver doves that sit a billing.

Once more the engine of her thoughts began:
O fairest mover on this mortal round,
Would thou wert as I am, and I a man,
My heart all whole as thine, thy heart my wound;
For one sweet look thy help I would assure thee,
Though nothing but my body's bane would cure thee

Give me my hand, saith he, why dost thou feel it?
Give me my heart, saith she, and thou shalt have it,
O! give it me, lest thy hard heart do steel it,
And being steel'd, soft sighs can never grave it:
Then, love's deep groans I never can regard,
Because Adonis' heart hath made mine hard.

For shame! he cries, let go, and let me go;
My day's delight is past, my horse is gone,
And 't is your fault I am bereft him so:
I pray you hence, and leave me here alone;
  For all my mind, my thought, my busy care,
  Is how to get my palfrey from the mare.

Thus she replies: thy palfrey, as he should,
Welcomes the warm approach of sweet desire:
Affection is a coal that must be cool'd;
Else, suffer'd, it will set the heart on fire.
  The sea hath bounds, but deep desire hath none
  Therefore, no marvel though thy horse be gone.

How like a jade he stood, tied to the tree,
Servilely mastered with a leathern rein;
But when he saw his love, his youth's fair fee,
He held such petty bondage in disdain;
  Throwing the base thong from his bending crest,
  Enfranchising his mouth, his back, his breast.

Who sees his true-love in her naked bed,
Teaching the sheets a whiter hue than white,
But, when his glutton eye so full hath fed,
His other agents aim at like delight?
  Who is so faint, that dare not be so bold
  To touch the fire, the weather being cold?

Let me excuse thy courser, gentle boy,
And learn of him, I heartily beseech thee,
To take advantage on presented joy;
Though I were dumb, yet his proceedings teach thee:
  O! learn to love; the lesson is but plain,
  And once made perfect, never lost again.

I know not love, quoth he, nor will not know it:
Unless it be a boar, and then I chase it;
'T is much to borrow, and I will not owe it;
My love to love is love but to disgrace it;
  For I have heard it is a life in death,
  That laughs, and weeps, and all but with a breath.

Who wears a garment shapeless and unfinish'd?
Who plucks the bud before one leaf put forth?
If springing things be any jot diminish'd,
They wither in their prime, prove nothing worth:

The colt that 's back'd and burden'd being young,
Loseth his pride, and never waxeth strong.

You hurt my hand with wringing; let us part,
And leave this idle theme, this bootless chat:
Remove your siege from my unyielding heart;
To love's alarms it will not ope the gate:
Dismiss your vows, your feigned tears, your flattery,
For where a heart is hard, they make no battery.

What! canst thou talk? (quoth she,) hast thou a tongue?
O, would thou hadst not, or I had no hearing!
Thy mermaid's voice hath done me double wrong!
I had my load before, now press'd with bearing:
Melodious discord, heavenly tune harsh-sounding,
Ear's deep sweet music, and heart's deep sore wounding.

Had I no eyes, but ears, my ears would love
That inward beauty and invisible;
Or, were I deaf, thy outward parts would move
Each part in me that were but sensible:
Though neither eyes nor ears, to hear nor see,
Yet should I be in love by touching thee.

Say, that the sense of feeling were bereft me,
And that I could not see, nor hear, nor touch,
And nothing but the very smell were left me,
Yet would my love to thee be still as much;
For from the stillitory of thy face excelling [ing
Comes breath perfum'd, that breedeth love by smell.

But O! what banquet wert thou to the taste,
Being nurse and feeder of the other four:
Would they not wish the feast might ever last,
And bid suspicion double lock the door,
Lest jealousy, that sour unwelcome guest,
Should by his stealing in disturb the feast?

Once more the ruby-colour'd portal opened,
Which to his speech did honey-passage yield;
Like a red morn, that ever yet betoken'd
Wreck to the sea-man, tempest to the field,
Sorrow to shepherds, woe unto the birds,
Gusts and foul flaws to herdmen and to herds.

This ill presage advisedly she marketh:
Even as the wind is hush'd before it raineth,
Or as the wolf doth grin before he barketh,
Or as the berry breaks before it staineth;
  Or like the deadly bullet of a gun,
  His meaning struck her ere his words begun.

And at his look she flatly falleth down,
For looks kill love, and love by looks reviveth:
A smile recures the wounding of a frown;
But blessed bankrupt that by love so thriveth!
  The silly boy, believing she is dead,
  Claps her pale cheek, till clapping makes it red;

And all amaz'd brake off his late intent,
For sharply he did think to reprehend her,
Which cunning love did wittily prevent:
Fair fall the wit that can so well defend her!
  For on the grass she lies, as she were slain,
  Till his breath breatheth life in her again.

He wrings her nose, he strikes her on the cheeks,
He bends her fingers, holds her pulses hard,
He chafes her lips; a thousand ways he seeks
To mend the hurt that his unkindness marr'd:
  He kisses her; and she, by her good will,
  Will never rise, so he will kiss her still.

The night of sorrow now is turn'd to day:
Her two blue windows faintly she up-heaveth,
Like the fair sun, when in his fresh array
He cheers the morn, and all the earth[1] relieveth:
  And as the bright sun glorifies the sky,
  So is her face illumin'd with her eye;

Whose beams upon his hairless face are fix'd,
As if from thence they borrow'd all their shine.
Were never four such lamps together mix'd,
Had not his clouded with his brow's repine;
  But hers, which through the crystal tears gave light,
  Shone like the moon in water seen by night.

O! where am I? quoth she, in earth or heaven,
Or in the ocean drench'd, or in the fire?
What hour is this? or morn or weary even?
Do I delight to die, or life desire?

[1] world: in ed. 1594.

But now I liv'd, and life was death's annoy;
But now I died, and death was lively joy.

O! thou didst kill me; kill me once again:
Thy eye's shrewd tutor, that hard heart of thine,
Hath taught them scornful tricks, and such disdain,
That they have murder'd this poor heart of mine;
And these mine eyes, true leaders to their queen,
But for thy piteous lips no more had seen.

Long may they kiss each other for this cure!
O! never let their crimson liveries wear,
And as they last, their verdure still endure,
To drive infection[1] from the dangerous year!
That the star-gazers, having writ on death,
May say, the plague is banish'd by thy breath.

Pure lips, sweet seals in my soft lips imprinted,
What bargains may I make, still to be sealing?
To sell myself I can be well contented,
So thou wilt buy, and pay, and use good dealing;
Which purchase if you make, for fear of slips
Set thy seal-manual on my wax-red lips.

A thousand kisses buys my heart from me,
And pay them at thy leisure, one by one.
What is ten hundred touches unto thee?
Are they not quickly told, and quickly gone?
Say, for non-payment that the debt should double,
Is twenty hundred kisses such a trouble?

Fair queen, quoth he, if any love you owe me,
Measure my strangeness with my unripe years:
Before I know myself, seek not to know me;
No fisher but the ungrown fry forbears:
The mellow plum doth fall, the green sticks fast,
Or being early pluck'd is sour to taste.

Look, the world's comforter, with weary gait,
His day's hot task hath ended in the west:
The owl, night's herald, shrieks, 't is very late;
The sheep are gone to fold, birds to their nest,
And coal-black clouds that shadow heaven's light,
Do summon us to part, and bid good night.

[1] Fragrant herbs were supposed to possess this power.

Now let me say good night; and so say you;
If you will say so, you shall have a kiss.
Good night, quoth she; and, ere he says adieu,
The honey-fee of parting tender'd is:
  Her arms do lend his neck a sweet embrace;
  Incorporate then they seem, face grows to face.

Till breathless he disjoin'd, and backward drew
The heavenly moisture, that sweet coral mouth,
Whose precious taste her thirsty lips well knew,
Whereon they surfeit, yet complain on drought:
  He with her plenty press'd, she faint with dearth,
  Their lips together glued, fall to the earth.

Now quick desire hath caught the yielding prey,
And glutton-like she feeds, yet never filleth;
Her lips are conquerors, his lips obey,
Paying what ransom the insulter willeth;
  Whose vulture thought doth pitch the price so high,
  That she will draw his lips' rich treasure dry.

And having felt the sweetness of the spoil,
With blindfold fury she begins to forage;
Her face doth reek and smoke, her blood doth boil,
And careless lust stirs up a desperate courage;
  Planting oblivion, beating reason back,
  Forgetting shame's pure blush, and honour's wrack.

Hot, faint, and weary, with her hard embracing,
Like a wild bird being tam'd with too much handling,
Or as the fleet-foot roe that 's tir'd with chasing,
Or like the froward infant still'd with dandling,
  He now obeys, and now no more resisteth,
  While she takes all she can, not all she listeth.

What wax so frozen but dissolves with tempering,
And yields at last to every light impression?
Things out of hope are compass'd oft with venturing,
Chiefly in love, whose leave exceeds commission:
  Affection faints not like a pale-fac'd coward,
  But then woos best, when most his choice is froward.

When he did frown, O! had she then gave over,
Such nectar from his lips she had not suck'd.
Foul words and frowns must not repel a lover;
What though the rose have prickles, yet 't is pluck'd

Were beauty under twenty locks kept fast,
Yet love breaks through, and picks them all at last.

For pity now she can no more detain him;
The poor fool prays her that he may depart:
She is resolv'd no longer to restrain him,
Bids him farewell, and look well to her heart,
The which, by Cupid's bow she doth protest,
He carries thence incaged in his breast.

Sweet boy, she says, this night I 'll waste in sorrow,
For my sick heart commands mine eyes to watch.
Tell me, love's master, shall we meet to-morrow?
Say, shall we? shall we? wilt thou make the match?
He tells her, no; to-morrow he intends
To hunt the boar with certain of his friends.

The boar! (quoth she) whereat a sudden pale,
Like lawn being spread upon the blushing rose,
Usurps her cheek: she trembles at his tale,
And on his neck her yoking arms she throws;
She sinketh down, still hanging by his neck,
He on her belly falls, she on her back.

Now is she in the very lists of love,
Her champion mounted for the hot encounter:
All is imaginary she doth prove,
He will not manage her, although he mount her;
That worse than Tantalus' is her annoy,
To clip[1] Elysium, and to lack her joy.

Even as poor birds, deceiv'd with painted grapes,
Do surfeit by the eye, and pine the maw,
Even so she languisheth in her mishaps,
As those poor birds that helpless berries saw.
The warm effects which she in him finds missing,
She seeks to kindle with continual kissing:

But all in vain; good queen, it will not be:
She hath assay'd as much as may be prov'd;
Her pleading hath deserv'd a greater fee;
She 's love, she loves, and yet she is not lov'd.
Fie, fie! he says, you crush me; let me go:
You have no reason to withhold me so.

[1] *Embrace.*

Thou hadst been gone, quoth she, sweet boy, ere this,
But that thou told'st me, thou wouldst hunt the boar.
O! be advis'd; thou know'st not what it is
With javelin's point a churlish swine to gore,
  Whose tushes never-sheath'd he whetteth still,
  Like to a mortal butcher, bent to kill.

On his bow-back he hath a battle set
Of bristly pikes, that ever threat his foes;
His eyes like glow-worms shine when he doth fret;
His snout digs sepulchres where'er he goes;
  Being mov'd, he strikes whate'er is in his way,
  And whom he strikes his cruel tushes slay.

His brawny sides, with hairy bristles armed,
Are better proof than thy spear's point can enter;
His short thick neck cannot be easily harmed;
Being ireful on the lion he will venture:
  The thorny brambles and embracing bushes,
  As fearful of him, part; through whom he rushes.

Alas! he nought esteems that face of thine,
To which love's eyes pay tributary gazes;
Nor thy soft hands, sweet lips, and crystal eyne,
Whose full perfection all the world amazes:
  But having thee at vantage, (wondrous dread!)
  Would root these beauties, as he roots the mead.

O! let him keep his loathsome cabin still:
Beauty hath nought to do with such foul fiends:
Come not within his danger[1] by thy will;
They that thrive well take counsel of their friends.
  When thou didst name the boar, not to dissemble,
  I fear'd thy fortune, and my joints did tremble.

Didst thou not mark my face? Was it not white?
Saw'st thou not signs of fear lurk in mine eye?
Grew I not faint? and fell I not downright?
Within my bosom, whereon thou dost lie,
  My boding heart pants, beats, and takes no rest,
  But like an earthquake shakes thee on my breast.

For where love reigns, disturbing jealousy
Doth call himself affection's sentinel;
Gives false alarms, suggesteth mutiny,
And in a peaceful hour doth cry, "kill, kill;"

[1] In his power.

Distempering gentle love in his desire,
As air and water do abate the fire.

This sour informer, this bate[1]-breeding spy,
This canker that eats up love's tender spring,
This carry-tale, dissentious jealousy,
That sometime true news, sometime false doth bring,
Knocks at my heart, and whispers in mine ear,
That if I love thee, I thy death should fear:

And more than so, presenteth to mine eye
The picture of an angry chafing boar,
Under whose sharp fangs on his back doth lie
An image like thyself, all stain'd with gore;
Whose blood upon the fresh flowers being shed,
Doth make them droop with grief, and hang the head.

What should I do, seeing thee so indeed,
That tremble at th' imagination?
The thought of it doth make my faint heart bleed,
And fear doth teach it divination:
I prophesy thy death, my living sorrow,
If thou encounter with the boar to-morrow.

But if thou needs wilt hunt, be rul'd by me;
Uncouple at the timorous flying hare,
Or at the fox, which lives by subtlety,
Or at the roe, which no encounter dare:
Pursue these fearful creatures o'er the downs,
And on thy well-breath'd horse keep with thy hounds.

And when thou hast on foot the purblind hare,
Mark the poor wretch, to overshut[2] his troubles,
How he out-runs the wind, and with what care
He cranks[3] and crosses with a thousand doubles:
The many musets[4] through the which he goes,
Are like a labyrinth to amaze his foes.

Sometimes he runs among a flock of sheep,
To make the cunning hounds mistake their smell;
And sometime where earth-delving conies keep,
To stop the loud pursuers in their yell;
And sometime sorteth[5] with a herd of deer.
Danger deviseth shifts; wit waits on fear·

[1] *Contention.* [2] Steevens reads: overshoot. [3] *Winds.* [4] The aperture in a hedge made by the hare in its frequent passage through it. [5] *Consorteth.*

For there his smell, with others being mingled,
The hot scent-snuffing hounds are driven to doubt,
Ceasing their clamorous cry, till they have singled
With much ado the cold fault cleanly out;
 Then do they spend their mouths: echo replies,
 As if another chase were in the skies.

By this, poor Wat, far off upon a hill,
Stands on his hinder legs with listening ear,
To harken if his foes pursue him still ·
Anon their loud alarums he doth hear;
 And now his grief may be compared well
 To one sore sick, that hears the passing bell.

Then shalt thou see the dew-bedabbled wretch
Turn, and return. indenting with the way;
Each envious brier his weary legs doth scratch,
Each shadow makes him stop, each murmur stay:
 For misery is trodden on by many,
 And being low, never reliev'd by any.

Lie quietly, and hear a little more;
Nay, do not struggle, for thou shalt not rise:
To make thee hate the hunting of the boar,
Unlike myself thou hear'st me moralize,
 Applying this to that, and so to so;
 For love can comment upon every woe.

Where did I leave?—No matter where, quoth he;
Leave me, and then the story aptly ends:
The night is spent. Why, what of that? quoth she
I am, quoth he, expected of my friends;
 And now 't is dark, and going I shall fall.
 In night, quoth she, desire sees best of all.

But if thou fall, O! then imagine this,
The earth, in love with thee, thy footing trips,
And all is but to rob thee of a kiss.
Rich preys make true-men thieves; so do thy lips
 Make modest Dian cloudy and forlorn,
 Lest she should steal a kiss, and die forsworn.

Now, of this dark night I perceive the reason:
Cynthia for shame obscures her silver shine,
Till forging Nature be condemn'd of treason,
For stealing moulds from heaven that were divine

Wherein she fram'd thee, in high heaven's despite,
To shame the sun by day, and her by night.

And therefore hath she brib'd the Destinies,
To cross the curious workmanship of nature;
To mingle beauty with infirmities,
And pure perfection with impure defeature;
Making it subject to the tyranny
Of mad mischances, and much misery;

As burning fevers, agues pale and faint,
Life-poisoning pestilence, and frenzies wood;[1]
The marrow-eating sickness, whose attaint
Disorder breeds by heating of the blood:
Surfeits, impostumes, grief, and damn'd despair,
Swear nature's death for framing thee so fair.

And not the least of all these maladies
But in one minute's fight brings beauty under:
Both favour, savour, hue, and qualities,
Whereat th' impartial gazer late did wonder,
Are on the sudden wasted, thaw'd, and done,
As mountain snow melts with the midday sun.

Therefore, despite of fruitless chastity,
Love-lacking vestals, and self-loving nuns,
That on the earth would breed a scarcity,
And barren dearth of daughters and of sons,
Be prodigal: the lamp that burns by night
Dries up his oil to lend the world his light.

What is thy body but a swallowing grave,
Seeming to bury that posterity
Which by the rights of time thou needs must have,
If thou destroy them not in dark obscurity?
If so, the world will hold thee in disdain,
Sith in thy pride so fair a hope is slain.

So in thyself thyself art made away,
A mischief worse than civil home-bred strife,
Or theirs whose desperate hands themselves do slay,
Or butcher sire that reaves his son of life.
Foul cankering rust the hidden treasure frets,
But gold that 's put to use more gold begets.

[1] *Mad.*

Nay then, quoth Adon, you will fall again
Into your idle over-handled theme:
The kiss I gave you is bestow'd in vain,
And all in vain you strive against the stream;
  For by this black-fac'd night, desire's foul nurse,
  Your treatise makes me like you worse and worse.

If love have lent you twenty thousand tongues,
And every tongue more moving than your own,
Bewitching like the wanton mermaid's songs,
Yet from mine ear the tempting tune is blown;
  For know, my heart stands armed in mine ear,
  And will not let a false sound enter there;

Lest the deceiving harmony should run
Into the quiet closure of my breast,
And then my little heart were quite undone,
In his bedchamber to be barr'd of rest.
  No, lady, no; my heart longs not to groan,
  But soundly sleeps, while now it sleeps alone.

What have you urg'd that I cannot reprove?
The path is smooth that leadeth on to danger;
I hate not love, but your device in love,
That lends embracements unto every stranger.
  You do it for increase: O strange excuse!
  When reason is the bawd to lust's abuse.

Call it not love, for love to heaven is fled,
Since sweating lust on earth usurp'd his name;
Under whose simple semblance he hath fed
Upon fresh beauty, blotting it with blame;
  Which the hot tyrant stains, and soon bereaves,
  As caterpillars do the tender leaves.

Love comforteth like sunshine after rain,
But lust's effect is tempest after sun;
Love's gentle spring doth always fresh remain,
Lust's winter comes ere summer half be done:
  Love surfeits not, lust like a glutton dies;
  Love is all truth, lust full of forged lies.

More I could tell, but more I dare not say;
The text is old, the orator too green.
Therefore, in sadness, now I will away;
My face is full of shame, my heart of teen:[1]

[1] *Sorrow.*

Mine ears, that to your wanton talk attended,
Do burn themselves for having so offended.

With this he breaketh from the sweet embrace
Of those fair arms which bound him to her breast,
And homeward through the dark lawn runs apace,
Leaves Love upon her back deeply distress'd.
Look, how a bright star shooteth from the sky,
So glides he in the night from Venus' eye;

Which after him she darts, as one on shore
Gazing upon a late-embarked friend,
Till the wild waves will have him seen no more,
Whose ridges with the meeting clouds contend:
So did the merciless and pitchy night
Fold in the object that did feed her sight.

Whereat amaz'd, as one that unaware
Hath dropp'd a precious jewel in the flood,
Or 'stonish'd as night wanderers often are,
Their light blown out in some mistrustful wood;
Even so confounded in the dark she lay,
Having lost the fair discovery of her way.

And now she beats her heart, whereat it groans,
That all the neighbour-caves, as seeming troubled,
Make verbal repetition of her moans:
Passion on passion deeply is redoubled.
Ah me! she cries, and twenty times, woe, woe!
And twenty echoes twenty times cry so.

She marking them, begins a wailing note,
And sings extemporally a woeful ditty;
How love makes young men thrall, and old men dote;
How love is wise in folly, foolish witty:
Her heavy anthem still concludes in woe,
And still the choir of echoes answer so.

Her song was tedious, and outwore the night,
For lovers' hours are long, though seeming short:
If pleas'd themselves, others, they think, delight
In such like circumstance, with such like sport:
Their copious stories, oftentimes begun,
End without audience, and are never done.

For who hath she to spend the night withal,
But idle sounds resembling parasites;
Like shrill-tongu'd tapsters answering every call,
Soothing the humour of fantastic wits?
  She says, 't is so: they answer all, 't is so;
  And would say after her, if she said no.

Lo! here the gentle lark, weary of rest,
From his moist cabinet mounts up on high,
And wakes the morning, from whose silver breast
The sun ariseth in his majesty;
  Who doth the world so graciously behold,
  That cedar-tops and hills seem burnish'd gold.

Venus salutes him with this fair good-morrow.
O thou clear god, and patron of all light,
From whom each lamp and shining star doth borrow
The beauteous influence that makes him bright,
  There lives a son that suck'd an earthly mother,
  May lend thee light, as thou dost lend to other.

This said, she hasteth to a myrtle grove,
Musing the morning is so much o'er-worn;
And yet she hears no tidings of her love:
She hearkens, for his hounds, and for his horn:
  Anon she hears them chaunt it lustily,
  And all in haste she coasteth[1] to the cry.

And as she runs, the bushes in the way
Some catch her by the neck, some kiss her face,
Some twin'd about her thigh to make her stay.
She wildly breaketh from their strict embrace,
  Like a milch doe, whose swelling dugs do ache,
  Hasting to feed her fawn hid in some brake

By this she hears the hounds are at a bay,
Whereat she starts, like one that spies an adder
Wreath'd up in fatal folds, just in his way,
The fear whereof doth make him shake and shudder
  Even so the timorous yelping of the hounds
  Appals her senses, and her spirit confounds.

For now she knows it is no gentle chase,
But the blunt boar, rough bear, or lion proud,
Because the cry remaineth in one place,
Where fearfully the dogs exclaim aloud;

[1] *Approaches.*

Finding their enemy to be so curst,
They all strain courtesy who shall cope him first.

This dismal cry rings sadly in her ear,
Through which it enters to surprise her heart;
Who, overcome by doubt and bloodless fear,
With cold-pale weakness numbs each feeling part:
Like soldiers, when their captain once doth yield,
They basely fly, and dare not stay the field.

Thus stands she in a trembling extasy,
Till cheering up her senses all[1] dismay'd,
She tells them, 't is a causeless fantasy,
And childish error that they are afraid;
Bids them leave quaking, bids them fear no more:
And with that word she spied the hunted boar;

Whose frothy mouth bepainted all with red,
Like milk and blood being mingled both together,
A second fear through all her sinews spread,
Which madly hurries her she knows not whither:
This way she runs, and now she will no further,
But back retires to rate the boar for murther.

A thousand spleens bear her a thousand ways;
She treads the path that she untreads again:
Her more than haste is mated with delays,[2]
Like the proceedings of a drunken brain;
Full of respect,[3] yet nought at all respecting,
In hand with all things, nought at all affecting.

Here kennel'd in a brake she finds a hound,
And asks the weary caitiff for his master;
And there another licking of his wound,
'Gainst venom'd sores the only sovereign plaster;
And here she meets another sadly scowling,
To whom she speaks, and he replies with howling.

When he hath ceas'd his ill-resounding noise,
Another flap-mouth'd mourner, black and grim,
Against the welkin vollies out his voice;
Another and another answer him,
Clapping their proud tails to the ground below,
Shaking their scratch'd ears, bleeding as they go.

[1] sore: in ed. 1596. [2] *Confounded.* [3] respects: ed. 1596.

Look, how the world's poor people are amazed
At apparitions, signs, and prodigies,
Whereon with fearful eyes they long have gazed,
Infusing them with dreadful prophecies;
  So she at these sad signs draws up her breath,
  And, sighing it again, exclaims on death.

Hard-favour'd tyrant, ugly, meagre, lean,
Hateful divorce of love, (thus chides she death)
Grim grinning ghost, earth's worm, what dost thou mean,
To stifle beauty, and to steal his breath,
  Who when he liv'd, his breath and beauty set
  Gloss on the rose, smell to the violet?

If he be dead,—O no! it cannot be,
Seeing his beauty, thou shouldst strike at it.
O yes! it may; thou hast no eyes to see,
But hatefully at random dost thou hit.
  Thy mark is feeble age; but thy false dart
  Mistakes that aim, and cleaves an infant's heart.

Hadst thou but bid beware, then he had spoke,
And hearing him thy power had lost his power.
The destinies will curse thee for this stroke;
They bid thee crop a weed, thou pluck'st a flower.
  Love's golden arrow at him should have fled,
  And not death's ebon dart, to strike him dead.

Dost thou drink tears, that thou provok'st such weeping?
What may a heavy groan advantage thee?
Why hast thou cast into eternal sleeping
Those eyes that taught all other eyes to see?
  Now Nature cares not for thy mortal vigour,
  Since her best work is ruin'd with thy rigour.

Here overcome, as one full of despair,
She vail'd her eye-lids, who, like sluices, stopped
The crystal tide that from her two cheeks fair
In the sweet channel of her bosom dropped;
  But through the flood-gates breaks the silver rain,
  And with his strong course opens them again.

O, how her eyes and tears did lend and borrow!
Her eyes seen in the tears, tears in her eye;
Both crystals, where they view'd each other's sorrow,
Sorrow that friendly sighs sought still to dry;

But like a stormy day, now wind, now rain,
Sighs dry her cheeks, tears make them wet again

Variable passions throng her constant woe,
As striving who should best become her grief;
All entertain'd, each passion labours so,
That every present sorrow seemeth chief
But none is best; then, join they all together,
Like many clouds consulting for foul weather.

By this far off she hears some huntsman hollow;
A nurse's song ne'er pleas'd her babe so well:
The dire imagination she did follow
This sound of hope doth labour to expel;
For now reviving joy bids her rejoice
And flatters her it is Adonis' voice.

Whereat her tears began to turn their tide,
Being prison'd in her eye, like pearls in glass;
Yet sometimes falls an orient drop beside,
Which her cheek melts, as scorning it should pass
To wash the foul face of the sluttish ground,
Who is but drunken, when she seemeth drown'd.

O hard-believing love, how strange it seems
Not to believe, and yet too credulous!
Thy weal and woe are both of them extremes;
Despair and hope make thee ridiculous:
The one doth flatter thee in thoughts unlikely,
In likely thoughts the other kills thee quickly.

Now she unweaves the web that she hath wrought;
Adonis lives, and Death is not to blame:
It was not she that call'd him all to nought;
Now she adds honours to his hateful name;
She clepes him king of graves, and grave for kings
Imperious supreme of all mortal things.

No, no, quoth she, sweet Death, I did but jest;
Yet pardon me, I felt a kind of fear,
When as I met the boar, that bloody beast,
Which knows no pity, but is still severe;
Then, gentle shadow, (truth I must confess)
I rail'd on thee, fearing my love's decease.

'T is not my fault: the boar provok'd my tongue;
Be wreak'd on him, invisible commander;
'T is he, foul creature, that hath done thee wrong;
I did but act, he 's author of thy slander.
Grief hath two tongues, and never woman yet
Could rule them both, without ten women's wit

Thus hoping that Adonis is alive,
Her rash suspect she doth extenuate;
And that his beauty may the better thrive,
With death she humbly doth insinuate:
Tells him of trophies, statues, tombs, and stories,
His victories, his triumphs, and his glories.

O Jove! quoth she, how much a fool was I,
To be of such a weak and silly mind,
To wail his death, who lives, and must not die,
Till mutual overthrow of mortal kind;
For he being dead, with him is beauty slain,
And, beauty dead, black chaos comes again.

Fie, fie, fond love! thou art so full of fear,
As one with treasure laden, hemm'd with thieves·
Trifles, unwitnessed with eye or ear,
Thy coward heart with false bethinking grieves.
Even at this word she hears a merry horn,
Whereat she leaps that was but late forlorn.

As falcons[1] to the lure, away she flies:
The grass stoops not, she treads on it so light;
And in her haste unfortunately spies
The foul boar's conquest on her fair delight:
Which seen, her eyes, as murder'd with the view,
Like stars asham'd of day, themselves withdrew

Or, as the snail, whose tender horns being hit,
Shrinks backward in his shelly cave with pain,
And there all smother'd up in shade doth sit,
Long after fearing to creep forth again:
So, at his bloody view, her eyes are fled
Into the deep-dark cabins of her head:

Where they resign their office and their light
To the disposing of her troubled brain;
Who bids them still consort with ugly night,
And never wound the heart with looks again;

[1] falcon: in ed. 1600.

Who, like a king perplexed in his throne,
By their suggestion gives a deadly groan,

Whereat each tributary subject quakes;
As when the wind, imprison'd in the ground,
Struggling for passage, earth's foundation shakes,
Which with cold terror doth men's minds confound.
This mutiny each part doth so surprise,
That from their dark beds once more leap her eyes,

And, being open'd, threw unwilling light
Upon the wide wound that the boar had trench'd
In his soft flank; whose wonted lily white
With purple tears, that his wound wept, was drench'd:
No flower was nigh, no grass, herb, leaf, or weed,
But stole his blood, and seem'd with him to bleed.

This solemn sympathy poor Venus noteth;
Over one shoulder doth she hang her head,
Dumbly she passions, franticly she doteth;
She thinks he could not die, he is not dead.
Her voice is stopp'd, her joints forget to bow,
Her eyes are mad that they have wept till now.

Upon his hurt she looks so stedfastly,
That her sight dazzling makes the wound seem three;
And then she reprehends her mangling eye,
That makes more gashes where no breach should be:
His face seems twain, each several limb is doubled;
For oft the eye mistakes, the brain being troubled.

My tongue cannot express my grief for one,
And yet, quoth she, behold two Adons dead!
My sighs are blown away, my salt tears gone,
Mine eyes are turn'd to fire, my heart to lead:
Heavy heart's lead, melt at mine eyes' red fire!
So shall I die by drops of hot desire.

Alas, poor world, what treasure hast thou lost!
What face remains alive that 's worth the viewing?
Whose tongue is music now? what canst thou boast
Of things long since, or any thing ensuing?
The flowers are sweet, their colours fresh and trim;
But true sweet beauty liv'd and died with him.

Bonnet nor veil henceforth no creature wear;
Nor sun nor wind will ever strive to kiss you:
Having no fair to lose, you need not fear;
The sun doth scorn you, and the wind doth hiss you:
But when Adonis liv'd, sun and sharp air
Lurk'd like two thieves, to rob him of his fair:

And therefore would he put his bonnet on,
Under whose brim the gaudy sun would peep,
The wind would blow it off, and, being gone,
Play with his locks: then, would Adonis weep,
And straight in pity of his tender years,
They both would strive who first should dry his tears.

To see his face, the lion walk'd along
Behind some hedge, because he would not fear[1] him;
To recreate himself when he hath sung,
The tiger would be tame, and gently hear him;
If he had spoke, the wolf would leave his prey,
And never fright the silly lamb that day.

When he beheld his shadow in the brook,
The fishes spread on it their golden gills:
When he was by, the birds such pleasure took,
That some would sing, some other in their bills
Would bring him mulberries, and ripe red cherries;
He fed them with his sight, they him with berries.

But this foul, grim, and urchin-snouted[2] boar,
Whose downward eye still looketh for a grave,
Ne'er saw the beauteous livery that he wore;
Witness the entertainment that he gave:
If he did see his face, why then, I know,
He thought to kiss him, and hath kill'd him so.

'T is true, 't is true: thus was Adonis slain.
He ran upon the boar with his sharp spear,
Who did[3] not whet his teeth at him again,
But by a kiss thought to persuade him there;
And nuzzling in his flank, the loving swine
Sheath'd, unaware, the tusk in his soft groin.

[1] *Alarm.* [2] An urchin, is a *hedge-hog*, it is so employed in "Titus Andronicus," Act II., sc. 3; but in "The Tempest," Act I., sc. 2. it rather means an *evil spirit*, or *fairy*. [3] would: in eds. 1594 and 1596.

Had I been tooth'd like him, I must confess,
With kissing him I should have kill'd him first:
But he is dead, and never did he bless
My youth with his, the more am I accurst.
With this she falleth in the place she stood,
And stains her face with his congealed blood.

She looks upon his lips, and they are pale;
She takes him by the hand, and that is cold;
She whispers in his ears a heavy tale,
As if they heard the woful words she told:
She lifts the coffer-lids that close his eyes,
Where lo! two lamps, burnt out, in darkness lies:

Two glasses, where herself herself beheld
A thousand times, and now no more reflect;
Their virtue lost, wherein they late excell'd,
And every beauty robb'd of his effect:
Wonder of time, quoth she, this is my spite,
That, thou[1] being dead, the day should yet be light

Since thou art dead, lo! here I prophesy,
Sorrow on love hereafter shall attend:
It shall be waited on with jealousy,
Find sweet beginning, but unsavoury end;
Ne'er settled equally, but high or low,
That all love's pleasure shall not match his woe.

It shall be fickle, false, and full of fraud;
Bud and be blasted in a breathing-while;
The bottom poison, and the top o'er-straw'd
With sweets, that shall the truest sight beguile:
The strongest body shall it make most weak,
Strike the wise dumb, and teach the fool to speak.

It shall be sparing, and too full of riot,
Teaching decrepit age to tread the measures;
The staring ruffian shall it keep in quiet,
Pluck down the rich, enrich the poor with treasures:
It shall be raging mad, and silly mild,
Make the young old, the old become a child.

It shall suspect, where is no cause of fear;
It shall not fear, where it should most mistrust;
It shall be merciful, and too severe,
And most deceiving, when it seems most just;

[1] you: in ed 1600.

Perverse it shall be, where it shows most toward;
Put fear to valour, courage to the coward.

It shall be cause of war, and dire events,
And set dissension 'twixt the son and sire;
Subject and servile to all discontents,
As dry combustious matter is to fire:
Sith in his prime death doth my love destroy,
They that love best, their loves shall not enjoy.

By this the boy, that by her side lay kill'd,
Was melted like a vapour from her sight,
And in his blood, that on the ground lay spill'd,
A purple flower sprung up, checquer'd with white;
Resembling well his pale cheeks, and the blood
Which in round drops upon their whiteness stood.

She bows her head the new-sprung flower to smell,
Comparing it to her Adonis' breath;
And says, within her bosom it shall dwell,
Since he himself is reft from her by death:
She crops the stalk, and in the breach appears
Green dropping sap, which she compares to tears.

Poor flower, quoth she, this was thy father's guise,
Sweet issue of a more sweet-smelling sire,
For every little grief to wet his eyes:
To grow unto himself was his desire,
And so 't is thine; but know, it is as good
To wither in my breast, as in his blood.

Here was thy father's bed, here in my breast;
Thou art the next of blood, and 't is thy right:
Lo! in this hollow cradle take thy rest,
My throbbing heart shall rock thee day and night:
There shall not be one minute in an hour,
Wherein I will not kiss my sweet love's flower.

Thus weary of the world, away she hies,
And yokes her silver doves; by whose swift aid
Their mistress mounted through the empty skies
In her light chariot quickly is convey'd;
Holding their course to Paphos, where their queen
Means to immure herself and not be seen.

THE RAPE OF LUCRECE.

"Lvcrece. London. Printed by Richard Field, for Iohn Harrison, and are to be sold at the signe of the white Greyhound in Paules Church-yard. 1594." 4to. 47 leaves.

"Lvcrece At London, Printed by P. S. for Iohn Harrison. 1598." 8vo. 36 leaves.

"Lvcrece London. Printed by I. H. for Iohn Harrison. 1600." 8vo. 36 leaves.

"Lvcrece. At London, Printed be N. O. for Iohn Harison. 1607." 8vo. 32 leaves.]

INTRODUCTION.

"Lucrece," as it is merely called in the earlier impressions, came out in the year following "Venus and Adonis," and it was printed for John Harrison, the publisher of the edition of "Venus and Adonis," in 1596. It had been previously entered, under a more explanatory title, in the Stationers' Registers:

"9 May 1594.

"Mr. Harrison, sen.] A booke intitled the Ravyshement of Lucrece."

Like, "Venus and Adonis," it was dedicated to the Earl of Southampton, but in a more confident and assured spirit.

This second production was, probably, not quite so popular as the first, and it was not again printed until 1598, for the same bookseller, who put forth a third edition of it in 1600: the fourth edition was issued in 1607: these are not so marked, and Malone tells us that he had heard of impressions in 1596 and 1602, but they have not since come to light; and our belief is, that "Lucrece" was only printed four times between 1594 and 1607. An edition in 1616 purports to have been "newly revised and corrected;" but, as Malone truly states, "it is the most inaccurate and corrupt of the ancient copies;" and he adds that "most of the alterations seem to have been made, because the reviser did not understand the poet's meaning." That Shakespeare had nothing to do with the revision and correction of this edition requires no proof; and so little was it esteemed, that it was not followed in its changes in the edition of 1624, which also professes to have been "newly revised." This last is accompanied by marginal notes, prosaically explanatory of the incidents poetically narrated.

The earliest mention of "Lucrece" occurs in the year in which it made its first appearance. Michael Drayton published his "Matilda," (a poem in seven-line stanzas, like "Lucrece") in 1594, and there we meet with the following passage:—

"Lucrece, of whom proud Rome hath boasted long,
Lately reviv'd to live another age,
And here arriv'd to tell of Tarquin's wrong,
Her chaste denial, and the tyrant's rage,
Acting her passions on our stately stage:
She is remember'd, all forgetting me,
Yet I as fair and chaste as e'er was she."

A difficulty here may arise out of the fifth line, as if Drayton were referring to a play upon the story of Lucrece, and it is very possible that one was then in existence. Thomas Heywood's tragedy, "The Rape of Lucrece," did not appear in print until 1608, and he could hardly have been old enough to have been the author of such a drama in 1594: he may, nevertheless, have availed himself of an elder play, and, according to the practice of the time, he may have felt warranted in publishing it as his own. It is likely, however, that Drayton's expressions are not to be taken literally, and that his meaning merely was, that the story of Lucrece had lately been revived, and brought upon the stage of the world: if this opinion be correct, the stanza we have above quoted contains a clear allusion to Shakespeare's "Lucrece;" and a question then presents itself, why Drayton entirely omitted it in the after impressions of his "Matilda?" He was a poet who, as we have shown in the Introduction to "Julius Cæsar," was in the habit of making extensive alterations in his productions, as they were severally reprinted, and the suppression of this stanza may have proceeded from many other causes than repentance of the praise he had bestowed upon a rival.

The edition of "Lucrece" we have taken as our text is the first, which, like "Venus and Adonis," was printed by Richard Field, though not on his own account. It may be stated on the whole to be an extremely creditable specimen of his typography: as the sheets were going through the press, some material errors were, however, observed in them, and they are therefore in several places corrected. This fact has hitherto escaped remark, but the variations are explained in our notes.

Modern editors have performed their task without due care, but of their want of attention we shall only here adduce two specimens. In one of the speeches in which Lucrece endeavours to dissuade Tarquin from his purpose, she tells him,

"Thou back'st reproach against *long-living* laud."

Which every modern editor misprints,

"Thou back'st reproach against *long-lived* laud."

Our second proof is from a later portion of the poem, just after Collatine has returned home, and meets his dishonoured wife: the true text, speaking of Collatine and Lucretia, is,

"*Both* stood like old acquaintance in a trance
Met far from home, wondering each other's chance."

Malone, and all editors after him, make nonsense of the couplet, by printing,

"*But* stood like old acquaintance in a trance," &c.

depriving the verb of its nominative, and destroying the whole force of the figure. It would be easy to add other instances of the same kind, but we refer for them to our notes.

TO THE RIGHT HONOURABLE

HENRY WRIOTHESLY,

EARL OF SOUTHAMPTON, AND BARON OF TICHFIELD.

THE love I dedicate to your lordship is without end; whereof this pamphlet, without beginning, is but a superfluous moiety. The warrant I have of your honourable disposition, not the worth of my untutored lines, makes it assured of acceptance. What I have done is yours; what I have to do is yours; being part in all I have, devoted yours. Were my worth greater, my duty would show greater[1]; mean time, as it is, it is bound to your lordship, to whom I wish long life, still lengthened with all happiness.

Your lordship's in all duty,

WILLIAM SHAKESPEARE.

[1] —my duty WOULD show greater;] Some of the later impressions, the editions of 1607 and 1624 for instance, read *should* for "would." In Malone's Shakspeare, by Boswell, the word "all," before "happiness," is omitted.

THE ARGUMENT.

Lucius Tarquinius (for his excessive pride surnamed Superbus) after he had caused his own father-in-law, Servius Tullius, to be cruelly murdered, and, contrary to the Roman laws and customs, not requiring or staying for the people's suffrages, had possessed himself of the kingdom, went, accompanied with his sons and other noblemen of Rome, to besiege Ardea: during which siege, the principal men of the army meeting one evening at the tent of Sextus Tarquinius, the king's son, in their discourses after supper every one commended the virtues of his own wife; among whom, Collatinus extolled the incomparable chastity of his wife Lucretia. In that pleasant humour they all posted to Rome; and intending by their secret and sudden arrival, to make trial of that which every one had before avouched, only Collatinus finds his wife (though it were late in the night) spinning amongst her maids: the other ladies were all found dancing and revelling, or in several disports; whereupon the noblemen yielded Collatinus the victory, and his wife the fame. At that time Sextus Tarquinius, being inflamed with Lucrece' beauty, yet smothering his passions for the present, departed with the rest back to the camp; from whence he shortly after privily withdrew himself, and was (according to his estate) royally entertained and lodged by Lucrece at Collatium. The same night he treacherously stealeth into her chamber, violently ravished her, and early in the morning speedeth away. Lucrece, in this lamentable plight, hastily dispatcheth messengers, one to Rome for her father, another to the camp for Collatine. They came, the one accompanied with Junius Brutus, the other with Publius Valerius; and finding Lucrece attired in mourning habit, demanded the cause of her sorrow. She, first taking an oath of them for her revenge, revealed the actor, and whole manner of his dealing, and withal suddenly stabbed herself: which done, with one consent they all vowed to root out the whole hated family of the Tarquins; and bearing the dead body to Rome, Brutus acquainted the people with the doer, and manner of the vile deed, with a bitter invective against the tyranny of the king; wherewith the people were so moved, that, with one consent and a general acclamation, the Tarquins were all exiled, and the state government changed from kings to consuls.

THE RAPE OF LUCRECE

FROM the besieged Ardea all in post,
Borne by the trustless wings of false desire,
Lust-breathed Tarquin leaves the Roman host,
And to Collatium bears the lightless fire
Which, in pale embers hid, lurks to aspire,
And girdle with embracing flames the waist
Of Collatine's fair love, Lucrece the chaste.

Haply that name of chaste unhappily set
This bateless edge on his keen appetite;
When Collatine unwisely did not let
To praise the clear unmatched red and white,
Which triumph'd in that sky of his delight;
Where mortal stars, as bright as heaven's beauties
With pure aspects did him peculiar duties.

For he the night before, in Tarquin's tent,
Unlock'd the treasure of his happy state;
What priceless wealth the heavens had him lent
In the possession of his beauteous mate;
Reckoning his fortune at such high proud rate,
That kings might be espoused to more fame,
But king nor peer to such a peerless dame.

O happiness! enjoy'd but of a few;
And, if possess'd, as soon decay'd and done,
As is the morning's silver-melting dew
Against the golden splendour of the sun;
An expir'd date, cancell'd ere well begun:
Honour and beauty, in the owner's arms,
Are weakly fortress'd from a world of harms.

Beauty itself doth of itself persuade
The eyes of men without an orator;
What needeth, then, apologies be made
To set forth that which is so singular?
Or why is Collatine the publisher
Of that rich jewel he should keep unknown
From thievish ears, because it is his own?

Perchance his boast of Lucrece' sovereignty
Suggested[1] this proud issue of a king,
For by our ears our hearts oft tainted be:
Perchance that envy of so rich a thing,
Braving compare, disdainfully did sting
His high-pitch'd thoughts, that meaner men should vaunt
That golden hap which their superiors want.

But some untimely thought did instigate
His all too timeless speed, if none of those:
His honour, his affairs, his friends, his state,
Neglected all, with swift intent he goes
To quench the coal which in his liver glows.
O rash, false heat! wrapt in repentant cold,
Thy hasty spring still blasts, and ne'er grows old.

When at Collatium this false lord arrived,
Well was he welcom'd by the Roman dame,
Within whose face beauty and virtue strived
Which of them both should underprop her fame:
When virtue bragg'd, beauty would blush for shame;
When beauty boasted blushes, in despite
Virtue would stain that o'er with silver white.

But beauty, in that white intituled,
From Venus' doves doth challenge that fair field;
Then, virtue claims from beauty beauty's red,
Which virtue gave the golden age to gild
Their silver cheeks, and call'd it then their shield;
Teaching them thus to use it in the fight,
When shame assail'd, the red should fence the white

This heraldry in Lucrece' face was seen,
Argued by beauty's red, and virtue's white:
Of either's colour was the other queen,
Proving from world's minority their right,
Yet their ambition makes them still to fight,

[1] *Instigated.*

  The sovereignty of either being so great,
  That oft they interchange each other's seat.

This silent war of lilies and of roses,
Which Tarquin view'd in her fair face's field,
In their pure ranks his traitor eye encloses;
Where, lest between them both it should be kill'd,
The coward captive vanquished doth yield
  To those two armies, that would let him go,
  Rather than triumph in so false a foe.

Now thinks he, that her husband's shallow tongue,
The niggard prodigal that prais'd her so,
In that high task hath done her beauty wrong,
Which far exceeds his barren skill to show:
Therefore, that praise which Collatine doth owe,
  Enchanted Tarquin answers with surmise,
  In silent wonder of still gazing eyes

This earthly saint, adored by this devil,
Little suspecteth the false worshipper,
For unstain'd thoughts do seldom dream on evil,
Birds never lim'd no secret bushes fear:
So guiltless she securely gives good cheer,
  And reverend welcome to her princely guest,
  Whose inward ill no outward harm express'd:

For that he colour'd with his high estate,
Hiding base sin in plaits of majesty;
That nothing in him seem'd inordinate,
Save sometime too much wonder of his eye,
Which, having all, all could not satisfy;
  But, poorly rich, so wanteth in his store,
  That cloy'd with much, he pineth still for more.

But she, that never cop'd with stranger eyes,
Could pick no meaning from their parling looks,
Nor read the subtle shining secrecies
Writ in the glassy margents of such books:
She touch'd no unknown baits, nor fear'd no hooks;
  Nor could she moralize his wanton sight,
  More than his eyes were open'd to the light.

He stories to her ears her husband's fame,
Won in the fields of fruitful Italy;
And decks with praises Collatine's high name,
Made glorious by his manly chivalry,
With bruised arms and wreaths of victory.
Her joy with heav'd-up hand she doth express,
And wordless so greets heaven for his success.

Far from the purpose of his coming thither,
He makes excuses for his being there:
No cloudy show of stormy blustering weather
Doth yet in his fair welkin once appear;
Till sable night, mother of dread and fear,
Upon the world dim darkness doth display,
And in her vaulty prison stows the day.

For then is Tarquin brought unto his bed,
Intending[1] weariness with heavy sprite;
For after supper long he questioned
With modest Lucrece, and wore out the night:
Now leaden slumber with life's strength doth fight,
And every one to rest themselves betake,
Save thieves, and cares, and troubled minds, that wake.

As one of which doth Tarquin lie revolving
The sundry dangers of his will's obtaining;
Yet ever to obtain his will resolving,
Though weak-built hopes persuade him to abstaining:
Despair to gain doth traffick oft for gaining;
And when great treasure is the meed proposed,
Though death be adjunct, there's no death supposed.

Those that much covet are with gain so fond,
That what they have not, that which they possess,
They scatter and unloose it from their bond,
And so, by hoping more, they have but less;
Or, gaining more, the profit of excess
Is but to surfeit, and such griefs sustain,
That they prove bankrupt in this poor rich gain.

The aim of all is but to nurse the life
With honour, wealth, and ease, in waning age;
And in this aim there is such thwarting strife,
That one for all, or all for one we gage;
As life for honour in fell battles' rage;

[1] *Pretending.*

Honour for wealth, and oft that wealth doth cost
The death of all, and all together lost.

So that in venturing ill, we leave to be
The things we are for that which we expect;
And this ambitious foul infirmity,
In having much, torments us with defect
Of that we have: so then we do neglect
The thing we have; and, all for want of wit,
Make something nothing by augmenting it.

Such hazard now must doting Tarquin make,
Pawning his honour to obtain his lust,
And for himself himself he must forsake.
Then, where is truth, if there be no self-trust?
When shall he think to find a stranger just,
When he himself himself confounds, betrays
To slanderous tongues, and wretched hateful days?

Now stole upon the time the dead of night,
When heavy sleep had clos'd up mortal eyes;
No comfortable star did lend his light,
No noise but owls' and wolves' death-boding cries:
Now serves the season that they may surprise
The silly lambs. Pure thoughts are dead and still,
While lust and murder wake, to stain and kill.

And now this lustful lord leap'd from his bed,
Throwing his mantle rudely o'er his arm,
Is madly toss'd between desire and dread;
Th' one sweetly flatters, th' other feareth harm;
But honest fear, bewitch'd with lust's foul charm,
Doth too too oft betake him to retire,
Beaten away by brain-sick rude desire.

His falchion on a flint he softly smiteth,
That from the cold stone sparks of fire do fly,
Whereat a waxen torch forthwith he lighteth,
Which must be lode-star to his lustful eye;
And to the flame thus speaks advisedly:
As from this cold flint I enforc'd this fire,
So Lucrece must I force to my desire.

Here, pale with fear, he doth premeditate
The dangers of his loathsome enterprise,
And in his inward mind he doth debate
What following sorrow may on this arise:
Then, looking scornfully, he doth despise
His naked armour of still slaughtered lust,
And justly thus controls his thoughts unjust.

Fair torch, burn out thy light, and lend it not
To darken her whose light excelleth thine;
And die, unhallow'd thoughts, before you blot
With your uncleanness that which is divine:
Offer pure incense to so pure a shrine:
Let fair humanity abhor the deed,
That spots and stains love's modest snow-white weed

O shame to knighthood, and to shining arms!
O foul dishonour to my household's grave!
O impious act, including all foul harms!
A martial man to be soft fancy's slave!
True valour still a true respect should have;
Then, my digression is so vile, so base,
That it will live engraven in my face.

Yea, though I die, the scandal will survive,
And be an eye-sore in my golden coat;
Some loathsome dash the herald will contrive,
To cipher me how fondly I did dote;
That my posterity, sham'd with the note,
Shall curse my bones, and hold it for no sin
To wish that I their father had not been.

What win I, if I gain the thing I seek?
A dream, a breath, a froth of fleeting joy.
Who buys a minute's mirth to wail a week,
Or sells eternity to get a toy?
For one sweet grape who will the vine destroy?
Or what fond beggar, but to touch the crown,
Would with the sceptre straight be stricken down?

If Collatinus dream of my intent,
Will he not wake, and in a desperate rage
Post hither, this vile purpose to prevent?
This siege that hath engirt his marriage,
This blur to youth, this sorrow to the sage,

This dying virtue, this surviving shame,
Whose crime will bear an ever-during blame.

O ! what excuse can my invention make,
When thou shalt charge me with so black a deed?
Will not my tongue be mute, my frail joints shake,
Mine eyes forego their light, my false heart bleed?
The guilt being great, the fear doth still exceed;
And extreme fear can neither fight nor fly,
But coward-like with trembling terror die.

Had Collatinus kill'd my son or sire,
Or lain in ambush to betray my life,
Or were he not my dear friend, this desire
Might have excuse to work upon his wife,
As in revenge or quital of such strife:
But as he is my kinsman, my dear friend,
The shame and fault finds no excuse nor end.

Shameful it is;—ay, if the fact be known:
Hateful it is;—there is no hate in loving:
I'll beg her love:—but she is not her own:
The worst is but denial, and reproving.
My will is strong, past reason's weak removing
Who fears a sentence, or an old man's saw,
Shall by a painted cloth be kept in awe.

Thus, graceless, holds he disputation
'Tween frozen conscience and hot burning will,
And with good thoughts makes dispensation,
Urging the worser sense for vantage still;
Which in a moment doth confound and kill
All pure effects, and doth so far proceed,
That what is vile shows like a virtuous deed.

Quoth he, she took me kindly by the hand,
And gaz'd for tidings in my eager eyes,
Fearing some hard news from the warlike band,
Where her beloved Collatinus lies.
O, how her fear did make her colour rise!
First red as roses that on lawn we lay,
Then, white as lawn, the roses took away.

And how her hand, in my hand being lock'd,
Forc'd it to tremble with her loyal fear!
Which struck her sad, and then it faster rock'd,
Until her husband's welfare she did hear;
Whereat she smiled with so sweet a cheer,
That had Narcissus seen her as she stood,
Self-love had never drown'd him in the flood.

Why hunt I, then, for colour or excuses?
All orators are dumb when beauty pleadeth;
Poor wretches have remorse in poor abuses;
Love thrives not in the heart that shadows dreadeth:
Affection is my captain, and he leadeth;
And when his gaudy banner is display'd,
The coward fights, and will not be dismay'd.

Then, childish fear, avaunt! debating, die!
Respect and reason, wait on wrinkled age!
My heart shall never countermand mine eye:
Sad pause and deep regard beseem the sage;
My part is youth, and beats these from the stage.
Desire my pilot is, beauty my prize;
Then, who fears sinking where such treasure lies?

As corn o'er-grown by weeds, so heedful fear
Is almost chok'd by unresisted lust.
Away he steals with open listening ear,
Full of foul hope, and full of fond mistrust;
Both which, as servitors to the unjust,
So cross him with their opposite persuasion,
That now he vows a league, and now invasion.

Within his thought her heavenly image sits,
And in the selfsame seat sits Collatine:
That eye which looks on her confounds his wits;
That eye which him beholds, as more divine,
Unto a view so false will not incline;
But with a pure appeal seeks to the heart,
Which, once corrupted, takes the worser part;

And therein heartens up his servile powers,
Who, flatter'd by their leader's jocund show,
Stuff up his lust, as minutes fill up hours;
And as their captain, so their pride doth grow,
Paying more slavish tribute than they owe.

By reprobate desire thus madly led,
The Roman lord marcheth to Lucrece' bed.

The locks between her chamber and his will,
Each one by him enforc'd retires his ward;
But as they open they all rate his ill,
Which drives the creeping thief to some regard:
The threshold grates the door to have him heard;
Night-wandering weesels shriek, to see him there;
They fright him, yet he still pursues his fear.

As each unwilling portal yields him way,
Through little vents and crannies of the place
The wind wars with his torch to make him stay,
And blows the smoke of it into his face,
Extinguishing his conduct in this case;
But his hot heart, with fond desire doth scorch,
Puffs forth another wind that fires the torch:

And being lighted, by the light he spies
Lucretia's glove, wherein her needle sticks:
He takes it from the rushes where it lies,
And griping it, the needle his finger pricks;
As who should say, this glove to wanton tricks
Is not inur'd; return again in haste;
Thou seest our mistress' ornaments are chaste.

But all these poor forbiddings could not stay him;
He in the worst sense construes their denial:
The doors, the wind, the glove, that did delay him,
He takes for accidental things of trial,
Or as those bars which stop the hourly dial;
Who with a ling'ring stay his course doth let,
Till every minute pays the hour his debt.

So, so, quoth he; these lets attend the time,
Like little frosts that sometime threat the spring,
To add a more rejoicing to the prime,
And give the sneaped[1] birds more cause to sing.
Pain pays the income of each precious thing; [sands,
Huge rocks, high winds, strong pirates, shelves and
The merchant fears, ere rich at home he lands.

[1] Nipped by the frost.

Now is he come unto the chamber-door,
That shuts him from the heaven of his thought,
Which with a yielding latch, and with no more,
Hath barr'd him from the blessed thing he sought
So from himself impiety hath wrought,
  That for his prey to pray he doth begin,
  As if the heavens should countenance his sin.

But in the midst of his unfruitful prayer,
Having solicited th' eternal power
That his foul thoughts might compass his fair fair,
And they would stand auspicious to the hour,
Even there he starts :—quoth he, I must deflower:
  The powers to whom I pray abhor this fact,
  How can they, then, assist me in the act?

Then Love and Fortune be my gods, my guide!
My will is back'd with resolution:
Thoughts are but dreams, till their effects be tried;
The blackest sin is clear'd with absolution;
Against love's fire fear's frost hath dissolution.
  The eye of heaven is out, and misty night
  Covers the shame that follows sweet delight.

This said, his guilty hand pluck'd up the latch,
And with his knee the door he opens wide.
The dove sleeps fast that this night-owl will catch:
Thus treason works ere traitors be espied.
Who sees the lurking serpent steps aside;
  But she, sound sleeping, fearing no such thing,
  Lies at the mercy of his mortal sting.

Into the chamber wickedly he stalks,
And gazeth on her yet-unstained bed.
The curtains being close, about he walks,
Rolling his greedy eye-balls in his head:
By their high treason is his heart misled;
  Which gives the watch-word to his hand full soon,
  To draw the cloud that hides the silver moon.

Look, as the fair and fiery pointed sun,
Rushing from forth a cloud, bereaves our sight;
Even so, the curtain drawn, his eyes begun
To wink, being blinded with a greater light:
Whether it i , that she reflects so bright,

That dazzleth them, or else some shame supposed,
But blind they are, and keep themselves enclosed.

O! had they in that darksome prison died,
Then had they seen the period of their ill
Then Collatine again, by Lucrece' side,
In his clear bed might have reposed still;
But they must ope, this blessed league to kill,
And holy-thoughted Lucrece to their sight
Must sell her joy, her life, her world's delight.

Her lily hand her rosy cheek lies under,
Cozening the pillow of a lawful kiss,
Who, therefore angry, seems to part in sunder,
Swelling on either side to want his bliss,
Between whose hills her head intombed is;
Where, like a virtuous monument, she lies,
To be admir'd of lewd unhallowed eyes.

Without the bed her other fair hand was,
On the green coverlet; whose perfect white
Show'd like an April daisy on the grass,
With pearly sweat, resembling dew of night.
Her eyes, like marigolds, had sheath'd their light,
And canopied in darkness sweetly lay,
Till they might open to adorn the day.

Her hair, like golden threads, play'd with her breath
O modest wantons! wanton modesty!
Showing life's triumph in the map of death,
And death's dim look in life's mortality:
Each in her sleep themselves so beautify,
As if between them twain there were no strife,
But that life liv'd in death, and death in life.

Her breasts, like ivory globes circled with blue,
A pair of maiden worlds unconquered;
Save of their lord, no bearing yoke they knew,
And him by oath they truly honoured
These worlds in Tarquin new ambition bred;
Who, like a foul usurper, went about
From this fair throne to heave the owner out.

What could he see, but mightily he noted?
What did he note, but strongly he desired?
What he beheld, on that he firmly doted,
And in his will his wilful eye he tired.[1]
With more than admiration he admired
   Her azure veins, her alabaster skin,
   Her coral lips, her snow-white dimpled chin.

As the grim lion fawneth o'er his prey,
Sharp hunger by the conquest satisfied,
So o'er this sleeping soul doth Tarquin stay,
His rage of lust by gazing qualified;
Slak'd, not suppress'd; for standing by her side,
   His eye, which late this mutiny restrains,
   Unto a greater uproar tempts his veins:

And they, like straggling slaves for pillage fighting,
Obdurate vassals fell exploits effecting,
In bloody death and ravishment delighting,
Nor children's tears, nor mothers' groans respecting,
Swell in their pride, the onset still expecting:
   Anon his beating heart, alarum striking,
   Gives the hot charge, and bids them do their liking.

His drumming heart cheers up his burning eye,
His eye commends the leading to his hand;
His hand, as proud of such a dignity,
Smoking with pride, march'd on to make his stand
On her bare breast, the heart of all her land,
   Whose ranks of blue veins, as his hand did scale,
   Left their round turrets destitute and pale.

They, mustering to the quiet cabinet
Where their dear governess and lady lies,
Do tell her she is dreadfully beset,
And fright her with confusion of their cries:
She, much amaz'd, breaks ope her lock'd-up eyes,
   Who, peeping forth this tumult to behold,
   Are by his flaming torch dimm'd and controll'd.

Imagine her as one in dead night
From forth dull sleep by dreadful fancy waking,
That thinks she hath beheld some ghastly sprite,
Whose grim aspect sets every joint a shaking,
What terror 't is! but she, in worser taking,

[1] *Fed*, as a falcon on his prey.

From sleep disturbed, heedfully doth view
The sight which makes supposed terror true.

Wrapp'd and confounded in a thousand fears,
Like to a new-kill'd bird she trembling lies;
She dares not look; yet, winking, there appears
Quick-shifting antics, ugly in her eyes:
Such shadows are the weak brain's forgeries;
Who, angry that the eyes fly from their lights,
In darkness daunts them with more dreadful sights

His hand, that yet remains upon her breast,
(Rude ram to batter such an ivory wall)
May feel her heart (poor citizen!) distress'd,
Wounding itself to death, rise up and fall,
Beating her bulk, that his hand shakes withal.
This moves in him more rage, and lesser pity,
To make the breach, and enter this sweet city.

First, like a trumpet, doth his tongue begin
To sound a parley to his heartless foe;
Who o'er the white sheet peers her whiter chin,
The reason of this rash alarm to know,
Which he by dumb demeanour seeks to show;
But she with vehement prayers urgeth still,
Under what colour he commits this ill.

Thus he replies: The colour in thy face
That even for anger makes the lily pale,
And the red rose blush at her own disgrace,
Shall plead for me, and tell my loving tale;
Under that colour am I come to scale
Thy never conquer'd fort: the fault is thine,
For those thine eyes betray thee unto mine.

Thus I forestall thee, if thou mean to chide:
Thy beauty hath ensnar'd thee to this night,
Where thou with patience must my will abide,
My will, that marks thee for my earth's delight,
Which I to conquer sought with all my might;
But as reproof and reason beat it dead,
By thy bright beauty was it newly bred.

I see what crosses my attempt will bring,
I know what thorns the growing rose defends,
I think the honey guarded with a sting;
All this beforehand counsel comprehends,
But will is deaf, and hears no heedful friends:
  Only he hath an eye to gaze on beauty,
  And dotes on what he looks, 'gainst law or duty.

I have debated, even in my soul,
What wrong, what shame, what sorrow I shall breed,
But nothing can affection's course control,
Or stop the headlong fury of his speed.
I know repentant tears ensue the deed,
  Reproach, disdain, and deadly enmity,
  Yet strive I to embrace mine infamy.

This said, he shakes aloft his Roman blade,
Which, like a falcon towering in the skies,
Coucheth the fowl below with his wings' shade,
Whose crooked beak threats, if he mount he dies:
So under his insulting falchion lies
  Harmless Lucretia, marking what he tells,
  With trembling fear, as fowl hear falcon's bells.

Lucrece, quoth he, this night I must enjoy thee:
If thou deny, then force must work my way,
For in thy bed I purpose to destroy thee.
That done, some worthless slave of thine I 'll slay,
To kill thine honour with thy life's decay;
  And in thy dead arms do I mean to place him,
  Swearing I slew him, seeing thee embrace him.

So thy surviving husband shall remain
The scornful mark of every open eye;
Thy kinsmen hang their heads at this disdain,
Thy issue blurr'd with nameless bastardy:
And thou, the author of their obloquy,
  Shalt have thy trespass cited up in rhymes,
  And sung by children in succeeding times.

But if thou yield, I rest thy secret friend:
The fault unknown is as a thought unacted;
A little harm, done to a great good end,
For lawful policy remains enacted.
The poisonous simple sometimes is compacted

In a pure compound; being so applied,
His venom in effect is purified.

Then, for thy husband and thy children's sake,
Tender my suit: bequeath not to their lot
The shame that from them no device can take,
The blemish that will never be forgot;
Worse than a slavish wipe, or birth-hour's blot;
For marks descried in men's nativity
Are nature's faults, not their own infamy.

Here, with a cockatrice' dead-killing eye,
He rouseth up himself, and makes a pause;
While she, the picture of pure piety,
Like a white hind under the gripe's[1] sharp claws,
Pleads in a wilderness, where are no laws,
To the rough beast that knows no gentle right,
Nor aught obeys but his foul appetite.

But when a black-fac'd cloud the world doth threat,
In his dim mist th' aspiring mountains hiding,
From earth's dark womb some gentle gust doth get,
Which blows these pitchy vapours from their biding,
Hindering their present fall by this dividing:
So his unhallowed haste her words delays,
And moody Pluto winks, while Orpheus plays.

Yet, foul night-waking cat, he doth but dally,
While in his hold-fast foot the weak mouse panteth:
Her sad behaviour feeds his vulture folly,
A swallowing gulf that even in plenty wanteth.
His ear her prayers admits, but his heart granteth
No penetrable entrance to her plaining:
Tears harden lust, though marble wears with raining

Her pity-pleading eyes are sadly fixed
In the remorseless wrinkles of his face;
Her modest eloquence with sighs is mixed,
Which to her oratory adds more grace.
She puts the period often from his place;
And 'midst the sentence so her accent breaks,
That twice she doth begin, ere once she speaks.

[1] Vulture.

She conjures him by high almighty Jove,
By knighthood, gentry, and sweet friendship's oath
By her untimely tears, her husband's love,
By holy human law, and common troth,
By heaven and earth, and all the power of both,
  That to his borrow'd bed he make retire,
  And stoop to honour, not to foul desire.

Quoth she, reward not hospitality
With such black payment as thou hast pretended;[1]
Mud not the fountain that gave drink to thee;
Mar not the thing that cannot be amended;
End thy ill aim before thy shoot be ended:
  He is no wood-man, that doth bend his bow
  To strike a poor unseasonable doe.

My husband is thy friend, for his sake spare me;
Thyself art mighty, for thine own sake leave me;
Myself a weakling, do not then ensnare me;
Thou look'st not like deceit, do not deceive me:
My sighs, like whirlwinds, labour hence to heave thee
  If ever man were mov'd with woman's moans,
  Be moved with my tears, my sighs, my groans.

All which together, like a troubled ocean,
Beat at thy rocky and wreck-threatening heart,
To soften it with their continual motion;
For stones dissolv'd to water do convert.
O, if no harder than a stone thou art,
  Melt at my tears and be compassionate!
  Soft pity enters at an iron gate.

In Tarquin's likeness I did entertain thee;
Hast thou put on his shape to do him shame?
To all the host of heaven I complain me,
Thou wrong'st his honour, wound'st his princely name
Thou art not what thou seem'st; and if the same,
  Thou seem'st not what thou art, a god, a king;
  For kings like gods should govern every thing.

How will thy shame be seeded in thine age,
When thus thy vices bud before thy spring?
If in thy hope thou dar'st do such outrage,
What dar'st thou not, when once thou art a king?
O, be remember'd! no outrageous thing

[1] *Intended.*

From vassal actors can be wip'd away;
Then, kings' misdeeds cannot be hid in clay.

This deed will make thee only lov'd for fear;
But happy monarchs still are fear'd for love:
With foul offenders thou perforce must bear,
When they in thee the like offences prove:
If but for fear of this, thy will remove;
For princes are the glass, the school, the book,
Where subjects' eyes do learn, do read, do look.

And wilt thou be the school where lust shall learn?
Must he in thee read lectures of such shame?
Wilt thou be glass, wherein it shall discern
Authority for sin, warrant for blame,
To privilege dishonour in thy name?
Thou back'st reproach against long-living laud,
And mak'st fair reputation but a bawd.

Hast thou command? by him that gave it thee,
From a pure heart command thy rebel will:
Draw not thy sword to guard iniquity,
For it was lent thee all that brood to kill.
Thy princely office how canst thou fulfil,
When, pattern'd by thy fault, foul sin may say,
He learn'd to sin, and thou didst teach the way?

Think but how vile a spectacle it were,
To view thy present trespass in another.
Men's faults do seldom to themselves appear;
Their own transgressions partially they smother:
This guilt would seem death-worthy in thy brother.
O, how are they wrapp'd in with infamies,
That from their own misdeeds askance their eyes!

To thee, to thee, my heav'd-up hands appeal,
Not to seducing lust, thy rash relier;
I sue for exil'd majesty's repeal;
Let him return, and flattering thoughts retire:
His true respect will prison false desire,
And wipe the dim mist from thy doting eyne,
That thou shalt see thy state, and pity mine.

Have done, quoth he: my uncontrolled tide
Turns not, but swells the higher by this let.
Small lights are soon blown out, huge fires abide,
And with the wind in greater fury fret:
The petty streams, that pay a daily debt
   To their salt sovereign with their fresh falls' haste,
   Add to his flow, but alter not his taste.

Thou art, quoth she, a sea, a sovereign king;
And lo! there falls into thy boundless flood
Black lust, dishonour, shame, misgoverning,
Who seek to stain the ocean of thy blood.
If all these petty ills shall change thy good,
   Thy sea within a puddle's womb is hersed,
   And not the puddle in thy sea dispersed.

So shall these slaves be king, and thou their slave;
Thou nobly base, they basely dignified;
Thou their fair life, and they thy fouler grave:
Thou loathed in their shame, they in thy pride:
The lesser thing should not the greater hide;
   The cedar stoops not to the base shrub's foot,
   But low shrubs wither at the cedar's root.

So let thy thoughts, low vassals to thy state—
No more, quoth he; by heaven, I will not hear thee:
Yield to my love: if not, enforced hate,
Instead of love's coy touch, shall rudely tear thee;
That done, despitefully I mean to bear thee
   Unto the base bed of some rascal groom,
   To be thy partner in this shameful doom.

This said, he sets his foot upon the light,
For light and lust are deadly enemies:
Shame, folded up in blind concealing night,
When most unseen, then most doth tyrannize.
The wolf hath seiz'd his prey, the poor lamb cries;
   Till with her own white fleece her voice controll'd
   Entombs her outcry in her lips' sweet fold:

For with the nightly linen that she wears,
He pens her piteous clamours in her head,
Cooling his hot face in the chastest tears
That ever modest eyes with sorrow shed.
O, that prone lust should stain so pure a bed!

The spots whereof could weeping purify,
Her tears should drop on them perpetually.

But she hath lost a dearer thing than life,
And he hath won what he would lose again;
This forced league doth force a further strife;
This momentary joy breeds months of pain:
This hot desire converts to cold disdain.
Pure chastity is rifled of her store,
And lust, the thief, far poorer than before.

Look, as the full-fed hound, or gorged hawk,
Unapt for tender smell, or speedy flight,
Make slow pursuit, or altogether balk
The prey wherein by nature they delight:
So surfeit-taking Tarquin fares this night:
His taste delicious, in digestion souring,
Devours his will, that liv'd by foul devouring.

O deeper sin, than bottomless conceit
Can comprehend in still imagination!
Drunken desire must vomit his receipt,
Ere he can see his own abomination.
While lust is in his pride, no exclamation
Can curb his heat, or rein his rash desire,
Till, like a jade, self-will himself doth tire.

And then, with lank and lean discolour'd cheek,
With heavy eye, knit brow, and strengthless pace,
Feeble desire, all recreant, poor, and meek,
Like to a bankrupt beggar wails his case:
The flesh being proud, desire doth fight with grace
For there it revels; and when that decays,
The guilty rebel for remission prays.

So fares it with this faultful lord of Rome,
Who this accomplishment so hotly chased;
For now against himself he sounds this doom,
That through the length of times he stands disgraced
Besides, his soul's fair temple is defaced
To whose weak ruins muster troops of cares,
To ask the spotted princess how she fares.

She says, her subjects with foul insurrection
Have batter'd down her consecrated wall,
And by their mortal fault brought in subjection
Her immortality, and made her thrall
To living death, and pain perpetual:
  Which in her prescience she controlled still,
  But her foresight could not fore-stall their will.

Even in this thought through the dark night he stealeth
A captive victor that hath lost in gain;
Bearing away the wound that nothing healeth,
The scar that will despite of cure remain;
Leaving his spoil perplex'd in greater pain.
  She bears the load of lust he left behind,
  And he the burden of a guilty mind.

He, like a thievish dog, creeps sadly thence,
She like a wearied lamb lies panting there;
He scowls, and hates himself for his offence,
She desperate with her nails her flesh doth tear;
He faintly flies, sweating with guilty fear;
  She stays, exclaiming on the direful night:
  He runs, and chides his vanish'd, loath'd delight.

He thence departs a heavy convertite,
She there remains a hopeless cast-away;
He in his speed looks for the morning light,
She prays she never may behold the day;
For day, quoth she, night's scapes doth open lay,
  And my true eyes have never practis'd how
  To cloke offences with a cunning brow.

They think not but that every eye can see
The same disgrace which they themselves behold,
And therefore would they still in darkness be,
To have their unseen sin remain untold;
For they their guilt with weeping will unfold,
  And grave, like water that doth eat in steel,
  Upon my cheeks what helpless shame I feel.

Here she exclaims against repose and rest,
And bids her eyes hereafter still be blind.
She wakes her heart by beating on her breast,
And bids it leap from thence, where it may find
Some purer chest to close so pure a mind.

Frantic with grief thus breathes she forth her spite
Against the unseen secrecy of night.

O, comfort-killing night, image of hell!
Dim register and notary of shame!
Black stage for tragedies and murders fell!
Vast sin-concealing chaos! nurse of blame!
Blind muffled bawd! dark harbour for defame!
Grim cave of death, whispering conspirator
With close-tongu'd treason and the ravisher!

O, hateful, vaporous, and foggy night!
Since thou art guilty of my cureless crime,
Muster thy mists to meet the eastern light,
Make war against proportion'd course of time:
Or if thou wilt permit the sun to climb
His wonted height, yet ere he go to bed,
Knit poisonous clouds about his golden head.

With rotten damps ravish the morning air;
Let their exhal'd unwholesome breaths make sick
The life of purity, the supreme fair,
Ere he arrive his weary noon-tide prick;
And let thy musty vapours march so thick,
That in their smoky ranks his smother'd light
May set at noon, and make perpetual night.

Were Tarquin night, as he is but night's child,
The silver-shining queen he would distain;
Her twinkling handmaids too, by him defil'd,
Through night's black bosom should not peep again:
So should I have copartners in my pain;
And fellowship in woe doth woe assuage,
As palmers' chat makes short their pilgrimage.

Where, now, I have no one to blush with me,
To cross their arms, and hang their heads with mine,
To mask their brows, and hide their infamy;
But I alone, alone must sit and pine,
Seasoning the earth with showers of silver brine;
Mingling my talk with tears, my grief with groans,
Poor wasting monuments of lasting moans.

O night! thou furnace of foul-reeking smoke,
Let not the jealous day behold that face
Which underneath thy black all-hiding cloak
Immodestly lies martyr'd with disgrace:
Keep still possession of thy gloomy place,
That all the faults which in thy reign are made
May likewise be sepulcher'd in thy shade.

Make me not object to the tell-tale day!
The light will show, character'd in my brow,
The story of sweet chastity's decay,
The impious breach of holy wedlock vow:
Yea, the illiterate, that know not how
To cipher what is writ in learned books,
Will quote[1] my loathsome trespass in my looks.

The nurse to still her child will tell my story,
And fright her crying babe with Tarquin's name;
The orator to deck his oratory
Will couple my reproach to Tarquin's shame;
Feast-finding minstrels, tuning my defame,
Will tie the hearers to attend each line,
How Tarquin wronged me, ı Collatine.

Let my good name, that senseless reputation,
For Collatine's dear love be kept unspotted:
If that be made a theme for disputation,
The branches of another root are rotted,
And undeserv'd reproach to him allotted,
That is as clear from this attaint of mine,
As I ere this was pure to Collatine.

O unseen shame! invisible disgrace!
O unfelt sore! crest-wounding, private scar!
Reproach is stamp'd in Collatinus' face,
And Tarquin's eye may read the mot[2] afar,
How he in peace is wounded, not in war.
Alas! how many bear such shameful blows,
Which not themselves, but he that gives them, knows

If, Collatine, thine honour lay in me,
From me by strong assault it is bereft.
My honey lost, and I, a drone-like bee,

[1] *Note, observe* [2] *Word, motto.*

Have no perfection of my summer left,
But robb'd and ransack'd by injurious theft:
  In thy weak hive a wandering wasp hath crept,
  And suck'd the honey which thy chaste bee kept.

Yet am I guilty of thy honour's wrack;
Yet for thy honour did I entertain him;
Coming from thee, I could not put him back,
For it had been dishonour to disdain him:
Besides, of weariness he did complain him,
  And talk'd of virtue.—O, unlook'd for evil,
  When virtue is profan'd in such a devil!

Why should the worm intrude the maiden bud,
Or hateful cuckoos hatch in sparrows' nests?
Or toads infect fair founts with venom mud?
Or tyrant folly lurk in gentle breasts?
Or kings be breakers of their own behests?
  But no perfection is so absolute,
  That some impurity doth not pollute.

The aged man that coffers up his gold,
Is plagu'd with cramps, and gouts, and painful fits,
And scarce hath eyes his treasure to behold,
But like still-pining Tantalus he sits,
And useless barns the harvest of his wits;
  Having no other pleasure of his gain,
  But torment that it cannot cure his pain.

So, then he hath it, when he cannot use it,
And leaves it to be master'd by his young;
Who in their pride do presently abuse it:
Their father was too weak, and they too strong;
To hold their cursed-blessed fortune long.
  The sweets we wish for turn to loathed sours,
  Even in the moment that we call them ours.

Unruly blasts wait on the tender spring,
Unwholesome weeds take root with precious flowers,
The adder hisses where the sweet birds sing,
What virtue breeds, iniquity devours;
We have no good that we can say is ours,
  But ill annexed opportunity
  Or kills his life, or else his quality.

O, Opportunity! thy guilt is great:
'T is thou that execut'st the traitor's treason;
Thou sett'st the wolf where he the lamb may get;
Whoever plots the sin, thou 'point'st the season:
'T is thou that spurn'st at right, at law, at reason:
  And in thy shady cell, where none may spy him,
  Sits sin to seize the souls that wander by him.

Thou mak'st the vestal violate her oath;
Thou blow'st the fire, when temperance is thaw'd;
Thou smother'st honesty, thou murder'st troth:
Thou foul abettor! thou notorious bawd!
Thou plantest scandal, and displacest laud:
  Thou ravisher, thou traitor, thou false thief
  Thy honey turns to gall, thy joy to grief!

Thy secret pleasure turns to open shame,
Thy private feasting to a public fast;
Thy smoothing titles to a ragged[1] name,
Thy sugar'd tongue to bitter wormwood taste:
Thy violent vanities can never last.
  How comes it then, vile Opportunity,
  Being so bad, such numbers seek for thee?

When wilt thou be the humble suppliant's friend,
And bring him where his suit may be obtain'd?
When wilt thou sort[2] an hour great strifes to end,
Or free that soul which wretchedness hath chained?
Give physic to the sick, ease to the pained?
  The poor, lame, blind, halt, creep, cry out for thee
  But they ne'er meet with Opportunity.

The patient dies while the physician sleeps;
The orphan pines while the oppressor feeds;
Justice is feasting while the widow weeps;
Advice is sporting while infection breeds:
Thou grant'st no time for charitable deeds.
  Wrath, envy, treason, rape, and murders rages.
  Thy heinous hours wait on them as their pages

When truth and virtue have to do with thee,
A thousand crosses keep them from thy aid:
They buy thy help; but sin ne'er gives a fee:

[1] *Broken, tarnished.* [2] *Select.*

He gratis comes, and thou art well appay'd,[1]
As well to hear, as grant what he hath said.
  My Collatine would else have come to me,
  When Tarquin did; but he was stay'd by thee

Guilty thou art of murder and of theft;
Guilty of perjury and subornation;
Guilty of treason, forgery, and shift;
Guilty of incest, that abomination:
An accessory by thine inclination
  To all sins past, and all that are to come,
  From the creation to the general doom.

Mis-shapen Time, copesmate of ugly night,
Swift subtle post, carrier of grisly care;
Eater of youth, false slave to false delight,
Base watch of woes, sin's pack-horse, virtue's snare;
Thou nursest all, and murderest all that are
  O hear me, then, injurious, shifting Time!
  Be guilty of my death, since of my crime

Why hath thy servant, Opportunity,
Betray'd the hours thou gav'st me to repose?
Cancell'd my fortunes, and enchained me
To endless date of never-ending woes?
Time's office is to fine[2] the hate of foes;
  To eat up errors by opinion bred,
  Not spend the dowry of a lawful bed.

Time's glory is to calm contending kings,
To unmask falsehood, and bring truth to light,
To stamp the seal of time in aged things,
To wake the morn, and sentinel the night,
To wrong the wronger till he render right;
  To ruinate proud buildings with thy hours,
  And smear with dust their glittering golden towers:

To fill with worm-holes stately monuments,
To feed oblivion with decay of things,
To blot old books, and alter their contents,
To pluck the quills from ancient ravens' wings,
To dry the old oak's sap, and cherish springs;
  To spoil antiquities of hammer'd steel,
  And turn the giddy round of Fortune's wheel

[1] *Satisfied.* [2] *End.*

To show the beldame daughters of her daughter,
To make the child a man, the man a child,
To slay the tiger that doth live by slaughter,
To tame the unicorn and lion wild;
To mock the subtle, in themselves beguil'd;
  To cheer the ploughman with increaseful crops,
  And waste huge stones with little water-drops

Why work'st thou mischief in thy pilgrimage,
Unless thou couldst return to make amends?
One poor retiring[1] minute in an age
Would purchase thee a thousand thousand friends,
Lending him wit that to bad debtors lends:
  O! this dread night, wouldst thou one hour come back,
  I could prevent this storm, and shun thy wrack.

Thou ceaseless lackey to eternity,
With some mischance cross Tarquin in his flight:
Devise extremes beyond extremity
To make him curse this cursed crimeful night:
Let ghastly shadows his lewd eyes affright,
  And the dire thought of his committed evil
  Shape every bush a hideous shapeless devil.

Disturb his hours of rest with restless trances,
Afflict him in his bed with bedrid groans;
Let there bechance him pitiful mischances,
To make him moan, but pity not his moans:
Stone him with harden'd hearts, harder than stones;
  And let mild women to him lose their mildness,
  Wilder to him than tigers in their wildness.

Let him have time to tear his curled hair,
Let him have time against himself to rave,
Let him have time of time's help to despair,
Let him have time to live a loathed slave;
Let him have time a beggar's orts to crave,
  And time to see one that by alms doth live,
  Disdain to him disdained scraps to give.

Let him have time to see his friends his foes,
And merry fools to mock at him resort;
Let him have time to mark how slow time goes

[1] *Returning.*

In time of sorrow, and how swift and short
His time of folly, and his time of sport:
  And ever let his unrecalling crime
  Have time to wail th' abusing of his time.

O Time, thou tutor both to good and bad,
Teach me to curse him that thou taught'st this ill!
At his own shadow let the thief run mad,
Himself himself seek every hour to kill!
Such wretched hands such wretched blood should spill
  For who so base should such an office have
  As slanderous death's-man to so base a slave?

The baser is he, coming from a king,
To shame his hope with deeds degenerate:
The mightier man, the mightier is the thing
That makes him honour'd, or begets him hate;
For greatest scandal waits on greatest state.
  The moon being clouded presently is miss'd,
  But little stars may hide them when they list.

The crow may bathe his coal-black wings in mire,
And unperceiv'd fly with the filth away;
But if the like the snow-white swan desire,
The stain upon his silver down will stay,
Poor grooms are sightless night, kings glorious day:
  Gnats are unnoted wheresoe'er they fly,
  But eagles gaz'd upon with every eye.

Out, idle words! servants to shallow fools,
Unprofitable sounds, weak arbitrators!
Busy yourselves in skill-contending schools;
Debate where leisure serves with dull debaters;
To trembling clients be you mediators:
  For me, I force[1] not argument a straw,
  Since that my case is past the help of law.

In vain I rail at Opportunity,
At Time, at Tarquin, and uncheerful night;
In vain I cavil with mine infamy,
In vain I spurn at my confirm'd despite:
This helpless smoke of words doth me no right.

[1] *Value.*

The remedy, indeed, to do me good,
Is to let forth my foul, defiled blood.

Poor hand, why quiver'st thou at this decree?
Honour thyself to rid me of this shame;
For if I die, my honour lives in thee,
But if I live, thou liv'st in my defame:
Since thou couldst not defend thy loyal dame,
And wast afear'd to scratch her wicked foe,
Kill both thyself and her for yielding so.

This said, from her be-tumbled couch she starteth,
To find some desperate instrument of death;
But this no slaughter-house no tool imparteth,
To make more vent for passage of her breath,
Which, thronging through her lips, so vanisheth
As smoke from Ætna, that in air consumes,
Or that which from discharged cannon fumes.

In vain, quoth she, I live; and seek in vain
Some happy mean to end a hapless life:
I fear'd by Tarquin's falchion to be slain,
Yet for the self-same purpose seek a knife;
But when I fear'd, I was a loyal wife.
So am I now:—O no! that cannot be:
Of that true type hath Tarquin rifled me.

O! that is gone, for which I sought to live,
And therefore now I need not fear to die.
To clear this spot by death, at least, I give
A badge of fame to slander's livery;
A dying life to living infamy.
Poor helpless help, the treasure stol'n away,
To burn the guiltless casket where it lay!

Well, well, dear Collatine, thou shalt not know
The stained taste of violated troth;
I will not wrong thy true affection so,
To flatter thee with an infringed oath;
This bastard graff shall never come to growth:
He shall not boast, who did thy stock pollute,
That thou art doting father of his fruit.

Nor shall he smile at thee in secret thought,
Nor laugh with his companions at thy state;
But thou shalt know thy interest was not bought
Basely with gold, but stolen from forth thy gate.
For me, I am the mistress of my fate,
  And with my trespass never will dispense,
  Till life to death acquit my forc'd offence.

I will not poison thee with my attaint,
Nor fold my fault in cleanly coin'd excuses;
My sable ground of sin I will not paint,
To hide the truth of this false night's abuses:
My tongue shall utter all; mine eyes, like sluices,
  As from a mountain spring that feeds a dale,
  Shall gush pure streams to purge my impure tale

By this, lamenting Philomel had ended
The well-tun'd warble of her nightly sorrow,
And solemn night with slow, sad gait descended
To ugly hell; when lo! the blushing morrow
Lends light to all fair eyes that light will borrow:
  But cloudy Lucrece shames herself to see,
  And therefore still in night would cloister'd be.

Revealing day through every cranny spies,
And seems to point her out where she sits weeping,
To whom she sobbing speaks: O eye of eyes!
Why pry'st thou through my window? leave thy peeping;
Mock with thy tickling beams eyes that are sleeping:
  Brand not my forehead with thy piercing light,
  For day hath nought to do what 's done by night

Thus cavils she with every thing she sees.
True grief is fond and testy as a child,
Who wayward once, his mood with nought agrees:
Old woes, not infant sorrows, bear them mild;
Continuance tames the one; the other wild,
  Like an unpractis'd swimmer plunging still,
  With too much labour drowns for want of skill.

So she, deep drenched in a sea of care,
Holds disputation with each thing she views,
And to herself all sorrow doth compare:
No object but her passion's strength renews,
And as one shifts, another straight ensues:

Sometime her grief is dumb, and hath no words;
Sometime 't is mad, and too much talk affords.

The little birds that tune their morning's joy,
Make her moans mad with their sweet melody;
For mirth doth search the bottom of annoy:
Sad souls are slain in merry company;
Grief best is pleas'd with grief's society:
True sorrow then is feelingly suffic'd,
When with like semblance it is sympathiz'd.

'T is double death to drown in ken of shore;
He ten times pines, that pines beholding food;
To see the salve doth make the wound ache more;
Great grief grieves most at that would do it good:
Deep woes roll forward like a gentle flood,
Who, being stopp'd, the bounding banks o'erflows.
Grief dallied with nor law nor limit knows.

You mocking birds, quoth she, your tunes entomb
Within your hollow swelling feather'd breasts,
And in my hearing be you mute and dumb:
My restless discord loves no stops nor rests;[1]
A woful hostess brooks not merry guests.
Relish your nimble notes to pleasing ears;
Distress likes dumps,[2] when time is kept with tears.

Come, Philomel, that sing'st of ravishment,
Make thy sad grave in my dishevel'd hair.
As the dank earth weeps at thy languishment,
So I at each sad strain will strain a tear,
And with deep groans the diapason bear:
For burden-wise I 'll hum on Tarquin still,
While thou on Tereus descant'st, better skill.[3]

And whiles against a thorn thou bear'st thy part,
To keep thy sharp woes waking, wretched I,
To imitate thee well, against my heart
Will fix a sharp knife, to affright mine eye,
Who, if it wink, shall thereon fall and die.
These means, as frets upon an instrument,
Shall tune our heart-strings to true languishment.

[1] *Terms in music* [2] *Melancholy music.* [3] i. e. *with* better skill · "descant" seems to have meant what we now call *variation.*

And for, poor bird, thou sing'st not in the day,
As shaming any eye should thee behold,
Some dark deep desert, seated from the way,
That knows not parching heat nor freezing cold,
Will we find out; and there we will unfold
   To creatures stern sad tunes to change their kinds:
   Since men prove beasts, let beasts bear gentle minds.

As the poor frighted deer, that stands at gaze,
Wildly determining which way to fly,
Or one encompass'd with a winding maze,
That cannot tread the way out readily;
So with herself is she in mutiny,
   To live or die which of the twain were better,
   When life is sham'd, and death reproach's debtor.

To kill myself, quoth she, alack! what were it,
But with my body my poor soul's pollution?
They that lose half, with greater patience bear it,
Than they whose whole is swallow'd in confusion.
That mother tries a merciless conclusion,
   Who having two sweet babes, when death takes one,
   Will slay the other, and be nurse to none.

My body or my soul, which was the dearer,
When the one pure, the other made divine?
Whose love of either to myself was nearer,
When both were kept for heaven and Collatine?
Ah me! the bark peel'd from the lofty pine,
   His love will wither, and his sap decay;
   So must my soul, her bark being peel'd away.

Her house is sack'd, her quiet interrupted,
Her mansion batter'd by the enemy;
Her sacred temple spotted, spoil'd, corrupted
Grossly engirt with daring infamy:
Then, let it not be call'd impiety,
   If in this blemish'd fort I make some hole,
   Through which I may convey this troubled soul.

Yet die I will not, till my Collatine
Have heard the cause of my untimely death,
That he may vow, in that sad hour of mine,
Revenge on him that made me stop my breath.
My stained blood to Tarquin I 'll bequeath,

Which by him tainted shall for him be spent,
And as his due writ in my testament.

My honour I 'll bequeath unto the knife
That wounds my body so dishonoured.
'T is honour to deprive dishonour'd life;
The one will live, the other being dead:
So of shame's ashes shall my fame be bred;
For in my death I murder shameful scorn:
My shame so dead, mine honour is new-born.

Dear lord of that dear jewel I have lost,
What legacy shall I bequeath to thee?
My resolution, love, shall be thy boast,
By whose example thou reveng'd may'st be.
How Tarquin must be us'd, read it in me:
Myself, thy friend, will kill myself, thy foe,
And for my sake serve thou false Tarquin so.

This brief abridgment of my will I make:—
My soul and body to the skies and ground;
My resolution, husband, do thou take;
Mine honour be the knife's that makes my wound;
My shame be his that did my fame confound;
And all my fame that lives disbursed be
To those that live, and think no shame of me.

Thou, Collatine, shalt oversee this will;[1]
How was I overseen that thou shalt see it!
My blood shall wash the slander of mine ill;
My life's foul deed my life's fair end shall free it.
Faint not, faint heart, but stoutly say, "so be it."
Yield to my hand; my hand shall conquer thee:
Thou dead, both die, and both shall victors be.

This plot of death when sadly she had laid,
And wip'd the brinish pearl from her bright eyes,
With untun'd tongue she hoarsely calls[2] her maid,
Whose swift obedience to her mistress hies;
For fleet-wing'd duty with thought's feathers flies.
Poor Lucrece' cheeks unto her maid seem so,
As winter meads when sun doth melt their snow.

[1] It was usual for testators to appoint not only executors, but overseers of their wills. Shakespeare did so. [2] called: in mod. eds.

Her mistress she doth give demure good-morrow,
With soft slow tongue, true mark of modesty,
And sorts a sad look to her lady's sorrow,
For why, her face wore sorrow's livery;
But durst not ask of her audaciously
Why her two suns were cloud-eclipsed so,
Nor why her fair cheeks over-wash'd with woe.

But as the earth doth weep, the sun being set,
Each flower moisten'd like a melting eye,
Even so the maid with swelling drops 'gan wet
Her circled eyne, enforc'd by sympathy
Of those fair suns set in her mistress' sky,
Who in a salt-wav'd ocean quench their light,
Which makes the maid weep like the dewy night.

A pretty while these pretty creatures stand.
Like ivory conduits coral cisterns filling:
One justly weeps, the other takes in hand
No cause but company of her drops spilling:
Their gentle sex to weep are often willing,
Grieving themselves to guess at others' smarts
And then they drown their eyes, or break their hearts:

For men have marble, women waxen, minds,
And therefore are they form'd as marble will,
The weak oppress'd, th' impression of strange kinds
Is form'd in them by force, by fraud, or skill:
Then, call them not the authors of their ill,
No more than wax shall be accounted evil,
Wherein is stamp'd the semblance of a devil.

Their smoothness, like a goodly champaign plain,
Lays open all the little worms that creep:
In men, as in a rough-grown grove, remain
Cave-keeping evils that obscurely sleep.
Through crystal walls each little mote will peep.
Though men can cover crimes with bold stern looks.
Poor women's faces are their own faults' books.

No man inveigh against the withered flower,
But chide rough winter that the flower hath kill'd.

[1] *Held.*

Not that devour'd, but that which doth devour,
Is worthy blame. O! let it not be hild[1]
Poor women's faults, that they are so fulfill'd
With men's abuses: those proud lords, to blame,
Make weak-made women tenants to their shame.

The precedent whereof in Lucrece view,
Assail'd by night, with circumstances strong
Of present death, and shame that might ensue
By that her death, to do her husband wrong:
Such danger to resistance did belong,
That dying fear through all her body spread;
And who cannot abuse a body dead?

By this, mild patience bid fair Lucrece speak
To the poor counterfeit of her complaining:
My girl, quoth she, on what occasion break
Those tears from thee, that down thy cheeks are raining?
If thou dost weep for grief of my sustaining,
Know, gentle wench, it small avails my mood:
If tears could help, mine own would do me good.

But tell me, girl, when went—(and there she stay'd
Till after a deep groan) Tarquin from hence?
Madam, ere I was up, replied the maid;
The more to blame my sluggard negligence:
Yet with the fault I thus far can dispense;
Myself was stirring ere the break of day,
And, ere I rose, was Tarquin gone away.

But, lady, if your maid may be so bold,
She would request to know your heaviness.
O peace! quoth Lucrece: if it should be told.
The repetition cannot make it less;
For more it is than I can well express:
And that deep torture may be call'd a hell,
When more is felt than one hath power to tell.

Go, get me hither paper, ink, and pen,—
Yet save that labour, for I have them here.
What should I say?—One of my husband's men
Bid thou be ready by and by, to bear
A letter to my lord, my love, my dear:
Bid him with speed prepare to carry it;
The cause craves haste, and it will soon be writ

[1] *Held.*

Her maid is gone, and she prepares to write,
First hovering o'er the paper with her quill.
Conceit and grief an eager combat fight;
What wit sets down is blotted straight with will;
This is too curious-good, this blunt and ill:
  Much like a press of people at a door
  Throng her inventions, which shall go before.

At last she thus begins: "Thou worthy lord
Of that unworthy wife that greeteth thee,
Health to thy person: next, vouchsafe t' afford
(If ever, love, thy Lucrece thou wilt see)
Some present speed to come and visit me.
  So I commend me from our house in grief:
  My woes are tedious, though my words are brief."

Here folds she up the tenour of her woe,
Her certain sorrow writ uncertainly.
By this short schedule Collatine may know
Her grief, but not her grief's true quality:
She dares not thereof make discovery,
  Lest he should hold it her own gross abuse,
  Ere she with blood had stain'd her stain'd excuse.

Besides, the life and feeling of her passion
She hoards, to spend when he is by to hear her;
When sighs and groans and tears may grace the fashion
Of her disgrace, the better so to clear her
From that suspicion which the world might bear her.
  To shun this blot she would not blot the letter
  With words, till action might become them better.

To see sad sights moves more than hear them told,
For then the eye interprets to the ear
The heavy motion that it doth behold,
When every part a part of woe doth bear:
'T is but a part of sorrow that we hear,
  Deep sounds make lesser noise than shallow fords,
  And sorrow ebbs, being blown with wind of words

Her letter now is seal'd, and on it writ
"At Ardea to my lord, with more than haste."
The post attends, and she delivers it,
Charging the sour-fac'd groom to hie as fast
As lagging fowls before the northern blast:

  Speed more than speed but dull and slow she deems.
  Extremity still urgeth such extremes.

The homely villain court'sies to her low,
And, blushing on her, with a stedfast eye
Receives the scroll, without or yea or no,
And forth with bashful innocence doth hie:
But they whose guilt within their bosoms lie,
  Imagine every eye beholds their blame,
  For Lucrece thought he blush'd to see her shame;

When, silly groom! God wot, it was defect
Of spirit, life, and bold audacity.
Such harmless creatures have a true respect
To talk in deeds, while others saucily
Promise more speed, but do it leisurely:
  Even so this pattern of a worn-out age
  Pawn'd honest looks, but lay'd no words to gage.

His kindled duty kindled her mistrust,
That two red fires in both their faces blazed;
She thought he blush'd, as knowing Tarquin's lust,
And, blushing with him, wistly on him gazed;
Her earnest eye did make him more amazed:
  The more she saw the blood his cheeks replenish,
  The more she thought he spied in her some blemish

But long she thinks till he return again,
And yet the duteous vassal scarce is gone.
The weary time she cannot entertain,
For now 't is stale to sigh, to weep, and groan:
So woe hath wearied woe, moan tired moan,
  That she her plaints a little while doth stay,
  Pausing for means to mourn some newer way.

At last she calls to mind where hangs a piece
Of skilful painting, made for Priam's Troy;
Before the which is drawn the power of Greece,
For Helen's rape the city to destroy,
Threatening cloud-kissing Ilion with annoy;
  Which the conceited[1] painter drew so proud,
  As heaven it seem'd to kiss the turrets bow'd.

[1] *Ingenious.*

A thousand lamentable objects there,
In scorn of nature, art gave lifeless life.
Many a dry drop seem'd a weeping tear,
Shed for the slaughter'd husband by the wife:
The red blood reek'd to show the painter's strife;
  And dying eyes gleam'd forth their ashy lights,
  Like dying coals burnt out in tedious nights.

There might you see the labouring pioneer
Begrim'd with sweat, and smeared all with dust;
And from the towers of Troy there would appear
The very eyes of men through loop-holes thrust,
Gazing upon the Greeks with little lust:
  Such sweet observance in this work was had,
  That one might see those far-off eyes look sad.

In great commanders grace and majesty
You might behold, triumphing in their faces;
In youth quick bearing and dexterity;
And here and there the painter interlaces
Pale cowards, marching on with trembling paces:
  Which heartless peasants did so well resemble, [ble.
  That one would swear he saw them quake and trem-

In Ajax and Ulysses, O, what art
Of physiognomy might one behold!
The face of either 'cipher'd either's heart;
Their face their manners most expressly told:
In Ajax' eyes blunt rage and rigour roll'd;
  But the mild glance that sly Ulysses lent,
  Show'd deep regard and smiling government.

There pleading might you see grave Nestor stand,
As 't were encouraging the Greeks to fight;
Making such sober action with his hand,
That it beguil'd attention, charm'd the sight.
In speech, it seem'd, his beard, all silver white,
  Wagg'd up and down, and from his lips did fly
  Thin winding breath, which purl'd up to the sky.

About him were a press of gaping faces,
Which seem'd to swallow up his sound advice;
All jointly listening, but with several graces,

As if some mermaid did their ears entice:
Some high, some low; the painter was so nice,
The scalps of many, almost hid behind,
To jump up higher seem'd, to mock the mind.

Here one man's hand lean'd on another's head,
His nose being shadow'd by his neighbour's ear;
Here one, being throng'd, bears back, all boll'n[1] and red
Another, smother'd, seems to pelt and swear;
And in their rage such signs of rage they bear,
As, but for loss of Nestor's golden words,
It seem'd they would debate with angry swords.

For much imaginary work was there;
Conceit deceitful, so compact, so kind,[2]
That for Achilles' image stood his spear,
Grip'd in an armed hand: himself behind
Was left unseen, save to the eye of mind.
A hand, a foot, a face, a leg, a head,
Stood for the whole to be imagined.

And from the walls of strong besieged Troy
When their brave hope, bold Hector, march'd to field,
Stood many Trojan mothers, sharing joy
To see their youthful sons bright weapons wield;
And to their hope they such odd action yield,
That through their light joy seemed to appear
(Like bright things stain'd) a kind of heavy fear.

And from the strond of Dardan, where they fought,
To Simois' reedy banks the red blood ran,
Whose waves to imitate the battle sought
With swelling ridges; and their ranks began
To break upon the galled shore, and than[3]
Retire again, till meeting greater ranks,
They join, and shoot their foam at Simois' banks.

To this well-painted piece is Lucrece come,
To find a face where all distress is steld[4].
Many she sees, where cares have carved some,
But none where all distress and dolour dwell'd,
Till she despairing Hecuba beheld,

[1] *Swollen.* [2] *Natural*, according to kind. [3] Often used, as here, for "then." [4] No other instance is known of the use of this word In Sonnet XXIV. we have *steel'd* used in a similar sense.

Staring on Priam's wounds with her old eyes,
Which bleeding under Pyrrhus' proud foot lies.

In her the painter had anatomiz'd
Time's ruin, beauty's wreck, and grim care's reign:
Her cheeks with chaps and wrinkles were disguis'd,
Of what she was no semblance did remain;
Here blue blood chang'd to black in every vein,
Wanting the spring that those shrunk pipes had fed,
Show'd life imprison'd in a body dead.

On this sad shadow Lucrece spends her eyes,
And shapes her sorrow to the beldam's woes,
Who nothing wants to answer but her cries,
And bitter words to ban her cruel foes:
The painter was no God to lend her those;
And therefore Lucrece swears he did her wrong,
To give her so much grief, and not a tongue.

Poor instrument, quoth she, without a sound,
I 'll tune thy woes with my lamenting tongue,
And drop sweet balm in Priam's painted wound,
And rail on Pyrrhus that hath done him wrong,
And with my tears quench Troy, that burns so long,
And with my knife scratch out the angry eyes
Of all the Greeks that are thine enemies.

Show me the strumpet that began this stir,
That with my nails her beauty I may tear.
Thy heat of lust, fond Paris, did incur
This load of wrath that burning Troy doth bear:
Thine eye kindled the fire that burneth here:
And here, in Troy, for trespass of thine eye,
The sire, the son, the dame, and daughter die.

Why should the private pleasure of some one
Become the public plague of many mo[1]?
Let sin, alone committed, light alone
Upon his head that hath transgressed so;
Let guiltless souls be freed from guilty woe.
For one's offence why should so many fall,
To plague a private sin in general?

[1] *More.*

Lo! here weeps Hecuba, here Priam dies,
Here manly Hector faints, here Troilus swounds;
Here friend by friend in bloody channel lies,
And friend to friend gives unadvised wounds,
And one man's lust these many lives confounds.
  Had doting Priam check'd his son's desire,
  Troy had been bright with fame, and not with fire

Here feelingly she weeps Troy's painted woes;
For sorrow, like a heavy hanging bell,
Once set on ringing, with his own weight goes;
Then little strength rings out the doleful knell:
So Lucrece, set a-work, sad tales doth tell
  To pencil'd pensiveness and colour'd sorrow; [row
  She lends them words, and she their looks doth bor

She throws her eyes about the painting, round,
And whom she finds forlorn she doth lament:
At last she sees a wretched image bound,
That piteous looks to Phrygian shepherds lent;
His face, though full of cares, yet show'd content.
  Onward to Troy with the blunt swains he goes,
  So mild, that patience seem'd to scorn his woes.

In him the painter labour'd with his skill
To hide deceit, and give the harmless show;
An humble gait, calm looks, eyes wailing still,
A brow unbent that seem'd to welcome woe;
Cheeks neither red nor pale, but mingled so
  That blushing red no guilty instance gave,
  Nor ashy pale the fear that false hearts have.

But, like a constant and confirmed devil,
He entertain'd a show so seeming just,
And therein so ensconc'd his secret evil,
That jealousy itself could not mistrust,
False-creeping craft and perjury should thrust
  Into so bright a day such black-fac'd storms,
  Or blot with hell-born sin such saint-like forms.

The well-skill'd workman this mild image drew
For perjur'd Sinon, whose enchanting story
The credulous old Priam after slew;
Whose words like wild-fire burnt the shining glory
Of rich-built Ilion, that the skies were sorry,

And little stars shot from their fixed places,
When their glass fell wherein they view'd their faces.

This picture she advisedly perused,
And chid the painter for his wondrous skill,
Saying, some shape in Sinon's was abused;
So fair a form lodg'd not a mind so ill:
And still on him she gaz'd; and gazing still,
Such signs of truth in his plain face she spied,
That she concludes the picture was belied.

It cannot be, quoth she, that so much guile—
(She would have said) can lurk in such a look;
But Tarquin's shape came in her mind the while,
And from her tongue, "can lurk" from "cannot" took,
"It cannot be" she in that sense forsook,
And turn'd it thus: it cannot be, I find,
But such a face should bear a wicked mind:

For even as subtle Sinon here is painted,
So sober-sad, so weary, and so mild,
(As if with grief or travail he had fainted)
To me came Tarquin armed; too[1] beguil'd[2]?
With outward honesty, but yet defil'd
With inward vice: as Priam him did cherish,
So did I Tarquin; so my Troy did perish.

Look, look! how listening Priam wets his eyes,
To see those borrow'd tears that Sinon sheds.
Priam, why art thou old, and yet not wise?
For every tear he falls a Trojan bleeds:
His eye drops fire, no water thence proceeds;
Those round clear pearls of his, that move thy pity
Are balls of quenchless fire to burn thy city.

Such devils steal effects from lightless hell,
For Sinon in his fire doth quake with cold,
And in that cold, hot-burning fire doth dwell;
These contraries such unity do hold,
Only to flatter fools, and make them bold:
So Priam's trust false Sinon's tears doth flatter,
That he finds means to burn his Troy with water.

[1] so · in mod eds. [2] *Masked, or in the guise of*

Here, all enrag'd, such passion her assails,
That patience is quite beaten from her breast
She tears the senseless Sinon with her nails,
Comparing him to that unhappy guest
Whose deed hath made herself herself detest:
At last she smilingly with this gives o'er;
Fool! fool! quoth she, his wounds will not be sore

Thus ebbs and flows the current of her sorrow,
And time doth weary time with her complaining.
She looks for night, and then she longs for morrow,
And both she thinks too long with her remaining.
Short time seems long in sorrow's sharp sustaining:
Though woe be heavy, yet it seldom sleeps;
And they that watch see time how slow it creeps.

Which all this time hath overslipp'd her thought,
That she with painted images hath spent,
Being from the feeling of her own grief brought
By deep surmise of others' detriment;
Losing her woes in shows of discontent.
It easeth some, though none it ever cured,
To think their dolour others have endured.

But now the mindful messenger, come back;
Brings home his lord and other company.
Who finds his Lucrece clad in mourning black;
And round about her tear-distained eye
Blue circles stream'd, like rainbows in the sky:
These water-galls in her dim element
Foretel new storms to those already spent.

Which when her sad-beholding husband saw,
Amazedly in her sad face he stares:
Her eyes, though sod in tears, look'd red and raw;
Her lively colour kill'd with deadly cares.
He hath no power to ask her how she fares;
Both stood like old acquaintance in a trance,
Met far from home, wondering each other's chance

At last he takes her by the bloodless hand,
And thus begins: What uncouth ill event
Hath thee befal'n, that thou dost trembling stand?

Sweet love, what spite hath thy fair colour spent?
Why art thou thus attir'd in discontent?
  Unmask, dear dear, this moody heaviness,
  And tell thy grief that we may give redress.

Three times with sighs she gives her sorrow fire,
Ere once she can discharge one word of woe:
At length, address'd to answer his desire,
She modestly prepares to let them know
Her honour is ta'en prisoner by the foe;
  While Collatine and his consorted lords
  With sad attention long to hear her words.

And now this pale swan in her watery nest
Begins the sad dirge of her certain ending.
Few words, quoth she, shall fit the trespass best,
Where no excuse can give the fault amending:
In me more woes than words are now depending;
  And my laments would be drawn out too long,
  To tell them all with one poor tired tongue.

Then, be this all the task it hath to say:
Dear husband, in the interest of thy bed
A stranger came, and on that pillow lay
Where thou wast wont to rest thy weary head;
And what wrong else may be imagined
  By foul enforcement might be done to me,
  From that, alas! thy Lucrece is not free.

For in the dreadful dead of dark midnight,
With shining falchion in my chamber came
A creeping creature, with a flaming light,
And softly cried, Awake, thou Roman dame,
And entertain my love; else lasting shame
  On thee and thine this night I will inflict,
  If thou my love's desire do contradict.

For some hard-favour'd groom of thine, quoth he,
Unless thou yoke thy liking to my will,
I'll murder straight, and then I'll slaughter thee,
And swear I found you where you did fulfil
The loathsome act of lust, and so did kill
  The lechers in their deed: this act will be
  My fame, and thy perpetual infamy.

With this I did begin to start and cry,
And then against my heart he set his sword,
Swearing, unless I took all patiently,
I should not live to speak another word;
So should my shame still rest upon record,
And never be forgot in mighty Rome
Th' adulterate death of Lucrece and her groom.

Mine enemy was strong, my poor self weak,
And far the weaker with so strong a fear:
My bloody judge forbad my tongue to speak;
No rightful plea might plead for justice there
His scarlet lust came evidence to swear
That my poor beauty had purloin'd his eyes,
And when the judge is rob'd, the prisoner dies.

O! teach me how to make mine own excuse,
Or, at the least, this refuge let me find:
Though my gross blood be stain'd with this abuse,
Immaculate and spotless is my mind;
That was not forc'd; that never was inclin'd
To accessory yieldings, but still pure
Doth in her poison'd closet yet endure.

Lo! here the hopeless merchant of this loss,
With head declin'd, and voice damm'd up with woe,
With sad set eyes, and wretched arms across,
From lips new waxen pale begins to blow
The grief away, that stops his answer so;
But wretched as he is, he strives in vain,
What he breathes out, his breath drinks up again.

As through an arch the violent roaring tide
Out-runs the eye that doth behold his haste,
Yet in the eddy boundeth in his pride
Back to the strait that forc'd him on so fast,
In rage sent out, recall'd in rage, being past;
Even so his sighs, his sorrows, make a saw,
To push grief on, and back the same grief draw.

Which speechless woe of his poor she attendeth,
And his untimely frenzy thus awaketh:
Dear lord, thy sorrow to my sorrow lendeth

Another power; no flood by raining slaketh.
My woe, too sensible, thy passion maketh
   More feeling painful: let it, then, suffice
   To drown one woe, one pair of weeping eyes.

And for my sake, when I might charm thee so,
For she that was thy Lucrece, now attend me:
Be suddenly revenged on my foe,
Thine, mine, his own: suppose thou dost defend me
From what is past, the help that thou shalt lend me
   Comes all too late, yet let the traitor die;
   For sparing justice feeds iniquity.

But ere I name him, you fair lords, quoth she,
(Speaking to those that came with Collatine)
Shall plight your honourable faiths to me,
With swift pursuit to venge this wrong of mine;
For 't is a meritorious fair design,
   To chase injustice with revengeful arms: [harms.
   Knights, by their oaths, should right poor ladies'

At this request, with noble disposition
Each present lord began to promise aid,
As bound in knighthood to her imposition,
Longing to hear the hateful foe bewray'd;
But she, that yet her sad task hath not said,
   The protestation stops. O! speak, quoth she,
   How may this forced stain be wip'd from me?

What is the quality of mine offence,
Being constrain'd with dreadful circumstance?
May my pure mind with the foul act dispense,
My low-declined honour to advance?
May any terms acquit me from this chance?
   The poison'd fountain clears itself again,
   And why not I from this compelled stain?

With this, they all at once began to say,
Her body's stain her mind untainted clears;
While with a joyless smile she turns away
The face, that map which deep impression bears
Of hard misfortune, carv'd in it with tears.
   No, no, quoth she; no dame, hereafter living,
   By my excuse shall claim excuse's giving.

Here, with a sigh as if her heart would break,
She throws forth Tarquin's name: "he, he," she says,
But more than "he" her poor tongue could not speak;
Till after many accents and delays,
Untimely breathings, sick and short assays,
  She utters this: he, he, fair lords, 't is he,
  That guides this hand to give this wound to me.

Even here she sheathed in her harmless breast
A harmful knife, that thence her soul unsheathed:
That blow did bail it from the deep unrest
Of that polluted prison where it breathed:
Her contrite sighs unto the clouds bequeathed
  Her winged sprite, and through her wounds doth fly
  Life's lasting date from cancel'd destiny.

Stone-still, astonish'd with this deadly deed,
Stood Collatine and all his lordly crew;
Till Lucrece' father, that beholds her bleed,
Himself on her self-slaughter'd body threw:
And from the purple fountain Brutus drew
  The murderous knife, and as it left the place,
  Her blood, in poor revenge, held it in chase;

And bubbling from her breast, it doth divide
In two slow rivers, that the crimson blood
Circles her body in on every side,
Who like a late-sack'd island vastly stood,
Bare and unpeopled, in this fearful flood.
  Some of her blood still pure and red remain'd,
  And some look'd black, and that false Tarquin stain'd

About the mourning and congealed face
Of that black blood a watery rigol[1] goes,
Which seems to weep upon the tainted place:
And ever since, as pitying Lucrece' woes,
Corrupted blood some watery token shows;
  And blood untainted still doth red abide,
  Blushing at that which is so putrify'd.

Daughter, dear daughter! old Lucretius cries,
That life was mine, which thou hast here deprived.
If in the child the father's image lies,

[1] *Circle.*

Where shall I live, now Lucrece is unlived?
Thou wast not to this end from me derived.
  If children pre-decease progenitors,
  We are their offspring, and they none of ours.

Poor broken glass, I often did behold
In thy sweet semblance my old age new-born;
But now that fair fresh mirror, dim and old,
Shows me a bare-bon'd death by time out-worn.
O! from thy cheeks my image thou hast torn,
  And shiver'd all the beauty of my glass,
  That I no more can see what once I was.

O time! cease thou thy course, and last no longer,
If they surcease to be that should survive.
Shall rotten death make conquest of the stronger,
And leave the faltering feeble souls alive?
The old bees die, the young possess their hive:
  Then, live sweet Lucrece; live again, and see
  Thy father die, and not thy father thee!

By this starts Collatine as from a dream,
And bids Lucretius give his sorrow place;
And then in key-cold Lucrece' bleeding stream
He falls, and bathes the pale fear in his face,
And counterfeits to die with her a space;
  Till manly shame bids him possess his breath,
  And live to be revenged on her death.

The deep vexation of his inward soul
Hath serv'd a dumb arrest upon his tongue;
Who, mad that sorrow should his use control,
Or keep him from heart-easing words so long,
Begins to talk; but through his lips do throng
  Weak words, so thick come in his poor heart's aid,
  That no man could distinguish what he said.

Yet sometime Tarquin was pronounced plain,
But through his teeth, as if the name he tore.
This windy tempest, till it blow up rain,
Held back his sorrow's tide to make it more;
At last it rains, and busy winds give o'er:
  Then, son and father weep with equal strife,
  Who should weep most, for daughter or for wife.

The one doth call her his, the other his,
Yet neither may possess the claim they lay.
The father says, She 's mine: O! mine she is,
Replies her husband: Do not take away
My sorrow's interest; let no mourner say
He weeps for her, for she was only mine,
And only must be wail'd by Collatine.

O! quoth Lucretius, I did give that life,
Which she too early and too late hath spill'd.
Woe, woe! quoth Collatine, she was my wife,
I ow'd her, and 't is mine that she hath kill'd,
"My daughter" and "my wife" with clamours fill'd
The dispers'd air, who holding Lucrece' life,
Answer'd their cries, "my daughter and my wife."

Brutus, who pluck'd the knife from Lucrece' side,
Seeing such emulation in their woe,
Began to clothe his wit in state and pride,
Burying in Lucrece' wound his folly's show.
He with the Romans was esteemed so
As silly jeering idiots are with kings,
For sportive words, and uttering foolish things:

But now he throws that shallow habit by,
Wherein deep policy did him disguise,
And arm'd his long-hid wits advisedly,
To check the tears in Collatinus' eyes.
Thou wronged lord of Rome, quoth he, arise:
Let my unsounded self, suppos'd a fool,
Now set thy long-experienc'd wit to school.

Why, Collatine, is woe the cure for woes?
Do wounds help wounds, or grief help grievous deeds
Is it revenge to give thyself a blow,
For his foul act by whom thy fair wife bleeds?
Such childish humour from weak minds proceeds;
Thy wretched wife mistook the matter so,
To slay herself that should have slain her foe.

Courageous Roman, do not steep thy heart
In such relenting dew of lamentations,
But kneel with me, and help to bear thy part,

To rouse our Roman gods with invocations,
That they will suffer these abominations,
  Since Rome herself in them doth stand disgraced,
  By our strong arms from forth her fair streets chased.

Now, by the Capitol that we adore,
And by this chaste blood so unjustly stained,
By heaven's fair sun that breeds the fat earth's store,
By all our country rights in Rome maintained,
And by chaste Lucrece' soul, that late complained
  Her wrongs to us, and by this bloody knife,
  We will revenge the death of this true wife.

This said, he struck his hand upon his breast,
And kiss'd the fatal knife to end his vow;
And to his protestation urg'd the rest,
Who, wondering at him, did his words allow;
Then, jointly to the ground their knees they bow,
  And that deep vow which Brutus made before,
  He doth again repeat, and that they swore.

When they had sworn to this advised doom
They did conclude to bear dead Lucrece thence;
To show her bleeding body thorough Rome,
And so to publish Tarquin's foul offence:
Which being done with speedy diligence,
  The Romans plausibly[1] did give consent
  To Tarquin's everlasting banishment.

[1] *With applause*

SONNETS.

"Shake-speares Sonnets. Neuer before Imprinted. At London By G. Eld for T. T. and are to be solde by William Aspley. 1609." 4to. 40 leaves.

"A Louers complaint. By William Shake-speare," occupies eleven pages at the end of this volume. The late Mr. Caldecot presented a copy of "Shakespeare's Sonnets" to the Bodleian Library, with the following imprint: "At London By G. Eld for T. T. and are to be solde by Iohn Wright, dwelling at Christ Church gate." It is no doubt the same edition as that "to be solde by William Aspley," for in other respects they agree exactly, excepting that the copy bearing the name of Iohn Wright has no date at the bottom of the title-page: it was very possibly cut off by the binder.

INTRODUCTION.

"SHAKESPEARE'S Sonnets" were printed under that title, and with the name of the poet in unusually large capital letters, in 1609. No Christian name is to be found until we arrive at "A Lover's Complaint," but "Shakespeare's Sonnets" is repeated at the head of the first of the series. Hence we may possibly be warranted in assuming that they were productions well known to have been for some time floating about among the lovers and admirers of poetry, and then collected into a volume. The celebrity of the author seems proved, if any proof of the kind were wanting, by the manner in which his "Sonnets" were put forth to the world.

There is one fact connected with the original publication of "Shakespeare's Sonnets" which has hitherto escaped remark, none of the commentators, apparently, being aware of it; viz. that although there were not two editions of them in 1609, there is an important difference in the title-pages of some copies of the impression of that year, which shows that a bookseller, not hitherto connected with the publication of any of our poet's works, was in some way concerned in the first edition of his "Sonnets." The usual imprint informs us, that they were printed by G. Eld, for T. T. and were to be sold by William Aspley (without any address); but the late Mr. Caldecot had a copy which stated that they were to be sold, not by William Aspley, (who had been one of the partners in "Much ado about Nothing," 1600, 4to., and "Henry IV.," part ii. 1600, 4to.) but by "John Wright, dwelling at Christ Church Gate." No other copy with which we are acquainted has this variation in the title-page, and possibly T. T. had some reason for having it cancelled, and for substituting the name of Aspley for that of Wright: the former might be better known to the ordinary buyers of such books, and to the two quarto plays in which he was interested, he, perhaps, did not think it necessary to append the place where his business was carried on.

The application of the initials T. T., on the title-page, is ascertained from the Registers of the Stationers' Company, where the subsequent entry is found:—

"20 May 1609.

Tho. Thorpe] A booke called Shakespeare's Sonnets."

Thorpe was a bookseller of considerable eminence, who

usually put his name at full length upon his title-pages, and why he did not do so in this instance, and also subscribed only T. T. to the dedication of the Sonnets, is a matter we should consider of little or no consequence, if it related to the productions of perhaps any other author but Shakespeare. It sometimes happened of old, that if it were suspected that a work might contain anything publicly or personally objectionable, the printer or the stationer only allowed their initials to appear in connection with it. That such was the case here, there is no sufficient ground for believing; and Eld avowed himself the printer, and Aspley the seller of "Shakespeare's Sonnets."

A question has arisen, and has been much disputed of late years, who was the individual to whom Thorpe dedicated these sonnets, and whom, in a very unprecedented and peculiar form, he addresses as "Mr. W. H." That form is precisely as follows, on a separate leaf immediately succeeding the title-page:—

TO. THE. ONLIE. BEGETTER. OF.
THESE. INSVING. SONNETS.
MR. W. H. ALL. HAPPINESSE.
AND. THAT. ETERNITIE.
PROMISED.
BY.
OUR. EVER-LIVING. POET.
WISHETH.
THE. WELL-WISHING.
ADVENTVRER. IN.
SETTING.
FORTH.

T. T.

We are not aware that there is another instance in our language, at that period, of a dedication of a similar kind, and in a similar style. It was not at all uncommon for booksellers to subscribe dedications; but it more frequently happened after the death of an author than during his life, and never, that we recollect, in a manner so remarkable. The discussion has been carried on with some pertinacity on the question, what person was addressed as "Mr. W. H.?" and various replies have been made to it. Farmer conjectured wildly that he might be William Hart, the poet's nephew, who was only born in 1600: Tyrwhitt guessed from a line in one of the sonnets (Son. XX.) that the name was W. Hughes, or Hews:

"A man in hue, all hues in his controlling"

which is thus printed in the 4to, 1609:

"A man in hew all *Hews* in his controwling."

Although the word "hue" is repeatedly spelt *hew* in the old edition, this is the only instance in which it is printed in Italic type, and with a capital letter, exactly the same as *Will*, in Sonnets CXXXV., CXXXVI., and CXLIII., where the author plays upon his own name. Dr. Drake imagined that

W. H. were the initials of Henry Wriothesly, Earl of Southampton, inverted ("Shakespeare and his Times," vol. ii. p. 62); and of late years Boaden, with great ingenuity, has contended that W. H. meant William Herbert, Earl of Pembroke[1]. This last notion seems too much taken for granted by Mr. C. Armitage Brown, in his very clever and, in many respects, original work, "Shakespeare's Autobiographical Poems," 8vo., 1838; but we own that we cannot accord in that, or in any other theory that has yet been advanced upon the point. We have no suggestion of our own to offer, and acquiescence in one opinion or in another in no way affects any position regarding them which we might be disposed to take up; but it seems to us the very height of improbability that a bookseller in the year 1609, when peculiar respect was paid to nobility and station, would venture to address an Earl and a Knight of the Garter merely as "Mr. W. H.[2]" However, notwithstanding the pains taken to settle the dispute, we hold it to be one of comparatively little importance, and it is certainly one upon which we are not likely to arrive at a final and satisfactory decision. To the desperate speculation of Chalmers, that not a few of the Sonnets were addressed to Queen Elizabeth, though maintained with considerable ability and learning, it is hardly necessary even to advert.

It is evident that the Sonnets were written at very different periods of Shakespeare's life, and under very different circumstances—some in youth, some in more advanced age; some when he was hopeful and happy, and some when he was desponding and afflicted at his own condition in life, and place in society. In many there are to be found most remarkable indications of self-confidence, and of assurance in the immortality of his verses, and in this respect the author's opinion was constant and uniform. He never scrupled to express it, and perhaps there is no writer of ancient or of modern times who, for the quantity of such writings left behind him, has so frequently or so strongly declared his firm

[1] In a small pamphlet, entitled "On the Sonnets of Shakespeare, identifying the Person to whom they were addressed, and elucidating several points in the Poet's History. By James Boaden." 8vo. 1838. The whole substance of the tract had been published in 1832 in a periodical work. We differ from Mr. Boaden with the more reluctance, because it appears that his notion was supported by the opinion of Mr. B. Heywood Bright, well known for his acuteness and learning, who, without any previous communication, had fallen upon the same conjecture before it was broached by Boaden.

[2] Upon this particular point we concur with Mr. Peter Cunningham, in a note to his excellent edition of Mr. T. Campbell's "Specimens of British Poets," (Essay, p. lxxi.) but we can by no means follow him in thinking that Shakespeare's Sonnets have been "over-rated," or that the Earl of Pembroke could not have been addressed in them, because he was only nine years old in 1598. Shakespeare had written sonnets at that date, according to the undoubted testimony of Meres, but those in which the Earl has been supposed to be addressed may have been produced at a considerably later period. Still, at the early age of eighteen or nineteen, which the Earl reached in 1609, it does not seem likely that Shakespeare would have thought it necessary, with so much vehemence, to urge him to marry.

belief that what he had written, in this department of poetry, "the world would not willingly let die." This conviction seems hardly reconcileable with the carelessness he appears to have displayed for the preservation of his dramatic writings. We know from Francis Meres that Shakespeare's Sonnets were scattered among his friends in 1598[3], and no doubt he continued to add to them from year to year; but it was left to a bookseller in 1609, perhaps, to cause them to be collected, and to be printed in a separate volume.

It is with reference to this circumstance that we understand Thorpe to address "Mr. W. H.," in the dedication, as "the only begetter of these ensuing sonnets." Boswell quoted a passage from Dekker's "Satiromastix," 1602, (and many other instances might be adduced) to prove that "begetter" only meant *obtainer* or *procurer*; and as Thorpe had been under some obligation to W. H., for collecting Shakespeare's scattered sonnets from various parties, for this reason, perhaps, he inscribed them to him. There is no doubt that "Mr. W. H." could not be "the *only* begetter" of the sonnets in any other sense, for it is indisputable that many of them are addressed to a woman; and though a male object might have been the cause of some of them, and particularly of the first twenty-six, he could not have been the cause of the last twenty-seven sonnets.

We have already mentioned Mr. Brown's work, "Shakespeare's Autobiographical Poems," which, with a few errors and inconsistencies of little moment, contains the best solution of various difficulties arising out of these Sonnets yet published. He contends that Shakespeare used the form of the sonnet as Spenser and many others employed stanzas of various descriptions, and that 152 of the 154 sonnets are divisible into six distinct poems. His arrangement of them is the following; and we think with him, that if they be read with this key, much will be intelligible which upon any other supposition must remain obscure:—

First Poem. Sonnets 1 to 26. To his friend, persuading him to marry.

Second Poem. Sonnets 27 to 55. To his friend, forgiving him for having robbed him of his mistress.

Third Poem. Sonnets 56 to 77. To his friend, complaining of his coldness, and warning him of life's decay.

Fourth Poem. Sonnets 78 to 101. To his friend, complaining that he prefers another poet's praises[4], and reproving him for faults that may injure his character.

[3] The following are the words Meres uses:—"As the soule of Euphorbus was thought to live in Pythagoras, so the sweete wittie soule of Ovid lives in mellifluous and hony-tongued Shakespeare: witnes his *Venus and Adonis*, his *Lucrece*, his sugred *Sonnets* among his private friends, &c."—*Palladis Tamia*, 1598, fo. 281, b.

[4] This is the poet whom Shakespeare (Son. lxxx.) calls "a better spirit," and of whom he also speaks in Son. lxxxiii. lxxxv. &c. Some have supposed that he meant Spenser, others Daniel; but Mr. P. Cunningham has pointed out an apparent allusion to Drayton, (and to his collection of Sonnets, published in 1594 under the title of "Idea's Mirror") in Shakespeare's twenty-first Sonnet, in these lines:-

Fifth Poem. Sonnets 102 to 126. To his friend, excusing himself for having been some time silent, and disclaiming the charge of inconstancy.

Sixth Poem. Sonnets 127 to 152. To his mistress, on her infidelity.

Mr. Brown asserts, and goes far to prove, that the sonnets in the first five of these divisions are consecutive, following up the same thought, and working out the same purpose. With regard to the "sixth poem," as he terms it, he contends that the sonnets have been confused, and that they are not, like the others, to be read in the order in which they were printed in the edition of 1609. He rejects the last two sonnets as no part of any of the six poems, and they are unquestionably somewhat incongruous.

Many years ago, long before the appearance of Mr. Brown's volume, it had occurred to us, as a mode merely of removing some of the difficulties attending this portion of the works of Shakespeare, that it was possible that he had consented to write some of them, not in his own person, but for individuals who asked his assistance. We entirely abandon that supposition, notwithstanding we are aware that such was not an uncommon practice in Shakespeare's age. Gascoigne, who died in 1577, mentions that he had been frequently so employed: the author of "The Forest of Fancy," 1579, tells us that he had written many of the poems it contains for persons "who had occasion to crave his help in that behalf;" and Sir John Harington, in his Epigrams, written probably about 1591, states expressly,

> "Verses are grown such merchantable ware,
> That now for Sonnets sellers are and buyers."

Marston, in his Satires, 1598, accuses "Roscio the tragedian" of having written some love-verses for Mutio, and he adds elsewhere that "absolute Castilio" had supplied himself in a similar manner, in order that he might pay acceptable court to his mistress. Therefore, if Shakespeare had now and then condescended to supply the wants of his friends in this way, who thus became possessed of his "sugred sonnets," as Meres calls them, it would, at all events, not have been without precedent.

Thorpe's edition of "Shakespeare's Sonnets" is a well printed volume, although not perhaps so good a specimen of the typography of that time, as Field's impressions of "Venus and Adonis" and "Lucrece." It is remarkable, that while

> "So is it not with me, as with that muse,
> Stirred by a painted beauty to his verse,
> Who heaven itself for ornament doth use,
> And every fair with his fair doth rehearse," &c.

It may be doubted whether in these, and the succeeding lines, Shakespeare had any individual reference. Drayton's "Idea's Mirror" has only been discovered of late years; and it seems not improbable that, like his "Endymion and Phœbe," (see the Bridgewater Catalogue, p. 108) he, for some reason, suppressed it. Only a single copy of each has been preserved.

most of Shakespeare's plays came from the press in the quarto editions in so slovenly and uncorrected a state, his minor poems have been handed down to us, perhaps, more accurately printed than those of any poets of the time, with the exception of Daniel and Drayton, who seem generally to have bestowed great pains upon their productions. At the end of the "Sonnets" is a poem, called "A Lover's Complaint;" and here, although it has no fresh title-page, we are assured that it is "by William Shake-speare." There could in fact be no doubt respecting the authorship of it; but on what occasion, or for what purpose it was written, we have no information.

The ensuing sonnets, with other poems, were reprinted in 1640, 8vo, with a frontispiece of the author, engraved by Marshall. It is an edition of no authority: it repeats and multiplies the errors of the previous separate impressions, and includes productions with which Shakespeare had no concern.

Our text is that of the 4to, 1609, in every case where a reason is not assigned for deviating from it. In all modern reprints various errors have been committed in consequence of carelessness of collation, or because one editor copied the mistakes of another: of these our notes will contain a sufficient indication.

SONNETS.

I.

FROM fairest creatures we desire increase,
That thereby beauty's rose might never die,
But as the riper should by time decease,
His tender heir might bear his memory:
But thou, contracted to thine own bright eyes,
Feed'st thy light's flame with self-substantial fuel,
Making a famine where abundance lies,
Thyself thy foe, to thy sweet self too cruel.
Thou that art now the world's fresh ornament,
And only herald to the gaudy spring,
Within thine own bud buriest thy content,
And, tender churl, mak'st waste in niggarding.
  Pity the world, or else this glutton be,
  To eat the world's due, by the grave and thee.

II.

When forty winters shall besiege thy brow,
And dig deep trenches in thy beauty's field,
Thy youth's proud livery, so gaz'd on now,
Will be a tatter'd weed, of small worth held:
Then, being ask'd where all thy beauty lies,
Where all the treasure of thy lusty days,
To say, within thine own deep-sunken eyes,
Were an all-eating shame, and thriftless praise.
How much more praise deserv'd thy beauty's use,
If thou couldst answer—"This fair child of mine
Shall sum my count, and make my old excuse,—"
Proving his beauty by succession thine.
  This were to be new made, when thou art old,
  And see thy blood warm, when thou feel'st it cold

III.

Look in thy glass, and tell the face thou viewest,
Now is the time that face should form another;
Whose fresh repair if now thou not renewest,
Thou dost beguile the world, unbless some mother.
For where is she so fair, whose un-ear'd[1] womb
Disdains the tillage of thy husbandry?
Or who is he so fond,[2] will be the tomb
Of his self-love, to stop posterity?
Thou art thy mother's glass, and she in thee
Calls back the lovely April of her prime:
So thou through windows of thine age shalt see,
Despite of wrinkles, this thy golden time.
  But if thou live, remember'd not to be,
  Die single, and thine image dies with thee.

IV.

Unthrifty loveliness, why dost thou spend
Upon thyself thy beauty's legacy?
Nature's bequest gives nothing, but doth lend;
And being frank, she lends to those are free.
Then, beauteous niggard, why dost thou abuse
The bounteous largess given thee to give?
Profitless usurer, why dost thou use
So great a sum of sums, yet canst not live?
For, having traffic with thyself alone,
Thou of thyself thy sweet self dost deceive.
Then how, when nature calls thee to be gone,
What acceptable audit canst thou leave?
  Thy unus'd beauty must be tomb'd with thee,
  Which, used, lives th'[3] executor to be.

V.

Those hours, that with gentle work did frame
The lovely gaze where every eye doth dwell,
Will play the tyrants to the very same,
And that unfair, which fairly doth excel:
For never-resting time leads summer on
To hideous winter, and confounds him there;
Sap check'd with frost, and lusty leaves quite gone,
Beauty o'er-snow'd and bareness every where:

[1] *Unploughed.* [2] *Foolish.* [3] thy: in mod. eds.

Then, were not summer's distillation left,
A liquid prisoner pent in walls of glass,
Beauty's effect with beauty were bereft,
Nor it, nor no remembrance what it was:
  But flowers distill'd, though they with winter meet
  Leese[1] but their show; their substance still lives sweet.

VI.

Then, let not winter's ragged hand deface
In thee thy summer, ere thou be distill'd:
Make sweet some phial; treasure thou some place
With beauty's treasure, ere it be self-kill'd.
That use is not forbidden usury,
Which happies those that pay the willing loan;
That 's for thyself to breed another thee,
Or ten times happier, be it ten for one:
Ten times thyself were happier than thou art,
If ten of thine ten times refigur'd thee.
Then what could death do if thou shouldst depart,
Leaving thee living in posterity?
  Be not self-will'd, for thou art much too fair
  To be death's conquest, and make worms thine heir.

VII.

Lo! in the orient when the gracious light
Lifts up his burning head, each under eye
Doth homage to his new-appearing sight,
Serving with looks his sacred majesty;
And having climb'd the steep-up heavenly hill,
Resembling strong youth in his middle age,
Yet mortal looks adore his beauty still,
Attending on his golden pilgrimage:
But when from high-most pitch with weary car,
Like feeble age, he reeleth from the day,
The eyes, 'fore duteous, now converted are
From his low tract, and look another way.
  So thou, thyself out-going in thy noon,
  Unlook'd on diest, unless thou get a son.

VIII.

Music to hear[2], why hear'st thou music sadly?
Sweets with sweets war not, joy delights in joy.
Why lov'st thou that which thou receiv'st not gladly,
Or else receiv'st with pleasure thine annoy?

[1] *Lose.* [2] Thou, whom it is music to hear.

If the true concord of well-tuned sounds,
By unions married, do offend thine ear,
They do but sweetly chide thee, who confounds
In singleness the parts that thou shouldst bear.
Mark, how one string, sweet husband to another,
Strikes each in each by mutual ordering;
Resembling sire and child and happy mother,
Who all in one one pleasing note do sing:
  Whose speechless song, being many, seeming one,
  Sings this to thee,—thou single wilt prove none.

IX.

Is it for fear to wet a widow's eye,
That thou consum'st thyself in single life?
Ah! if thou issueless shalt hap to die,
The world will wail thee like a makeless[1] wife;
The world will be thy widow, and still weep,
That thou no form of thee hast left behind,
When every private widow well may keep,
By children's eyes, her husband's shape in mind.
Look, what an unthrift in the world doth spend,
Shifts but his place, for still the world enjoys it;
But beauty's waste hath in the world an end,
And, kept unus'd, the user so destroys it.
  No love toward others in that bosom sits,
  That on himself such murderous shame commits.

X.

For shame! deny that thou bear'st love to any,
Who for thyself art so unprovident.
Grant, if thou wilt, thou art belov'd of many,
But that thou none lov'st is most evident;
For thou art so possess'd with murderous hate,
That 'gainst thyself thou stick'st not to conspire,
Seeking that beauteous roof to ruinate,
Which to repair should be thy chief desire.
O, change thy thought, that I may change my mind!
Shall hate be fairer lodg'd than gentle love?
Be, as thy presence is, gracious and kind,
Or, to thyself, at least, kind-hearted prove:
  Make thee another self, for love of me,
  That beauty still may live in thine or thee.

[1] Used indifferently for *mateless*.

XI.

As fast as thou shalt wane, so fast thou growest
In one of thine, from that which thou departest:
And that fresh blood which youngly thou bestowest,
Thou may'st call thine, when thou from youth convertest.
Herein lives wisdom, beauty, and increase;
Without this, folly, age, and cold decay:
If all were minded so, the times should cease,
And threescore year would make the world away.
Let those whom nature hath not made for store,
Harsh, featureless, and rude, barrenly perish:
Look, whom she best endow'd, she gave the more;
Which bounteous gift thou shouldst in bounty cherish.
  She carv'd thee for her seal, and meant thereby,
  Thou shouldst print more, not let that copy die.

XII.

When I do count the clock that tells the time,
And see the brave day sunk in hideous night;
When I behold the violet past prime,
And sable curls all silver'd o'er with white;
When lofty trees I see barren of leaves,
Which erst from heat did canopy the herd,
And summer's green all girded up in sheaves,
Borne on the bier with white and bristly beard;
Then, of thy beauty do I question make,
That thou among the wastes of time must go,
Since sweets and beauties do themselves forsake,
And die as fast as they see others grow;
  And nothing 'gainst time's scythe can make defence,
  Save breed, to brave him, when he takes thee hence.

XIII.

O, that you were yourself! but, love, you are
No longer yours, than you yourself here live.
Against this coming end you should prepare,
And your sweet semblance to some other give:
So should that beauty which you hold in lease,
Find no determination: then, you were
Yourself again, after yourself's decease,
When your sweet issue your sweet form should bear.

Who lets so fair a house fall to decay,
Which husbandry in honour might uphold,
Against the stormy gusts of winter's day,
And barren rage of death's eternal cold?
O! none but unthrifts. Dear my love, you know,
You had a father: let your son say so.

XIV.

Not from the stars do I my judgment pluck,
And yet, methinks, I have astronomy,
But not to tell of good, or evil luck,
Of plagues, or dearths, or seasons' quality;
Nor can I fortune to brief minutes tell,
Pointing to each his thunder, rain, and wind;
Or say with princes if it shall go well,
By oft predict that I in heaven find:
But from thine eyes my knowledge I derive,
And, constant stars, in them I read such art,
As truth and beauty shall together thrive,
If from thyself to store thou wouldst convert;
Or else of thee this I prognosticate,
Thy end is truth's and beauty's doom and date.

XV.

When I consider every thing that grows
Holds in perfection but a little moment;
That this huge stage presenteth nought but shows,
Whereon the stars in secret influence comment;
When I perceive that men as plants increase,
Cheered and check'd even by the selfsame sky,
Vaunt in their youthful sap, at height decrease,
And wear their brave state out of memory;
Then, the conceit of this inconstant stay
Sets you most rich in youth before my sight,
Where wasteful time debateth with decay,
To change your day of youth to sullied night;
And, all in war with time, for love of you,
As he takes from you, I engraft you new.

XVI.

But wherefore do not you a mightier way
Make war upon this bloody tyrant, time,
And fortify yourself in your decay
With means more blessed than my barren rhyme?

Now stand you on the top of happy hours,
And many maiden gardens, yet unset,
With virtuous wish would bear your living flowers,
Much liker than your painted counterfeit:
So should the lines of life that life repair,
Which this, time's pencil, or my pupil pen,
Neither in inward worth, nor outward fair,
Can make you live yourself in eyes of men.
  To give away yourself, keeps yourself still,
  And you must live, drawn by your own sweet skill.

XVII.

Who will believe my verse in time to come,
If it were fill'd with your most high deserts?
Though yet, heaven knows, it is but as a tomb
Which hides your life, and shows not half your parts.
If I could write the beauty of your eyes,
And in fresh numbers number all your graces,
The age to come would say, "this poet lies;
Such heavenly touches ne'er touch'd earthly faces."
So should my papers, yellow'd with their age,
Be scorn'd, like old men of less truth than tongue,
And your true rights be term'd a poet's rage,
And stretched metre of an antique song;
  But were some child of yours alive that time,
  You should live twice—in it, and in my rhyme.

XVIII.

Shall I compare thee to a summer's day?
Thou art more lovely and more temperate:
Rough winds do shake the darling buds of May,
And summer's lease hath all too short a date.
Sometime too hot the eye of heaven shines,
And often is his gold complexion dimm'd,
And every fair from fair sometime declines,
By chance, or nature's changing course, untrimm'd;
But thy eternal summer shall not fade,
Nor lose possession of that fair thou owest;
Nor shall death brag thou wander'st in his shade,
When in eternal lines to time thou growest.
  So long as men can breathe, or eyes can see,
  So long lives this, and this gives life to thee.

XIX.

Devouring Time, blunt thou the lion's paws,
And make the earth devour her own sweet brood;
Pluck the keen teeth from the fierce tiger's jaws,
And burn the long-liv'd phœnix in her blood:
Make glad and sorry seasons as thou fleets,
And do whate'er thou wilt, swift-footed Time,
To the wide world, and all her fading sweets;
But I forbid thee one most heinous crime:
O! carve not with thy hours my love's fair brow,
Nor draw no lines there with thine antique pen;
Him in thy course untainted do allow,
For beauty's pattern to succeeding men.
  Yet, do thy worst, old Time: despite thy wrong,
  My love shall in my verse ever live young.

XX.

A woman's face, with nature's own hand painted,
Hast thou, the master-mistress of my passion;
A woman's gentle heart, but not acquainted
With shifting change, as is false women's fashion:
An eye more bright than theirs, less false in rolling,
Gilding the object whereupon it gazeth;
A man in hue, all hues in his controlling,
Which steals men's eyes, and women's souls amazeth;
And for a woman wert thou first created;
Till nature, as she wrought thee, fell a-doting,
And by addition me of thee defeated,
By adding one thing to my purpose nothing.
  But since she prick'd thee out for women's pleasure,
  Mine be thy love, and thy love's use their treasure.

XXI.

So is it not with me, as with that muse
Stirr'd by a painted beauty to his verse,
Who heaven itself for ornament doth use,
And every fair with his fair doth rehearse;
Making a couplement of proud compare,
With sun and moon, with earth and sea's rich gems,
With April's first-born flowers, and all things rare
That heaven's air in this huge rondure hems.
O! let me, true in love, but truly write,
And then, believe me, my love is as fair

As any mother's child, though not so bright
As those gold candles fix'd in heaven's air:
Let them say more that like of hear-say well,
I will not praise, that purpose not to sell.

XXII.

My glass shall not persuade me I am old,
So long as youth and thou are of one date;
But when in thee time's furrows I behold,
Then look I death my days should expiate;
For all that beauty that doth cover thee,
Is but the seemly raiment of my heart,
Which in thy breast doth live, as thine in me.
How can I, then, be elder than thou art?
O! therefore, love, be of thyself so wary,
As I, not for myself, but for thee will,
Bearing thy heart, which I will keep so chary
As tender nurse her babe from faring ill.
Presume not on thy heart, when mine is slain;
Thou gav'st me thine, not to give back again.

XXIII.

As an unperfect actor on the stage,
Who with his fear is put besides his part,
Or some fierce thing replete with too much rage,
Whose strength's abundance weakens his own heart;
So I, for fear of trust, forget to say
The perfect ceremony of love's rite,
And in mine own love's strength seem to decay,
O'er-charg'd with burden of mine own love's might.
O! let my books be, then, the eloquence
And dumb presagers of my speaking breast,
Who plead for love, and look for recompense,
More than that tongue that more hath more express'd.
O! learn to read what silent love hath writ
To hear with eyes belongs to love's fine wit.

XXIV.

Mine eye hath play'd the painter, and hath steel'd
Thy beauty's form in table of my heart:
My body is the frame wherein 't is held,
And perspective it is best painter's art;

For through the painter must you see his skill,
To find where your true image pictur'd lies;
Which in my bosom's shop is hanging still,
That hath his windows glazed with thine eyes.
Now, see what good turns eyes for eyes have done:
Mine eyes have drawn thy shape, and thine for me
Are windows to my breast, where-through the sun
Delights to peep, to gaze therein on thee;
Yet eyes this cunning want to grace their art,
They draw but what they see, know not the heart.

XXV.

Let those who are in favour with their stars
Of public honour and proud titles boast,
Whilst I, whom fortune of such triumph bars,
Unlook'd for joy in that I honour most.
Great princes' favourites their fair leaves spread,
But as the marigold at the sun's eye;
And in themselves their pride lies buried,
For at a frown they in their glory die.
The painful warrior, famoused for fight,[1]
After a thousand victories once foil'd,
Is from the book of honour razed quite,
And all the rest forgot for which he toil'd:
Then, happy I, that love and am beloved,
Where I may not remove, nor be removed.

XXVI.

Lord of my love, to whom in vassalage
Thy merit hath my duty strongly knit,
To thee I send this written embassage,
To witness duty, not to show my wit:
Duty so great, which wit so poor as mine
May make seem bare, in wanting words to show it,
But that I hope some good conceit of thine
In thy soul's thought, all naked, will bestow it;
Till whatsoever star that guides my moving,
Points on me graciously with fair aspect,
And puts apparel on my tattered loving,
To show me worthy of thy sweet respect:
Then may I dare to boast how I do love thee; [me.
Till then, not show my head where thou may'st prove

[1] worth: in old eds. Theobald made the change.

XXVII.

Weary with toil I haste me to my bed,
The dear repose for limbs with travel tired;
But then begins a journey in my head,
To work my mind, when body's work's expired:
For then my thoughts (from far where I abide)
Intend a zealous pilgrimage to thee,
And keep my drooping eyelids open wide,
Looking on darkness which the blind do see:
Save that my soul's imaginary sight
Presents thy shadow to my sightless view,
Which, like a jewel hung in ghastly night,
Makes black night beauteous, and her old face new.
  Lo! thus by day my limbs, by night my mind,
  For thee, and for myself, no quiet find.

XXVIII.

How can I, then, return in happy plight,
That am debarr'd the benefit of rest?
When day's oppression is not eas'd by night,
But day by night, and night by day, oppress'd?
And each, though enemies to either's reign,
Do in consent shake hands to torture me;
The one by toil, the other to complain
How far I toil, still farther off from thee.
I tell the day, to please him thou art bright,
And dost him grace when clouds do blot the heaven:
So flatter I the swart-complexion'd night,
When sparkling stars twire not, thou gild'st the even:
  But day doth daily draw my sorrows longer,
  And night doth nightly make grief's length seem stronger.

XXIX.

When in disgrace with fortune and men's eyes,
I all alone beweep my outcast state,
And trouble deaf heaven with my bootless cries,
And look upon myself, and curse my fate,
Wishing me like to one more rich in hope,
Featur'd like him, like him with friends possess'd,
Desiring this man's art, and that man's scope,
With what I most enjoy contented least;
Yet in these thoughts myself almost despising,

Haply I think on thee, and then my state
(Like to the lark at break of day arising
From sullen earth) sings hymns at heaven's gate:
For thy sweet love remember'd such wealth brings
That then I scorn to change my state with kings.

XXX.

When to the sessions of sweet silent thought
I summon up remembrance of things past,
I sigh the lack of many a thing I sought,
And with old woes new wail my dear time's waste·
Then, can I drown an eye, unus'd to flow,
For precious friends hid in death's dateless night,
Ana weep afresh love's long since cancell'd woe,
And moan th' expense of many a vanish'd sight.
Then, can I grieve at grievances fore-gone,
And heavily from woe to woe tell o'er
The sad account of fore-bemoaned moan,
Which I new pay, as if not paid before:
But if the while I think on thee, dear friend,
All losses are restor'd, and sorrows end.

XXXI.

Thy bosom is endeared with all hearts,
Which I by lacking have supposed dead,
And there reigns love, and all love's loving parts,
And all those friends which I thought buried.
How many a holy and obsequious[1] tear
Hath dear religious love stol'n from mine eye,
As interest of the dead, which now appear
But things remov'd, that hidden in thee lie!
Thou art the grave where buried love doth live,
Hung with the trophies of my lovers gone,
Who all their parts of me to thee did give;
That due of many now is thine alone:
Their images I lov'd I view in thee,
And thou (all they) hast all the all of me.

XXXII.

If thou survive my well-contented day,
When that churl death my bones with dust shall cover
And shalt by fortune once more re-survey
These poor rude lines of thy deceased lover,

[1] *Funereal.*

Compare them with the bettering of the time;
And though they be out-stripp'd by every pen,
Reserve them for my love, not for their rhyme,
Exceeded by the height of happier men.
O! then vouchsafe me but this loving thought:
"Had my friend's muse grown with this growing age,
A dearer birth than this his love had brought,
To march in ranks of better equipage:
But since he died, and poets better prove,
Theirs for their style I 'll read, his for his love."

XXXIII.

Full many a glorious morning have I seen
Flatter the mountain tops with sovereign eye,
Kissing with golden face the meadows green,
Gilding pale streams with heavenly alchymy;
Anon permit the basest clouds to ride
With ugly rack on his celestial face,
And from the forlorn world his visage hide,
Stealing unseen to west with this disgrace.
Even so my sun one early morn did shine,
With all triumphant splendour on my brow;
But out, alack! he was but one hour mine,
The region cloud hath mask'd him from me now.
Yet him for this my love no whit disdaineth;
Suns of the world may stain, when heaven's sun [staineth.

XXXIV.

Why didst thou promise such a beauteous day,
And make me travel forth without my cloak,
To let base clouds o'ertake me in my way,
Hiding thy bravery in their rotten smoke?
'T is not enough that through the cloud thou break,
To dry the rain on my storm-beaten face,
For no man well of such a salve can speak,
That heals the wound, and cures not the disgrace:
Nor can thy shame give physic to my grief;
Though thou repent, yet I have still the loss:
Th' offender's sorrow lends but weak relief
To him that bears the strong offence's cross.[1]
Ah! but those tears are pearl, which thy love sheds,
And they are rich and ransom all ill deeds.

[1] loss: in old eds. Malone made the change.

XXXV.

No more be griev'd at that which thou hast done:
Roses have thorns, and silver fountains mud;
Clouds and eclipses stain both moon and sun,
And loathsome canker lives in sweetest bud.
All men make faults, and even I in this,
Authorizing thy trespass with compare;
Myself corrupting, salving thy amiss,
Excusing thy sins more than thy sins are:
For to thy sensual fault I bring in sense,
Thy adverse party is thy advocate,
And 'gainst myself a lawful plea commence.
Such civil war is in my love and hate,
  That I an accessary needs must be
  To that sweet thief which sourly robs from me.

XXXVI.

Let me confess that we two must be twain,
Although our undivided loves are one:
So shall those blots that do with me remain,
Without thy help by me be borne alone.
In our two loves there is but one respect,
Though in our lives a separable spite,
Which though it alter not love's sole effect,
Yet doth it steal sweet hours from love's delight.
I may not evermore acknowledge thee,
Lest my bewailed guilt should do thee shame;
Nor thou with public kindness honour me,
Unless thou take that honour from thy name:
  But do not so; I love thee in such sort,
  As, thou being mine, mine is thy good report.

XXXVII.

As a decrepit father takes delight
To see his active child do deeds of youth,
So I, made lame by fortune's dearest spite,
Take all my comfort of thy worth and truth;
For whether beauty, birth, or wealth, or wit,
Or any of these all, or all, or more,
Entitled in thy parts do crowned sit,
I make my love engrafted to this store:

So then I am not lame, poor, nor despis'd,
Whilst that this shadow doth such substance give,
That I in thy abundance am suffic'd,
And by a part of all thy glory live.
  Look what is best, that best I wish in thee:
  This wish I have; then, ten times happy me!

XXXVIII.

How can my muse want subject to invent,
While thou dost breathe, that pour'st into my verse
Thine own sweet argument, too excellent
For every vulgar paper to rehearse?
O! give thyself the thanks, if aught in me
Worthy perusal stand against thy sight;
For who 's so dumb that cannot write to thee,
When thou thyself dost give invention light?
Be thou the tenth muse, ten times more in worth
Than those old nine which rhymers invocate;
And he that calls on thee, let him bring forth
Eternal numbers to out-live long date.
  If my slight muse do please these curious days,
  The pain be mine, but thine shall be the praise.

XXXIX.

O! how thy worth with manners may I sing,
When thou art all the better part of me?
What can mine own praise to mine own self bring?
And what is 't but mine own, when I praise thee?
Even for this let us divided live,
And our dear love lose name of single one,
That by this separation I may give
That due to thee which thou deserv'st alone.
O absence! what a torment wouldst thou prove,
Were it not thy sour leisure gave sweet leave
To entertain the time with thoughts of love,
Which time and thoughts so sweetly doth[1] deceive,
  And that thou teachest how to make one twain,
  By praising him here, who doth hence remain.

XL.

Take all my loves, my love; yea, take them all:
What hast thou then more than thou hadst before?

[1] dost: in old eds.

No love, my love, that thou may'st true love call:
All mine was thine before thou hadst this more.
Then, if for my love thou my love receivest,
I cannot blame thee, for my love thou usest;
But yet be blam'd, if thou thyself deceivest
By wilful taste of what thyself refusest.
I do forgive thy robbery, gentle thief,
Although thou steal thee all my poverty;
And yet love knows it is a greater grief
To bear love's wrong, than hate's known injury.
  Lascivious grace, in whom all ill well shows,
  Kill me with spites, yet we must not be foes.

XLI.

Those pretty wrongs that liberty commits,
When I am sometime absent from thy heart,
Thy beauty and thy years full well befits,
For still temptation follows where thou art.
Gentle thou art, and therefore to be won,
Beauteous thou art, therefore to be assailed;
And when a woman woos, what woman's son
Will sourly leave her till she have prevailed.
Ah me! but yet thou might'st my seat forbear,
And chide thy beauty and thy straying youth,
Who lead thee in their riot even there
Where thou art forc'd to break a two-fold truth;
  Hers, by thy beauty tempting her to thee,
  Thine, by thy beauty being false to me.

XLII.

That thou hast her, it is not all my grief,
And yet it may be said, I lov'd her dearly;
That she hath thee, is of my wailing chief,
A loss in love that touches me more nearly.
Loving offenders, thus I will excuse ye:—
Thou dost love her, because thou know'st I love her;
And for my sake even so doth she abuse me,
Suffering my friend for my sake to approve her.
If I lose thee, my loss is my love's gain,
And losing her, my friend hath found that loss;
Both find each other, and I lose both twain,
And both for my sake lay on me this cross:
  But here 's the joy; my friend and I are one.
  Sweet flattery!—then, she loves but me alone.

XLIII.

When most I wink, then do mine eyes best see,
For all the day they view things unrespected;
But when I sleep, in dreams they look on thee,
And darkly bright are bright in dark directed.
Then thou, whose shadow shadows doth make bright,
How would thy shadow's form, form happy show
To the clear day with thy much clearer light,
When to unseeing eyes thy shade shines so?
How would, I say, mine eyes be blessed made
By looking on thee in the living day,
When in dead night thy fair imperfect shade
Through heavy sleep on sightless eyes doth stay?
  All days are nights to see, till I see thee, [me.
  And nights bright days, when dreams do show thee

XLIV.

If the dull substance of my flesh were thought,
Injurious distance should not stop my way;
For, then, despite of space, I would be brought
From limits far remote where thou dost stay.
No matter then, although my foot did stand
Upon the farthest earth remov'd from thee;
For nimble thought can jump both sea and land,
As soon as think the place where he would be.
But ah! thought kills me, that I am not thought,
To leap large lengths of miles when thou art gone,
But that, so much of earth and water wrought,
I must attend time's leisure with my moan;
  Receiving nought by elements so slow
  But heavy tears, badges of either's woe.

XLV.

The other two, slight air and purging fire,
Are both with thee, wherever I abide;
The first my thought, the other my desire,
These present-absent with swift motion slide:
For when these quicker elements are gone
In tender embassy of love to thee,
My life, being made of four, with two alone
Sinks down to death, oppress'd with melancholy,
Until life's composition be recured
By those swift messengers return'd from thee,

Who even but now come back again, assured
Of thy fair health, recounting it to me:
  This told, I joy; but then, no longer glad,
  I send them back again, and straight grow sad.

XLVI.

Mine eye and heart are at a mortal war,
How to divide the conquest of thy sight;
Mine eye my heart thy picture's sight would bar,
My heart mine eye the freedom of that right.
My heart doth plead, that thou in him dost lie,
(A closet never pierc'd with crystal eyes)
But the defendant doth that plea deny,
And says in him thy fair appearance lies.
To 'cide[1] this title is impannelled
A quest of thoughts, all tenants to the heart;
And by their verdict is determined
The clear eye's moiety,[2] and the dear heart's part:
  As thus; mine eye's due is thine outward part,
  And my heart's right thine inward love of heart

XLVII.

Betwixt mine eye and heart a league is took,
And each doth good turns now unto the other.
When that mine eye is famish'd for a look,
Or heart in love with sighs himself doth smother,
With my love's picture then my eye doth feast,
And to the painted banquet bids my heart:
Another time mine eye is my heart's guest,
And in his thoughts of love doth share a part:
So, either by thy picture or my love,
Thyself away art present still with me;
For thou not farther than my thoughts canst move,
And I am still with them, and they with thee;
  Or, if they sleep, thy picture in my sight
  Awakes my heart to heart's and eye's delight.

XLVIII.

How careful was I, when I took my way,
Each trifle under truest bars to thrust:
That to my use it might unused stay
From hands of falsehood, in sure wards of trust!

[1] *Decide.* [2] Not merely *half*, but any portion or share.

But thou, to whom my jewels trifles are,
Most worthy comfort, now my greatest grief,
Thou, best of dearest, and mine only care,
Art left the prey of every vulgar thief.
Thee have I not lock'd up in any chest,
Save where thou art not, though I feel thou art,
Within the gentle closure of my breast,
From whence at pleasure thou may'st come and part;
  And even thence thou wilt be stol'n, I fear,
  For truth proves thievish for a prize so dear.

XLIX.

Against that time, if ever that time come,
When I shall see thee frown on my defects,
When as thy love hath cast his utmost sum,
Call'd to that audit by advis'd respects;
Against that time, when thou shalt strangely pass,
And scarcely greet me with that sun, thine eye;
When love, converted from the thing it was,
Shall reasons find of settled gravity;
Against that time do I ensconce me here,
Within the knowledge of mine own desert,
And this my hand against myself uprear,
To guard the lawful reasons on thy part:
  To leave poor me thou hast the strength of laws,
  Since why to love I can allege no cause.

L.

How heavy do I journey on the way,
When what I seek (my weary travel's end)
Doth teach that ease and that repose to say,
"Thus far the miles are measur'd from thy friend!"
The beast that bears me, tired with my woe,
Plods dully on[1] to bear that weight in me,
As if by some instinct the wretch did know,
His rider lov'd not speed being made from thee.
The bloody spur cannot provoke him on
That sometimes anger thrusts into his hide,
Which heavily he answers with a groan,
More sharp to me than spurring to his side:
  For that same groan doth put this in my mind,
  My grief lies onward, and my joy behind.

[1] duly: in old eds. Malone made the change.

LI.

Thus can my love excuse the slow offence
Of my dull bearer, when from thee I speed:
From where thou art why should I haste me thence?
Till I return of posting is no need.
O! what excuse will my poor beast then find,
When swift extremity can seem but slow?
Then should I spur, though mounted on the wind;
In winged speed no motion shall I know:
Then can no horse with my desire keep pace;
Therefore desire, (of perfect love being made)
Shall neigh (no dull flesh) in his fiery race;
But love, for love, thus shall excuse my jade;
  Since from thee going he went wilful-slow,
  Towards thee I 'll run, and give him leave to go

LII.

So am I as the rich, whose blessed key
Can bring him to his sweet up-locked treasure,
The which he will not every hour survey,
For blunting the fine point of seldom pleasure,
Therefore, are feasts so solemn and so rare,
Since seldom coming, in the long year set
Like stones of worth, they thinly placed are,
Or captain jewels in the carcanet.
So is the time that keeps you as my chest,
Or as the wardrobe which the robe doth hide,
To make some special instant special-blest,
By new unfolding his imprison'd pride.
  Blessed are you, whose worthiness gives scope,
  Being had, to triumph, being lack'd, to hope.

LIII.

What is your substance, whereof are you made,
That millions of strange shadows on you tend?
Since every one hath, every one, one shade,
And you, but one, can every shadow lend.
Describe Adonis, and the counterfeit
Is poorly imitated after you;
On Helen's cheek all art of beauty set,
And you in Grecian tires are painted new:
Speak of the spring, and foison[1] of the year,
The one doth shadow of your beauty show,

[1] *Plenty.*

The other as your bounty doth appear;
And you in every blessed shape we know.
  In all external grace you have some part,
  But you like none, none you, for constant heart.

LIV.

O, how much more doth beauty beauteous seem,
By that sweet ornament which truth doth give!
The rose looks fair, but fairer we it deem
For that sweet odour which doth in it live.
The canker[1]-blooms have full as deep a dye,
As the perfumed tincture of the roses;
Hang on such thorns, and play as wantonly
When summer's breath their masked buds discloses;
But, for their virtue only is their show,
They live unwoo'd, and unrespected fade;
Die to themselves. Sweet roses do not so;
Of their sweet deaths are sweetest odours made:
  And so of you, beauteous and lovely youth,
  When that shall fade, my[2] verse distils your truth.

LV.

Not marble, nor the gilded monuments
Of princes, shall out-live this powerful rhyme;
But you shall shine more bright in these contents
Than unswept stone, besmear'd with sluttish time.
When wasteful war shall statues overturn,
And broils root out the work of masonry,
Nor Mars his sword, nor war's quick fire shall burn
The living record of your memory.
'Gainst death and all-oblivious enmity
Shall you pace forth: your praise shall still find room
Even in the eyes of all posterity,
That wear this world out to the ending doom.
  So, till the judgment that yourself arise,
  You live in this, and dwell in lovers' eyes.

LVI.

Sweet love, renew thy force; be it not said,
Thy edge should blunter be than appetite,
Which but to-day by feeding is allay'd,
To-morrow sharpen'd in his former might:

[1] *Dog-rose.* [2] by: in old [illegible] Malone made the change.

So, love, be thou; although to-day thou fill
Thy hungry eyes, even till they wink with fulness,
To-morrow see again, and do not kill
The spirit of love with a perpetual dulness.
Let this sad interim like the ocean be
Which parts the shore, where two contracted new
Come daily to the banks, that when they see
Return of love more blest may be the view;
Or call it winter, which being full of care, [rare
Makes summer's welcome thrice more wish'd, more

LVII.

Being your slave, what should I do but tend
Upon the hours and times of your desire?
I have no precious time at all to spend,
Nor services to do, till you require.
Nor dare I chide the world-without-end hour,
Whilst I, my sovereign, watch the clock for you.
Nor think the bitterness of absence sour,
When you have bid your servant once adieu:
Nor dare I question with my jealous thought,
Where you may be, or your affairs suppose:
But, like a sad slave, stay and think of nought,
Save where you are, how happy you make those.
So true a fool is love, that in your will
(Though you do any thing) he thinks no ill.

LVIII.

That God forbid, that made me first your slave,
I should in thought control your times of pleasure,
Or at your hand th' account of hours to crave,
Being your vassal, bound to stay your leisure!
O! let me suffer (being at your beck)
Th' imprison'd absence of your liberty;
And patience, tame to sufferance, bide each check,
Without accusing you of injury.
Be where you list; your charter is so strong,
That you yourself may privilege your time:
Do what you will, to you it doth belong
Yourself to pardon of self-doing crime.
I am to wait, though waiting so be hell,
Not blame your pleasure, be it ill or well.

LIX.

If there be nothing new, but that which is
Hath been before, how are our brains beguil'd,
Which, labouring for invention, bear amiss
The second burden of a former child?
O! that record could with a backward look,
Even of five hundred courses of the sun,
Show me your image in some antique book,
Since mind at first in character was done;
That I might see what the old world could say
To this composed wonder of your frame;
Whether we are mended, or where better they,
Or whether revolution be the same.
O! sure I am, the wits of former days
To subjects worse have given admiring praise.

LX.

Like as the waves make towards the pebbled shore,
So do our minutes hasten to their end;
Each changing place with that which goes before,
In sequent toil all forwards do contend.
Nativity, once in the main of light,
Crawls to maturity, wherewith being crown'd,
Crooked eclipses 'gainst his glory fight,
And time that gave doth now his gift confound.
Time doth transfix the flourish set on youth,
And delves the parallels in beauty's brow;
Feeds on the rarities of nature's truth,
And nothing stands but for his scythe to mow:
And yet to times in hope my verse shall stand,
Praising thy worth, despite his cruel hand.

LXI.

Is it thy will, thy image should keep open
My heavy eyelids to the weary night?
Dost thou desire my slumbers should be broken,
While shadows, like to thee, do mock my sight?
Is it thy spirit that thou send'st from thee
So far from home, into my deeds to pry:
To find out shames and idle hours in me,
The scope and tenour of thy jealousy?
O no! thy love, though much, is not so great:
It is my love that keeps mine eye awake;

Mine own true love that doth my rest defeat,
To play the watchman ever for thy sake:
  For thee watch I, whilst thou dost wake elsewhere,
  From me far off, with others all too near.

LXII.

Sin of self-love possesseth all mine eye,
And all my soul, and all my every part;
And for this sin there is no remedy,
It is so grounded inward in my heart.
Methinks no face so gracious is as mine,
No shape so true, no truth of such account;
And for myself mine own worth do define,
As I all other in all worths surmount.
But when my glass shows me myself indeed,
Beated and chopp'd with tann'd antiquity,
Mine own self-love quite contrary I read;
Self so self-loving were iniquity.
  'T is thee (myself) that for myself I praise,
  Painting my age with beauty of thy days.

LXIII.

Against my love shall be, as I am now,
With time's injurious hand crush'd and o'erworn;
When hours have drain'd his blood, and fill'd his brow
With lines and wrinkles; when his youthful morn
Hath travell'd on to age's steepy night;
And all those beauties, whereof now he 's king,
Are vanishing, or vanish'd out of sight,
Stealing away the treasure of his spring;
For such a time do I now fortify
Against confounding age's cruel knife,
That he shall never cut from memory
My sweet love's beauty, though my lover's life;
  His beauty shall in these black lines be seen,
  And they shall live, and he in them still green.

LXIV.

When I have seen by Time's fell hand defaced
The rich proud cost of out-worn buried age;
When sometime lofty towers I see down-rased,
And brass eternal, slave to mortal rage:

When I have seen the hungry ocean gain
Advantage on the kingdom of the shore,
And the firm soil win of the watery main,
Increasing store with loss, and loss with store:
When I have seen such interchange of state,
Or state itself confounded to decay,
Ruin hath taught me thus to ruminate—
That time will come and take my love away.
  This thought is as a death, which cannot choose
  But weep to have that which it fears to lose.

LXV.

Since brass, nor stone, nor earth, nor boundless sea,
But sad mortality o'er-sways their power,
How with this rage shall beauty hold a plea,
Whose action is no stronger than a flower?
O! how shall summer's honey-breath hold out
Against the wreckful siege of battering days,
When rocks impregnable are not so stout,
Nor gates of steel so strong, but time decays?
O fearful meditation! where, alack,
Shall time's best jewel from time's chest lie hid?
Or what strong hand can hold his swift foot back?
Or who his spoil of beauty can forbid?
  O none! unless this miracle have might,
  That in black ink my love may still shine bright

LXVI.

Tir'd with all these, for restful death I cry;—
As, to behold desert a beggar born,
And needy nothing trimm'd in jollity,
And purest faith unhappily forsworn,
And gilded honour shamefully misplac'd,
And maiden virtue rudely strumpeted,
And right perfection wrongfully disgrac'd,
And strength by limping sway disabled,
And art made tongue-tied by authority,
And folly (doctor-like) controlling skill,
And simple truth miscall'd simplicity,
And captive good attending captain ill:
  Tir'd with all these, from these would I be gone,
  Save that to die I leave my love alone.

LXVII.

Ah! wherefore with infection should he live,
And with his presence grace impiety,
That sin by him advantage should achieve,
And lace[1] itself with his society?
Why should false painting imitate his cheek,
And steal dead seeing of his living hue?
Why should poor beauty indirectly seek
Roses of shadow, since his rose is true?
Why should he live, now nature bankrupt is,
Beggar'd of blood to blush through lively veins?
For she hath no exchequer now but his,
And, proud of many, lives upon his gains.
O! him she stores, to show what wealth she had
In days long since, before these last so bad.

LXVIII.

Thus is his cheek the map of days out-worn,
When beauty liv'd and died as flowers do now,
Before these bastard signs of fair were borne,
Or durst inhabit on a living brow;
Before the golden tresses of the dead,
The right of sepulchres, were shorn away,
To live a second life on second head;
Ere beauty's dead fleece made another gay.
In him those holy antique hours are seen,
Without all ornament, itself, and true,
Making no summer of another's green,
Robbing no old to dress his beauty new;
And him as for a map doth nature store,
To show false art what beauty was of yore.

LXIX.

Those parts of thee that the world's eye doth view,
Want nothing that the thought of hearts can mend;
All tongues (the voice of souls) give thee that due,[2]
Uttering bare truth, even so as foes commend.
Thine outward thus with outward praise is crown'd
But those same tongues that give thee so thine own,
In other accents do this praise confound,
By seeing farther than the eye hath shown.
They look into the beauty of thy mind,

[1] *Trim, adorn.* [2] end: in old eds. Tyrwhitt made the change.

And that, in guess, they measure by thy deeds; [kind,
Then (churls) their thoughts, although their eyes were
To thy fair flower add the rank smell of weeds:
  But why thy odour matcheth not thy show,
  The solve[1] is this;—that thou dost common grow.

LXX.

That thou art blam'd shall not be thy defect,
For slander's mark was ever yet the fair;
The ornament of beauty is suspect,
A crow that flies in heaven's sweetest air.
So thou be good, slander doth but approve
Thy worth the greater, being woo'd of time;
For canker vice the sweetest buds doth love,
And thou present'st a pure unstained prime.
Thou hast past by the ambush of young days,
Either not assail'd, or victor being charged;
Yet this thy praise cannot be so thy praise,
To tie up envy, evermore enlarged:
  If some suspect of ill mask'd not thy show,
  Then, thou alone kingdoms of hearts shouldst owe.

LXXI.

No longer mourn for me when I am dead,
Than you shall hear the surly sullen bell
Give warning to the world that I am fled
From this vile world, with vilest worms to dwell:
Nay, if you read this line, remember not
The hand that writ it; for I love you so,
That I in your sweet thoughts would be forgot,
If thinking on me then should make you woe.
O! if (I say) you look upon this verse,
When I perhaps compounded am with clay,
Do not so much as my poor name rehearse,
But let your love even with my life decay;
  Lest the wise world should look into your moan,
  And mock you with me after I am gone.

LXXII.

O! lest the world should task you to recite
What merit liv'd in me, that you should love
After my death, dear love, forget me quite,
For you in me can nothing worthy prove;

[1] *Solution.*

Unless you would devise some virtuous lie,
To do more for me than mine own desert,
And hang more praise upon deceased I,
Then niggard truth would willingly impart.
O! lest your true love may seem false in this,
That you for love speak well of me untrue,
My name be buried where my body is,
And live no more to shame nor me nor you.
  For I am sham'd by that which I bring forth,
  And so should you, to love things nothing worth.

LXXIII.

That time of year thou may'st in me behold,
When yellow leaves, or none, or few, do hang
Upon those boughs which shake against the cold,
Bare ruin'd choirs, where late the sweet birds sang.
In me thou seest the twilight of such day
As after sun-set fadeth in the west,
Which by and by black night doth take away,
Death's second self, that seals up all in rest:
In me thou seest the glowing of such fire,
That on the ashes of his youth doth lie,
As the death-bed whereon it must expire,
Consum'd with that which it was nourish'd by. [strong,
  This thou perceiv'st, which makes thy love more
  To love that well which thou must leave ere long:

LXXIV.

But be contented: when that fell arrest
Without all bail shall carry me away,
My life hath in this line some interest,
Which for memorial still with thee shall stay:
When thou reviewest this, thou dost review
The very part was consecrate to thee.
The earth can have but earth, which is his due;
My spirit is thine, the better part of me:
So then thou hast but lost the dregs of life,
The prey of worms, my body being dead;
The coward conquest of a wretch's knife,
Too base of thee to be remembered.
  The worth of that is that which it contains,
  And that is this, and this with thee remains.

LXXV.

So are you to my thoughts, as food to life,
Or as sweet-season'd showers are to the ground;
And for the peace of you I hold such strife
As 'twixt a miser and his wealth is found:
Now proud as an enjoyer, and anon
Doubting the filching age will steal his treasure;
Now counting best to be with you alone,
Then better'd that the world may see my pleasure:
Sometime all full with feasting on your sight,
And by and by clean starved for a look;
Possessing or pursuing no delight,
Save what is had or must from you be took.
Thus do I pine and surfeit day by day;
Or gluttoning on all, or all away.

LXXVI.

Why is my verse so barren of new pride,
So far from variation or quick change?
Why, with the time, do I not glance aside
To new-found methods and to compounds strange?
Why write I still all one, ever the same,
And keep invention in a noted weed,
That every word doth almost tell my name,
Showing their birth, and where they did proceed?
O! know, sweet love, I always write of you,
And you and love are still my argument;
So, all my best is dressing old words new,
Spending again what is already spent:
For as the sun is daily new and old,
So is my love, still telling what is told.

LXXVII.

Thy glass will show thee how thy beauties wear,
Thy dial how thy precious minutes waste;
The vacant leaves thy mind's imprint will bear,
And of this book this learning may'st thou taste:
The wrinkles which thy glass will truly show,
Of mouthed graves will give thee memory;
Thou by thy dial's shady stealth may'st know
Time's thievish progress to eternity.
Look, what thy memory cannot contain,
Commit to these waste blanks, and thou shalt find

Those children nurs'd, deliver'd from thy brain,
To take a new acquaintance of thy mind.
  These offices, so oft as thou wilt look,
  Shall profit thee, and much enrich thy book.

LXXVIII.

So oft have I invok'd thee for my muse,
And found such fair assistance in my verse,
As every alien pen hath got my use,
And under thee their poesy disperse.
Thine eyes that taught the dumb on high to sing,
And heavy ignorance aloft to fly,
Have added feathers to the learned's wing,
And given grace a double majesty.
Yet be most proud of that which I compile,
Whose influence is thine, and born of thee:
In others' works thou dost but mend the style,
And arts with thy sweet graces graced be;
  But thou art all my art, and dost advance
  As high as learning my rude ignorance.

LXXIX.

Whilst I alone did call upon thy aid,
My verse alone had all thy gentle grace;
But now my gracious numbers are decay'd,
And my sick muse doth give another place.
I grant, sweet love, thy lovely argument
Deserves the travail of a worthier pen;
Yet what of thee thy poet doth invent,
He robs thee of, and pays it thee again.
He lends thee virtue, and he stole that word
From thy behaviour; beauty doth he give,
And found it in thy cheek; he can afford
No praise to thee but what in thee doth live.
  Then, thank him not for that which he doth say,
  Since what he owes thee, thou thyself dost pay.

LXXX.

O! how I faint when I of you do write,
Knowing a better spirit doth use your name,
And in the praise thereof spends all his might,
To make me tongue-tied, speaking of your fame:

But since your worth (wide as the ocean is)
The humble as the proudest sail doth bear,
My saucy bark, inferior far to his,
On your broad main doth wilfully appear.
Your shallowest help will hold me up afloat,
Whilst he upon your soundless deep doth ride;
Or, being wreck'd, I am a worthless boat,
He of tall building, and of goodly pride:
Then, if he thrive, and I be cast away,
The worst was this—my love was my decay.

LXXXI.

Or I shall live your epitaph to make,
Or you survive when I in earth am rotten:
From hence your memory death cannot take,
Although in me each part will be forgotten.
Your name from hence immortal life shall have,
Though I, once gone, to all the world must die:
The earth can yield me but a common grave,
When you entombed in men's eyes shall lie.
Your monument shall be my gentle verse,
Which eyes not yet created shall o'er-read;
And tongues to be your being shall rehearse,
When all the breathers of this world are dead;
You still shall live (such virtue hath my pen,)
Where breath most breathes, even in the mouths of men.

LXXXII.

I grant thou wert not married to my muse,
And, therefore, may'st without attaint o'er-look
The dedicated words which writers use
Of their fair subject, blessing every book.
Thou art as fair in knowledge as in hue,
Finding thy worth a limit past my praise;
And, therefore, art enforc'd to seek anew
Some fresher stamp of the time-bettering days.
And do so, love; yet when they have devis'd
What strained touches rhetoric can lend,
Thou, truly fair, wert truly sympathiz'd
In true plain words, by thy true-telling friend;
And their gross painting might be better used
Where cheeks need blood: in thee it is abused.

LXXXIII.

I never saw that you did painting need,
And, therefore, to your fair no painting set;
I found, or thought I found, you did exceed
The barren tender of a poet's debt:
And, therefore, have I slept in your report,
That you yourself, being extant, well might show
How far a modern quill doth come too short,
Speaking of worth, what worth in you doth grow.
This silence for my sin you did impute,
Which shall be most my glory, being dumb;
For I impair not beauty being mute,
When others would give life, and bring a tomb.
  There lives more life in one of your fair eyes,
  Than both your poets can in praise devise.

LXXXIV.

Who is it that says most? which can say more,
Than this rich praise, that you alone are you?
In whose confine immured is the store,
Which should example where your equal grew.
Lean penury within that pen doth dwell,
That to his subject lends not some small glory;
But he that writes of you, if he can tell
That you are you, so dignifies his story,
Let him but copy what in you is writ,
Not making worse what nature made so clear,
And such a counterpart shall fame his wit,
Making his style admired every where.
  You to your beauteous blessings add a curse,
  Being fond on praise, which makes your praises worse.

LXXXV.

My tongue-tied muse in manners holds her still,
While comments of your praise, richly compil'd,
Reserve their character with golden quill,
And precious phrase by all the muses fil'd.
I think good thoughts, whilst other write good words,
And, like unletter'd clerk, still cry "Amen"
To every hymn that able spirit affords,
In polish'd form of well-refined pen.
Hearing you prais'd, I say, "'t is so, 't is true,"

And to the most of praise add something more,
But that is in my thought, whose love to you,
Though words come hindmost, holds his rank before:
  Then, others for the breath of words respect,
  Me for my dumb thoughts, speaking in effect.

LXXXVI.

Was it the proud full sail of his great verse,
Bound for the prize of all too precious you,
That did my ripe thoughts in my brain inherse,
Making their tomb the womb wherein they grew?
Was it his spirit, by spirits taught to write
Above a mortal pitch, that struck me dead?
No, neither he, nor his compeers by night
Giving him aid, my verse astonished:
He, nor that affable familiar ghost,
Which nightly gulls him with intelligence,
As victors of my silence cannot boast.
I was not sick of any fear from thence;
  But when your countenance fill'd up his line,
  Then lack'd I matter; that enfeebled mine.

LXXXVII.

Farewell: thou art too dear for my possessing,
And like enough thou know'st thy estimate:
The charter of thy worth gives thee releasing;
My bonds in thee are all determinate.
For how do I hold thee but by thy granting?
And for that riches where is my deserving?
The cause of this fair gift in me is wanting,
And so my patent back again is swerving.
Thyself thou gav'st, thy own worth then not knowing
Or me, to whom gav'st it, else mistaking;
So thy great gift, upon misprision growing,
Comes home again, on better judgment making.
  Thus have I had thee, as a dream doth flatter,
  In sleep a king, but waking, no such matter.

LXXXVIII.

When thou shalt be dispos'd to set me light,
And place my merit in the eye of scorn,
Upon thy side against myself I 'll fight,
And prove thee virtuous, though thou art forsworn:

With mine own weakness being best acquainted,
Upon thy part I can set down a story
Of faults conceal'd, wherein I am attainted,
That thou, in losing me, shalt win much glory:
And I by this will be a gainer too;
For bending all my loving thoughts on thee,
The injuries that to myself I do,
Doing thee vantage, double vantage me.
  Such is my love, to thee I so belong,
  That for thy right myself will bear all wrong.

LXXXIX.

Say that thou didst forsake me for some fault
And I will comment upon that offence:
Speak of my lameness, and I straight will halt,
Against thy reasons making no defence.
Thou canst not, love, disgrace me half so ill,
To set a form upon desired change,
As I 'll myself disgrace: knowing thy will,
I will acquaintance strangle, and look strange;
Be absent from thy walks; and in my tongue
Thy sweet beloved name no more shall dwell,
Lest I (too much profane) should do it wrong,
And haply of our old acquaintance tell.
  For thee, against myself I 'll vow debate,
  For I must ne'er love him whom thou dost hate.

XC.

Then, hate me when thou wilt; if ever, now:
Now, while the world is bent my deeds to cross,
Join with the spite of fortune, make me bow,
And do not drop in for an after loss.
Ah! do not, when my heart hath scap'd this sorrow,
Come in the rearward of a conquer'd woe;
Give not a windy night a rainy morrow,
To linger out a purpos'd overthrow.
If thou wilt leave me, do not leave me last,
When other petty griefs have done their spite,
But in the onset come: so shall I taste
At first the very worst of fortune's might;
  And other strains of woe, which now seem woe,
  Compar'd with loss of thee, will not seem so.

XCI.

Some glory in their birth, some in their skill,
Some in their wealth, some in their body's force;
Some in their garments, though new-fangled ill;
Some in their hawks and hounds, some in their horse
And every humour hath his adjunct pleasure,
Wherein it finds a joy above the rest;
But these particulars are not my measure:
All these I better in one general best.
Thy love is better than high birth to me,
Richer than wealth, prouder than garments' cost,
Of more delight than hawks or horses be;
And having thee, of all men's pride I boast:
   Wretched in this alone, that thou may'st take
   All this away, and me most wretched make.

XCII.

But do thy worst to steal thyself away,
For term of life thou art assured mine;
And life no longer than thy love will stay,
For it depends upon that love of thine:
Then, need I not to fear the worst of wrongs,
When in the least of them my life hath end.
I see a better state to me belongs
Than that which on thy humour doth depend.
Thou canst not vex me with inconstant mind,
Since that my life on thy revolt doth lie.
O! what a happy title do I find,
Happy to have thy love, happy to die:
   But what 's so blessed fair that fears no blot?
   Thou may'st be false, and yet I know it not.

XCIII.

So shall I live, supposing thou art true,
Like a deceived husband; so love's face
May still seem love to me, though alter'd new;
Thy looks with me, thy heart in other place:
For there can live no hatred in thine eye;
Therefore, in that I cannot know thy change.
In many's looks the false heart's history
Is writ in moods, and frowns, and wrinkles strange;
But heaven in thy creation did decree,
That in thy face sweet love should ever dwell;

Whate'er thy thoughts or thy heart's workings be,
Thy looks should nothing thence but sweetness tell.
  How like Eve's apple doth thy beauty grow,
  If thy sweet virtue answer not thy show!

XCIV.

They that have power to hurt, and will do none,
That do not do the thing they most do show,
Who, moving others, are themselves as stone,
Unmoved, cold, and to temptation slow;
They rightly do inherit heaven's graces,
And husband nature's riches from expense;
They are the lords and owners of their faces,
Others but stewards of their excellence.
The summer's flower is to the summer sweet,
Though to itself it only live and die;
But if that flower with base infection meet,
The basest weed outbraves his dignity;
  For sweetest things turn sourest by their deeds.
  Lilies that fester smell far worse than weeds.

XCV.

How sweet and lovely dost thou make the shame,
Which, like a canker in the fragrant rose,
Doth spot the beauty of thy budding name?
O, in what sweets dost thou thy sins enclose!
That tongue that tells the story of thy days,
(Making lascivious comments on thy sport)
Cannot dispraise but in a kind of praise;
Naming thy name blesses an ill report.
O! what a mansion have those vices got,
Which for their habitation chose out thee,
Where beauty's veil doth cover every blot,
And all things turn to fair that eyes can see!
  Take heed, dear heart, of this large privilege;
  The hardest knife ill us'd doth lose his edge.

XCVI.

Some say, thy fault is youth, some wantonness;
Some say, thy grace is youth, and gentle sport;
Both grace and faults are lov'd of more and less:
Thou mak'st faults graces that to thee resort

As on the finger of a throned queen
The basest jewel will be well esteem'd,
So are those errors that in thee are seen
To truths translated, and for true things deem'd.
How many lambs might the stern wolf betray,
If like a lamb he could his looks translate !
How many gazers mightst thou lead away,
If thou wouldst use the strength of all thy state '
  But do not so ; I love thee in such sort,
  As thou being mine, mine is thy good report.

XCVII.

How like a winter hath my absence been
From thee, the pleasure of the fleeting year !
What freezings have I felt, what dark days seen,
What old December's bareness every where !
And yet this time remov'd was summer's time ;
The teeming autumn, big with rich increase,
Bearing the wanton burden of the prime,
Like widow'd wombs after their lords' decease :
Yet this abundant issue seem'd to me
But hope of orphans, and unfather'd fruit ;
For summer and his pleasures wait on thee,
And, thou away, the very birds are mute ;
  Or, if they sing, 't is with so dull a cheer,
  That leaves look pale, dreading the winter 's near.

XCVIII.

From you have I been absent in the spring,
When proud-pied April, dress'd in all his trim,
Hath put a spirit of youth in every thing,
That heavy Saturn laugh'd and leap'd with him :
Yet nor the lays of birds, nor the sweet smell
Of different flowers in odour and in hue,
Could make me any summer's story tell,
Or from their proud lap pluck them where they grew
Nor did I wonder at the lily's white,
Nor praise the deep vermilion in the rose ;
They were but sweet, but figures of delight,
Drawn after you ; you pattern of all those.
  Yet seem'd it winter still, and, you away,
  As with your shadow I with these did play :

XCIX.

The forward violet thus did I chide:—
Sweet thief, whence didst thou steal thy sweet that
If not from my love's breath? the purple pride [smells,
Which on thy soft cheek for complexion dwells,
In my love's veins thou hast too grossly dyed.
The lily I condemned for thy hand,
And buds of marjoram had stol'n thy hair:
The roses fearfully on thorns did stand,
One blushing shame, another white despair;
A third, nor red nor white, had stolen of both,
And to this robbery had annex'd thy breath;
But, for his theft, in pride of all his growth
A vengeful canker eat him up to death.
More flowers I noted, yet I none could see,
But sweet or colour it had stol'n from thee.

C.

Where art thou, Muse, that thou forget'st so long
To speak of that which gives thee all thy might?
Spend'st thou thy fury on some worthless song,
Darkening thy power to lend base subjects light?
Return, forgetful Muse, and straight redeem
In gentle numbers time so idly spent:
Sing to the ear that doth thy lays esteem,
And gives thy pen both skill and argument.
Rise, resty Muse, my love's sweet face survey,
If Time have any wrinkle graven there;
If any, be a satire to decay,
And make Time's spoils despised every where.
Give my love fame faster than Time wastes life;
So thou prevent'st his scythe, and crooked knife.

CI.

O truant Muse! what shall be thy amends,
For thy neglect of truth in beauty dyed?
Both truth and beauty on my love depends;
So dost thou too, and therein dignified.
Make answer, Muse: wilt thou not haply say,
"Truth needs no colour, with his colour fix'd;
Beauty no pencil, beauty's truth to lay;
But best is best, if never intermix'd."
Because he needs no praise, wilt thou be dumb?

Excuse not silence so; for 't lies in thee
To make him much out-live a gilded tomb,
And to be prais'd of ages yet to be.
  Then, do thy office, Muse: I teach thee how
  To make him seem long hence as he shows now.

CII.

My love is strengthen'd, though more weak in seeming;
I love not less, though less the show appear:
That love is merchandiz'd, whose rich esteeming
The owner's tongue doth publish every where.
Our love was new, and then but in the spring,
When I was wont to greet it with my lays;
As Philomel in summer's front doth sing,
And stops his pipe in growth of riper days:
Not that the summer is less pleasant now,
Than when her mournful hymns did hush the night,
But that wild music burdens every bough,
And sweets grown common lose their dear delight.
  Therefore, like her, I sometime hold my tongue,
  Because I would not dull you with my song.

CIII.

Alack! what poverty my muse brings forth,
That having such a scope to show her pride,
The argument, all bare, is of more worth,
Than when it hath my added praise beside.
O! blame me not, if I no more can write:
Look in your glass, and there appears a face,
That over-goes my blunt invention quite,
Dulling my lines, and doing me disgrace.
Were it not sinful, then, striving to mend,
To mar the subject that before was well?
For to no other pass my verses tend,
Than of your graces and your gifts to tell;
  And more, much more, than in my verse can sit,
  Your own glass shows you, when you look in it.

CIV.

To me, fair friend, you never can be old,
For as you were, when first your eye I ey'd,
Such seems your beauty still. Three winters cold
Have from the forests shook three summers' pride;

Three beauteous springs to yellow autumn turn'd,
In process of the seasons have I seen;
Three April perfumes in three hot Junes burn'd,
Since first I saw you fresh, which yet are green.
Ah! yet doth beauty, like a dial hand,
Steal from his figure, and no pace perceived;
So your sweet hue, which methinks still doth stand,
Hath motion, and mine eye may be deceived:
  For fear of which, hear this, thou age unbred.—
  Ere you were born was beauty's summer dead.

CV.

Let not my love be call'd idolatry,
Nor my beloved as an idol show,
Since all alike my songs and praises be,
To one, of one, still such, and ever so.
Kind is my love to-day, to-morrow kind,
Still constant in a wondrous excellence;
Therefore, my verse to constancy confin'd,
One thing expressing, leaves out difference.
Fair, kind, and true, is all my argument,
Fair, kind, and true, varying to other words;
And in this change is my invention spent,
Three themes in one, which wondrous scope affords.
  Fair, kind, and true, have often liv'd alone,
  Which three, till now, never kept seat in one.

CVI.

When in the chronicle of wasted time
I see descriptions of the fairest wights,
And beauty making beautiful old rhyme,
In praise of ladies dead, and lovely knights;
Then, in the blazon of sweet beauty's best,
Of hand, of foot, of lip, of eye, of brow,
I see their antique pen would have express'd
Even such a beauty as you master now.
So all their praises are but prophecies
Of this our time, all you prefiguring;
And for they look'd but with divining eyes,
They had not skill enough your worth to sing:
  For we, which now behold these present days,
  Have eyes to wonder, but lack tongues to praise.

CVII.

Not mine own fears, nor the prophetic soul
Of the wide world, dreaming on things to come,
Can yet the lease of my true love control,
Suppos'd as forfeit to a confin'd doom.
The mortal moon hath her eclipse endur'd,
And the sad augurs mock their own presage;
Incertainties now crown themselves assur'd,
And peace proclaims olives of endless age.
Now, with the drops of this most balmy time
My love looks fresh, and death to me subscribes,
Since, spite of him, I 'll live in this poor rhyme,
While he insults o'er dull and speechless tribes:
  And thou in this shalt find thy monument,
  When tyrants' crests, and tombs of brass are spent.

CVIII.

What 's in the brain that ink may character,
Which hath not figur'd to thee my true spirit?
What 's new to speak, what now to register,
That may express my love, or thy dear merit?
Nothing, sweet boy; but yet, like prayers divine,
I must each day say o'er the very same,
Counting no old thing old, thou mine, I thine,
Even as when first I hallow'd thy fair name.
So that eternal love, in love's fresh case,
Weighs not the dust and injury of age;
Nor gives to necessary wrinkles place,
But makes antiquity for aye his page;
  Finding the first conceit of love there bred,
  Where time and outward form would show it dead

CIX.

O! never say that I was false of heart,
Though absence seem'd my flame to qualify.
As easy might I from myself depart,
As from my soul, which in thy breast doth lie.
That is my home of love: if I have rang'd,
Like him that travels, I return again,
Just to the time, not with the time exchang'd;
So that myself bring water for my stain.
Never believe, though in my nature reign'd

All frailties that besiege all kinds of blood,
That it could so preposterously be stain'd,
To leave for nothing all thy sum of good;
  For nothing this wide universe I call,
  Save thou, my Rose; in it thou art my all.

CX.

Alas! 't is true, I have gone here and there,
And made myself a motley to the view;
Gor'd mine own thoughts, sold cheap what is most dear,
Made old offences of affections new:
Most true it is, that I have look'd on truth
Askance and strangely; but, by all above,
These blenches[1] gave my heart another youth,
And worse essays prov'd thee my best of love.
Now all is done, save[2] what shall have no end:
Mine appetite I never more will grind
On newer proof, to try an older friend,
A god in love, to whom I am confin'd.
  Then, give me welcome, next my heaven the best,
  Even to thy pure, and most most loving breast.

CXI.

O! for my sake do you with fortune chide,
The guilty goddess of my harmful deeds,
That did not better for my life provide
Than public means, which public manners breeds:
Thence comes it that my name receives a brand;
And almost thence my nature is subdu'd
To what it works in, like the dyer's hand.
Pity me, then, and wish I were renew'd,
Whilst, like a willing patient, I will drink
Potions of eysel[3] 'gainst my strong infection;
No bitterness that I will bitter think,
Nor double penance, to correct correction.
  Pity me, then, dear friend, and I assure ye,
  Even that your pity is enough to cure me.

CXII.

Your love and pity doth th' impression fill
Which vulgar scandal stamp'd upon my brow;

[1] To blench is to *start from*. [2] have: in old eds. Tyrwhitt made the change. [3] *Vinegar*.

For what care I who calls me well or ill,
So you o'er-green my bad, my good allow?
You are my all-the-world, and I must strive
To know my shames and praises from your tongue;
None else to me, nor I to none alive,
That my steel'd sense or changes, right or wrong.
In so profound abysm I throw all care
Of others' voices, that my adder's sense
To critic and to flatterer stopped are.
Mark how with my neglect I do dispense:—
  You are so strongly in my purpose bred,
  That all the world besides methinks they are dead [1]

CXIII.

Since I left you mine eye is in my mind,
And that which governs me to go about
Doth part his function, and is partly blind,
Seems seeing, but effectually is out;
For it no form delivers to the heart
Of bird, of flower, or shape, which it doth latch:[2]
Of his quick objects hath the mind no part,
Nor his own vision holds what it doth catch;
For if it see the rud'st or gentlest sight,
The most sweet favour, or deformed'st creature,
The mountain or the sea, the day or night,
The crow or dove, it shapes them to your feature.
  Incapable of more, replete with you,
  My most true mind thus maketh mine untrue.[3]

CXIV.

Or whether doth my mind, being crown'd with you,
Drink up the monarch's plague, this flattery?
Or whether shall I say, my eye saith true,
And that your love taught it this alchymy,
To make, of monsters and things indigest,
Such cherubins as your sweet self resemble,
Creating every bad a perfect best,
As fast as objects to his beams assemble?
O! 't is the first: 't is flattery in my seeing,
And my great mind most kingly drinks it up:
Mine eye well knows what with his gust is 'greeing,
And to his palate doth prepare the cup:

[1] methinks y' are dead: in old cop. Dyce omits "they" [2] lack in old eds. Malone made the change. [3] Used as a substantive.

  If it be poison'd, 't is the lesser sin
  That mine eye loves it, and doth first begin.

CXV.

Those lines that I before have writ do lie,
Even those that said I could not love you dearer;
Yet then my judgment knew no reason why
My most full flame should afterwards burn clearer.
But reckoning time, whose million'd accidents
Creep in 'twixt vows, and change decrees of kings,
Tan sacred beauty, blunt the sharp'st intents,
Divert strong minds t' the course of altering things;
Alas! why, fearing of time's tyranny,
Might I not then say, "now I love you best,"
When I was certain o'er incertainty,
Crowning the present, doubting of the rest?
  Love is a babe; then, might I not say so,
  To give full growth to that which still doth grow?

CXVI.

Let me not to the marriage of true minds
Admit impediments: love is not love,
Which alters when it alteration finds,
Or bends with the remover to remove:
O no! it is an ever-fixed mark,
That looks on tempests, and is never shaken;
It is the star to every wandering bark,
Whose worth 's unknown, although his height be taken
Love 's not Time's fool, though rosy lips and cheeks
Within his bending sickle's compass come;
Love alters not with his brief hours and weeks,
But bears it out even to the edge of doom.
  If this be error, and upon me proved,
  I never writ, nor no man ever loved.

CXVII.

Accuse me thus: that I have scanted all
Wherein I should your great deserts repay;
Forgot upon your dearest love to call,
Whereto all bonds do tie me day by day;
That I have frequent been with unknown minds,
And given to time your own dear-purchas'd right;
That I have hoisted sail to all the winds
Which should transport me farthest from your sight ·

Book both my wilfulness and errors down,
And on just proof surmise accumulate;
Bring me within the level of your frown,
But shoot not at me in your waken'd hate,
  Since my appeal says, I did strive to prove
  The constancy and virtue of your love.

CXVIII.

Like as, to make our appetites more keen,
With eager[1] compounds we our palate urge;
As, to prevent our maladies unseen,
We sicken to shun sickness when we purge;
Even so, being full of your ne'er-cloying sweetness,
To bitter sauces did I frame my feeding;
And, sick of welfare, found a kind of meetness
To be diseas'd, ere that there was true needing.
Thus policy in love, t' anticipate
The ills that were not, grew to faults assur'd,
And brought to medicine a healthful state,
Which, rank of goodness, would by ill be cur'd;
  But thence I learn, and find the lesson true,
  Drugs poison him that so fell sick of you.

CXIX.

What potions have I drunk of syren tears,
Distill'd from limbecks foul as hell within,
Applying fears to hopes, and hopes to fears,
Still losing when I saw myself to win!
What wretched errors hath my heart committed,
Whilst it hath thought itself so blessed never!
How have mine eyes out of their spheres been fitted,
In the distraction of this madding fever!
O benefit of ill! now I find true,
That better is by evil still made better;
And ruin'd love, when it is built anew,
Grows fairer than at first, more strong, far greater.
  So I return rebuk'd to my content,
  And gain by ill thrice more than I have spent.

CXX.

That you were once unkind befriends me now,
And for that sorrow, which I then did feel,
Needs must I under my transgression bow,
Unless my nerves were brass or hammer'd steel.

[1] Fr. *aigre*, sour.

For if you were by my unkindness shaken,
As I by yours, you have pass'd a hell of time;
And I, a tyrant, have no leisure taken
To weigh how once I suffer'd in your crime.
O! that our night of woe might have remember'd
My deepest sense, how hard true sorrow hits;
And soon to you, as you to me, then tender'd
The humble salve which wounded bosoms fits!
  But that your trespass now becomes a fee;
  Mine ransoms yours, and yours must ransom me.

CXXI.

'T is better to be vile, than vile esteemed,
When not to be receives reproach of being;
And the just pleasure lost, which is so deemed,
Not by our feeling, but by others' seeing:
For why should others' false adulterate eyes
Give salutation to my sportive blood?
Or on my frailties why are frailer spies,
Which in their wills count bad what I think good?
No, I am that I am; and they that level
At my abuses, reckon up their own:
I may be straight, though they themselves be bevel
By their rank thoughts my deeds must not be shown
  Unless this general evil they maintain,
  All men are bad, and in their badness reign.

CXXII.

Thy gift, thy tables, are within my brain
Full character'd with lasting memory,
Which shall above that idle rank remain,
Beyond all date, even to eternity;
Or, at the least, so long as brain and heart
Have faculty by nature to subsist;
Till each to ras'd oblivion yield his part
Of thee, thy record never can be miss'd.
That poor retention could not so much hold,
Nor need I tallies thy dear love to score;
Therefore to give them from me was I bold,
To trust those tables that receive thee more:
  To keep an adjunct to remember thee,
  Were to import forgetfulness in me.

CXXIII.

No ! Time, thou shalt not boast that I do change :
Thy pyramids, built up with newer might,
To me are nothing novel, nothing strange ;
They are but dressings of a former sight.
Our dates are brief, and therefore we admire
What thou dost foist upon us that is old,
And rather make them born to our desire,
Than think that we before have heard them told.
Thy registers and thee I both defy,
Not wondering at the present, nor the past ;
For thy records and what we see do lie,
Made more or less by thy continual haste.
This I do vow, and this shall ever be,
I will be true, despite thy scythe and thee.

CXXIV.

If my dear love were but the child of state,
It might for fortune's bastard be unfathered,
As subject to time's love, or to time's hate,
Weeds among weeds, or flowers with flowers gathered.
No, it was builded far from accident ;
It suffers not in smiling pomp, nor falls
Under the blow of thralled discontent,
Whereto th' inviting time our fashion calls :
It fears not policy, that heretic,
Which works on leases of short number'd hours,
But all alone stands hugely politic,
That it nor grows with heat, nor drowns with showers.
To this I witness call the fools of time,
Which die for goodness, who have liv'd for crime.

CXXV.

Were 't aught to me I bore the canopy,
With my extern the outward honouring,
Or laid great bases for eternity,
Which prove more short than waste or ruining ?
Have I not seen dwellers on form and favour
Lose all, and more, by paying too much rent ;
For compound sweet foregoing simple savour,
Pitiful thrivers, in their gazing spent ?
No ; let me be obsequious in thy heart,
And take thou my oblation, poor but free.

Which is not mix'd with seconds, knows no art,
But mutual render, only me for thee.
  Hence, thou suborn'd informer! a true soul,
  When most impeach'd, stands least in thy control.

CXXVI.

O thou, my lovely boy! who in thy power
Dost hold Time's fickle glass, his sickle, hour;
Who hast by waning grown, and therein show'st
Thy lovers withering, as thy sweet self grow'st;
If nature, sovereign mistress over wrack,
As thou goest onwards still will pluck thee back
She keeps thee to this purpose, that her skill
May time disgrace, and wretched minutes kill.
Yet fear her, O thou minion of her pleasure!
She may detain, but not still keep her treasure:
Her audit, though delay'd, answer'd must be,
And her quietus is to render thee.

CXXVII.

In the old age black was not counted fair,
Or if it were, it bore not beauty's name;
But now is black beauty's successive heir,
And beauty slander'd with a bastard shame;
For since each hand hath put on nature's power,
Fairing the foul with art's false borrow'd face
Sweet beauty hath no name, no holy bower,
But is profan'd, if not lives in disgrace.
Therefore, my mistress' eyes are raven black,
Her eyes so suited; and they mourners seem
At such, who, not born fair, no beauty lack,
Slandering creation with a false esteem:
  Yet so they mourn, becoming of their woe,
  That every tongue says, beauty should look so.

CXXVIII.

How oft, when thou, my music, music playest,
Upon that blessed wood, whose motion sounds
With thy sweet fingers, when thou gently swayest
The wiry concord that mine ear confounds,
Do I envy those jacks,[1] that nimble leap
To kiss the tender inward of thy hand,
Whilst my poor lips, which should that harvest reap,
At the wood's boldness by thee blushing stand.

[1] The *keys* of the virginal.

To be so tickled, they would change their state
And situation with those dancing chips,
O'er whom thy fingers walk with gentle gait,
Making dead wood more bless'd than living lips.
  Since saucy jacks so happy are in this,
  Give them thy fingers, me thy lips to kiss.

CXXIX.

Th' expense of spirit in a waste of shame
Is lust in action; and till action, lust
Is perjur'd, murderous, bloody, full of blame,
Savage, extreme, rude, cruel, not to trust;
Enjoy'd no sooner but despised straight;
Past reason hunted, and no sooner had,
Past reason hated, as a swallow'd bait,
On purpose laid to make the taker mad:
Mad in pursuit, and in possession so;
Had, having, and in quest to have, extreme:
A bliss in proof,—and prov'd, a very woe;[1]
Before, a joy propos'd; behind, a dream.
  All this the world well knows, yet none knows well
  To shun the heaven that leads men to this hell.

CXXX.

My mistress' eyes are nothing like the sun;
Coral is far more red than her lips' red:
If snow be white, why then her breasts are dun;
If hairs be wires, black wires grow on her head.
I have seen roses damask'd, red and white,
But no such roses see I in her cheeks;
And in some perfumes is there more delight
Than in the breath that from my mistress reeks.
I love to hear her speak, yet well I know
That music hath a far more pleasing sound:
I grant I never saw a goddess go;
My mistress, when she walks, treads on the ground.
  And yet, by heaven, I think my love as rare
  As any she belied with false compare.

CXXXI.

Thou art as tyrannous, so as thou art,
As those whose beauties proudly make them cruel;
For well thou know'st, to my dear doting heart

[1] and proud and very woe: in old eds. Malone made the change.

Thou art the fairest and most precious jewel.
Yet, in good faith, some say that thee behold,
Thy face hath not the power to make love groan:
To say they err I dare not be so bold,
Although I swear it to myself alone.
And, to be sure that is not false I swear,
A thousand groans, but thinking on thy face,
One on another's neck, do witness bear,
Thy black is fairest in my judgment's place.
In nothing art thou black, save in thy deeds,
And thence this slander, as I think, proceeds.

CXXXII.

Thine eyes I love, and they, as pitying me,
Knowing thy heart torments[1] me with disdain,
Have put on black, and loving mourners be,
Looking with pretty ruth upon my pain.
And, truly, not the morning sun of heaven
Better becomes the grey cheeks of the east,
Nor that full star that ushers in the even
Doth half that glory to the sober west,
As those two mourning eyes become thy face.
O! let it, then, as well beseem thy heart
To mourn for me, since mourning doth thee grace,
And suit thy pity like in every part;
Then will I swear, beauty herself is black,
And all they foul that thy complexion lack.

CXXXIII.

Beshrew that heart, that makes my heart to groan
For that deep wound it gives my friend and me!
Is 't not enough to torture me alone,
But slave to slavery my sweet'st friend must be?
Me from myself thy cruel eye hath taken,
And my next self thou harder hast engrossed:
Of him, myself, and thee, I am forsaken;
A torment thrice threefold thus to be crossed.
Prison my heart in thy steel bosom's ward,
But, then, my friend's heart let my poor heart bail;
Whoe'er keeps me, let my heart be his guard;
Thou canst not then use rigour in my jail:
And yet thou wilt; for I, being pent in thee,
Perforce am thine, and all that is in me.

[1] torment: in old eds.

CXXXIV.

So, now I have confess'd that he is thine,
And I myself am mortgag'd to thy will;
Myself I 'll forfeit, so that other mine
Thou wilt restore, to be my comfort still:
But thou wilt not, nor he will not be free,
For thou art covetous, and he is kind;
He learn'd but, surety-like, to write for me,
Under that bond that him as fast doth bind.
The statute[1] of thy beauty thou wilt take,
Thou usurer, that put'st forth all to use,
And sue a friend, came debtor for my sake;
So him I lose through my unkind abuse.
  Him have I lost; thou hast both him and me:
  He pays the whole, and yet am I not free.

CXXXV.

Whoever hath her wish, thou hast thy *Will*,[2]
And *Will* to boot, and *Will* in over-plus;
More than enough am I, that vex thee still,
To thy sweet will making addition thus.
Wilt thou, whose will is large and spacious,
Not once vouchsafe to hide my will in thine?
Shall will in others seem right gracious,
And in my will no fair acceptance shine?
The sea, all water, yet receives rain still,
And in abundance addeth to his store:
So thou, being rich in *Will*, add to thy *Will*
One will of mine, to make thy large *Will* more.
  Let no unkind, no fair beseechers kill:
  Think all but one, and me in that one *Will*.

CXXXVI.

If thy soul check thee that I come so near,
Swear to thy blind soul that I was thy *Will*,
And will, thy soul knows, is admitted there;
Thus far for love, my love-suit, sweet, fulfil.
Will will fulfil the treasure of thy love,
Ay, fill it full with wills, and my will one.

[1] *Security*. [2] Whoever hath her wish, thou hast thy *Will*: As there is in this and the next sonnet, as well as in Sonnet cxliii, an obvious play upon the Christian name of the poet, we have printed it exactly as it stands in the quarto, 1609, and as it probably stood in the manuscript from which it was printed.

In things of great receipt with ease we prove,
Among a number one is reckon'd none:
Then, in the number let me pass untold,
Though in thy stores' account I one must be;
For nothing hold me, so it please thee hold
That nothing me, a something sweet to thee:
  Make but my name thy love, and love that still
  And then thou lov'st me,—for my name is *Will.*

CXXXVII.

Thou blind fool, Love, what dost thou to mine eyes
That they behold, and see not what they see?
They know what beauty is, see where it lies,
Yet what the best is, take the worst to be.
If eyes, corrupt by over-partial looks,
Be anchor'd in the bay where all men ride,
Why of eyes' falsehood hast thou forged hooks,
Whereto the judgment of my heart is tied?
Why should my heart think that a several plot,[1]
Which my heart knows the wide world's common place
Or mine eyes seeing this, say, this is not,
To put fair truth upon so foul a face?
  In things right true my heart and eyes have erred,
  And to this false plague are they now transferred.

CXXXVIII.[2]

When my love swears that she is made of truth,
I do believe her, though I know she lies,
That she might think me some untutor'd youth,
Unlearned in the world's false subtleties.
Thus vainly thinking that she thinks me young,
Although she knows my days are past the best,
Simply I credit her false-speaking tongue:
On both sides thus is simple truth suppress.
But wherefore says she not, she is unjust?
And wherefore say not I, that I am old?
O! love's best habit is in seeming trust,
And age in love loves not to have years told:
  Therefore I lie with her, and she with me,
  And in our faults by lies we flatter'd be.

[1] A piece of ground which has been "common," or uninclosed, but has been separated and made private property. [2] This sonnet, with variations, was first printed in "The Passionate Pilgrim," 1599. It is inserted hereafter as it stands in that work, that the reader may have an opportunity of comparing the two copies.

CXXXIX.

O! call not me to justify the wrong,
That thy unkindness lays upon my heart;
Wound me not with thine eye, but with thy tongue,
Use power with power, and slay me not by art.
Tell me thou lov'st elsewhere; but in my sight,
Dear heart, forbear to glance thine eye aside: [might
What need'st thou wound with cunning, when thy
Is more than my o'er-press'd defence can 'bide?
Let me excuse thee: ah! my love well knows
Her pretty looks have been mine enemies,
And therefore from my face she turns my foes,
That they elsewhere might dart their injuries.
  Yet do not so; but since I am near slain,
  Kill me out-right with looks, and rid my pain.

CXL.

Be wise as thou art cruel; do not press
My tongue-tied patience with too much disdain;
Lest sorrow lend me words, and words express
The manner of my pity-wanting pain.
If I might teach thee wit, better it were,
Though not to love, yet, love, to tell me so;
As testy sick men, when their deaths be near,
No news but health from their physicians know:
For, if I should despair, I should grow mad,
And in my madness might speak ill of thee;
Now this ill-wresting world is grown so bad,
Mad slanderers by mad ears believed be.
  That I may not be so, nor thou belied, [wide.
  Bear thine eyes straight, though thy proud heart go

CXLI.

In faith I do not love thee with mine eyes,
For they in thee a thousand errors note;
But 't is my heart that loves what they despise,
Who in despite of view is pleas'd to dote.
Nor are mine ears with thy tongue's tune delighted;
Nor tender feeling, to base touches prone,
Nor taste, nor smell, desire to be invited
To any sensual feast with thee alone:
But my five wits, nor my five senses can[1]
Dissuade one foolish heart from serving thee,

[1] See note to "King Lear," Act III, sc. iv.

Who leave unsway'd the likeness of a man,
Thy proud heart's slave and vassal wretch to be
Only my plague thus far I count my gain,
That she that makes me sin awards me pain.

CXLII.

Love is my sin, and thy dear virtue hate,
Hate of my sin, grounded on sinful loving.
O! but with mine compare thou thine own state,
And thou shalt find it merits not reproving;
Or, if it do, not from those lips of thine,
That have profan'd their scarlet ornaments,
And seal'd false bonds of love as oft as mine,
Robb'd others' beds revenues of their rents.
Be it lawful I love thee, as thou lov'st those
Whom thine eyes woo as mine importune thee:
Root pity in thy heart, that when it grows,
Thy pity may deserve to pitied be.
If thou dost seek to have what thou dost hide,
By self-example may'st thou be denied!

CXLIII.

Lo! as a careful housewife runs to catch
One of her feather'd creatures broke away,
Sets down her babe, and makes all swift dispatch
In pursuit of the thing she would have stay;
Whilst her neglected child holds her in chace,
Cries to catch her whose busy care is bent
To follow that which flies before her face,
Not prizing her poor infant's discontent:
So run'st thou after that which flies from thee,
Whilst I, thy babe, chase thee afar behind;
But if thou catch thy hope, turn back to me,
And play the mother's part, kiss me, be kind:
So will I pray that thou may'st have thy *Will*,
If thou turn back, and my loud crying still.

CXLIV.[1]

Two loves I have of comfort and despair,
Which like two spirits do suggest[2] me still:
The better angel is a man, right fair,
The worser spirit a woman, colour'd ill.

[1] This sonnet, with some variations, will be found hereafter in "The Passionate Pilgrim" [2] *Tempt.*

To win me soon to hell, my female evil
Tempteth my better angel from my side,
And would corrupt my saint to be a devil,
Wooing his purity with her foul pride.
And whether that my angel be turn'd fiend,
Suspect I may, yet not directly tell:
But being both from me, both to each friend,
I guess one angel in another's hell:
  Yet this shall I ne'er know, but live in doubt.
  Till my bad angel fire my good one out.

CXLV.

Those lips that Love's own hand did make,
Breath'd forth the sound that said, "I hate."
To me that languish'd for her sake;
But when she saw my woeful state,
Straight in her heart did mercy come,
Chiding that tongue, that ever sweet
Was us'd in giving gentle doom,
And taught it thus anew to greet.
"I hate," she alter'd with an end,
That follow'd it as gentle day
Doth follow night, who, like a fiend,
From heaven to hell is flown away:
  "I hate" from hate away she threw,
  And sav'd my life, saying—"not you."

CXLVI.

Poor soul, the center of my sinful earth,
Fool'd by those rebel powers that thee array,[1]
Why dost thou pine within, and suffer dearth,
Painting thy outward walls so costly gay?
Why so large cost, having so short a lease,
Dost thou upon thy fading mansion spend?
Shall worms, inheritors of this excess,
Eat up thy charge? is this thy body's end?
Then, soul, live thou upon thy servant's loss,
And let that pine to aggravate thy store;
Buy terms divine in selling hours of dross;
Within be fed, without be rich no more:
  So shalt thou feed on death, that feeds on men,
  And, death once dead, there 's no more dying then.

[1] Old ed. reads: My sinful earth these rebel powers that thee array Malone made the change.

CXLVII.

My love is as a fever, longing still
For that which longer nurseth the disease;
Feeding on that which doth preserve the ill,
Th' uncertain sickly appetite to please.
My reason, the physician to my love,
Angry that his prescriptions are not kept,
Hath left me, and I desperate now approve,
Desire is death, which physic did except.
Past cure I am, now reason is past care,
And frantic mad with ever-more unrest:
My thoughts and my discourse as mad men's are,
At random from the truth vainly express'd;
For I have sworn thee fair, and thought thee bright
Who art as black as hell, as dark as night.

CXLVIII.

O me! what eyes hath love put in my head,
Which have no correspondence with true sight!
Or, if they have, where is my judgment fled,
That censures falsely what they see aright?
If that be fair whereon my false eyes dote,
What means the world to say it is not so?
If it be not, then love doth well denote
Love's eye is not so true as all men's: no,
How can it? O! how can love's eye be true,
That is so vex'd with watching and with tears?
No marvel, then, though I mistake my view;
The sun itself sees not, till heaven clears.
O cunning love! with tears thou keep'st me blind,
Lest eyes well-seeing thy foul faults should find.

CXLIX.

Canst thou, O Cruel! say, I love thee not,
When I, against myself, with thee partake?[1]
Do I not think on thee, when I forgot
Am of myself, all tyrant, for thy sake?
Who hateth thee that I do call my friend?
On whom frown'st thou that I do fawn upon?
Nay, if thou low'rst on me, do I not spend
Revenge upon myself with present moan?
What merit do I in myself respect,
That is so proud thy service to despise,

[1] *Take part.*

When all my best doth worship thy defect,
Commanded by the motion of thine eyes?
  But, love, hate on, for now I know thy mind:
  Those that can see thou lov'st, and I am blind.

CL.

O! from what power hast thou this powerful might,
With insufficiency my heart to sway?
To make me give the lie to my true sight,
And swear that brightness doth not grace the day?
Whence hast thou this becoming of things ill,
That in the very refuse of thy deeds
There is such strength and warrantise of skill,
That in my mind thy worst all best exceeds?
Who taught thee how to make me love thee more,
The more I hear and see just cause of hate?
O! though I love what others do abhor,
With others thou shouldst not abhor my state:
  If thy unworthiness rais'd love in me,
  More worthy I to be belov'd of thee.

CLI.

Love is too young to know what conscience is;
Yet who knows not, conscience is born of love?
Then, gentle cheater, urge not my amiss,
Lest guilty of my faults thy sweet self prove:
For, thou betraying me, I do betray
My nobler part to my gross body's treason;
My soul doth tell my body that he may
Triumph in love; flesh stays no farther reason,
But rising at thy name, doth point out thee
As his triumphant prize. Proud of this pride,
He is contented thy poor drudge to be,
To stand in thy affairs, fall by thy side.
  No want of conscience hold it, that I call
  Her love, for whose dear love I rise and fall.

CLII.

In loving thee thou know'st I am forsworn,
But thou art twice forsworn, to me love swearing;
In act thy bed-vow broke, and new faith torn,
In vowing new hate after new love bearing.
But why of two oaths' breach do I accuse thee,

When I break twenty? I am perjur'd most;
For all my vows are oaths but to misuse thee,
And all my honest faith in thee is lost:
For I have sworn deep oaths of thy deep kindness,
Oaths of thy love, thy truth, thy constancy;
And to enlighten thee, gave eyes to blindness,
Or made them swear against the thing they see;
  For I have sworn thee fair: more perjur'd I,
  To swear against the truth so foul a lie!

CLIII.

Cupid laid by his brand, and fell asleep:
A maid of Dian's this advantage found,
And his love-kindling fire did quickly steep
In a cold valley-fountain of that ground;
Which borrow'd from this holy fire of love
A dateless lively heat, still to endure,
And grew a seething bath, which yet men prove,
Against strange maladies a sovereign cure.
But at my mistress' eye love's brand new-fired,
The boy for trial needs would touch my breast;
I sick withal, the help of bath desired,
And thither hied, a sad distemper'd guest,
  But found no cure: the bath for my help lies
  Where Cupid got new fire, my mistress' eyes.

CLIV.

The little Love-god lying once asleep,
Laid by his side his heart-inflaming brand,
Whilst many nymphs, that vow'd chaste life to keep,
Came tripping by; but in her maiden hand
The fairest votary took up that fire
Which many legions of true hearts had warm'd:
And so the general of hot desire
Was, sleeping, by a virgin hand disarm'd.
This brand she quenched in a cool well by,
Which from love's fire took heat perpetual,
Growing a bath, and healthful remedy
For men diseas'd; but I, my mistress' thrall,
  Came there for cure, and this by that I prove,
  Love's fire heats water, water cools not love.

A LOVER'S COMPLAINT.

A LOVER'S COMPLAINT

FROM off a hill whose concave womb re-worded
A plaintful story from a sistering vale,
My spirits t' attend this double voice accorded,
And down I laid to list the sad-tun'd tale;
Ere long espy'd a fickle maid full pale,
Tearing of papers, breaking rings a-twain,
Storming her world with sorrow's wind and rain.

Upon her head a platted hive of straw,
Which fortified her visage from the sun,
Whereon the thought might think sometime it saw
The carcase of a beauty spent and done:
Time had not scythed all that youth begun.
Nor youth all quit; but, spite of heaven's fell rage,
Some beauty peep'd through lattice of sear'd age.

Oft did she heave her napkin to her eyne,
Which on it had conceited characters,
Laundering the silken figures in the brine
That season'd woe had pelleted in tears,
And often reading what contents it bears;
As often shrieking undistinguish'd woe
In clamours of all size, both high and low.

Sometimes her level'd eyes their carriage ride,
As they did battery to the spheres intend;
Sometime, diverted, their poor balls are tied
To the orbed earth; sometimes they do extend
Their view right on; anon their gazes lend
To every place at once, and no where fix'd,
The mind and sight distractedly commix'd.

Her hair, nor loose, nor tied in formal plat,
Proclaim'd in her a careless hand of pride;
For some, untuck'd, descended her sheav'd[1] hat,
Hanging her pale and pined cheek beside;
Some in her threaden fillet still did bide,
And, true to bondage, would not break from thence,
Though slackly braided in loose negligence.

A thousand favours from a maund[2] she drew
Of amber, crystal, and of bedded jet,
Which one by one she in a river threw,
Upon whose weeping margent she was set;
Like usury, applying wet to wet,
Or monarchs' hands, that let not bounty fall
Where want cries "some," but where excess begs all

Of folded schedules had she many a one,
Which she perus'd, sigh'd, tore, and gave the flood;
Crack'd many a ring of posied gold and bone,
Bidding them find their sepulchres in mud;
Found yet more letters sadly pen'd in blood,
With sleided[3] silk feat and affectedly
Enswath'd, and seal'd to curious secrecy.

These often bath'd she in her fluxive eyes,
And often kiss'd, and often 'gan[4] to tear;
Cry'd, O false blood! thou register of lies,
What unapproved witness dost thou bear!
Ink would have seem'd more black and damned here.
This said, in top of rage the lines she rents,
Big discontent so breaking their contents.

A reverend man that graz'd his cattle nigh,
Sometime a blusterer, that the ruffle knew
Of court, of city, and had let go by
The swiftest hours, observed as they flew,
Towards this afflicted fancy fastly drew;
And, privileged by age, desires to know,
In brief, the grounds and motives of her woe.

So slides he down upon his grained bat,
And comely-distant sits he by her side;

[1] *Straw.* [2] *Basket.* [3] *Untwisted.—Percy.* [4] gave: in old eds Malone made the change.

When he again desires her, being sat,
Her grievance with his hearing to divide:
If that from him there may be aught applied,
Which may her suffering ecstasy assuage,
'T is promis'd in the charity of age.

Father, she says, though in me you behold
The injury of many a blasting hour,
Let it not tell your judgment I am old;
Not age, but sorrow, over me hath power:
I might as yet have been a spreading flower,
Fresh to myself, if I had self-applied
Love to myself, and to no love beside.

But woe is me! too early I attended
A youthful suit, it was to gain my grace;
O! one by nature's outwards so commended,
That maidens' eyes stuck over all his face:
Love lack'd a dwelling, and made him her place;
And when in his fair parts she did abide,
She was new lodg'd, and newly deified.

His browny locks did hang in crooked curls,
And every light occasion of the wind
Upon his lips their silken parcels hurls:
What 's sweet to do, to do will aptly find;
Each eye that saw him did enchant the mind,
For on his visage was in little drawn,
What largeness thinks in paradise was sawn.[1]

Small show of man was yet upon his chin:
His phœnix down began but to appear,
Like unshorn velvet, on that termless skin,
Whose bare out-brag'd the web it seem'd to wear;
Yet show'd his visage by that cost most[2] dear,
And nice affections wavering stood in doubt
If best were as it was, or best without.

His qualities were beauteous as his form,
For maiden-tongu'd he was, and thereof free;
Yet, if men mov'd him, was he such a storm
As oft 'twixt May and April is to see,

[1] The northern provincialism for *sown*.—*Boswell*. [2] more: in old eds.

When winds breathe sweet, unruly though they be.
His rudeness so, with his authoriz'd youth,
Did livery falseness in a pride of truth.

Well could he ride, and often men would say,
"That horse his mettle from his rider takes:
Proud of subjection, noble by the sway,
What rounds, what bounds, what course, what stop he makes!"
And controversy hence a question takes,
Whether the horse by him became his deed,
Or he his manage by the well-doing steed.

But quickly on this side the verdict went.
His real habitude gave life and grace
To appertainings and to ornament,
Accomplish'd in himself, not in his case:
All aids, themselves made fairer by their place,
Came[1] for additions, yet their purpos'd trim
Piec'd not his grace, but were all grac'd by him.

So on the tip of his subduing tongue,
All kind of arguments and question deep,
All replication prompt, and reason strong,
For his advantage still did wake and sleep:
To make the weeper laugh, the laugher weep,
He had the dialect and different skill,
Catching all passions in his craft of will:

That he did in the general bosom reign
Of young, of old; and sexes both enchanted,
To dwell with him in thoughts, or to remain
In personal duty, following where he haunted:
Consents, bewitch'd, ere he desire have granted;
And dialogued for him what he would say,
Ask'd their own wills, and made their wills obey.

Many there were that did his picture get,
To serve their eyes, and in it put their mind;
Like fools that in th' imagination set
The goodly objects which abroad they find
Of lands and mansions, theirs in thought assign'd;
And labouring in more pleasures to bestow them,
Than the true gouty landlord which doth owe them.

[1] 'Can' in old eds.

So many have, that never touch'd his hand,
Sweetly suppos'd them mistress of his heart.
My woeful self, that did in freedom stand,
And was my own fee-simple, (not in part)
What with his art in youth, and youth in art,
Threw my affections in his charmed power,
Reserv'd the stalk, and gave him all my flower.

Yet did I not, as some my equals did,
Demand of him, nor, being desir'd, yielded;
Finding myself in honour so forbid,
With safest distance I mine honour shielded.
Experience for me many bulwarks builded
Of proofs new-bleeding, which remain'd the foil
Of this false jewel, and his amorous spoil.

But ah! who ever shunn'd by precedent
The destin'd ill she must herself assay?
Or forc'd examples, 'gainst her own content,
To put the by-pass'd perils in her way?
Counsel may stop a while what will not stay;
For when we rage, advice is often seen
By blunting us to make our wits more keen.

Nor gives it satisfaction to our blood,
That we must curb it upon others' proof,
To be forbid the sweets that seem so good,
For fear of harms that preach in our behoof.
O appetite, from judgment stand aloof!
The one a palate hath that needs will taste,
Though reason weep, and cry, "it is thy last."

For farther I could say, "this man 's untrue,"
And knew the patterns of his foul beguiling;
Heard where his plants in others' orchards grew,
Saw how deceits were gilded in his smiling;
Knew vows were ever brokers to defiling;
Thought characters, and words, merely but art
And bastards of his foul adulterate heart.

And long upon these terms I held my city,
Till thus he 'gan besiege me: "Gentle maid,
Have of my suffering youth some feeling pity,
And be not of my holy vows afraid:

That 's to you sworn, to none was ever said;
For feasts of love I have been call'd unto,
Till now did ne'er invite, nor never vow.

All my offences that abroad you see,
Are errors of the blood, none of the mind:
Love made them not: with acture[1] they may be,
Where neither party is nor true nor kind:
They sought their shame that so their shame did find,
And so much less of shame in me remains,
By how much of me their reproach contains.

Among the many that mine eyes have seen,
Not one whose flame my heart so much as warmed,
Or my affection put to the smallest teen,[2]
Or any of my leisures ever charmed:
Harm have I done to them, but ne'er was harmed;
Kept hearts in liveries, but mine own was free,
And reign'd, commanding in his monarchy.

Look here, what tributes wounded fancies sent me,
Of paled pearls, and rubies red as blood;
Figuring that they their passions likewise lent me
Of grief and blushes, aptly understood
In bloodless white and the encrimson'd mood;
Effects of terror and dear modesty,
Encamp'd in hearts, but fighting outwardly.

And lo! behold these talents of their hair,
With twisted metal amorously impleach'd,[3]
I have receiv'd from many a several fair,
(Their kind acceptance weepingly beseech'd)
With the annexions of fair gems enrich'd,
And deep-brain'd sonnets, that did amplify
Each stone's dear nature, worth, and quality.

The diamond; why, 't was beautiful and hard,
Whereto his invis'd[4] properties did tend,
The deep-green emerald, in whose fresh regard
Weak sights their sickly radiance do amend;
The heaven-hued sapphire, and the opal blend
With objects manifold: each several stone,
With wit well blazon'd, smil'd, or made some moan.

[1] *Action.* [2] *Sorrow.* [3] *Plaited.* [4] *Unseen*

Lo! all these trophies of affections hot,
Of pensiv'd and subdued desires the tender,
Nature hath charg'd me that I hoard them not,
But yield them up where I myself must render;
That is, to you, my origin and ender:
For these, of force, must your oblations be,
Since I their altar, you enpatron me.

O! then, advance of yours that phraseless hand,
Whose white weighs down the airy scale of praise;
Take all these similes to your own command,
Hallow'd with sighs that burning lungs did raise,
What me, your minister, for you obeys,
Works under you; and to your audit comes
Their distract parcels in combined sums.

Lo! this device was sent me from a nun,
Or sister sanctified, of holiest note;
Which late her noble suit in court did shun,
Whose rarest havings made the blossoms[1] dote:
For she was sought by spirits of richest coat,
But kept cold distance, and did thence remove,
To spend her living in eternal love.

But O, my sweet! what labour is 't to leave
The thing we have not, mastering what not strives?
Paling[2] the place which did no form receive;
Playing patient sports in unconstrained gyves?
She that her fame so to herself contrives,
The scars of battle scapeth by the flight,
And makes her absence valiant, not her might.

O, pardon me, in that my boast is true!
The accident which brought me to her eye,
Upon the moment did her force subdue,
And now she would the caged cloister fly;
Religious love put out religion's eye:
Not to be tempted, would she be immur'd,[3]
And now, to tempt all, liberty procur'd.

How mighty then you are, O hear me tell!
The broken bosoms that to me belong,

[1] Flower of the young nobility. [2] Playing: in old eds. Malone made the change. [3] enur'd: in old ed. Malone made the change

Have emptied all their fountains in my well,
And mine I pour your ocean all among:
I strong o'er them, and you o'er me being strong,
Must for your victory us all congest,
As compound love to physic your cold breast.

My parts had power to charm a sacred sun,
Who, disciplin'd, I dieted[1] in grace,
Believ'd her eyes, when they t' assail begun,
All vows and consecrations giving place.
O most potential love! vow, bond, nor space,
In thee hath neither sting, knot, nor confine,
For thou art all, and all things else are thine.

When thou impressest, what are precepts worth
Of stale example? When thou wilt inflame,
How coldly those impediments stand forth
Of wealth, of filial fear, law, kindred, fame?
Love's arms are peace, 'gainst rule, 'gainst sense, 'gainst shame;
And sweetens, in the suffering pangs it bears,
The aloes of all forces, shocks, and fears.
Now, all these hearts that do on mine depend,
Feeling it break, with bleeding groans they pine;
And supplicant their sighs to you extend,
To leave the battery that you make 'gainst mine,
Lending soft audience to my sweet design,
And credent soul to that strong-bonded oath,
That shall prefer and undertake my troth."

This said, his watery eyes he did dismount,
Whose sights till then were level'd on my face;
Each cheek a river running from a fount
With brinish current downward flow'd apace.
O, how the channel to the stream gave grace!
Who, glaz'd with crystal, gate the glowing roses
That flame through water which their hue incloses.

O father! what a hell of witchcraft lies
In the small orb of one particular tear;
But with the inundation of the eyes
What rocky heart to water will not wear?

[1] From the quarto, 1609, the property of Lord F. Egerton. Malone's copy at Oxford has "I died" for "and dieted," which he substituted at the suggestion of a correspondent.

What breast so cold that is not warmed here?
O[1] cleft effect! cold modesty, hot wrath,
Both fire from hence and chill extincture hath!

For lo! his passion, but an art of craft,
Even there resolv'd my reason into tears:
There my white stole of chastity I daff'd;
Shook off my sober guards, and civil fears:
Appear to him, as he to me appears,
All melting; though our drops this difference bore,
His poison'd me, and mine did him restore.

In him a plenitude of subtle matter,
Applied to cautels, all strange forms receives,
Of burning blushes, or of weeping water,
Or swooning paleness; and he takes and leaves,
In either's aptness, as it best deceives
To blush at speeches rank, to weep at woes,
Or to turn white, and swoon at tragic shows:

That not a heart which in his level came,
Could scape the hail of his all-hurting aim,
Showing fair nature is both kind and tame,
And veil'd in them, did win whom he would maim
Against the thing he sought he would exclaim;
When he most burn'd in heart-wish'd luxury,
He preach'd pure maid, and prais'd cold chastity.

Thus, merely with the garment of a grace
The naked and concealed fiend he cover'd;
That th' unexperienc'd gave the tempter place,
Which, like a cherubin, above them hover'd.
Who, young and simple, would not be so lover'd?
Ah me! I fell; and yet do question make,
What I should do again for such a sake.

O, that infected moisture of his eye!
O, that false fire, which in his cheek so glowed!
O, that forc'd thunder from his heart did fly!
O, that sad breath his spungy lungs bestowed!
O, all that borrow'd motion, seeming owed,
Would yet again betray the fore-betray'd,
And new pervert a reconciled maid!

[5] Or: in old ed. Malone made the change.

THE PASSIONATE PILGRIM.

The Passionate Pilgrime By W. Shakespeare. At London Printed for W. Iaggard, and are to be sold by W. Leake, at the Greyhound in Paules Churchyard. 1599." 16mo. 30 leaves.

The title-page first given to the edition of 1612 ran thus: "The Passionate Pilgrime. Or Certaine Amorous Sonnets, betweene Venus and Adonis, newly corrected and augmented. By W. Shakespere. The third Edition. Wherevnto is newly added two Loue-Epistles, the first from Paris to Hellen, and Hellen's answere backe againe to Paris. Printed by W. Iaggard. 1612." The title-page substituted for the above differs in no other respect but in the omission of "By W. Shakespere."

INTRODUCTION.

In the following pages we have reprinted "The Passionate Pilgrim," 1599, as it came from the press of W. Jaggard,[1] with the exception only of the orthography. Malone omitted several portions of it; some because they were substantially repetitions of poems contained elsewhere, and others because they appeared to have been improperly assigned to Shakespeare: one piece, the last in the tract, is not inserted at all in Boswell's edition, although Malone reprinted it in 1780, and no reason is assigned for rejecting it. We have given the whole, and in our notes we have stated the particular circumstances belonging to such pieces, as there is reason to believe did not come from the pen of our great dramatist. "The Passionate Pilgrim" was reprinted by W. Jaggard, in 1612, with additions, and the facts attending the publication of the two impressions are peculiar.

In 1598, Richard Barnfield put his name to a small collection of productions in verse, entitled "The Encomion of Lady Pecunia," which contained more than one poem attributed to Shakespeare in "The Passionate Pilgrim," 1599: the first was printed by John, and the last by William Jaggard. Boswell suggests, that John Jaggard in 1598 might have stolen Shakespeare's verses and attributed them to Barnfield; but the answer to this supposition is two-fold—first, that Barnfield formally, and in his own name, printed them as his in 1598; and next, that he reprinted them under the same circumstances in 1605, notwithstanding they had been in the mean time assigned to Shakespeare[2]. The truth seems to be

[1] It professes to be "printed *for* W. Jaggard," but he was probably the typographer, and W. Leake the bookseller. Leake published an edition of "Venus and Adonis" in 1602, contrary to what is stated on p 911.

[2] This edition of Barnfield's work was unknown to bibliographers until a copy of it was met with in the library of Lord Francis Egerton. See the Bridgewater Catalogue, 1837, p. 21. It was not a mere reprint of the edition of 1598, but it was really "newly corrected and enlarged" by the author, as stated on the title-page; so that Barnfield's attention was particularly directed to the contents of his small volume, and perhaps to the manner in which part of them had been stolen by W. Jaggard in 1599. It is to be remarked also that John Jaggard was not concerned in the second edition of Barnfield's "Encomion," as he had been in the first: it was printed by

that W. Jaggard took them in 1599 from Barnfield's publication, printed by John Jaggard in 1598. In 1612 W. Jaggard went even more boldly to work; for in the impression of "The Passionate Pilgrim" of that year[3], he not only repeated Barnfield's poems of 1598, but included two of Ovid's Epistles, which had been translated by Thomas Heywood, and printed by him with his name in his "Troja Britannica," 1609. The epistles were made, with some little ambiguity, to appear in "The Passionate Pilgrim" of 1612, to have been also the work of Shakespeare. When, therefore, Heywood published his next work in 1612, he exposed the wrong that had been thus done to him, and claimed the performances as his own. (See the Reprint of "The Apology for Actors," by the Shakespeare Society, pp. 62 and 66.) He seems also to have taken steps against W. Jaggard; for the latter cancelled the title-page of "The Passionate Pilgrim," 1612, which contained the name of Shakespeare, and substituted another without any name, so far discrediting Shakespeare's right to any of the poems the work contained, although some were his beyond all dispute. Malone's copy in the Bodleian Library has both title-pages.

To what extent, therefore, we may accept W. Jaggard's assertion of the authorship of Shakespeare of the poems in "The Passionate Pilgrim," is a question of some difficulty[4]. Two Sonnets, with which the little volume opens are contained (with variations, on which account we print them again here) in Thorpe's edition of "Shakespeare's Sonnets," 1609: three other pieces (also with changes) are found in "Love's Labour 's Lost," which had been printed the year before "The Passionate Pilgrim" originally came out:—

W. I. (probably W. Iaggard, the very person who had committed the theft in 1599) and it was "to be sold by Iohn Hodgets." Both editions contain the tribute to Spenser, Daniel Drayton, and Shakespeare: the lines to the latter would hardly have been reprinted in 1605, if Barnfield had supposed that Shakespeare had in any way given his sanction to the transference of two pieces from the "Encomion" to "The Passionate Pilgrim."

[3] On the title-page it is called "the third edition," but no second edition is known, although it is very probable that it had been republished in the interval between 1599 and 1612.

[4] Nicholas Breton seems to have written his "Passionate Shepherd," 1604, in imitation of the title and of the style of some of the poems in the "Passionate Pilgrim." The only known copy of this production is in private hands. It is very possible that a second edition of "The Passionate Pilgrim" (that of 1612, as we have observed, is called "the *third* impression") came out about 1604, and that on this account Breton was led to imitate the title, and the form of verse of some of the pieces in it. As "The Passionate Shepherd" is a great curiosity, not being even mentioned by bibliographers, and as it is thus connected with the name and works of Shakespeare, an exact copy of the title-page may be acceptable:—

"The Passionate Shepheard, or The Shepheardes Loue: set downe in Passions to his Shepheardesse Aglaia. With many excellent conceited Poems and pleasant Sonnets, fit for young heads to passe away idle houres. London Imprinted by E. Allde for Iohn Tappe, and are to bee solde at his Shop, at the Tower-Hill, neere the Bulwarke Gate. 1604." 4to.

another, and its "answer," notoriously belong to Marlowe and Raleigh; a sonnet, with some slight differences, had been printed as his in 1596, by a person of the name of Griffin; while one production appeared in "England's Helicon" in 1600, under the signature of *Ignoto*. The various circumstances attending each poem, wherever any remark seemed required, are stated in our notes, and it is not necessary therefore to enter farther into the question here.

It ought to be mentioned, that although the signatures at the bottom of the pages are continued throughout, after the poem beginning, "Lord, how mine eyes throw gazes to the east!" we meet with a new and dateless title-page, which runs thus:—"Sonnets to sundry Notes of Musicke. At London Printed for W. Iaggard, and are to be sold by W. Leake, at the Greyhound in Paules Churchyard." Hence we may infer that all the productions inserted after this division had been set by popular composers: that some of them had received this distinction, evidence has descended to our day: we refer particularly to the lyrical poem, "My flocks feed not," (p. 965) and to the well-known lines, "Live with me and be my love," (p. 966) the air to which seems to have been so common, that it was employed by Deloney as a ballad-tune. See his "Strange Histories," 1607, p. 28 of the reprint by the Percy Society.

One object with W. Jaggard in 1612, when he republished "The Passionate Pilgrim" with unwarrantable additions, was probably to swell the bulk of it; and so much had he felt this want in 1599, that, excepting the three last leaves, all the rest of the volume is printed on one side of the paper only, a peculiarity we do not recollect to belong to any other work of the time: by the insertion of Heywood's translations from Ovid, this course was rendered unnecessary in 1612, and although the volume is still of small bulk, it was not so insignificant in its appearance as it had been in 1599[5]. Only a single copy of the edition of 1599, we believe, has been preserved, and that is among Capell's books in the library of Trinity College, Cambridge. No other copy of "The Passionate Pilgrim" of 1612 has the two title-pages, with and without the name of Shakespeare, but that formerly belonging to Malone, and bequeathed by him, with so many other valuable rarities, to the Bodleian Library.

"The Passionate Pilgrim," 1599, concludes with a piece of moral satire, "Whilst as fickle fortune smil'd," &c., and we have followed it by a poem found only in a publication by Robert Chester, dated 1601[6]. Malone preceded "The Phœnix

[5] It is as small a poetical volume as we remember to have seen, excepting a copy of George Peele's "Tale of Troy," which was reprinted in 1604, of the size of an inch and a half high by an inch broad. It contains some curious variations from the text of the first edition in 1589. 4to.

[6] It is called "Love's Martyr, or Rosalin's Complaint." Of the author or editor nothing is known; but he is not to be confounded with Charles Chester, called Carlo Buffone in Ben Jonson's "Every Man out of his Humour," and respecting whom see Nash's "Pierce

and the Turtle," by the song "Take, O! take those lips away:" this we have not thought it necessary to repeat, because we have given the whole of it, exactly in the same words, in "Measure for Measure," Act iv. sc. 1. The first verse only is found in Shakespeare, and the second, which is much inferior, in Beaumont and Fletcher's "Bloody Brother." It may be doubted, therefore, whether Shakespeare wrote it, or, like Beaumont and Fletcher, only introduced part of it into his play as a popular song of the time.

Penniless," 1592, (Shakespeare Society's reprint, pp. 38 99) and Thoms's "Anecdotes and Traditions," (printed for the Camden Society) p. 56. Charles Chester is several times mentioned by name in "Skialetheia," a collection of Epigrams and Satires, by E. Guilpin, printed in 1598, as well as in "Ulysses upon Ajax," 1596.

THE PASSIONATE PILGRIM.

I.[1]

When my love swears that she is made of truth
I do believe her, though I know she lies,
That she might think me some untutor'd youth
Unskilful in the world's false forgeries.
Thus vainly thinking that she thinks me young,
Although I know my years be past the best,
I smiling credit her false speaking tongue,
Out-facing faults in love with love's ill rest.
But wherefore says my love that she is young?
And wherefore say not I that I am old?
O! love's best habit is a soothing tongue,
And age, in love, loves not to have years told.
  Therefore I 'll lie with love, and love with me,
  Since that our faults in love thus smother'd be.

II.[2]

Two loves I have of comfort and despair,
Which like two spirits do suggest me still:
The better angel is a man, right fair,
The worser spirit a woman, colour'd ill.
To win me soon to hell, my female evil
Tempteth my better angel from my side,
And would corrupt a saint to be a devil,
Wooing his purity with her fair pride:
And whether that my angel be turn'd fiend,
Suspect I may, but not directly tell;
For being both to me, both to each friend,
I guess one angel in another's hell.
  The truth I shall not know, but live in doubt,
  Till my bad angel fire my good one out.

[1] This sonnet is substantially the same as Sonnet cxxxviii. in the quarto published by Thorpe, in 1609. [2] This sonnet is also included in the collection of 1609, (Sonnet cxliv.) but with some verbal variations.

III.[1]

Did not the heavenly rhetorick of thine eye,
'Gainst whom the world could not hold argument,
Persuade my heart to this false perjury?
Vows for thee broke deserve not punishment.
A woman I forswore; but I will prove,
Thou being a goddess, I forswore not thee:
My vow was earthly, thou a heavenly love;
Thy grace being gain'd cures all disgrace in me.
My vow was breath, and breath a vapour is:
Then thou fair sun, that on this earth dost shine,
Exhale this vapour now; in thee it is:
If broken, then it is no fault of mine.
If by me broke, what fool is not so wise
To break an oath, to win a paradise?

IV.

Sweet Cytherea, sitting by a brook,
With young Adonis, lovely, fresh and green,
Did court the lad with many a lovely look,
Such looks as none could look but beauty's queen.
She told him stories to delight his ear;
She show'd him favours to allure his eye;
To win his heart, she touch'd him here and there:
Touches so soft still conquer chastity.
But whether unripe years did want conceit,
Or he refus'd to take her figur'd[2] proffer,
The tender nibbler would not touch the bait,
But smile and jest at every gentle offer:
Then, fell she on her back, fair queen, and toward
He rose and ran away; ah, fool too froward!

V.[3]

If love make me forsworn, how shall I swear to love?
O! never faith could hold, if not to beauty vow'd:
Though to myself forsworn, to thee I'll constant prove;
Those thoughts, to me like oaks, to thee like osiers bow'd.

[1] This sonnet is found in "Love's Labour 's Lost," but with some slight variations, published in 1598. [2] We may suspect, notwithstanding the concurrence of the two ancient editions in our text, that the true reading was *sugar'd*, the long *s* having been, as in other places, mistaken for the letter *f*. [3] This poem, with variations, is read by Sir Nathaniel, in "Love's Labour 's Lost."

Study his bias leaves, and makes his book thine eyes,
Where all those pleasures live, that art can comprehend
If knowledge be the mark, to know thee shall suffice;
Well learned is that tongue that well can thee commend;
All ignorant that soul that sees thee without wonder,
Which is to me some praise, that I thy parts admire:
Thine eye Jove's lightning seems, thy voice his dreadful thunder,
Which (not to anger bent) is music and sweet fire.
Celestial as thou art, O! do not love that wrong,
To sing the heavens' praise with such an earthly tongue.

VI.

Scarce had the sun dried up the dewy morn,
And scarce the herd gone to the hedge for shade,
When Cytherea, all in love forlorn,
A longing tarriance for Adonis made,
Under an osier growing by a brook,
A brook, where Adon us'd to cool his spleen:
Hot was the day; she hotter that did look
For his approach, that often there had been.
Anon he comes, and throws his mantle by,
And stood stark naked on the brook's green brim;
The sun look'd on the world with glorious eye,
Yet not so wistly as this queen on him:
He, spying her, bounc'd in, whereas he stood:
O Jove! quoth she, why was not I a flood?

VII.

Fair is my love, but not so fair as fickle,
Mild as a dove, but neither true nor trusty;
Brighter than glass, and yet, as glass is, brittle,
Softer than wax, and yet as iron rusty:
A lily pale, with damask dye to grace her,
None fairer, nor none falser to deface her.

Her lips to mine how often hath she joined,
Between each kiss her oaths of true love swearing!
How many tales to please me hath she coined,
Dreading my love, the loss whereof still fearing!
Yet in the midst of all her pure protestings,
Her faith, her oaths, her tears, and all were jestings.

She burn'd with love, as straw with fire flameth;
She burn'd out love, as soon as straw out burneth:
She fram'd the love, and yet she foil'd the framing;
She bade love last, and yet she fell a turning.
   Was this a lover, or a lecher whether?
   Bad in the best, though excellent in neither.

VIII.[1]

If music and sweet poetry agree,
As they must needs, the sister and the brother,
Then, must the love be great twixt thee and me,
Because thou lov'st the one, and I the other.
Douland to thee is dear, whose heavenly touch
Upon the lute doth ravish human sense:
Spenser to me, whose deep conceit is such,
As passing all conceit needs no defence.
Thou lov'st to hear the sweet melodious sound
That Phœbus' lute (the queen of music) makes;
And I in deep delight am chiefly drown'd
Whenas himself to singing he betakes.
   One god is god of both, as poets feign,
   One knight loves both, and both in thee remain.

IX.

Fair was the morn, when the fair queen of love,[2]
   *   *   *   *   *   *   *   *
Paler for sorrow than her milk-white dove,
For Adon's sake, a youngster proud and wild;
Her stand she takes upon a steep up hill:
Anon Adonis comes with horn and hounds;
She silly queen, with more than love's good will,
Forbade the boy he should not pass those grounds.
Once, (quoth she) did I see a fair sweet youth
Here in these brakes deep-wounded with a boar,
Deep in the thigh, a spectacle of ruth!
See, in my thigh, (quoth she,) here was the sore.
   She showed hers; he saw more wounds than one,
   And blushing fled, and left her all alone.

[1] This poem was published in 1598, in Richard Barnfield's "Encomion of Lady Pecunia." There is little doubt that it is his property, notwithstanding it appeared in the "Passionate Pilgrim," 1599; and it was reprinted as Barnfield's in the new edition of his "Encomion," in 1605. [2] The next line is lost.

X.

Sweet rose, fair flower, untimely pluck'd, soon faded,
Pluck'd in the bud, and faded in the spring!
Bright orient pearl, alack! too timely shaded,
Fair creature, kill'd too soon by death's sharp sting!
  Like a green plum that hangs upon a tree,
  And falls, (through wind) before the fall should be

I weep for thee, and yet no cause I have;
For why? thou left'st me nothing in thy will.
And yet thou left'st me more than I did crave;
For why? I craved nothing of thee still:
  O yes, (dear friend,) I pardon crave of thee:
  Thy discontent thou didst bequeath to me.

XI.[1]

Venus with Adonis sitting by her,
Under a myrtle shade, began to woo him:
She told the youngling how god Mars did try her,
And as he fell to her, she fell to him.[2]
Even thus, (quoth she) the warlike god embrac'd me;
And then she clipp'd Adonis in her arms;
Even thus, (quoth she) the warlike god unlac'd me,
As if the boy should use like loving charms:
Even thus, (quoth she) he seized on my lips,
And with her lips on his did act the seizure;
And as she fetched breath, away he skips,
And would not take her meaning, nor her pleasure.
  Ah! that I had my lady at this bay,
  To kiss and clip me till I ran away!

XII.

Crabbed age and youth
  Cannot live together;
Youth is full of pleasance,
  Age is full of care:
Youth like summer morn,
  Age like winter weather;

[1] This sonnet, with considerable variations, is the third in a collection of seventy-two sonnets, published in 1596, under the title of "Fidessa," with the name of B. Griffin, as the author. A syllabic defect in the first line is there remedied by the insertion of "young" before "Adonis." A manuscript of the time, now before us, is without the epithet, and has the initials W. S. at the end. [2] The line so stands in both editions of "The Passionate Pilgrim," and in the contemporaneous manuscript; but in Griffin's "Fidessa," it is: And as he fell to her, so fell she to him.

Youth like summer brave,
  Age like winter bare.
Youth is full of sport,
Age's breath is short;
  Youth is nimble, age is lame:
Youth is hot and bold,
Age is weak and cold;
  Youth is wild, and age is tame.
Age, I do abhor thee,
Youth, I do adore thee;
  O, my love, my love is young!
Age, I do defy thee;
O, sweet shepherd! hie thee,
  For methinks thou stay'st too long

XIII.

Beauty is but a vain and doubtful good,
A shining gloss that fadeth suddenly;
A flower that dies, when first it 'gins to bud;
A brittle glass, that 's broken presently:
  A doubtful good, a gloss, a glass, a flower,
  Lost, faded, broken, dead within an hour.

And as goods lost are seld or never found,
As faded gloss no rubbing will refresh;
As flowers dead lie wither'd on the ground,
As broken glass no cement can redress;
  So beauty blemish'd once, for ever lost,
  In spite of physic, painting, pain, and cost.

XIV.

Good night, good rest. Ah! neither be my share.
She bade good night, that kept my rest away;
And daff'd me to a cabin hang'd with care,
To descant on the doubts of my decay.
  Farewell, quoth she, and come again to-morrow:
  Fare well I could not, for I supp'd with sorrow.

Yet at my parting sweetly did she smile,
In scorn or friendship, nill I construe whether:
'T may be, she joy'd to jest at my exile,
'T may be, again to make me wander thither;
  "Wander," a word for shadows like thyself,
  As take the pain, but cannot pluck the pelf.

XV.

Lord, how mine eyes throw gazes to the east!
My heart doth charge the watch, the morning rise
Doth cite each moving sense from idle rest.
Not daring trust the office of mine eyes,
  While Philomela sits and sings, I sit and mark,
  And wish her lays were tuned like the lark;

For she doth welcome day-light with her ditty.
And drives away dark dismal-dreaming night:
The night so pack'd, I post unto my pretty;
Heart hath his hope, and eyes their wished sight;
  Sorrow chang'd to solace, solace mix'd with sorrow;
  For why? she sigh'd, and bade me come to-morrow.

Were I with her, the night would post too soon;
But now are minutes added to the hours;
To spite me now, each minute seems a moon;[1]
Yet not for me, shine sun to succour flowers!
  Pack night, peep day, good day, of night now borrow:
  Short, night, to-night, and length thyself to-morrow.

XVI.[2]

It was a lording's daughter,
The fairest one of three,
That liked of her master
As well as well might be,
Till looking on an Englishman,
The fairest that eye could see,
  Her fancy fell a turning.

Long was the combat doubtful,
That love with love did fight,
To leave the master loveless,
Or kill the gallant knight:

an hour: in old eds. Steevens made the change; *moon* having the sense of *month*. [2] This is the first piece in the division of "The Passionate Pilgrim," 1599, called "Sonnets to sundry Notes of Music." As the signatures of the pages run on throughout the small volume, we have continued to mark the poems by numerals in the order in which they were printed.

To put in practice either,
Alas! it was a spite
  Unto the silly damsel.

But one must be refused,
More mickle was the pain,
That nothing could be used,
To turn them both to gain;
For of the two the trusty knight
Was wounded with disdain:
  Alas! she could not help it.

Thus art with arms contending
Was victor of the day,
Which by a gift of learning
Did bear the maid away;
Then lullaby, the learned man
Hath got the lady gay:
  For now my song is ended.

XVII[1].

On a day (alack the day!)
Love, whose month was ever May,
Spied a blossom passing fair,
Playing in the wanton air:
Through the velvet leaves the wind,
All unseen, 'gan passage find;
That the lover (sick to death)
Wish'd himself the heaven's breath,
Air (quoth he) thy cheeks may blow;
Air, would I might triumph so!
But, alas! my hand hath sworn
Ne'er to pluck thee from thy thorn:
Vow, alack! for youth unmeet:
Youth, so apt to pluck a sweet.
Thou for whom Jove would swear
Juno but an Ethiop were;
And deny himself for Jove,
Turning mortal for thy love.

[1] This poem, in a more complete state, and with the addition of two lines only found there, may be seen in "Love's Labour's Lost." The poem is also printed in "England's Helicon," (sign. H.) a miscellany of poetry, first published in 1600, (reprinted in 1812,) where "W. Shakespeare" is appended to it.

XVIII.[1]

My flocks feed not,
My ewes breed not,
My rams speed not
All is amiss:
Love is dying,[2]
Faith's defying,
Heart's denying,[3]
Causer of this.
All my merry jigs are quite forgot,
All my lady's love is lost (God wot):
Where her faith was firmly fix'd in love,
There a nay is plac'd without remove.
One silly cross
Wrought all my loss:
O frowning Fortune, cursed fickle dame!
For now I see
Inconstancy
More in women than in men remain.

In black mourn I,
All fears scorn I,
Love hath forlorn me,
Living in thrall:
Heart is bleeding,
All help needing,
O cruel speeding!
Fraughted with gall!
My shepherd's pipe can sound no deal,[4]
My wether's bell rings doleful knell;
My curtail dog that wont to have play'd,
Plays not at all, but seems afraid;
My sighs so deep[5],
Procure to weep,

[1] In "England's Helicon," 1600, this poem immediately follows "On a day (alack the day!)" but it is there entitled, "The unknown Shepherd's Complaint," and it is subscribed *Ignoto*. Hence, we may suppose that the compiler of that collection knew that it was not by Shakespeare, although it had been attributed to him in "The Passionate Pilgrim," of the year preceding. It had appeared anonymously, with the music, in 1597, in a collection of Madrigals, by Thomas Weelkes. [2] Love's denying: in "England's Helicon." [3] Heart's renying: in "England's Helicon." [4] *Part.* [5] Both editions of "The Passionate Pilgrim," have *With* for *My*, which last not only is necessary for the sense, but is confirmed as the true reading by Weelkes' Madrigals, 1597.

In howling-wise, to see my doleful plight.
How sighs resound
Through heartless ground,
Like a thousand vanquish'd men in bloody fight!

Clear wells spring not,
Sweet birds sing not,
Green plants bring not
Forth their dye:[1]
Herds stand weeping,
Flocks all sleeping,
Nymphs back peeping
Fearfully:
All our pleasure known to us poor swains,
All our merry meetings on the plains,
All our evening sport from us is fled;
All our love is lost, for love is dead.
Farewell, sweet lass,[2]
Thy like ne'er was
For a sweet content, the cause of all my moan[3]
Poor Coridon
Must live alone,
Other help for him I see that there is none.

XIX.[4]

When as thine eye hath chose the dame,
And stall'd the deer that thou shouldst strike,

[1] So both editions of "The Passionate Pilgrim," and "England's Helicon." Malone preferred the passage as it stands in Weelkes' Madrigals:

"Loud bells ring not
Cheerfully."

[2] "The Passionate Pilgrim," and "England's Helicon," both have *love* for *lass*, which the rhyme shows to be the true reading, as it stands in Weelkes' Madrigals, 1597. [3] So "England's Helicon" and Weelkes' Madrigals: "The Passionate Pilgrim," 1599, has *woe* for *moan*. [4] In some modern editions, the stanzas of this poem have been given in an order different to that in which they stand in "The Passionate Pilgrim," 1599: to that order we restore them, and that text we follow, excepting where it is evidently corrupt. The line, "As well as partial fancy like," we have corrected by a manuscript of the time. The edition of 1599 reads: "As well as fancy party all might," which is decidedly wrong. Malone substituted "As well as fancy, partial *tike*." The manuscript by which we have corrected the fourth line of the stanza also gives the two last lines of it thus:—

"Ask counsel of some other head,
Neither unwise nor yet unwed."

But no change from the old printed copy is here necessary. In the manuscript the whole has Shakespeare's initials at the end.

Let reason rule things worthy blame,
As well as partial fancy like:
  Take counsel of some wiser head,
  Neither too young, nor yet unwed.

And when thou com'st thy tale to tell,
Smooth not thy tongue with filed talk,
Lest she some subtle practice smell;
A cripple soon can find a halt:
  But plainly say thou lov'st her well,
  And set thy person forth to sell.[1]

What though her frowning brows be bent,
Her cloudy looks will clear ere night;
And then too late she will repent
That thus dissembled her delight;
  And twice desire, ere it be day,
  That which with scorn she put away.

What though she strive to try her strength,
And ban and brawl, and say thee nay,
Her feeble force will yield at length,
When craft hath taught her thus to say,—
  "Had women been so strong as men,
  In faith you had not had it then."

And to her will frame all thy ways:
Spare not to spend, and chiefly there
Where thy desert may merit praise,
By ringing in thy lady's ear:
  The strongest castle, tower, and town,
  The golden bullet beats it down.

Serve always with assured trust,
And in thy suit be humble, true;
Unless thy lady prove unjust,
Seek never thou to choose a new.
  When time shall serve, be thou not slack
  To proffer, though she put thee back.

The wiles and guiles that women work,
Dissembled with an outward show,

[1] So the manuscript in our possession, and another that Malone used: the old copies read, with obvious corruption,
"And set *her* person forth to *sale*."

The tricks and toys that in them lurk,
The cock that treads them shall not know.
Have you not heard it said full oft,
A woman's nay doth stand for nought?

Think, women still to strive with men
To sin, and never for to saint:
There is no heaven; be holy then,
When time with age shall them attaint.
Were kisses all the joys in bed,
One woman would another wed.

But soft! enough,—too much, I fear;
Lest that my mistress hear my song,
She will not stick to warm my ear[1],
To teach my tongue to be so long:
Yet will she blush, here be it said,
To hear her secrets so bewray'd.

XX.[2]

Live with me and be my love,
And we will all the pleasures prove,
That hills and valleys, dales and fields,
And the craggy mountain yields.

There will we sit upon the rocks,
And see the shepherds feed their flocks
By shallow rivers, to whose falls
Melodious birds sing madrigals.

There will I make thee a bed of roses,
With a thousand fragrant posies;
A cap of flowers, and a kirtle
Embroider'd all with leaves of myrtle.

[1] So the manuscript in our possession: "The Passionate Pilgrim," 1599, has it, "She will not stick to round me on th' ear." [2] This poem, here incomplete, and what is called "Love's Answer," still more imperfect, may be seen at length in "Percy's Reliques," Vol. I. They belong to Christopher Marlowe and Sir Walter Raleigh: the first is assigned by name to Marlowe, in "England's Helicon," 1600, (sign A 2) and the last appears in the same collection, under the name of *Ignoto*, which was a signature sometimes adopted by Sir Walter Raleigh. They are, besides, assigned to both these authors in Walton's "Angler," (p. 149, edit. 1808) under the titles of "The milk-maid's song," and "The Milk-maid's Mother's answer."